TRADITION AND CHANGE
IN AUSTRALIAN LAW

SALES CENTRES AND AGENTS

HEAD OFFICE: 44-50 Waterloo Road NORTH RYDE NSW 2113
Tel: (02) 936 6444 Fax: (02) 888 2287

4th Floor 167 Phillip Street SYDNEY NSW 2000
Tel: (02) 235 0766 Fax: (02) 221 4004

568 Lonsdale Street MELBOURNE Vic 3000
Tel: (03) 670 7888 Fax: (03) 670 0138

1st Floor 40 Queen Street BRISBANE Qld 4000
Tel: (07) 221 6688 Fax: (07) 220 0084

9th Floor St George's Centre 81 St George's Terrace PERTH WA 6000
Tel: (09) 321 8583 Fax: (09) 324 1910

Sales Representative Keith Peterson GPO Box 384 ADELAIDE SA 5001
Tel/Fax: (08) 295 7644 Mobile: 018 84 3052

Preferred Stockist The Bookworld 30 Smith Street DARWIN NT 0800
Tel: (089) 81 5277 Fax: (089) 411 226

Sales Representative Peter Stewart PO Box 1689 AUCKLAND NZ
Tel: (09) 366 7204 Fax: (09) 366 6828

CANADA

The Carswell Company Ltd
Ontario

HONG KONG

Bloomsbury Books Ltd

MALAYSIA

Malayan Law Journal Sdn Bhd

SINGAPORE

Butterworths Asia

UNITED KINGDOM

Sweet & Maxwell Ltd
London

USA

Wm W Gaunt & Sons, Inc
Holmes Beach, Florida

Tradition and Change in Australian Law

by

PATRICK PARKINSON

MA (Oxon), LLM (Illinois)
Associate Professor in Law, University of Sydney

THE LAW BOOK COMPANY LIMITED
1994

Published in Sydney by

The Law Book Company Limited
   44-50 Waterloo Road, North Ryde, NSW
   568 Lonsdale Street, Melbourne, Victoria
   40 Queen Street, Brisbane, Queensland
   81 St George's Terrace, Perth, WA

National Library of Australia
   Cataloguing-in-Publication entry

Parkinson, Patrick.
   Tradition and change in Australian law.

   Includes index.
   ISBN 0 455 21292 9.

   1. Law—Australia—History. I. Title.

349.94

Designed and edited by Debbie Duncan

Typeset in Times Roman, 10 on 12 point, by Mercier Typesetters Pty Ltd,
   Granville, NSW
   Printed by Ligare Pty Ltd, Riverwood, NSW

PREFACE

There are many different ways to introduce the law to students for the first time. Some books set out to introduce legal method, the courts and other aspects of the modern legal system. Others take a more theoretical perspective, introducing students to the law through the interpretative filters of critical theory.

This book begins from the premise that law cannot be understood properly without an awareness that law is, in its very essence, traditional. This is not the same, of course, as saying that the legal profession is resistant to change or that lawyers tend to be politically conservative. Both of those things may well be true, but that is not what is meant by emphasising the significance of law as tradition. Rather, what is significant about the traditionality of law is that law involves a constant dialogue between the present and the past. Legal reasoning, formally at least, relies upon finding authorities, many of them the work of judges long dead, or Parliaments long since dissolved. Yet law is constantly changing, and not only because present day Parliaments continually pour out new enactments. Change occurs continuously in the law, but it does so only by means of the processes ordained within the legal tradition.

This book also places emphasis on the history both of Australian legal institutions, and of the idea of law in the western legal tradition. Australian law cannot truly be understood without a deep awareness of its history. A description of the modern day institutions of the law would only provide knowledge of what those institutions are, and not why they came to be. History provides a context which explains that which could otherwise seem incomprehensible; and it helps us to evaluate our rules and our institutions afresh. To understand why something came into being is an indispensable first stage to evaluating why, if at all, it should continue to be. There is an inherent tendency in all institutions to find reasonable justifications for why things are as they are. Often, however, history may show that what is now, need not have been; that those things which seem writ in stone are themselves the product of particular circumstances and accidents of history. At other times, an awareness of origins may give new meaning to aspects of the tradition which seem unnecessary or irrelevant in the modern era, and enable us to treat old traditions with a renewed respect.

However, the history which it is necessary to study is not merely, or even mainly, the history of institutions or rules, but also of legal theory. For this reason, one of the aims of this book is to introduce students to some of the major ideas about law and legal reasoning which have shaped the development of Australian law today. Australian law is a part of the western legal tradition as a whole, and shares with the civil law countries of continental Europe, some common perceptions of the nature of law and the role of law in society.

Of course, that tradition is under attack in some circles. Perhaps there will be those who would wish that this book had taken a more critical approach to its subject matter, and had given more extensive coverage to contemporary movements such as feminist legal theory and critical legal studies. No doubt those who are teachers will make up for these deficiencies in their own courses. If discussion of these contemporary movements does not fill the pages of this book, it is not because the author is unaware of them or regards them as unimportant. Rather, it is because at this juncture, it is difficult to know which ideas will last. Like the 1990s, the 1960s was, in many ways a period of great social change, yet the intellectual heroes of that generation are now merely names in the index of discarded ideas. From the intellectual ferment of the North American academy in particular, there is no doubt much which will prove to be of lasting value; but all that glisters is not gold. Indeed, a close reading of feminist legal theory or the writings associated with critical legal studies, results in a prism effect. What is often portrayed as a single source of light refracts, through that prism, into a great variety of different perceptions and inconsistent world views.

Many have counselled against endeavouring to write a history of one's own age. The distance of time offers the benefit of perspective. More particularly, with the greater perspective of time, we may come to see more clearly that some ideas which are claimed today as being of universal application, are in fact deeply rooted in the cultural soil from which they grew.

With a profound understanding of the Australian legal tradition, its history, its formative ideas, its modes of thought and means of change, there is a strong foundation both for critique of the law, and for a sense of perspective which will be useful in evaluating those critiques. It is with that aim in mind, that this book has been written.

The book departs from the normal convention of using gender neutral language in the historical sections of the book where to have been gender neutral would have been completely inaccurate as a matter of history.

I am grateful to the secretarial staff and librarians of the University of Sydney Law School for the extensive assistance they have given me during the time in which this book was being written. I also owe an intellectual debt to many people. The debt I owe to numerous scholars both in Australia and overseas will be apparent from these pages. I am also indebted to many of my colleagues at the University of Sydney. My own understanding of legal ideas has benefited greatly from their stimulus. Many of the themes and ideas in this book were first developed when I was teaching in the first year law course, Legal Institutions. The syllabus and materials of that course resulted from the contributions of a large number of the staff over a period of time. My especial thanks must go to Professor Christine Chinkin, now of the University of Southampton, with whom I began to write a different sort of book, and with whom I have had many interesting discussions about the tradition of law in Australia. I am also grateful to Ross Anderson, Don Rothwell and Wojciech Sadurski for comments on individual chapters.

My thanks are due also to Judith Fox and Anne Maree O'Neill of The Law Book Company for their constant encouragement and considerable patience. This book was meant to be completed a very long time ago. In retrospect, I am glad it wasn't. My thanks finally for the continuing encouragement of my wife, Mimi, who has also shown very great patience with this, and other, writing projects.

The challenge for the future of Australian law is to develop its inherited legal tradition to meet the changing needs and aspirations of Australian society at the end of the 20th century. In shaping that tradition, the words of the Apostle Paul seem apt:

"Test all things; hold fast to the things which are good."

(1 Thessalonians 5:21)

PATRICK PARKINSON

Sydney
August 1994

TABLE OF CONTENTS

PART FOUR: LEGAL REASONING

TABLE OF CASES

TABLE OF STATUTES

Part One

Australia and the Western Legal Tradition

Chapter 1

THE TRADITION OF LAW IN AUSTRALIA

1.1 Characteristics of the Australian Legal Tradition

In its legal institutions, as in other aspects of its national life, Australia bears indelibly the marks of its birth. The legal and political institutions of Australia find their roots, not in the traditions of its native inhabitants, but in the traditions of a colonial power which imported its understanding of law and social organisation with the landing of the first white settlers in 1788. That history has meant that the tradition of law in Australia is received rather than indigenous, the product of evolution not of revolution, and monocultural rather than multicultural. All three of these characteristics are very significant for a proper understanding of Australian law.

1.1.1   A received tradition

The Australian legal tradition cannot be understood without an appreciation of the idea of law as it was developed through some seven centuries in Britain prior to the settlement of Australia, and the various institutions through which that idea of law was, and still is, expressed. Governor Phillip's Commission in 1787 required him to establish courts which would apply English law; and while these were rudimentary in the early years, and military in character, by 1824, a court system on the English model had been established in New South Wales and Van Diemen's Land. These legal institutions were given from Westminster through Acts of the British Parliament. Its governors were men exported from Britain who were largely comfortable with English values and institutions. When representative government emerged in the 1840s and 1850s, it followed English traditions in most respects.

Even after more than 200 years since white settlement, the Australian legal tradition still maintains a close similarity with that in England. Certainly, during these two centuries, Australian law has developed distinctive features which differentiate Australian institutions from those existing in the United Kingdom. Examples include the existence of a written constitution, the regulation of industrial relations by means of legally binding awards and compulsory arbitration (although the significance of centrally-fixed awards is diminishing), the development of a Family Court, and the establishment of an Administrative Appeals Tribunal which has the power to review administrative decisions of government on their merits.[1]

3

In matters of detail, the laws of the Australian colonies differed from England in many respects from the beginnings of white settlement. Yet despite these distinctive features, the underlying patterns of thought reflect the common law tradition as received from Britain.

Central to this, is that, until recently, Australian courts have seen themselves as bound by the precedential authority of English courts.[2] Since the common law was received from England, the English courts were treated as the authoritative expositors of that law to the extent that it was appropriate for Australian conditions. Until the 1970s and 1980s, Australian courts were subordinate to a final court of appeal in London, known as the Privy Council. Australian courts saw that they had an important role in the maintenance of the common law as received from Britain. Far from being anxious to assert their independence they showed a remarkable subservience and deference to English precedents.[3] It is only in the last few years that a nationalist consciousness has emerged in Australian law, and the apron strings which tied Australian law to English law have been loosened.

The tradition of law in Australia is thus a received tradition. It is none the worse for that. Few legal traditions are indigenous. Borrowing by one country from the legal traditions of another has a long history.[4] The common law tradition is also one which spread through much of the world by means of English colonial expansion. Despite manifold differences between the laws of Australia, Canada, Great Britain, New Zealand, and the United States, all these countries share, with many other countries, the same common law tradition which allows each to draw upon the experience of the others, and which gives to them a commonality which transcends national boundaries and cultural differences. The Australian legal tradition is thus not isolated from that of other nations.

Furthermore, the common law forms part of a wider tradition of law, which has been termed the "western legal tradition". The common law reflects an understanding of the nature and function of law which is shared with the "civil law" tradition[5] which took hold in continental Europe. The civil law developed in Europe from the 12th century onwards, during the same period as the common law was developing in England. However, unlike the common law, which developed out of the practice and procedure of the royal courts, the civil law was founded upon the study of Roman law.[6]

In many respects, these two traditions of law are distinct. Roman law had a much more profound influence upon the substance of law in Europe than it did in England. The two traditions grew in different soil, and largely independent from each other. However, nationalistic accounts of the development of the law have sometimes obscured the connections between them. At the level of ideas, the two systems of law represent a single western tradition,[7] with a shared understanding that law has a central role to play in all social organisation. This is scarcely surprising, for the common law and civil law traditions were subject to the same formative influences. They grew in different soil but each was exposed to the same elements. Each was imbued with the same ideas of the nature and significance of law in society. In particular, at the level of ideas about law, each was affected by Greek, Roman, and Judaeo-Christian thought.

It is therefore meaningful to speak of a western legal tradition, as opposed to merely a common law tradition, for throughout western Europe, there were prevalent ideas about law and society which gained wide currency through the teaching of the church and the universities. These played a vital role in shaping modern western ideas about law, and the influence of those ideas continues today. The extent of European colonial expansion was such that much of the world has been influenced either by the common law or the civil law.

1.1.2   An evolved tradition

Australians adopted the English tradition of law not only because it was imposed upon them initially by the English colonial government, but also because they had no alternative vision. Australia was, in this, quite unlike the United States. Both of these societies had their modern origins in English colonialisation.[8] Yet the United States of America was different in that it experienced a revolution. The settlers overthrew the government, and they did so not only in the name of self-rule, although that was important to them, but also in pursuit of an ideal. Many of the early settlers of the American colonies were fleeing from religious persecution in Europe, and religious principles influenced much of their formative political thought. The American revolution was also affected considerably by enlightenment ideas of natural rights. These were considered inalienable and required constitutional protection. Thus, following the American War of Independence, the American colonies were born again as the United States, with a set of shared values which united a disparate nation in a vision of the common good.

Australia, however, knew none of these things. Certainly, those who sailed to its "fatal shore" were aware that they were starting a new life; but this was not expressed politically. The early colonists carried with them no vision of a new order. There was a First Fleet, but there were no Pilgrim Fathers. Nor was there any revolution in government which brought to birth a new political system. There was a Rum Rebellion,[9] but no Boston Tea Party.[10]

Of course, Australians developed for themselves a distinct self-image and identity. They wrote their own novels, created their own art, and composed their own ballads. However, the mythology which gave to Australians a sense of value was bound up with the land rather than the government. A largely urban society, at least by the 20th century, celebrated itself as a people of the bush. Curiously, it had found its identity in the land just as the Aboriginals had done thousands of years earlier. Thus, the identity which Australians developed for themselves did not involve a distinctive legal or political tradition. There were many things which were distinctively Australian by the end of the 19th century, but its legal tradition was not amongst them.

To say that the origins of the Australian legal and political tradition were found in British history is not to suggest that the early settlers necessarily had fond memories of the British system, nor even that all shared the same memory of it. Many early settlers were Welsh, Scottish, or Irish, and had no particular admiration for English law and government. Some of the early settlers with most experience of the law had seen it from within the shadow of the gallows. Nor was women's experience of English law necessarily the same as men's. There is no reason to believe that in the collective memory of the 19th century colonists, there was a particular respect for English law and legal institutions.

Nonetheless, Australians generally showed no desire to break the close legal and political ties with Britain until the last few years.[11] While there has been much discussion recently of breaking the final imperial ties by becoming a republic, republican sentiment in Australia has hitherto been held only by a minority.[12] It was only in 1986 that the Australian States gained formal independence from the sovereignty of the British Parliament at Westminster. Their independence was not the culmination of any great struggle for freedom. Such independence had been available to them as long ago as 1931, but was not taken up.[13]

The close relationship between Australian law and English law may again be contrasted with the United States, where the interpretation of the common law was markedly influenced by the American Revolution. Although Americans adopted the common law, and American law continues to exhibit a family resemblance to that in Australia and Britain, American law was marked by an emphasised discontinuity with its British origins whereas Australian courts laid stress on the historic continuity. The Americans quickly developed their own case law and precedents in the years following the Declaration of Independence. English precedents were still followed, since legal authority had to be located somewhere and often English case law was the only source of authority available. However, they were followed selectively.[14] Thus, American and English law began to diverge, and while leading English precedents established in the 19th century continued to influence American law, by the early 20th century almost all legal authority in America was indigenous.[15] Increasingly the content of American law was influenced by the Bill of Rights in the United States' Constitution. Thus American law, since the American War of Independence, is, like Australian law, a product of evolutionary development,[16] but it evolved through the course of the 19th and 20th centuries on a different path from the law in Britain and its surviving empire.

1.1.3   A monocultural tradition

A third feature of Australian law is that its legal institutions and traditions are monocultural in character, reflecting its English origins. In other countries, British colonial policy did make room for some local customs and cultural values within its legal system, especially in regard to marriage and family relations. It allowed the possibility that different laws could apply to the different ethnic groups within the one polity. [17] Even in New Zealand, the white settlers made a treaty with the Maori, known as the Treaty of Waitangi in 1840, which provided at least some recognition then that the Maori people had certain entitlements within the overall framework of British sovereignty. [18] While the terms of that treaty were vague, and had the effect of legitimising British sovereignty, the treaty has in recent years provided a basis for the Maori people to assert claims against the white majority.

By contrast, Aboriginal culture was as little recognised by the colonial authorities as were their land rights. There was no official acknowledgment that the land was obtained by conquest, or at least that the white advance had displaced Aboriginal peoples. The early settlers of New South Wales regarded the Aboriginal peoples as too primitive to be treated as having an indigenous culture and social organisation which deserved respect within the dominant legal system. [19] The pattern of the ensuing years was one of dispossession of Aboriginal peoples from their traditional lands, and decimation of their population through violence and disease. It was followed later by policies of segregation on reserves designed to protect them, and eventual assimilation into the white Australian culture. [20] A significant feature of this policy of assimilation was the removal of Aboriginal children from their families, and their upbringing within white society. [21]

In recent years, there has been increasing recognition by the Commonwealth, and State and Territory governments, of the rights, needs and legitimate claims of Aboriginal people. Some accommodation has been made in the laws of various States to the distinctive traditions and culture of Aborigines, and there has been an increasing awareness of the importance of preserving and protecting their cultural heritage. Recommendations of law reform bodies and other commissions have indicated that the recognition of Aboriginal customary law should be taken much further. [22]

In the same way as the legal tradition paid no regard to the distinctive traditions of the indigenous peoples, so it has as yet, been little affected by the waves of migration from countries other than the British Isles. For more than 150 years after the first white settlement of Australia, the extent of migration from countries other than the British Isles was not sufficiently large to change the essentially British character of Australian society and of its legal institutions. That migration first occurred in the 19th century. Chinese came to Australia in large numbers during the Gold Rush period of the 1850s, and continued to arrive thereafter. As well, small numbers of migrants came from various other countries. The adoption of an explicit "white Australia" policy from the beginning of the 20th century[23] ensured the continuing dominance of British traditions in Australian life. At the outbreak of World War II, publicists boasted that 98 per cent of the population was either born in the British Isles or descended from families in the British Isles. [24]

However, since that time, much has changed. The gradual abandonment of a culturally restrictive immigration policy in the years following World War II, and the large size of the migrant intake since then, has led Australia to embrace the concept of being a multicultural society with diminishing links to Britain and Europe. In 1986, over 20 per cent of Australian residents had been born overseas. Of these, 56 per cent were born in a non-English speaking country and 16.5 per cent had come from Asia. [25] The proportion of Australian residents who were born in non-English speaking countries has increased since 1986 and will continue to do so. The numbers of immigrants from Britain, expressed as a percentage of the total migrant intake each year, declined substantially between 1966 and 1986. In the period 1966-1970, migrants from the United Kingdom and Ireland represented 46 per cent of the total migrant intake. By 1986, the figure was 20 per cent. [26] In 1989-90, 42 per cent of the settler arrivals had been born in Asia (of which the majority were born in South-East Asia), 32 per cent were born in Europe (21 per cent were from the United Kingdom) and 12 per cent were born in Oceania. [27]

The challenge for today is to adapt the legal system to the demands which this places upon it. [28] At one level, this raises issues of access to justice. People of non-English speaking backgrounds have particular needs for interpreting services, and for education in the norms of Australian law which are culturally alien to their own traditions. Beyond this, the substance of Australian law may need to be adapted to reflect the cultural mosaic of Australian society. This raises the question of whether, and to what extent, the majority culture is willing to give due recognition to the values and belief systems of non-"western" ethnic minorities. [29] The development of a multicultural society in Australia raises the possibility of conflicting values held by members of different communities. In endeavouring to accommodate and compromise between different community values, the issue which has to be addressed is to determine which "western" values are so fundamental that no compromise can be made with conflicting minority traditions.

1.1.4   A patriarchal tradition?

The tradition of law in Australia also originated within a world in which men dominated public life and the women's role was seen to be in the home. Folklore had it that "the hand which rocks the cradle rules the world"; but in reality, these were two quite distinct roles, and they were assigned to different genders. Women were seen as the custodians of the hearth, and the notion that they could, or should, also play a role in public life was a quite alien one. Of course, for centuries, women had worked inside the home in cottage industries and outside the home in agriculture, selling produce, and, after the industrial revolution, in the factories. The emergence of hospitals and offices had also seen women employed as nurses and in clerical occupations. However, leadership was seen as a male preserve, and men ran the government, the law, agriculture, business and the professions. Thus, the legal profession was an exclusively male domain until this century. The judiciary was drawn from the ranks of the male legal profession, and inevitably, the substance of the law, which was shaped by the judiciary, often reflected male perceptions of the world. [30]

The domination by men was expressed in and through the law. In the common law, the traditional position was that married women had no legal existence apart from their husbands, and that the husband was regarded as her representative in social life. This was expressed most famously by Sir William Blackstone in his *Commentaries on the Laws of England* (1765):

> "By marriage, the husband and wife are one person in law; that is, the very being or legal existence of the woman is suspended during the marriage, or at least incorporated and consolidated into that of the husband: under whose wing, protection and cover she performs every thing." [31]

Blackstone went on to express the view that "even the disabilities, which the wife lies under, are for the most part intended for her protection and benefit. So great a favourite is the female sex of the laws of England." [32]

Thus, while the western legal tradition emphasised the importance of the individual, the individuality of women and children was often hidden within the family unit, headed by the husband and father. This had many ramifications in English and Australian law. Until the late 19th century, men held property on behalf of the family unit. On marriage, a woman's property passed into the control of her husband. The only way in which a married woman could maintain ownership of her wealth separately was if the property was held on trust by others for her benefit. [33] Furthermore, a married woman could only seek redress for a legal wrong done to her if she had her husband's concurrence. Another aspect of the law's attitude to the family was that the family was regarded largely as a private domain free from the law's intrusion, while the law reinforced male headship of the domestic unit. [34]

It was only in the 20th century that the exclusion of women from public life began to be seriously challenged. Few gains were made without struggle. Women did not have the vote until it was first granted to them in South Australia in 1894, [35] and thereafter in the other Australian colonies. They were not admitted to the legal profession in Australia until the 20th century, and the appointment of the first female judges to State supreme courts and the High Court of Australia has only occurred in recent years.

Historically, the patriarchal structures of society were reflected in the law and within the legal profession. Yet to what extent may it be said that the legal tradition itself is intrinsically a male tradition? In the view of some feminist scholars, the legal system is irredeemably masculine and law is synonymous with male dominance in society. For example, Catharine MacKinnon writes:

"The rule of law and the rule of men are one thing, indivisible, at once official and unofficial—officially circumscribed, unofficially not. State power, embodied in law, exists throughout society as male power at the same time as the power of men over women throughout society is organised as the power of the state . . . However autonomous of class the liberal state may appear, it is not autonomous of sex. Male power is systemic. Coercive, legitimated, and epistemic, it is the regime." [36]

In this view of law as a patriarchal tradition, law not only reflects the dominance of men in society, but it rules in accordance with masculine patterns of relating. In the same vein, Polan writes that: "The whole structure of law—its hierarchical organisation; its combative, adversarial format; and its undeviating bias in favour of rationality over all other values—defines it as a fundamentally patriarchal institution." [37] Another strand of feminist writing, influenced by the work of Carol Gilligan, [38] has sought to discover the way in which law might be different if women's "different voice", the different values and patterns of relating which are particularly associated with femininity, were to have a greater influence upon the law and its structures. [39]

Other feminist writers do not see law as intrinsically a masculine tradition. Rather, feminist critiques of law have emphasised the discordance between the law's rhetoric of equality and justice, and its treatment of women in particular areas of the law. In this view, the feminist project is seen to be to expose ways in which law's apparent neutrality and impartiality disguise gendered patterns and forms of discrimination, and to use law as a means of change. Thus, while the substance of law is seen as far from gender neutral, the tradition of law is capable of being used to effect change, in order to bring reality into line with law's rhetoric and professed values. [40]

1.2   The Traditionality of Law

The theme of tradition and change in Australian law focuses attention on an important aspect of law: its traditionality. It is of the essence of law that it is traditional. Whether one is describing the legal system of a country based upon the English common law tradition, whether one is examining the law of a European country based upon the medieval interpretation of Roman law, or whether the legal system under discussion is based upon custom, as with the Aboriginal peoples of Australia, analysis of the law involves an understanding of how the past has authority for the present. The sources of those traditions vary from one legal system to another. In interpreting the modern law of Australia, lawyers have recourse to a variety of authoritative documents, judgments and pronouncements—Acts of Parliament, whether State or federal, judgments of courts in previous cases, and sometimes, opinions of learned writers—within which the present law is said to be contained. In societies where law is based on custom, the tradition which is invoked may well be an oral one, or one which has authority merely by virtue of common and habitual application in the past.

Law is traditional, not merely in the sense that it contains traditions, rituals and ceremonies. More than this, Krygier argues that law contains three significant elements which are to be found in all traditions, and which are central to its existence and identity. [41] These are origins in the past, present authority and inter-generational transmission.

1.2.1   Origins in the past

Traditions, by definition, either originated some considerable time in the past, or are believed to have done so by those who maintain those traditions. Traditions cannot be created. It is only through hindsight that sometimes we may be able to see that in some event, and at some particular time, a tradition began. Like other complex traditions, law contains and preserves a large body of beliefs, assumptions, rituals and materials which have been deposited over generations. [42]

Of course, law is not in its entirety, the product of distant origin and generational transmission. The Parliaments of Australia produce new laws and regulations by the hundreds and thousands each year. Much law which falls to be applied by the courts is statutory law of quite recent origin. Yet even this new law is an accretion to, or a modification of, the previous body of law which has been built up over years and centuries. The new law presupposes the old, builds upon it, or alters it in various ways. Furthermore, when lawyers and judges are interpreting an entirely new statute, they read it with the aid of the past. That is, they bring to the reading of it, various traditions of interpretation going back centuries, and various assumptions about the law which are long standing. [43] Thus even new legislation takes its place within the legal tradition. [44] The language chosen by these drafting statutes is language which will be understood by those who are entrusted with the interpretation of the enactments. There is a symbiotic relationship between the drafters and the interpreters with each operating according to conventions of legal language which are mutually understood. A new statute, therefore, does not operate in a vacuum. It presupposes a large body of existing law and takes its place within that corpus of law.

1.2.2   Present authority

The second characteristic of a tradition, is that it has a present authority and significance for the lives and activities of those who participate in that tradition. In law, the past not only is significant, but it is authoritatively present. The past is not merely utilised. It is institutionalised. Nowhere is this more clear than in the process of legal reasoning. Legal reasoning involves a process of justifying arguments for or against a particular proposition by reference to accepted interpretations of historical legal materials, mainly statutes and cases.

In this process of reasoning, there is what one commentator has called "a wonderful elision of time".[45] The enactments of federal Parliament in 1904 are treated as carrying the authority of the present Parliament. The statements of judges long dead are seen to be as relevant and important as those of the living.[46] In this way, time is almost transcended and the past speaks into the present with continuing authority. One Canadian report stated:

> "In no other branch of learning (except perhaps religion) does received wisdom enjoy a preferred position over newly revealed insights. In law however, statute and code, precedent and doctrine acquire authority in part through longevity."[47]

The comparison with religion is instructive.[48] As in religious traditions, such as the Judaeo-Christian tradition and the Islamic faith, authority rests in various received texts; in many, if not most, religious groupings, certain people are designated within the tradition as authoritative expositors of those texts. In the same way, lawyers also ascribe authority to particular texts, and have both particular traditions of interpretation, and in the judiciary, an authoritative community of interpretation.

It is not self-evident that cases should be decided by a process of reference back in time to the past. The decisions of judges in past ages may only reflect the wisdom and values of their time. There are other ways in which disputes might be resolved: by compromise, by appeals to right conduct, by regard to what is fair or moral. All of these are reference points for the resolution of disputes within other societies, and in certain contexts, within Australian society. Yet, in the Australian legal tradition, these reference points are not evoked by courts called upon to adjudicate in disputes. Disputes are resolved by reference to legal rights, and those rights are determined by reference to past authority and precedent.

However, the role of the past in legal reasoning is a complex one. It would be inaccurate to say that the past *determines* the present, for if that were so, law would only evolve through new enactments by State or Federal Parliaments, and the extension and development of existing rules to new fact situations by judges. Yet these are not the only means of change in law. Despite an emphasis on historic continuity and a reference to the past as a justification for decisions in the present, law is in a constant state of evolution and flux. Law responds to, and is affected by, the society of which it is an integral part. As that society changes, the legal system must, to a greater or lesser extent, keep pace. Sometimes that change is surreptitious with judges altering the law to adapt it to modern conditions while proclaiming that the decision stands in historic continuity with the past. Sometimes the change is brought about more openly.[49] The Australian Constitution provides an example of a foundational law which has only occasionally been amended since its enactment in 1900. Yet the meaning now attributed to various key sections of the constitution, and the overall position of the Commonwealth vis à vis the States in relation to constitutional law is radically different from that which prevailed in the first 15 years after the enactment of the Constitution. Australia could not have a 20th century society, competing economically in world markets and participating in international discourse, if its law reflected the values and beliefs of a 19th century world. Law must evolve and change if it is to continue to reflect community values and assist, rather than hinder, efficiency in social organisation.

Thus, in law, the past is a source of continuing authority, guidance and reference, but it is interpreted through the eyes of the present. In these respects, the study of law may be compared and contrasted with the study of history. It has been said that history also inevitably involves a process of interpreting the past through the eyes of the present.[50] Yet law is different from the study of history in that it is not concerned with historical accuracy but with the meaning ascribed to that past by subsequent generations. What matters in law is not so much what the law was in the past, but what it has been understood to be by previous authoritative interpreters. Furthermore, the past is often reinterpreted to conform with the needs of the present; not infrequently, judges will refer to the continuing authority of an old precedent, while distinguishing it so that it is regarded as inapplicable to the instant case. It follows that law is always evolving, as the past goes through continual reinterpretation.

1.2.3   Inter-generational transmission

The third characteristic of tradition is that it has been handed down through the generations.[51] It is a feature of the Australian legal tradition, as with that of some other countries, such as England, that there is a strong pressure to conformity with the values, principles and interpretative methods of the tradition. Acceptance in the higher echelons of the profession is dependent upon adherence to that tradition—its culture, its language, its practices, its methods of reasoning, its rituals, and its codes of conduct, both written and unwritten. In this way, the tradition is both maintained, and passed on to successive acolytes.

1.2.4   The development of traditions

Traditions progress and build upon what has gone before. They are dynamic rather than static, for the continuities between past and present do not exclude evolution and change. Krygier writes that characteristic of traditions is "a dialectical interplay between inherited layers which pervade and . . . mould the present, and the constant renewals and reshapings of these inheritances, in which authorised interpreters and guardians of the tradition and lay participants indulge, and must indulge."[52]

Yet it is in the nature of traditions that at a level of fundamental precepts and values, there is always a line of continuity. As Alasdair MacIntyre has written in the context of a tradition of thought:

> "[I]t is central to the conception of such a tradition that the past is never something merely to be discarded, but rather that the present is intelligible only as a commentary upon and response to the past in which the past, if necessary and if possible, is corrected and transcended, yet corrected and transcended in a way that leaves the present open to being in turn corrected and transcended by some yet more adequate future point of view."[53]

Legal traditions are different inasmuch as they do not usually evolve in pursuance of truth, but rather in pursuance of efficiency, social order and societal consensus. As the values and circumstances of the community change, the law will tend to adapt accordingly. In the light of present conditions, particular past rules may be seen to be inadequate or inappropriate. However, the western legal tradition shares the characteristic of all traditions that change and growth has occurred continuously over generations and centuries, with each generation building upon the work of previous generations.[54] It is essential to the nature of a tradition that the change is evolutionary. If fundamental beliefs and principles are discarded, and discontinuity with the past becomes the dominant pattern, then there will come a point at which the tradition itself ceases to exist. Following such turbulent change, it may be a long time before new traditions become established, and become part of the fabric of the social order.

1.3   Tradition and Legitimacy

Why is there such an emphasis within the legal system on tradition—on the authority of the past to determine the present? And why is that tradition preserved and guarded jealously, so that younger generations of lawyers feel a pressure to conformity in maintaining it?

1.3.1   Tradition and the political order

First, continuity with tradition is important for the legitimacy of the legal and political order. The foundational question for any legal system is where ultimate authority should reside. Who or what is the final arbiter of the law which will govern the community? That question has been answered in different ways by different societies. In some societies that question is answered by ascribing ultimate authority to God as revealed in a holy book or in other sacred writings. At times in the history of the western legal tradition, ultimate authority has been ascribed to "natural law"—perceived as a timeless law evident in the natural order and discernible by reason. In other societies, ultimate authority has vested in a monarch. Judges have always been the servants of the ultimate authority within a legal system, exercising a delegated authority within that legal order.

The resolution of the foundational question of authority in English law dates back to the constitutional conflicts of the 17th century between the English monarch and Parliament, which led for a while, during the Cromwellian era, to the abolition of the monarchy.[55] The supremacy of Parliament, under the ultimate formal authority of the monarch, was established by the end of the 17th century, and that constitutional structure was inherited in Australia with the monarch being represented by the Governor-General and the Governors of various States. Judges and administrators, in applying Australian law, and the police in enforcing it, derive their authority to do so from the acceptance within the community of that basic constitutional settlement. They must be seen to be giving effect to the intentions of Parliament when interpreting legislation, and must defer to the ultimate authority of the relevant Parliament within the constitutional order.

For as long as the community accepts the cohesive authority of a shared tradition, even if it knows little of its origins and has scarcely reflected upon its justification, a certain stability is assured for government. This means that the basic constitutional settlement of the nation is not being questioned and resolved afresh in each generation. Like Britain, Australia has not lurched through the last 200 years from one political experiment to another.

Stability, of course, is not a good in itself. There is little good in the stability of an oppressive regime. Yet it is the nature of oppressive regimes, marked as they usually are by the exercise of arbitrary power and self-interested governance, that rarely can they claim to be the legitimate heirs of a society's legal traditions, for their government and laws are not the product of an evolved social consensus. As Professor Tay has written:

> "In all societies, it is often forgotten, law is not merely the utterance of power; it both represents and produces a significant degree of social consensus. Without that, law would lose its distinctive character, its legitimacy as promoting and safeguarding the normal capacity of human beings to live together, to respect each others' humanity. Law thus stands halfway between violence and education, and partakes of both."[56]

Of course, governments which base their authority on long-standing traditions of law can sometimes become oppressive through the moral decay of their ruling elites, or because of the neglect of those entrusted with the preservation of that tradition. The existence of a legal tradition is not in itself a safeguard against corruption. The values which are handed down, values such as a commitment to substantive equality before the law, to natural justice and to fundamental human rights, need to be internalised and reaffirmed by each successive generation of lawyers and judges. Nonetheless, even in societies which have experienced extensive moral decay, or in which notions of fairness and justice are most distorted, the legal tradition can act as a brake upon arbitrary power. The mask of law's neutrality and legitimacy cannot be kept on without some adherence to its precepts. The rule of law stands inherently for the propositions that power should not be the final arbiter in human affairs, and that every human being has the right to the application of legal rules by due process of law.[57] Even those who are most corrupted by power can sometimes be haunted by the memory of the law's higher ideals. Furthermore, judges and lawyers steeped in the values of the legal tradition have often stood up to rulers seeking to exercise arbitrary power and to violate human rights, even at the cost of their positions.[58]

As stability is not a good in itself, nor is antiquity. Traditions may sometimes be regarded as dead weights upon a contemporary society. Karl Marx expressed this negative aspect of traditions when he wrote:

> "Men make their own history, but they do not make it just as they please; they do not make it under circumstances chosen by themselves, but under circumstances directly encountered, given and transmitted from the past. The tradition of all the dead generations weighs like a nightmare on the brain of the living."[59]

Yet even when traditions as handed down are flawed by the weaknesses and blind spots of previous generations, they may contain within them not only the capacity to change, but the impetus to promote that change. For all but the last century or so, countries which have formed part of the western legal tradition have tolerated slavery. At the same time, it has been a constant theme of western legal thought that in at least certain ways, all people should be deemed equal before the law. This was treated by the Greeks and Romans as being consistent with slavery and other distinctions between classes. Nonetheless, Plato saw the principle of equality before the law as arising from "our equality of birth by nature".[60] The recognition that all human beings were equal under God in Judaeo-Christian teaching also informed the western legal tradition, and the impact of the Enlightenment on western thought further reinforced the principle that all people should be treated as equal before the law. The abolition of slavery in Britain following the campaign by evangelical Christians such as William Wilberforce, and its eventual abolition in the United States following the Emancipation Proclamation of Abraham Lincoln,[61] harmonised the law with a basic premise of the western legal tradition. In the same way, this tradition of equality before the law represents a basis upon which claims to substantively equal treatment can be made when there is discrimination by race, gender or otherwise. The appeal to equality is most compelling when it represents an appeal to the essential values underlying the western legal tradition, rather than being presented within a framework of complete rejection of that tradition.

There are good reasons not to despise traditions in the name of progress. Like other aspects of a society's culture, its legal tradition can be destroyed, but not easily restored again. It represents a heritage which is valuable at least because it is an integral part of a society's history, shared values and present character. Certain features of a legal tradition may be outmoded, but it is the nature of traditions that their value is not only in their functional utility. Traditions join the present to the past, and in so doing help to integrate the present culture with its origins. The wholesale abandonment of its traditions cuts a society loose from its moorings.

A further reason for respect of traditions is that only by showing such a general respect for a nation's legal heritage can the present generation demonstrate a basis for future generations to respect its own contribution to legal ordering, and thereby ensure the stability of the political order. By maintaining respect for the accumulated wisdom of the past, it becomes more difficult for future generations to cast aside those values which are recognised within the tradition as fundamental.[62] Perhaps the most influential exponent of this aspect of tradition was Edmund Burke, who criticised the revolutionaries in France at the end of the 18th century for tearing down rather than repairing what was defective in the existing order. He wrote of the French that "you began ill, because you began by despising everything that belonged to you," and he warned against those who destroy the inherited fabric of society and thereby teach those who come after them "as little to respect their contrivances, as they had themselves respected the institutions of their forefathers". He concluded that in a society which had no sense of continuity, "men would become little better than the flies of a summer."[63]

Regimes which are rotten to the core may need to be overthrown, but as the history of France after the French Revolution demonstrated, the danger of despising all that has gone before, and starting afresh, is that for generations afterwards a society may stagger from one constitutional experiment to another, with much violence and bloodshed on its path.

1.3.2 The legitimacy of legal rules

A second important quality of tradition is that it imbues law with the authority of multi-generational collaboration. It is a feature of all long-standing traditions of law that they have a core of legal rules and principles which are deemed to be foundational precepts. They represent a basic structure of rights, obligations, entitlements and prohibitions which are essential for social harmony. Over time, these foundational rules of the society may develop, adapt and become more sophisticated, but the maturing law builds upon that basic structure. Furthermore, it is an aspect of these foundational laws that they are seen to be derived in some broad sense from the community and reflect the values of that community. They are the product of a tradition which transcends generations, and, in the case of the common law particularly, also transcends national boundaries.

This transcendent authority of the law, from which particular legal rules gain a derivative legitimacy, results, at least in part,[64] from a sense that law is essential to the life of a community and that the law which we have reflects the accumulated wisdom of past generations which has been handed down to the present. This involvement of past generations in developing the laws of the present is not necessarily true of specific rules, which may owe their authority to an Act of Parliament which was brought into force last year, or a decision which was handed down by the High Court of Australia yesterday. Not all rules can claim to be produced by the accumulated wisdom of many generations. Some particular rules may not be the product of very much wisdom at all. However, as has been discussed, new rules of law do not completely replace existing laws, rather they modify the existing corpus of law, and must fit within it. No one generation can work out for itself, as if beginning on a fresh sheet of paper, the balances which need to be struck between competing and conflicting rights, or the extent to which and the reasons for which essentially autonomous human beings should owe obligations to one another. The balances which have been struck between competing rights often have to be reconsidered and adjusted as societal needs and values change; nonetheless this process occurs by adaptation of the solutions and compromises of previous generations, and only rarely by abrogation of them.

Thus, particular legal rules gain an important degree of legitimacy from their location within a body of rules which do represent the work of many generations. And it is the recognition that the law as a whole represents a multi-generational achievement which gives the law a life and authority of its own. Even if citizens disagree with individual rules, or perceive injustice in individual cases, the traditionality of law, and the respect which judges accord to precedent, is a factor in giving it a sufficient level of acceptance to play a role as adjudicator in bitter conflicts and as arbiter of competing claims. The shared acceptance of the legal tradition, and respect for its inherent authority, provides a focal point for ultimate unity in the face of the very conflicts which the law is called upon to resolve.

1.4   Tradition and Change

Precisely because traditions have their origins in the past, they are likely to be influenced, for good or ill, by the values of the past. They necessarily reflect the values and culture of the generations in which they developed, and need to be reviewed critically in the light of changes in the circumstances, needs and values of contemporary society. Legal traditions which have developed in a male-dominated world may reflect male perspectives, consciously or otherwise. They may likewise have been shaped by the needs of those who have most wealth and education, with the result that the law tends to be inaccessible to the population as a whole.

Thus, a legal tradition must constantly undergo adaptation and renewal in order to meet the changing needs of society. In particular, it faces continually the challenge of inclusion. For the legitimacy which the legal tradition provides to the political order is dependent upon its acceptance as belonging to the people. It is in this respect that the tradition of law in Australia is most in need of renewal. For as long as Australians saw themselves as Britons in a different land, for as long as they were content to retain the close ties with the mother country, it mattered little that their law was so heavily dependent upon British borrowings. The sense of ownership of the legal tradition was tied to the sense of belonging to the wider British "family". All that is changing now. Increasingly, it is perceived that divergence between Britain and Australia is both inevitable and desirable.[65] Britain's sphere of economic involvement has shifted from the British Commonwealth to the European Union. Australia is beginning to perceive the need to locate itself economically and politically within Asia and the Pacific. With such changes in orientation, it is no longer enough for Australia to rely on a borrowed tradition, resting upon a derivative legitimacy. Australian legislatures and courts have recognised the need for Australian law to pursue its own path, drawing assistance from England and other common law countries, but ultimately seeking its own solutions to problems of law and society. This process began perhaps, with the enactment of the Constitution of the Commonwealth of Australia in 1900, and has gathered pace since the 1960s.

The challenge of inclusion is to encourage a sense that the Australian legal tradition is one which "belongs" to all parts of the community.[66] This involves some reconciliation between white Australians and the Aboriginal community. It involves the adaptation of Australian law to the needs of a multicultural society. It also involves recognising where the application of the law has a discriminatory impact on women. Feminist legal scholars have been active in demonstrating areas of the law where the rules which are in place act detrimentally to women, or where the legal system fails to take account of women's perspectives. The challenge of inclusion also involves adapting the legal system to the needs and rights of children, especially as defendants in criminal cases and witnesses in court proceedings. A continual concern is that all sections of the community should have access to affordable justice. It is through this process of continual re-examination that the legal tradition is adapted in each generation to the needs and values of the community.

An important issue for Australian law now, is how to effect these changes while maintaining continuities within the legal tradition. Not every pressure group can be accommodated, not everyone's values and lifestyles in a pluralistic society can be equally respected. In coping with the tension between tradition and change it is essential to identify and hold onto those core values, principles and beliefs which are at the heart of the tradition. These are moral, political and procedural principles which together give content to a society's central ideas about justice, democracy and civil order. A monocultural tradition may successfully adapt itself to cultural pluralism only if it avoids lapsing into moral relativism.

The themes of tradition and change in Australian law are the themes of this book. The tradition needs to be identified and explored within its historic origins both as an idea as part of the western legal tradition, and in its detailed development through the course of English history. The constitutional inheritance from England and the manner in which Australia achieved independence in a legal sense are traced. The tension between the past and the present in terms of legal reasoning is explored through the doctrine of precedent and the changes in approach to statutory interpretation.

Australian law is in a process of transition. The transition is on many levels and in many different areas. Essentially however, the legal tradition is changing in response to the challenge of inclusion, to make it relevant to our present needs, and to give a changing society a renewed sense of ownership of a tradition which developed centuries ago, on the other side of the world.

NOTES

1. Crawford, J, "Australian Law After Two Centuries" (1988) 11 Sydney LR 444.
2. See further, below, Chapter 6.
3. See below, 5.3.3.
4. Watson, A, *The Evolution of Law* (John Hopkins UP, Baltimore, 1985).
5. The term "civil law" has two distinct meanings. As used above, the term refers to the tradition of law in Europe which traces its origins to interpretation of the Ius Civilis, the "civil law" of the Roman Emperor Justinian. See further, below, Chapter 2. The term is also used in contrast with the criminal law, and in this context refers to that branch of the law which deals with disputes and competing entitlements, where the punitive powers of the criminal law are not invoked.
6. The knowledge of Roman law did not survive continuously through the centuries following the decline and fall of the Roman Empire. Rather it was rediscovered at the end of the 11th century, and became the subject of intense scholarly study thereafter. See further, below, Chapter 2.
7. The existence of a western legal tradition which unites the common law systems and the civil law countries (based on Roman law), has been questioned. For a defence of the concept, see David, R, "On the Concept of 'Western' Law" (1983) 52 Univ of Cincinnati LR 126. See also Sawer, G, "The Western Conception of Law" *International Encyclopedia of Comparative Law* (Tubingen, The Hague, 1975), Vol II, Ch 1.
8. This is not true specifically of all 50 States in the present Union. Parts of the United States, such as Louisiana, were originally under French control. Louisiana retains certain civil law ideas. On the West Coast, the Spanish had a formative influence, notably in California.
9. See further, Fitzgerald, R, and Hearn, M, *Bligh, Macarthur and the Rum Rebellion* (Kangaroo Press, Sydney, 1988).
10. The Boston Tea Party was an incident in December 1773 prior to the American War of Independence, in which colonists disguised as Indians boarded three ships in Boston Harbour, and threw tea overboard in protest at the taxation imposed by the British government on goods imported into the American colonies.
11. For discussion of this in the High Court of Australia, see *China Ocean Shipping Co v South Australia* (1979) 145 CLR 172, in particular, the debate between Stephen and Murphy JJ.
12. In five surveys between 1953 and 1981, the Morgan Gallup poll in the Bulletin did not record a percentage greater than 28 per cent in support of a republic. McMillan, J, Evans, G, and Storey, H, *Australia's Constitution: Time for Change?* (Law Foundation of New South Wales and Allen and Unwin, Sydney, 1983), p 178. For a history of republican sentiment in Australia, see Grassby, A, *The Australian Republic* (Pluto Press, Sydney, 1993).

13. See below, Chapter 5.
14. See, eg, *Van Ness v Pacard* (1829) 27 US 137.
15. See Pound, R, *The Spirit of the Common Law* (Marshall Jones, Francestown, NH, 1921); Jones, H W, "The Common Law in the United States: English Themes and American Variations" in H W Jones (ed) *Political Separation and Legal Continuity* (American Bar Association, Atlanta, 1976), p 91.
16. For a discussion of the evolutionary metaphor within Anglo-American jurisprudence see Elliott, D, "The Evolutionary Tradition in Jurisprudence" (1985) 85 Columbia LR 38.
17. See, eg, Nygh, P, "Malaysia, Singapore, Australia and Papua New Guinea: The Common Law Approach to Interpersonal Law in Marriage Relations" (1972) 3 *Lawasia* 137.
18. For over 100 years, this treaty lay dormant, and had little ongoing significance for the legal relationship between whites and Maoris. In recent years, the treaty has been given considerable prominence as a basis for the recognition of indigenous Maori rights.
19. See below, Chapter 5. In a landmark decision, *Mabo v Queensland (No 2)* (1992) 175 CLR 1, the High Court at last gave recognition to aboriginal native title at common law, and overturned the position that New South Wales should be treated as terra nullius, unoccupied territory, at the time of its white settlement. See further, below, 5.1.3.
20. See further McRae, H, Nettheim, G, and Beacroft, L, *Aboriginal Legal Issues* (Law Book Co, Sydney, 1991), pp 9-32; Gumbert, M, *Neither Justice Nor Reason* (University of Queensland Press, St Lucia, 1984); Bird, G, *The Process of Law in Australia— Intercultural Perspectives* (2nd ed, Butterworths, Sydney, 1993), pp 24-38.
21. See Read, P, *The Stolen Generations. The Removal of Aboriginal Children in New South Wales 1883 to 1969* (New South Wales Ministry of Aboriginal Affairs, Sydney, 1982).
22. See Australian Law Reform Commission, Report No 31, *The Recognition of Aboriginal Customary Laws* (AGPS, Canberra, 1986); *National Report of the Royal Commission into Aboriginal Deaths in Custody* (AGPS, Canberra, 1991).
23. This was put in place especially through the *Immigration Restriction Act* 1901 (Cth). Section 3 required prospective migrants to take a dictation test of 50 words in a European language. By an amending Act in 1905, the word "European" was replaced by the words "a prescribed language" to avoid giving offence to Japan and India. The "white Australia" policy was also carried into effect by the *Pacific Island Labourers Act* 1901 which provided for the deportation of all such labourers by 1905. A few were later allowed to remain on compassionate grounds. See further, Clark, M, *A Short History of Australia* (3rd ed, NAL Penguin, New York 1986), pp 196-199.
24. Clark, M, op cit, p 269.
25. Australian Bureau of Statistics, *Overseas Born Australians 1988: A Statistical Profile* (ABS, Canberra, 1989), p 47.
26. Ibid, p 46.
27. Bureau of Immigration Research, *Settler Arrivals 1989-1990* (AGPS, Canberra, 1991).
28. Bird, G, op cit; Australian Law Reform Commission, Report No 57, *Multiculturalism and the Law* (AGPS, Canberra, 1992).
29. See below, Chapter 10.
30. For discussion, see Finlay, L, "Breaking Women's Silence in Law: The Dilemma of the Gendered Nature of Legal Reasoning" (1989) 64 *Notre Dame Law Review* 886.
31. Blackstone, W, *Commentaries on the Laws of England* (1765), Bk 1, Vol 1, Ch 15. For discussion, see Parker, S, Parkinson, P, and Behrens, J, *Australian Family Law in Context* (Law Book Co, Sydney, 1994), pp 307-308.
32. Blackstone, W, ibid.
33. A trust is a form of ownership in which the legal title of the property is held by trustees who have the responsibility for its management, and the property is looked after on behalf of those who are the "beneficiaries" of the trust.
34. See O'Donovan, K, *Sexual Divisions in the Law* (Weidenfeld and Nicolson, London, 1985); Olsen, F, "The Myth of State Intervention in the Family" (1985) 18 Univ of Michigan J of Law Reform 835.
35. New Zealand led the world in granting women the vote in 1893. South Australia gave women the vote in 1894. The vote was granted to women in England only after World War I.
36. MacKinnon, C, *Toward a Feminist Theory of the State* (Harvard UP, Cambridge, 1989), p 170.

37. Polan, D, "Towards a Theory of Law and Patriarchy" in D Kairys (ed), *The Politics of Law: A Progressive Critique* (Pantheon, New York, 1982), p 303. A similar view is implicit in the writings of Australian scholars Regina Graycar and Jenny Morgan. They refer to the mainstream tradition of law as the "malestream". See Graycar, R, and Morgan, J, *The Hidden Gender of Law* (Federation Press, Sydney, 1992), p 6. For a critique of their work, see Hill, J, and Loughlan, P, "Feminism and Doll's Houses" (1993) 15 Sydney LR 373.

38. Gilligan, C, *In a Different Voice: Psychological Theory and Women's Development* (Harvard UP, Cambridge, 1982).

39. For discussion, see Graycar, R, and Morgan, J, op cit, pp 50-55. See also Frug, M J, "Progressive Feminist Legal Scholarship: Can We Claim a Different Voice?" (1992) 15 *Harvard Women's Law Journal* 37.

40. For a discussion of different feminist approaches to law, see Naffine, N, *Law and the Sexes* (Allen and Unwin, Sydney, 1990), Ch 1.

41. Krygier, M, "Law as Tradition" (1986) 5 *Law and Philosophy* 237 at 240-251.

42. Ibid at 241.

43. See below, Chapter 9.

44. Krygier, M, "The Traditionality of Statutes" (1988) 1 *Ratio Juris* 20.

45. Vining, J, *The Authoritative and the Authoritarian* (University of Chicago Press, Chicago, 1986), p 9.

46. As Professor Blackshield has written: "Great individual judges of the past are a living presence, reinforced by accretions of anecdote and parable and cultural folklore which give us a sense of working with them in a vast continuous enterprise." Blackshield, A, "The Legitimacy and Authority of Judges" (1987) 10 UNSWLJ 155 at 157.

47. Consultative Group on Research and Education in Law, *Law and Learning: A Report to the Social Science and Humanities Research Council of Canada* (1983) (the Arthurs Report), cited in Weisbrot, D, *Australian Lawyers* (Longman Cheshire, Melbourne, 1990), p 8.

48. Professor Berman argues that law shares four features in common with religion: the use of rituals, the importance of tradition, the reliance upon authority and the claim of universality. See Berman, H, *The Interaction of Law and Religion* (SCM Press, London, 1974), pp 31-39.

49. See below, Chapter 8.

50. Carr, E H, wrote in *What is History?* (Penguin, Harmondsworth, 1964), pp 29-30: "The relation between a historian and his facts is one of equality, of give-and-take . . . As he works, both the interpretation and the selection and ordering of his facts undergo subtle and perhaps partly unconscious changes, through the reciprocal action of one on the other. And this reciprocal action also involves reciprocity between present and past, since the historian is part of the present and the facts belong to the past."

51. Krygier, M, "Law as Tradition" (1986) 5 *Law and Philosophy* 237 at 250.

52. Krygier, M, "Thinking Like a Lawyer" in W Sadurski (ed), *Ethical Dimensions of Legal Theory* (Rodopi, Amsterdam, 1991), p 68.

53. MacIntyre, A, *After Virtue* (2nd ed, Duckworths, London, 1985), p 146.

54. Berman, H, *Law and Revolution* (Harvard UP, Cambridge, Mass, 1983), p 5.

55. See below, Chapter 4.

56. Tay, A, "The Role of Law in the 20th Century: From Law to Laws to Social Science" (1991) 13 Syd LR 247 at 251-252.

57. See the discussion of the rule of law as seen in English law during the 18th century: 4.7.1.

58. See, eg, the account of events in Malaysia: Trindade, F, "The Removal of the Malaysian Judges" (1990) 106 LQR 51.

59. Marx, K, "The 18th Brumaire of Louis Bonaparte" in K Marx and F Engels, *Selected Works* (Progress Publishers, Moscow, 1969), Vol 1, p 398.

60. Plato, *Menexenus* 239a. See further, Kelly, J, *A Short History of Western Legal Theory* (Clarendon, Oxford, 1992), pp 29-30, 37, 70-72.

61. This became effective from 1 January 1863.

62. This view is reflected in American constitutional law. In determining which rights should be treated as so fundamental that they should receive the protection of the 14th amendment to the United States Constitution (the due process clause), four members of the Supreme Court of the United States said that the court should look to "traditionally protected interests". Scalia J, with whom three other members agreed, said that the purpose of limiting judicial activism in this way is "to prevent future generations lightly casting aside important traditional values". *Michael H v Gerald D* (1989) 491 US 110 at 122, n 2.

63. Burke, E, *Reflections on the Revolution in France* (1790) cited, and discussed, in Kronman, A, "Precedent and Tradition" (1990) Yale LJ 1029 at 1048ff. For a critique of Kronman's views see Luban, D, "Legal Traditionalism" (1991) 43 Stanford LR 1035.
64. The reverence for law in popular consciousness may also be attributed to the impact of the Judaeo-Christian tradition in shaping western values and, related to this, the various forms of natural law theory. See below, Chapter 2.
65. See, eg, Mason, Sir Anthony, "Future Directions in Australian Law" (1987) 13 Monash ULR 149.
66. See below, Chapter 10.

Chapter 2

THE WESTERN IDEA OF LAW

To understand the tradition of law in Australia, it is necessary to understand the idea of law which has prevailed throughout the western world. From England, Australia inherited the substance of the common law, its methodology, values and fundamental precepts; but the idea of law to which the common law gave specific content was of much greater antiquity, and it was an idea shared with those countries which had a civil law system. This idea of law offered an understanding of the nature and function of law in society, and its significance for order and good government. In this chapter, we examine some of the central characteristics of that tradition, its origins, development and formative influences, and the ideas about law which remain significant today.

Many of the features of the western legal tradition are so familiar that it is tempting to see them as universal. However, this is far from the case. If such ideas are becoming universal, then it is only because of the pervasive influence of western values and ideas throughout the world. In turn, the western legal tradition has been affected, to a certain extent, by the values of other legal orders.

2.1   Characteristics of the Western Legal Tradition

There are three characteristics of the western legal tradition which are particularly noteworthy, and which distinguish it from the place of law in other cultures.[1] The first is the autonomy of law; the second is its centrality in social ordering; the third is its moral authority.

2.1.1   The autonomy of law

Law, in western thought, is an autonomous discipline. That is, it is conceptually distinct from custom, morality, religion or politics,[2] and a clear differentiation is made between legal institutions and other types of institutions, and between legal rules and other kinds of rules. Moral norms and legal norms may coincide but are not synonymous with one another. Laws may originate in the customs of a community, but are distinct from customs inasmuch as not all customs are law, and not all laws originate in custom. Laws may have a religious rationale, but the source of their authority and binding nature is not religious obligation, but civic duty.

24

Thus, courts in Australia punish criminal infringements and enforce contractual obligations not merely because the majority of the population would approve of this, nor because such action is sanctioned by the teachings of a particular faith, but because the law of the land allows, and indeed instructs, the courts to act in this way. Similarly, laws may reflect the will of a government, but the will of the government is not, in itself, law, and indeed the laws of the land may at times thwart the will of a government.

Law is not autonomous in the sense that it is free from the influences of politics, religion, economics and those factors of culture, upbringing and worldview which influence the beliefs and attitudes of individual judges. The content of law is shaped, perhaps even dictated, by the social forces which are the context of law's operation; but the values of these social forces are not simply reproduced in the western legal tradition as legal norms. They have to be reconstructed within law and to be accepted as law. That is, the language of other disciplines and belief systems is not merely translated into law, but rewritten as law, converted into legal norms of rights and obligations, and of lawful and unlawful acts.[3] The vindication of those rights occurs through legal procedures, and the law takes on a life of its own as it develops the content and scope of those rights through its normal processes of legal reasoning and the establishment of legal precedents.

The autonomy of law in western societies is reflected in the fact that it has its own institutions, its own profession or professions, its own university discipline, professional literature, technical language and peculiar etiquette. The discipline of law is a distinct one. It is characterised in all western countries by a tendency towards the formal organisation of the law into categories and legal concepts, with an emphasis upon consistency in the application of legal norms. However, as Harold Berman points out, legal scholarship stands in a complex dialectical relationship to the legal institutions it studies since:

> "on the one hand the learning describes those institutions but on the other hand the legal institutions, which would otherwise be disparate and unorganised, become conceptualised and systematised, and thus transformed, by what is said about them in learned treatises and articles and in the classroom."[4]

A further feature of the western idea of law is that the law is seen as a coherent whole, a body of law which has developed gradually over the centuries, rather than a random collection of particular laws, each one developed in an ad hoc fashion to fill the needs of a given moment. From this body of law, new principles may be generated which are seen to be implicit in the existing rules, and in this way the law develops and grows by reference to its own logic and established precepts. Thus, it often finds renewal and adapts to changing circumstances by looking afresh at the principles contained within its own tradition.

The autonomy of law seems so obvious to the western mind that it is difficult to conceive of a civilisation which does not organise itself in the same way. Yet examples abound, both historically and in the present day. A contrast may be drawn between the western idea of law and the concept of law in traditional Aboriginal culture. Aboriginal communities certainly have laws.[5] However, these laws are inseparable from Aboriginal custom and religion. They are as much a part of custom and culture as Aboriginal music or dance. The leaders of Aboriginal communities maintain their laws as they maintain other traditions of the tribal community. Aboriginal laws require no distinctive hierarchy of judges to uphold them, nor is there a distinctive "profession" associated with them. This does not mean that Aboriginal customary law is any less "law" than the laws of western societies. It differs from western law, however, in that Aboriginal customary law is not autonomous. The rise of fundamentalist Islam provides another example of where law and religion may be inextricably interwined. Where legal principles are derived directly from sacred writings, and owe their authority to the divine will, law ceases to have an authority which is independent from that of the religion. Islamic groups which seek to adopt the Shar'ia law of the Koran as the basis of a national legal system, deny the autonomy of law.

As law in some societies may be only an aspect of a community's custom or religion, so in some societies it may be nothing more than a manifestation of political power. Where monarchs have exercised absolute power, no distinction could be made between political power and the law. The Roman jurist, Ulpian, writing in about 215 AD, wrote of a society which was tending in that direction when he stated that "the emperor's will has the force of statute."[6] However, when people bind their rulers by constitutions or other legal limits, the law asserts its independence from political power, and subjugates political power to its authority.

2.1.2   The centrality of law

The second prominent characteristic of the western legal tradition is the centrality of law as a means of social ordering. Law pervades every aspect of modern society, and is a primary means of social control. Laws regulate business and labour relations extensively; laws govern political life through constitutional precepts, and the decision making of public officials through elaborate systems of administrative law; laws provide a framework for family relations, including both the entry into, and exit from, marriage, and increasingly, in dealing with the various disputes which arise on the breakdown of de facto relationships. Laws govern dealings between people, both by giving effect to contracts if freely and fairly made, and by imposing other obligations not to cause harm to one another.

This centrality of law has a long history in western legal thought. Adda Bozeman writes that:

"[I]t would be difficult not to conclude from the records that law has consistently been trusted in the West as the main carrier of shared values, the most effective agent of social control, and the only reliable principle capable of moderating and reducing the reign of passion, arbitrariness and caprice in human life."[7]

Furthermore, law is seen as a primary means of social change. Political parties campaign for control of the legislative body as well as the executive, and law provides an important means of giving effect to the policies of the government, along with fiscal management and education. Law, in itself, is perceived as having not only a coercive value, but also an educative power. It sends messages, as well as mandating particular conduct.

Geoffrey Sawer emphasises the pervasiveness of legal ordering in observing the paradox that law is seen as essential even by revolutionaries who demonstrate hostility to lawyers:

"[T]he lawyer as an individual or a type has often been exceedingly unpopular and lawyers have often been the first to suffer in revolutionary situations. Nevertheless, lawyers . . . have also always been prominent in the councils of rulers and of revolutionaries alike. A respect for and even a demand for the legal approach to the structuring or ordering of social relations has kept triumphing over the periodic dissatisfactions with the particular structure or order achieved at a particular time and place . . . it is still the predominant western view that theories of the disappearance of law, or of its replacement by social administration, are utopian."[8]

The centrality and pervasiveness of law in western society is nonetheless far from universal. There are other means of social ordering which have power in other societies. Religion and custom can be significant factors in shaping human behaviour, as can etiquette, honour, and national loyalty. Law plays a less pronounced role in societies which can appeal to other bases for moulding behaviour. The appeal to Islamic tradition or to communist values, is a call to do certain things or to behave in certain ways for reasons other than adherence to legal rules.

In particular, the centrality of law in western societies may be contrasted with the tradition of eastern cultures such as those of China and Japan. Traditionally, the Chinese recognised enacted or "positive" law, called "fa", which meant the rules prescribed by an earthly ruler. However, the Chinese were generally suspicious of fa. It was seen to be much better for the preservation of harmony and order in the universe, that social relations should be governed by "li", the ethics, taboos, ceremonies and customs of the community. The distrust of fa is demonstrated in the introduction to the oldest datable code of law in China, the *Tso Chuan* (535 BC) in which it was said:

"The ancient kings, who weighed matters very carefully before establishing ordinances, did not [write down] their systems of punishments, fearing to awaken a litigious spirit among the people. But since all crimes cannot be prevented, they set up the barrier of righteousness, bound the people by administrative ordinances, treated them according to just usage, guarded them with good faith, and surrounded them with benevolence . . . But when the people know that there are laws regulating punishments, they have no respectful fear of authority. A litigious spirit awakes, invoking the letter of the law, and trusting that evil actions will not fall under its provisions."[9]

A similar pattern may be seen in Japan, where honour and good faith are more important factors in maintaining relations than the law.[10] In the latter half of the 19th century, Japan adopted a legal system which was modelled substantially on the legal codes of continental Europe. This "western" idea of law was, however, grafted onto traditional Japanese methods of social ordering. Japanese society is ordered by a series of social rules known as "giri", which specify the conduct to be observed in a great variety of interpersonal relationships. Society is reliant on observation of the giri to a much greater extent than it is reliant on law. In the event of disputes, the initial appeal would be to the giri. Indeed, much emphasis is placed on the importance of negotiating with sincerity,[11] with compromise and reconciliation being more important than the vindication of legal rights. Law thus has a place, but it is far from central. Indeed, resort to the law may be considered shameful in Japanese society.

2.1.3   The moral authority of law

A third feature of the western legal tradition is that the law commands a high level of respect in western societies which is independent of popular acceptance either of the merits of particular laws or of the level of respect shown to the law makers. Law, thus, is not only autonomous; it tends to be disembodied in people's consciousness from the law makers, and derives authority and respect from a deep sense within the community that the law ought to be obeyed, not merely for fear of sanction, but from a feeling of positive obligation.

Descriptions of law as an instrument for giving effect to the policies of those in power, or as a collection of rules governing political, social and economic relations, or in terms of law's function in regulating society, provide a wholly inadequate description of law in themselves. They miss the important element that law, in the western legal tradition, is not only generally obeyed, but believed in. It is not only, or even mainly fear of sanctions which secures obedience to law (although some laws, such as speeding laws, may be an exception). People have an emotional commitment to such values as the desire for equal treatment before the law, the claim to an impartial hearing, the need for consistency in the application of rules, and the principle that governments are themselves subject to law. People appeal to their legal rights, and to the obligations of others towards them, as a standard to be adhered to in their private dealings with one another, and as an objective indication of right conduct. Law, in popular consciousness, thus represents what one ought to do morally, as well as legally, and the appeal to law is an appeal to voluntary compliance out of respect for the rightness of the law's demands.

The adherence to law, in other words, has a quasi-sacred quality in the western legal tradition. Fidelity to law, adherence by governments to the rule of law, and the importance of procedural fairness in the application of laws, represent fundamental values in western societies. As Harold Berman writes:

> "Law itself, in all societies, encourages the belief in its own sanctity. It puts forward its claim to obedience in ways that appeal not only to the material, impersonal, finite, rational interests of the people who are asked to observe it but also to their faith in a truth, a justice, that transcends social utility . . . Even Joseph Stalin had to reintroduce into Soviet law elements which would make his people believe in its inherent rightness—emotional elements, sacred elements; for otherwise the persuasiveness of law would have totally vanished, and even Stalin could not rule solely by threat of force." [12]

This respect for law in western countries, and its quasi-sacred authority in popular consciousness, is not universal. Indeed, in some ways, respect for law is a fragile quality. The experience of a number of western countries in recent years demonstrates that a strong adherence to the fundamental precepts of the western legal tradition can co-exist with the breakdown of law and order in some parts of the community. This breakdown is often associated with poverty; but on its own, this is an inadequate explanation. Many countries are poor, yet the levels of violent crime are very much lower than in some western countries. When people become alienated from a society, and perceive themselves as destined to be the have-nots within a nation where levels of wealth are high, respect for the rule of law will often give way to violent and destructive tendencies. Respect for law cannot be taken for granted. It is always dependent, ultimately, on people's sense of belonging to a society. Where law is seen purely as an instrument of repression, it ceases to be effective as law at all.

2.2   The Origins of the Western Legal Tradition

All of these characteristics of the western legal tradition reflect its historic origins. Specifically, the western idea of law developed from a combination of Roman, Greek, and Judaeo-Christian thought. These all played a role in shaping our ideas about law as a result of a revival of classical learning from the late 11th century onwards. Roman law provided the basis for the civil law systems of continental Europe, and for much of the canon law of the church. However, Roman law was inextricably intertwined with Greek and Christian influences, for it was studied within the context of a worldview which was derived from Aristotelian philosophy as reinterpreted by Christian theology. Indeed, Christianity was to the formation of the western legal tradition as the womb is to human life. The history of western law cannot be understood in isolation from religious influences, for at every level of society, and in every aspect of social and political life, these influences were pervasive. It was largely through the influence of church teachers and writers that classical ideas from Greece and Rome gained so much currency, and when Roman law was revived in the 11th and 12th centuries, the methodology which was used to study the Roman law texts was the same methodology of scholasticism, derived from Greek dialectical reasoning, which was used to explain, harmonise and reconcile the Scriptures. Furthermore, the Christian theology of revelation was married with the Roman and Greek ideas of natural law to form the intellectual underpinnings of the medieval legal system.

The western idea of law, derived from these formative influences, has always been an evolving one. Many of the fundamental ideas about law which influenced legal thought for centuries are no longer widely held in modern western thought. Conversely, modern ideas about the nature and function of law would have been alien to legal theorists even two centuries ago. Yet the western idea of law has developed as all traditions develop. Present ideas about law are only intelligible as a commentary upon and response to the past,[13] and legal theory has developed either by building upon, or in seeking to correct, what has gone before. Even if some theories about law which dominated western legal thought for centuries are no longer current, they have given to the modern world a legacy of many of its foundational precepts and most commonly invoked ideas.

2.2.1   The rediscovery of roman law

The influence of Roman law on the western legal tradition may be traced to the rediscovery of certain Roman law texts towards the end of the 11th century, and their intensive study by medieval scholars from that time onwards.[14] Roman law had, of course, influenced Europe during the heyday of the Roman Republic and Empire, in particular from the first century BC to the third century AD. At the height of its influence, Rome had dominion over much of Europe. By the 11th century, however, it was merely a distant memory. In 395 AD, it had split into two empires, the western empire based upon Rome itself, and an eastern empire centred in Constantinople. The western empire fell in 476 AD, when the last emperor of the West was deposed, but already in 410 AD, the empire was crumbling. In that year, Alaric and his Visigoth soldiers had conquered and plundered Rome. After the fall of the western empire, Roman civilisation thereafter lingered on only in the East, where it became subject to Greek and oriental influences. The old western empire of Rome passed to the control of Germanic tribes.

Nonetheless, it was significant for the revival of Roman law in the 11th century that the political idea, as opposed to the political reality, of a Roman empire in the west continued. In particular, it experienced a renewal with the coronation by the Pope in 800 AD of Charlemagne, ruler of the Franks, as Emperor of Rome. Charlemagne sought to give to his Frankish empire some of the traditional dignity associated with the Roman empire. After the fall of Charlemagne's successors, known as the Carolingians, the title of Roman emperor passed to the German kings (c 950 AD).

The Holy Roman Empire, centred upon Germany, had an ideological meaning to northern and western Europe which transcended the limits of the military and political power of these rulers. As a practical matter, the Holy Roman emperors did not have temporal dominion over all of Christendom, even in the West. Temporal authority in places such as Britain which were further from the heartland of German influence, was exercised by local and national rulers. But the Holy Roman Empire suggested a historic continuity between the old Roman empire and the Europe of the ninth century and beyond, and with that, the continuing theoretical relevance of Roman law.

However, Roman law could not, practically, have much influence since its detail was long since lost. Parts of it had survived in collective memory in the customs of local communities, but the dominant influences upon custom were derived from other sources. The methods of dispute resolution which were common to much of western Europe, such as trials by ordeal, and the appeal to supernatural intervention, were the product of pagan religious ideas. To a limited extent, classical learning had been preserved through the monasteries, but the revival of Roman law awaited the rediscovery of certain manuscripts in northern Italy in the late 11th century, which could provide details of its content.

2.2.2   The texts of Justinian

The texts which were rediscovered at that time were those associated with the Emperor Justinian who ruled the eastern empire between 527 and 565 AD, at a time when Roman influence was well into its twilight years. Justinian had sought to collect and preserve the learning of classical Roman law by bringing it all together in a number of volumes. In the medieval period, these texts came to be known collectively as the *Corpus Juris Civilis*. The *Corpus Juris* of Justinian was the product of a remarkable enterprise in collecting and organising the various sources of Roman law, which was carried out by Justinian's minister Tribonianus. Most of it was first issued in 533-534 AD. It was a much needed gathering and ordering of the law applicable in the empire. By this stage, the primary sources of Roman law were twofold. First, there were the decisions, decrees and laws of the Roman emperors. Secondly, there were the writings of the jurists. The jurists were experts in the law who gave advice and opinions on difficult issues of law to litigants and judges. These opinions came to be collected in books. The jurists were not inclined to philosophical speculation or conceptual analysis. Rather their concentration was upon specific cases and legal problems which arose in Roman society.

Over several centuries, a vast body of writing on the law was thus gathered. Inevitably, there were many conflicting opinions in this vast body of literature, deriving from different jurists in different time periods. By the fifth century, attempts had been made to state which of the jurists had particular authority. Five writers from the second and third centuries AD, Papinian, Paul, Gaius, Ulpian and Modestinus, gained this status.[15] However, Justinian recognised the need to go beyond merely the ascription of special authority to a few men. Some reordering of this vast body of writing was needed. The *Corpus Juris* collected the imperial laws and selected from the writings of the most prominent jurists. Some attempt was made to eliminate contradictions by amending the texts to suit the need for an orderly account.

The *Corpus Juris* comprised a number of different parts—the Digest, the Code, the Novels and the Institutes. The longest of these books was the Digest. It ran to thousands of pages, and contained extracts from the opinions of Roman jurists on a wide variety of legal questions, ordered according to a basic system of topics. The Code comprised the laws of the Roman emperors who preceded Justinian. The Novels contained Justinian's own laws, while the Institutes was a short textbook designed to introduce the law to new students. The purpose of Justinian's collection was to preserve the best of the classical Roman law and to reform the law of his own time.

The rediscovery of these texts thus gave a vast degree of material on Roman law to the scholars of the late 11th century and beyond. But why study Roman law at all? They did not study these texts to seek insight into a past civilisation. This was not an age when antiquity was valued for its own sake. A partial answer is that Roman law was far more detailed and sophisticated than any customs or traditions which had emerged since then, and in comparison to Roman law, local laws and customs were not considered worthy of study. Roman law represented an ideal of what law ought to be.[16] Furthermore, with the perceived continuity between Rome and the germanic Holy Roman Empire, it was understood as representing in some sense, a law for the Empire which was of continuing validity. A further reason for the intensive study of Roman law was that it provided a major source of answers where local customary law was too primitive and limited to offer solutions. It provided a means of filling gaps in customary law, and was accessible because it was written and ordered.[17] However, a major reason for studying Roman law was also to be found in the worldview of the medieval scholars. This was the age of the authoritative text, in which scholars were avidly seeking after truth in whatever sphere it might be found. Religious truth was to be found in the Bible and the teachings of the Church Fathers; and these scholars saw law as well as theology as being truth to be discovered. To the Roman law texts and to such of the writings of Aristotle as were then known, these scholars gave a quasi-sacred authority.[18]

The intensive study of Roman law began at the end of the 11th century in a number of cities, including Orleans, Pavia, Ravenna, Rome and Verona. Most well known as a centre of learning was Bologna. Its fame became established with Irnerius (c 1055-c 1130) who in about 1088 began to lecture there on Justinian's texts. The study of Roman law attracted students from all over Europe, despite the difficulties and dangers of travel in that period. Fifty years after Irnerius began teaching in Bologna, there were sometimes thousands of students in the city. [19] In this new interest in learning (not only about Roman law, but also canon law) there developed a "university". The word "university" is derived from the Latin word "universitas", which was the name given to the associations of students which were formed to organise study and to employ teachers at Bologna and in other cities. In Italy, the university began, therefore, as a body organised by students. Teachers were not members of the universitas. In Paris, a university of a different model was founded, in which professorial control was the basis. [20] In the same period, universities were also founded elsewhere, including at Oxford and, later, at Cambridge. Apart from law, students studied theology, medicine and the liberal arts.

2.2.3   The glossators and commentators

These scholars of the late 11th and 12th centuries set about studying and harmonising the Justinian texts, especially the Digest. This work took the form of making notes or glosses to the text; thus the scholars became known as the glossators. The work of the glossators lasted from the beginning of the 12th century until approximately the middle of the 13th century. Initially, these glosses were written between the lines and the margins of the Roman text by students. As time went on, however, they became more and more extensive, and eventually the work of the glossator school was presented, along with his own work, by Accursius, who produced a great textbook which came to be known as the "Standard Gloss", and formed the basis of future generations' understanding of the Corpus Juris. The work of the glossators was primarily the exposition of the text, with detailed treatments of specific difficulties. There was, within this mass of writing, however, some tendency to want to formulate more general rules from the mass of detail in the Digest.

The work of systematisation was continued by the commentators, of whom the most famous was the Italian, Bartolus (1313-1357). These scholars wrote detailed commentaries on the text. They classified, distinguished, and refined concepts, using Aristotelian logic. Like the glossators, the commentators were still essentially legal technicians, but the needs of the time required them to adapt Roman law concepts to grapple with current legal problems. Gradually, the commentators built up a substantial literature based upon their discussion of various problems and expert opinions.

From the work of the glossators and commentators, a systematic exposition of Roman law emerged. This was a version of Roman law quite different from the law which Cicero was familiar with, or to which Ulpian and Modestinus devoted themselves. It would, indeed, have been scarcely recognisable to the compilers of the Justinian corpus. Nonetheless, this transformed version of Roman law suited the needs of the Middle Ages. Through the work of the glossators and commentators, the Justinian texts experienced a slow but sure metamorphosis to become a working law for medieval continental Europe. As scholars who had been trained in the universities became judges so they used Roman law concepts in deciding cases where there was no applicable local law. They also interpreted local laws within the general framework of Roman law. In this way, Roman law ideas were received into national legal systems, and were later refined by adaptation and application even to international problems. Gradually, local customary law was displaced.

2.2.4   The humanist scholars

For as long as the scholastics insisted upon the quasi-sacred nature of Justinian's texts, little progress and development could occur. Legal scholarship was confined to further elaboration upon the Digest through commentaries. By the 15th century, this approach was under attack. Criticism of the reverence attached to the Digest increased by the end of the 15th century, with the awareness that there was an older and more reliable manuscript of the Digest than the one which had been used in Bologna. The knowledge of this Florentine manuscript undermined the sacrosanctity of the commentaries based upon the Bologna version. The humanist scholars of the 16th century, interested in the classical texts for their own sake, and committed to a fresh understanding of the sources in their historical context, discarded the glosses and the commentaries which had stood between the reader and the text, and which had acquired an authority greater than the texts themselves.

The study of Roman law for what it taught about Rome, rather than for what it taught about law, helped the humanist jurists to a new understanding of the relationship between law and society. As Professor Stein writes:[21]

> "Humanist jurists thus saw that the state of the Roman law was in some sense related to the political state of the Roman society, and in charting its developments, they noted parallels with the political changes which were going on in their own time. They saw in the study of ancient law lessons for legal and constitutional reform. But the more they related Roman law to what they had discovered about Roman society, the more they realised how different was their own 16th century society from that of ancient Rome. That led them to ask which stage of Roman law should be the best exemplar for them and then to question whether it was really appropriate to try to apply Roman law to contemporary society at all."

The awareness that Roman law need no longer be seen as authoritative for the law of their period, led the humanists to a new freedom in their treatment of the Roman law materials. Huguenot scholars such as Hugues Doneau (Donellus) (1527-1591) who taught at the University of Bourges, began to rearrange the Roman law materials in a more logical and systematic order which allowed the internal coherence of the law to be more readily appreciated.[22] With this new understanding of the law, systematic treatments of national laws were written. One of the most famous was by the Dutch writer Hugo Grotius (1583-1645). Grotius is most well known for his systematic exposition of international law in *De Jure Belli ac Pacis* (1625),[23] but he also wrote an account of Dutch law.[24]

It was a long time before this movement had any appreciable impact upon the substance of the civil law as practised in Europe. The glosses and commentaries of the earlier medieval scholars continued to be regarded as authoritative for many years. However, gradually, the work of the academic humanists began to influence national law, and the foundations were laid for modern systems of law in the civil law countries.

2.2.5   *Roman law, canon law and the common law*

As a result of the work of the glossators and commentators, much of the basic legal vocabulary of Europe is derived from Roman law, and also a significant part of its historic substance. Roman law also provided a basis for much of the canon law of the church. Canon law was the other great subject of legal study in the universities, and the study of canon law and Roman law side by side meant that inevitably, canon law borrowed concepts and solutions from Roman law.[25] The canon law provided for the church a vast system of law, by which it was governed. It was through law that the content of the faith was laid down for the church. That law should be used to govern the church reflected the worldview of the medieval period. It was thought that since God ruled the world through natural laws, it was appropriate for the church to use law to govern itself. Law had received divine approval.

Canon law was derived from a number of sources, including papal decrees, the decisions of church councils, some decrees of the early Frankish kings, the Bible and writings of the Church Fathers. In matters of faith and doctrine, these were necessarily the primary sources. However, the church was also a major institution with vast amounts of property, and its own order of government. It used law to regulate itself internally, and to govern its relations with secular authorities—for it was an institution which stood substantially outside the authority of national rulers. Church and state represented parallel systems of government standing alongside one another, and inter-relating with one another, each with its own law. The church also had exclusive jurisdiction over the lives of lay people in matters such as family law and inheritance. In some areas, such as certain contracts and in relation to church property, the church courts had a concurrent jurisdiction with secular courts. The dividing line of jurisdiction was frequently unclear, but these difficulties tended to be worked out through co-operation and compromise.

In England, the influence of Roman law was much less pronounced, since, as will be seen in the next chapter, the English common law developed in a manner quite different to the way law developed from Roman law in continental Europe. The common law grew from the practice of hearing cases in the royal courts; its learning was transmitted through apprenticeship schools attached to the Inns of Court in London, and in isolation from the classical study of Roman law in the universities. However, the isolation was not total. It took a while for a distinct legal profession to develop, and before it did, those exercising judicial office on behalf of the monarch were often men learned in Roman law and canon law. One of the earliest writers on the common law, Henry De Bracton, was considerably influenced by his study of Roman law principles.[26] Roman law continued to be used as a source of law thereafter. The borrowing was not extensive, but certain judges were disposed towards it, notably the great 18th century judge, Lord Mansfield.[27]

2.2.6   Scholasticism and legal method

The medieval study of Roman law in the universities by the glossators and commentators utilised a method of study which became known as "scholasticism". It was the same method as was used to analyse scripture and the teachings of the Church Fathers in order to harmonise and rationalise apparently conflicting texts and principles. It was no accident that law and theology should adopt the same method. Both were working with authoritative texts. The texts of Justinian were seen to have a universal and permanent quality, a codification of law as it ought to be, an embodiment of reason. The underlying assumption of its study was that this thread of reason ran through the somewhat diverse sayings of the jurists, and that discordant texts could, therefore, be reconciled. Similarly the Scriptures, were, and still are, considered by Christians to be authoritative in matters of faith and life, and to contain a fundamental unity of message despite the diversity of human authorship. To the medieval mind, both law and theology expressed truth in their respective spheres, and the work of scholars was to draw out that truth. The lawyer and the theologian were thus both "people of the book".

Scholasticism drew its characteristic methodology from Plato and Aristotle and, in particular, the principles of dialectical reasoning, but it transformed that methodology to accord with the worldview of the time. It was not Aristotle's ideas as originally presented which led to the transformation of Roman law into an elaborate system of law by the medieval scholars. Rather it was Aristotle as understood and interpreted in another age, with a different agenda to that of Aristotle himself.

"Dialectic" is derived from the Greek word for conversation or dialogue. It was a method of analysis which the Roman lawyers themselves had used during the classical era of Roman law, but which was taken much further by the medieval scholars. A simple form of dialectic reasoning used by the Scholastics began with the posing of a question relating to an apparent contradiction within the authoritative materials. The posing of a quaestio would be followed by a propositio stating authorities and reasons which supported one position. The oppositio gave authorities and reasons for the contrary proposition. Finally, a solutio or conclusio would result, showing why a propositio might be sustainable despite the contrary proposition, or why it might need to be qualified or abandoned. However, it was inherent in their belief in the law as coherent, and in all its parts authoritative, that contradictory propositions could be held together to produce a synthesis.

The scholastics had a variety of techniques for resolving contradictions and reconciling apparently opposing points of view. One of these was by deriving a general rule from the specific rules which were apparently in opposition. How, for example, might one reconcile the teaching of the Old and New Testaments which forbade killing with the examples of cases where killing appeared to be justified? Roman law recognised that in certain specific contexts, force could be used to repel force. It was characteristic of the Roman approach to such matters that this was not perceived as a general principle but rather it arose from specific circumstances connected primarily with the protection of property. The scholastic jurists did create a general principle, however, and from their analysis of a variety of contexts came the concept that in certain circumstances the limited use of force was justified. The same principles provided the basis for the notion of a "just war".

Important to the dialectical method also was the definition of concepts by distinction, which involved the analysis of a class (or genus) into species and subspecies, and conversely the logical techniques which formed species into a class and classes into larger classes. Together with this were two types of logic. Deductive logic moved from the general to the particular. A general rule might be stated in relation to a particular class, and necessarily that applied to all the species and subspecies of that class. Conversely, inductive logic moves from the particular to the general by identifying the common element in particular cases, from which general principles might be derived.

Aristotle distinguished carefully between logic which could create certainties and logic which could only lead to probabilities. "Apodictic" reasoning was the only form of reasoning which could create certainties. This involved beginning with premises which were known to be true necessarily. If, however, the premises with which the discussion began were not necessarily true, but merely widely accepted, then nothing derived from those premises could be imbued with a greater certainty than the premises themselves. To this form of reasoning alone, he applied the word "dialectic". The transformation of Aristotelian philosophy by the medieval scholars was in deriving absolute truths of law and justice from the authoritative legal texts, which modern minds would realise could not be premises founded upon known truths. It was because the texts of Justinian were imbued by the medieval scholars with quasi-scriptural authority that they could be used as the basis of civil law.

The importance of the scholastic contribution to law was in its effort to create a system of law based upon the synthesis of opposing norms and the creation of general concepts. Through this process, each part of the law was seen as being related to the whole, and the whole was in turn related to each part. Law was seen to be a "corpus", a coherent body of law based upon an integrated system of rules and principles. The scholastic method was thus influential in the formation of a methodology for the study of modern law. The medieval scholars gave to the western legal tradition its characteristic methods of analysis and synthesis of authoritative texts, by which cases could be synthesised into rules, rules into more general principles, and those principles into a coherent system. [28]

2.3   Natural Law

It was also in the study of Roman law, and in an intertwining of Greek, Roman and Christian thought, that one of the most influential ideas about law was forged. This was the concept of natural law. The theory of natural law has been described as "a common affirmation about the possibility of arriving at objective standards, and a common procedure for doing so— looking for a purposive order in nature and man." [29] It provided a theory of law which dominated western thought until the 18th century.

Natural law has meant different things to different people through the ages. In Greek thought, natural law was an aspect of the search for meaning and purpose in the world. It was thus part of an explanation for why things happened as they did. [30] The focus of inquiry was otherwise in certain Roman writings and in early Christian thought, when theories about the nature and validity of law and the state were uppermost. As natural law theory developed in Roman law, it posited the idea that there are natural principles of law which are common to humanity. Later, in Christian thought, its particular meaning was as an ideal by which all human laws may be judged.

2.3.1   Greek and Roman ideas of natural law

Views on the source of such natural laws, and their substance, varied between different Greek and Roman philosophers. One of the popular understandings of natural law is that it is derived from observation of nature, so that just as nature follows various physical laws, so there are moral norms which are observable in the natural order. [31] At its most basic level, this meant for some philosophers that there were certain laws which were "natural" because they were observable throughout the animal kingdom. This view was expressed, for example, by the Roman author Ulpian, a third century writer whose views were transmitted to medieval scholars through Justinian's Digest. He defined natural law as "that which all animals have been taught by nature . . . From it comes the union of man and woman called by us matrimony, and therewith the procreation and rearing of children; we find in fact that animals in general, the very wild beasts, are marked by acquaintance with this law." [32]

Nonetheless, observation of the "natural order" had within it the danger that nature could equally be used to justify oppression. So it was in the Platonic dialogue *Gorgias*, in which the view is presented by Callicles that might makes right. Callicles argued that the laws of the community are established by the weak to prevent the strong from acquiring what naturally belonged to them. In his view, nature decrees that the strong should rule over the weak, and true justice is for the more powerful to have more than the less powerful. This justified stronger states invading weaker ones "according to the law of nature". [33]

A more sophisticated view of the laws which may be discerned in the natural order is to be found in the writings of Aristotle, and such was the status of Aristotle for medieval thinkers, that his views had a lasting impact upon European thought. Aristotle did not have a developed theory of natural law, and much of his emphasis is upon utilising reason to make decisions in ethics and politics, rather than deriving abstract principles from nature. [34] Nonetheless, his writings gave support to natural law ideas by positing a view of nature that everything contained an essential purpose. "For what each thing is when fully developed," Aristotle wrote, "we call its nature." [35] His method of analysis, which involved determining the essential nature of a thing from its purpose or end, was called the "teleological" method. From such observations of the natural order, ethical norms could be derived. Thus, in Book I of *The Politics*, Aristotle wrote that:

> "In the first place, there must be a union of those who cannot exist without each other; namely of male and female, that the race may continue (and this is a union which is formed, not of choice but because, in common with other animals and with plants, mankind have a natural desire to leave behind them an image of themselves)". [36]

For Aristotle, the family was an association established by nature, and so was the state, since the result of human association is the community of the state, which represents a common existence in order to provide for the needs of life, and continues for the sake of a good life. Aristotle concluded from these observations that "man is by nature a being inclined to a civic existence." [37]

Aristotle's ideas of a natural order did not lead him to principles of egalitarianism. In his natural order, men could dominate women, and slavery was justified, [38] for there was a natural hierarchy of superiority and inferiority. Furthermore, to fulfil the purposes for which people organised into states, it was necessary that the state be ruled by aristocrats who had the leisure and education to lead the state in a life of virtue.[39]

The idea that there was a natural law derived from observation of nature, contained within it the qualification that such natural laws were not self-evident. They required discovery by processes of reason. This requirement of reason was emphasised most strongly in the writings of the Roman advocate and statesman Cicero (106-43 BC) who, drawing his ideas from Stoic philosophy, argued that there were natural laws for the conduct of individuals, and these precepts were discernible by reason. They had their origin in the divine will and did not depend for their validity and status as law on being recorded as law by any human authority. These were the elemental principles of justice, and only laws which were in harmony with these principles could truly be called laws.[40] The most famous exposition of Cicero's ideas of natural law is in Chapter 22 of *De Re Publica*, in which a response is given to the argument that law and justice are merely a product of government, and varied widely from one nation to another. Cicero wrote:

> "True law is right reason in agreement with nature diffused among all men; constant and unchanging, it should call men to their duties by its precepts, and averts from wrongdoing by its prohibitions . . . We cannot be freed from its obligations by senate or people, and we need not look outside ourselves for an expounder or interpreter of it. And there will not be different laws at Rome and at Athens, or different laws now and in the future, but one eternal and unchangeable law will be valid for all nations and all times."[41]

Such law, wrote Cicero, was promulgated by God,[42] but discernible by reason. This "reason" was a capacity of moral reason which raised humans above the level of beasts and enabled people to distinguish between good and evil, and to understand what accorded with the true nature of mankind. Cicero's understanding of what nature demanded led him to argue against the idea that people should pursue mere self-interest. Rather, the social nature of human existence required that people had a duty to be kind to others and to share goods. He wrote accordingly that:

> "To take away wrongfully from another, and for one man to advance his own interest by the disadvantage of another man is more contrary to nature than death, than poverty, than pain, than any other evil".[43]

Cicero, and other writers, contrasted the ius civile, the civil law of Rome, with the ius gentium, the law of nations, which was a philosophical concept referring to the common elements of all legal systems.[44] This was closely related to, or perhaps synonymous with the ius naturale, natural law. However, in Ulpian's writings, the ius naturale was contrasted with the ius gentium, and treated as an ideal order which was not entirely fulfilled by existing laws. For Ulpian, natural law explained various human institutions, but it also had the capacity to challenge them. In particular, he regarded slavery as contrary to the law of nature, since "all men were born free,"[45] even though slavery was an accepted institution in Roman society. Cicero also had expressed the view that all people were morally equal because of their capacity to reason. [46] Thus, the idea of a natural law had the potential not merely to explain and justify existing human and legal institutions, but to challenge them in the name of a higher order. It was a potential which was to bear fruit many centuries later in the concept of natural human rights which fuelled 18th century revolutions.

2.3.2   *The discordance between natural law and civil law*

The gap between the law of nature and the civil laws of existing societies posed for philosophers the problem of how to reconcile the idea that this natural law could be perceived by reason, with the reality that governments had not always enacted such laws in civil society. The explanations which gained currency, in particular from Christian theology, posited the idea of a fall from a perfect, or "natural" order, and the loss of an age of innocence. [47] Such a view of a lost golden age was put forward by the Roman author Seneca (1-65 AD), [48] and similar arguments, based on the doctrine of the Fall, [49] were used by Christian writers. Augustine of Hippo argued that mankind, as originally created by God, was not intended to be subject to the oppression of government nor to be enslaved. [50] Such institutions were the result of the fall from that original created order. Ambrose (c 340-397) and Isidore of Seville (c 560-636) both treated possession of all things in common as part of the natural law. Private property was necessitated by the loss of innocence, a view which was to be echoed by 18th century writers.

Thus, the idea of natural law which passed into western thought from the Greek philosophers, the Roman jurists and the Church Fathers, was that there were universal moral laws, capable of perception in the natural order which was permeated with reason, and derived from God who was the source of that reason. The Apostle Paul's writings appeared to indicate further that there was a natural law which was not merely discoverable by reason but intuitive—written on people's hearts by conscience. [51]

2.3.3   *Aquinas, eternal law and natural law*

It was Thomas Aquinas, who, writing in the 13th century, refined earlier ideas about natural law and developed a theology of law which was to remain the dominant understanding of law for the next five centuries. Thomas Aquinas (1225-74 AD) was born in Italy, [52] and was a Dominican friar. He taught at the University of Paris and in Italy, and was responsible for a systematic exploration of philosophy and theology which profoundly affected thinking in the western world for centuries thereafter, and in particular, within the Catholic church. The major theme of Aquinas' writings was how to unify diverse aspects of human experience, and divergent intellectual traditions. These traditions were derived from the

Scriptures, the writings of the Church Fathers, and the Greek philosophers, notably Aristotle, whom he called simply "the Philosopher". The underlying premise of Aquinas' work was that there could be no dichotomy between faith and reason, and that the various diverse viewpoints deriving from Greek and Christian thought were, therefore, reconcilable.[53]

In his most famous work, the *Summa Theologica*, Aquinas devoted a section to a treatise on law, in which he sought to reconcile Christian understandings of the authority of divine law, as revealed in the Scriptures, with Greek and Roman ideas of natural law, as represented particularly by the writings of Aristotle and Cicero. He also sought to explain the place within this of human law. He defined law as "an ordinance of reason for the common good, made by him who has care of the community, and promulgated."[54]

Aquinas argued that there were four types of law.[55] There was first the eternal law, which existed in the mind of God. This is not the law which God has revealed in the Scriptures, but "the very Idea of the government of things in God, the Ruler of the universe."[56] In the words of one commentator, it is the "timeless, universal order . . . providence perceived as law."[57] This law was not in general available to human perception, but elements could be perceived through natural law and divine law. Aquinas defined natural law as that part of the eternal law which could be known by intelligent creatures using the light of natural reason. Other aspects of the eternal law had been given by revelation. Aquinas called this the divine law, which was the law God had revealed to take mankind beyond the limitations imposed by its own unaided understanding. This was contained in the Old and New Testaments, and became law when it was made so by the church.[58] The final source of law was human law, which was derived from natural law and constituted its specific application. Human law, the positive law of a community, was necessary to give specific content to the general principles of natural law. Furthermore, it was part of the natural order of things that the state had authority to make laws on those matters which were morally indifferent.[59]

In his ideas of natural law, Aquinas sought to reconcile reason with providence by using Aristotle's teleological idea that everything had an essential end or purpose to which it naturally inclined. Providence directs creation towards its natural ends, and to that extent it might be thought that there was no place for reason or free will. To this logical difficulty with the idea of providence, Aquinas responded that humans were unique in that they were allowed to participate in that providence through natural reason. The natural law which humans perceive by reason, inclines people to that proper end which is given by the providence of eternal law.[60] Mankind differs from the rest of creation in that it is aware of its purpose, and reasons accordingly. Aquinas recognised, however, that people did not always do what they ought to do by natural inclination. It required reason to turn natural inclinations into practical actions, and reason could sometimes be distorted by "passion, or evil habit, or an evil occupation of nature".[61] Furthermore, the specific application of principles to particular cases was not always deducible by logical necessity.[62]

For Aquinas, the content of natural law, at least in terms of broad principles, was self-evident. The principles were discernible by "practical reason", and flowed from a first premise, that "good is to be done and pursued, and evil is to be avoided."[63] This somewhat vague principle had more specific applications. Self-preservation was a natural and, therefore, good inclination, as were sexual intercourse and education of offspring. Mankind also had a natural inclination to know the truth about God and to live in society.[64] The social nature of mankind justified laws concerning such matters as buying and selling. Elsewhere in Aquinas' writings, it is apparent that he saw theft, adultery, homosexuality, usury, drunkenness, gluttony, suicide, murder and the violation of promises as contrary to natural law.[65]

2.3.4 Aquinas and civil disobedience

In discussing the relationship between these sources of law, and the problem of conflict between them, Aquinas addressed an issue which has exercised legal and political philosophers since the death of Socrates:[66] the problem of when it is morally right to disobey the law of the political community of which one is a member, and if indeed, it is ever right to overthrow a government. Such disobedience to law is known as "civil disobedience".[67]

Aquinas answered the question of when human laws ought to be obeyed by stating that a law is just, and therefore binding in conscience, when it is ordered for the common good, and thus consistent with natural law. He wrote, "every law laid down by men has the force of law in that it flows from natural law. If on any head, it is at variance with natural law, it will not be law, but spoilt law."[68] The commands of unjust laws did not need to be obeyed, except to avoid scandal or riot, "for which cause a man should even yield his right".[69] However, a law which is contrary to divine law—such as a law commanding idolatry—should never be obeyed.[70]

This view that sometimes disobedience to human law was justified, and even mandatory, represented a much older tradition of Christian thought. The early Christians emphasised that the general authority of secular rulers emanated from the divine will. In the Epistle to the Romans the Apostle Paul wrote:

"Everyone must submit himself to the governing authorities, for there is no authority except that which God has established. The authorities which exist have been established by God. Consequently, he who rebels against the authority is rebelling against what God has instituted, and those who do so will bring judgment on themselves. For rulers hold no terror for those who do right, but for those who do wrong."[71]

However, this affirmation of the general authority of rulers, which is also to be found in the teachings of Christ,[72] did not imply that all rulers enjoyed the favour of God or that they could be trusted to rule justly. Paul himself wrote many of his epistles from prison, and eventually was martyred during the persecutions of the Emperor Nero's reign (c 64 AD). Furthermore, the "Book of Revelation", the last book of the *New Testament*, was a veiled warning of the capacity of rulers, and in particular, Roman emperors, to be instruments of oppression. Consequently, the instruction to obey civic authorities was qualified in Christian teaching: in the case of conflict, Christians should obey God, and not human rulers. This was reflected in the life of the early church, which at times survived "underground" in the catacombs of Rome. A theory of civil disobedience was also articulated by the Christian writer, Origen in the middle of the third century. He wrote that:

"Where the law of nature, that is of God, enjoins precepts contradictory to the written laws, consider whether reason does not compel a man to dismiss the written code and the intention of the lawgivers far from his mind, and to devote himself to the divine Lawgiver and to choose to live according to His word, even if in doing this he must endure dangers and countless troubles and death and shame."[73]

Aquinas' views reflected this tension in Christian thought. On the one hand, temporal authority was given by God. Aquinas married this idea with Aristotle's teleological version of natural law: rulers govern in order to direct people towards their own good or to the common good. Yet, on the other hand, the ruler was subject himself to the laws of God and civil disobedience may, in some circumstances, be a moral duty. Aquinas argued, however, that rulers were not subject to their own laws. He took the view that a ruler is above the law with respect to its constraining force, for no one can be constrained by himself.[74] There was an obligation upon rulers to apply the law to themselves, but it was only a moral one. Some of Aquinas' contemporaries went further in articulating a concept of the rule of law as a constitutional principle, such that the authority of kings was limited by their duty to be subject to the laws of the land. While this view was expressed by a number of writers within Europe, it was perhaps most strongly expressed in England.[75]

These ideas about the rule of law and the moral validity of civil disobedience were to have important repercussions in 17th century England and 18th century America, for in these contexts, they came to provide a moral and legal justification for revolution. They led, in each country, to the establishment of a new political order which laid the foundations for their modern democratic structures. From a mixture of the British and American models of government, the Australian federal structure emerged at the beginning of the 20th century.

2.3.5 Natural law after Aquinas

Aquinas provided a philosophy of law which integrated Christian thought with the strongly held beliefs in a natural law. However, his synthesis of Christian teaching with Aristotelian philosophy did not pass without challenge theologically. His view that mankind has a natural aptitude for virtue went against the less optimistic view of human nature (in its fallen state) contained in the writings of Augustine. It was an idea which was again to be challenged strongly in the Reformation, notably by Calvin. To the Reformers, the virtue which mankind had before the Fall was lost in that rebellion against God's commands. Mankind's reason was a tarnished reason, and mankind's will was a depraved will. Hence the notion that mankind's unaided reason could discern the natural good was an idea rejected by some Protestant theologians.

Nonetheless, Aquinas' view that natural law was fully accessible to human reason had one important consequence: it meant that belief in the existence of God, and knowledge of the divine will as revealed in the Scriptures, was not a necessary condition for having a theory of natural law. This was perceived by the "late-scholastic" writers of the 16th century such as Fernando de Vasquez and Gabriel Vasquez, and the idea that natural law was simply what reason commands, separated from any theological context, was taken up in England after the Reformation.[76] Thus, Hooker, in his *Laws of Ecclesiastical Polity* (1594), wrote that the law, which used to be called the law of nature, may most fittingly be called the Law of Reason, and that its principles are "investigable by Reason, without the help of Revelation supernatural or divine".[77]

This line of thinking led in due course to the idea that natural law could be completely secularised. The Dutch Protestant writer, Hugo Grotius (1583-1645) is often accredited with the first secularisation of natural law.[78] He is also regarded as the founder of international law, for although the possibility of a law binding nations had been perceived by earlier writers,[79] it was Grotius who first put forward principles of international law on a rational and organised basis. In his great work, *De Jure Belli ac Pacis* (*The Law of War and Peace*), first published in 1625, Grotius used natural law ideas as the basis for the elaboration of an international legal order to regulate relations between states. A foundational principle was that treaties should be observed (pacta sunt servanda); this was derived from one of the rules necessary for civil society—that promises shold be kept. Grotius also based his theory of just wars on the fundamental natural right of self-defence. Grotius observed, in introducing his work,[80] that natural law was not dependent upon revelation, although he himself regarded the notion that there is no God as one of "the utmost wickedness", and affirmed his own belief that natural law derived its origin ultimately from God, by whom nature was created. The significance of Grotius for natural law theory was not that he separated natural law from theology (for he still had a worldview formed by Christian belief) but rather that he separated natural law from the theologians.[81] Hitherto, it had been seen as an adjunct to theological exploration. Grotius turned it to a purely secular purpose, and furthermore, devised principles which were derived from reason and which were not dependent on being part of a larger philosophical and theological system of thought. Thereafter, natural law theories were developed without a dependence upon a theological framework, but rather were based upon logical argument from demonstrable principles, and by the 18th century, secular theories of natural law abounded.[82]

2.4   Natural Rights and the Legitimacy of Government

A further application of natural law ideas was made in the late 17th century in developing theories for the moral basis of civil society. It was the ideas of Thomas Hobbes (1588-1679) and John Locke (1632-1704) which are particularly associated with the formation of modern political theories of the state. Both of them wrote in England during the 17th century which was a time of civil turmoil and of questioning about the legitimacy of government.[83] Locke was especially important in that he provided a basis for the recognition by a political community of the natural rights of its members, an idea which was to bear fruit in the American Revolution, and in the Bill of Rights which was grafted onto the United States Constitution thereafter.

In many ways, Hobbes and Locke offered entirely contrasting visions of civil society, but both began with the same intellectual premise, that there was a "state of nature" which could be treated, at least for the purposes of argument, as existing prior to the formation of civil society. This "state of nature" was not determined by empirical observation, nor was it ever stated necessarily to have a historical or geographic existence. Rather, it was an intellectual construct, based upon premises about human nature, from which certain ideas about the necessity of civil society could follow. However, while Hobbes and Locke shared the same starting point in considering what was the natural state of people living in a community without a structure of government, their theories about that state of nature differed markedly.

2.4.1   Hobbes and the justification for autocracy

For Hobbes, in his famous work *Leviathan* (1651), the state of nature was a society at war with itself. Hobbes sought to build his theories without any recourse to metaphysical ideas about the nature and purpose of mankind. He left behind the teleology of Aristotle and the theological worldview of Aquinas, and focused only on what he regarded to be certain and empirically observable[84]—that people have desires and aversions, which is to them their meaning of good and evil.[85]

Hobbes, therefore, rejected the notion of interpersonal obligations which had a normative validity independent of the desires and aversions of individuals. Additionally, he argued, people have an inherent instinct towards self-preservation. This he regarded as the first precept of the law of nature since it was nature's most urgent imperative instinct. The result of the uncontrolled pursuit of (often conflicting) desires, meant that the state of nature was one where there could be no security, nor any of the optimal conditions which were necessary for building, for industry, for overseas trade, and for the flourishing of learning and the arts. In the state of nature, concluded Hobbes, human life would be "solitary, poor, nasty, brutish and short".[86] He qualified this stark description by defining the state of war as inhering not in actual fighting, but in the known disposition thereto, since in the state of nature, there could be no assurance of peace and safety. The evil to be avoided by civil government essentially was the constant insecurity which would exist without it, and it was this perilous condition in the state of nature which required and justified government to preserve order.

From his description of the state of nature, it followed that there were laws of nature which were discernible by reason as being necessary to take humankind out of this state of war, and to allow for mutual self-preservation. In total, he identified some 19 laws of nature. Hobbes, who disavowed all authority of a religious nature for the purposes of devising his theory, found he could summarise all these laws in the same "golden rule" which Christ had annunciated 16 centuries earlier: you must love your neighbour as yourself.[87] The difficulty, as Hobbes saw it, was that people do not naturally lay aside their "passions" for the sake of the common good, and covenants needed to be backed up by the sword in order to be effective. This justified the existence of an unlimited and absolute ruler. Hobbes' social contract was one in which people surrendered their natural liberty to a sovereign who would maintain peace. The only obligation of that sovereign, he argued, was to preserve the lives of the citizens, for that was the sovereign's reason for existence. In this sense, Hobbes' ideas of natural law were quite different to those of other theorists. Hobbes saw no reason to prescribe for law a particular moral content, nor was he prepared to test its substance by any external standard of reasonableness. It was sufficient reason to require obedience to law and to civil authority, that such authority was necessary to preserve order. In Hobbes' theory, the fundamental quality which the sovereign should possess is effectiveness, not reasonableness or moral sensibility.

Hobbes' ideas about the justification for dictatorship laid the intellectual foundations for absolute government which continue into modern times. As Kelly writes:

"In general, Hobbes' Leviathan came to afford a plausible model of absolute government, a type of which later ages, into our own time, were able to show all too many examples: dictatorships for which, at any rate according to modern western notions about the minimum civil rights of the individual, nothing could be said except that they provided a sort of peace, a sort of security, even if an arbitrary police power and the prison camp were its modes."[88]

The unconscious echoes of Hobbes continue to be heard in the international debates about human rights violations in certain nations. Defenders of dictatorship point to the provision of the "human rights" of food, shelter and other sorts of basic subsistence as a justification for violating other human rights such as free speech and freedom of association.

2.4.2   Locke and the idea of fundamental human rights

It was Hobbes' near-contemporary, John Locke, who first gave voice to the modern western notion that individuals have certain fundamental human rights which governments should not violate, and that arbitrary and absolute government was incompatible with human freedom.

John Locke had a rather less pessimistic view than Hobbes about the natural condition of humankind without government. Locke's *Second Treatise on Civil Government* was published in 1690, and has been described as "the most influential work on natural law ever written."[89] In it, he put forward a theory that government existed to protect the natural rights of its citizens, rights which existed in the state of nature. Unlike Hobbes, Locke's ideas were placed specifically within a Christian worldview, and his fundamental premises were that the natural order was ordained by God, that God had prescribed rules of conduct which were discoverable by reason and objectively valid, and that such rules could be known with certainty.[90] Locke assumed the idea of natural law in the *Second Treatise*, and saw no need to spell out a detailed theory of it. He had written a work on natural law before,[91] and was to turn to the subject again before his death.[92]

In Locke's "state of nature", all people were of equal status, and all had natural rights: rights to life, liberty and property which inhered in each individual. He wrote:

> "To understand political power aright, and derive it from its original, we must consider what state all men are naturally in, and that is a state of perfect freedom to order their actions and dispose of their possessions and persons as they think fit, within the bounds of the law of nature, without asking leave, or depending upon the will of any other man.
>
> A state also of equality, wherein all the power and jurisdiction is reciprocal, no one having more than another; there being nothing more evident than that creatures of the same rank, promiscuously born to all the same advantages of nature, and the use of the same faculties, should be equal one amongst another without subordination or subjection."[93]

Civil government was based upon the consent of each individual to abide by the rules of the community. This was the social contract. In Locke's view, that social contract existed for the purpose that the natural rights of each individual should be better protected thereby. Government was necessary so that there was a common and independent arbiter of disputes, and it was also necessary to guard and protect each person's rights. Power was given to government as a form of trust for the benefit of the people. Locke focused upon the right of property, but in defining this he included the rights people have in their persons as well as their goods. Thus, he included the rights to life and liberty as well.

In Locke's view, there could be no justification for arbitrary government, since the legislative power

"is not, nor possibly can be, absolutely arbitrary over the lives and fortunes of the people. For it being but the joint power of every member of society given up to that person or assembly which is legislator, it can be no more than those persons had in a state of Nature before they entered into society, and gave it up to the community. For nobody can transfer to another more power than he has in himself, and nobody has an absolute arbitrary power over himself or over any other, to destroy his own life, or take away the life or property of another."[94]

Locke saw the basic human rights of individuals as inalienable. His social contract did not contemplate that one could surrender those rights voluntarily to an absolute ruler, nor that one could accept voluntary enslavement.

It followed from Locke's ideas about the role of government that he should endorse the possibility of revolution, which he termed the "appeal to heaven", when government failed to uphold those rights. Revolution was only acceptable, however, if the majority in a society took that decision, since the social contract bound the individual to the majority. In Locke's theory, the consent to civil government need not be explicit. Consent could be given tacitly by living within the territorial limits of the state without active resistance. However, what was especially novel about his ideas, in contrast to earlier theorists, was his insistence that rights inhered in the individual, and that the societal contract was one between all individuals, rather than, more vaguely, a contract between government and governed.

Locke endeavoured, also, to offer an explanation of the natural right of individuals to own property privately. He argued that the right of owning property was derived from the need for self-preservation, which required that people be able to appropriate what they needed for subsistence. The earth's natural resources were held in common, but the mixing of an individual's labour with those natural resources justified the resultant produce being treated as that person's private property. The only theoretical limit he placed upon the acquisition of private wealth was that people should leave "enough, and as good" for others to appropriate to their needs.[95] Numerous 18th century philosophers followed Locke in advancing natural law justifications for private property. In contrast, some 18th century writers, notably Rousseau and Linguet, attacked Locke's views. Linguet, writing in 1767, regarded civil institutions which protected private property as engaged in a conspiracy against the majority of the human race. Their views were to influence Karl Marx in formulating his ideas about private property in the following century. [96]

Like many other books which have had a significant impact upon society, Locke's book gained much of its importance from the period in which it was published. It was more a political tract than a carefully reasoned philosophical treatise; many of its premises were merely asserted, rather than argued convincingly. Yet in its statement of the limitations on government, in its affirmation of fundamental rights, and in its arguments which allowed for the possibility and necessity of revolution, Locke's work spoke powerfully to the situation of his time in England, in which Parliament had overthrown a monarch for the second time in 50 years, in which it had asserted fundamental political rights, and in which it had firmly declared limitations upon the prerogative of the Crown. [97]

Locke's book was successful in England because it offered a basis for legitimising the constitutional order which had emerged from the conflicts of that century. Indeed it was, in many respects, an apologia for the English Revolution of 1688, which had been the culmination of a half century of conflict between the Crown and Parliament, and of constitutional experimentation. Subsequently, Locke's work was influential in the American colonies because it offered a moral basis for challenging the royal prerogative in terms of colonial rule. The idea that human beings had natural rights which were inalienable, and that civil society exists for the purpose of ensuring those rights, was a powerful belief in justifying the overthrow of a regime which was geographically distant and insensitive to the political demands of the American leaders. [98] Locke's ideas also took root in France, being popularised in particular by Voltaire, who regarded Locke as one of the great progressive thinkers of the age.

Thus, the idea of rights, the appeal to natural and fundamental entitlements which represent limits beyond which governments may not trespass, passed into western consciousness through John Locke, and became an article of faith through the French and American revolutions. It had itself been inspired by the emphasis in protestant Christian thought on an individual's responsibility before God, and by the struggle over the legitimacy of government which dominated English politics for much of the 17th century. [99]

2.4.3   *Rousseau and the general will*

The notion of a social contract was given a different basis by the French philosopher Jean Jacques Rousseau (1712-1778). The extent to which Rousseau accepted the idea of natural law is debatable; certainly, he was a fierce critic of the idea that pure reason, uninfluenced by emotive and intuitive feelings, could offer a firm basis for morality. Both the heart and reason had to be involved in understanding moral obligations, and people needed to listen to the inner voice of conscience. Rousseau did not respect the logical and rationalistic accounts of natural law which had dominated the thought of previous generations. Nor did he share with Locke a belief that there was a state of nature which offered a starting point in understanding what civil society ought to be. Rosseau's state of nature was one in which humankind was still at a primitive stage of development, without a capacity for co-operative behaviour. It was no garden of Eden, and nor did individuals in such a state fulfil their human potential. Yet he agreed with Locke that in that state of nature, human beings were free and equal, and the need was to reconcile that natural freedom and equality with society and government.

In *The Social Contract* (1762), he described a form of contract in which people surrendered their rights to the whole community. He wrote:

"Each of us puts his person and all his power in common under the supreme direction of the general will, and, in our corporate capacity, we receive each member as an indivisible part of the whole." [100]

Thus, in Rousseau's vision of society, the individual personality of each contracting party was replaced by a collective body, and this act of association gave to that body its unity, identity, life and will.

The general will was expressed in legislation made through the participation of all members of the community. Rousseau's idea of democracy could not be satisfied by representative government. It was also central to Rousseau's conception of the general will that it should not be arrived at by an accumulation of the self-interested votes of a majority. The general will was not, in this way, synonymous with the result of any and every democratic process. Rather, it was reached when people placed the good of the community ahead of self-interest. Nor was the general will synonymous with what others had called "natural law", for it need not be the same in every society. [101] Discovery of the general will meant the discovery of what was good only for the political community of which one was a member. Rousseau's idea of the general will thus had a somewhat mystical quality. He offered little by way of explanation of how one might distinguish between the actual will of a majority, and the general will. Nonetheless, Rousseau emphasised the importance of education, and conceived of the possibility that an individual who consistently disagreed with the general will might be "forced to be free".

Rousseau's thought provided an important shift in the way of conceiving political obligation. He substituted the civic state for a providential natural order. No longer was the focus upon obedience to natural laws because (as in the view of Aquinas) they represented God's will, nor because (as in Aristotelian thought) one thereby fulfilled a teleological destiny. Rousseau offered a theory of democracy, while still insisting on the idea that law should have an intrinsic moral quality, that is, a disposition towards the fulfilment of the common good. In 19th century England, the distinction between the existence of law and its moral quality was to be more sharply drawn.

2.5   The Rise of Legal Positivism

2.5.1   *The reaction against natural law*

Natural law sustained three forms of attack in the 18th and 19th centuries respectively, which together appeared to have dealt it a mortal blow as a sustainable moral and legal philosophy. The first attack was empirical. Writers such as Montesquieu (1689-1755) observed that the laws of different nations vary considerably according to their history, tradition and circumstances, despite the unifying influence of Roman law in continental Europe. Montesquieu published his famous work, *The Spirit of Laws*, in 1748. In it, he argued from the empirical evidence that there was an observable principle in the history of the laws of different nations. Laws should be adapted to the people for whom they are framed. He wrote:

"They should be related to the climate of each country, to the quality of its soil, to its situation and extent, to the principal occupation of the natives, whether husbandmen, huntsmen or shepherds; they should be related to the degree of liberty which the constitution will bear; to the religion of the inhabitants, to their inclinations, riches, numbers, commerce, manners and customs." [102]

Montesquieu's ideas led later generations to the study of law from comparative, anthropological and sociological perspectives. By emphasising not only that regional and national laws did in fact differ from one another, but that those differences were explicable and justifiable, Montesquieu undermined the notion that there was a universal natural law, discernible by reason, to which human laws ought to conform.

A second form of attack on natural law was philosophical, and the criticism was of the basis on which principles of natural law claimed to be derived. The challenge was to the idea that law could, in any meaningful sense, be "natural", that is, derived from nature. The philosophical challenge is usually attributed to the Scottish philosopher, David Hume (1711-1776). [103] In his *Treatise of Human Nature* published in 1739, Hume observed that moral systems derived from the idea of natural law continually made a logically improper leap, from discussing what is and is not, to a discussion of what ought, and ought not to be. As later philosophers took up the critique, natural law was seen as being open to the challenge that one cannot derive a theory of moral obligation from statements of empirical fact. Specifically, it was invalid to reason that because the nature of humankind was this, or that, therefore, it followed that people ought to do this, or that.

After Hume, it became fashionable to regard the inference from facts to norms as an illicit one, and it was thought that this provided an irrefutable argument against the validity of all theories of natural law. However, the assumption that the inference is illicit, and that natural law theories are necessarily dependent upon this inference, has been strongly challenged in recent years. Alasdair MacIntyre has argued in the context of moral theory that the inference from facts to norms is only illicit if one abandons Aristotle's teleological conception that human beings exist to fulfil their essential nature. [104] If mankind has a purpose in the world, and each person has a potential as a human being that he or she should strive to reach, then it is legitimate to reason from the nature of mankind to moral precepts which enable us to realise our true nature and fulfil our destiny as human beings. In the same way, with a conception of the nature of human beings within civic society, and with a vision for what society ought to be, it is possible to discern laws which are natural and essential if that society is going to function in accordance with its purposes, and if the individuals within it are to fulfil their potential as human beings.

Another, different, defence of natural law as a rational concept has been made by the most prominent of the contemporary natural law theorists, John Finnis. Finnis argues that the ideas of Thomas Aquinas were not dependent upon derivation from speculations about the nature or purpose of humanity, nor about good and evil, but rather were self-evident and underived. He writes:

"When discerning what is good, to be pursued (prosequendum), intelligence is operating in a different way, yielding a different logic, from when it is discerning what is the case (historically, scientifically or metaphysically); but there is no good reason for asserting that the latter operations of intelligence are more rational than the former." [105]

Nonetheless, Hume's was not the only attack on the idea of natural law. Another prominent critic was Jeremy Bentham (1748-1832), perhaps the most influential British political and social thinker of his generation. Bentham criticised natural law for its subjectivism:

"A great multitude of people are continually talking of the law of nature; and then they go on giving you their sentiments about what is right and what is wrong: and these sentiments, you are to understand, are so many chapters and sections of the Law of Nature." [106]

Bentham was an untiring social reformer, and was, in this respect, part of a much larger reform movement which affected England at the end of the 18th century and in the first half of the 19th century. This reform movement was, to some extent, led by evangelical Christians affected by the Wesleyan Revival such as William Wilberforce (1759-1833) and later, Lord Shaftesbury (1801-1885). However, the pressure for change in the social conditions of society came from a variety of sources, and Bentham was the leading intellectual voice of the reform movement. He was most influential in the area of penal reform. Bentham saw in the ideas of natural law, and in the artifice which surrounded the English common law of his day, a confusion which hindered the progress of reform. To Bentham, talk of natural law and natural rights simply obscured clear thinking about law. Indeed, he was especially critical of the French *Declaration of the Rights of Man and the Citizen*. He denounced natural rights as "simple nonsense . . . rhetorical nonsense—nonsense upon stilts." [107] Bentham is identified with the third great attack on natural law. This challenge was to the validity of describing natural law as "law". The theories of legal positivism, which are associated in the last century with John Austin, and in this century with Hans Kelsen and H L A Hart, were the result of that challenge.

Bentham advocated a new science of law and of legislation. By "science" he meant not the making of generalisations derived from empirical observation and experimentation, but rather, the careful analysis of law through classification and subclassification. Bentham's methodology, known as "bi-partite" or "dichotomous" division, could be traced back to the scholastics, and to Aristotle before them. [108] It involved the subdivision of a broad class into two mutually exclusive and exhaustive subspecies, and then further subdivision of each of these, followed by yet further subdivision until no further differentiation was necessary. Together with this process of classification, he insisted on the accurate use of terminology to describe these different classes and subclasses, and the adoption of precise and morally neutral vocabulary to describe aspects of law and politics. Bentham is most well known for his science of legislation, which was based upon his principle of utilitarianism. The utilitarian position is that policies should be chosen which will lead to the greatest happiness of the greatest number. He also wrote a considered treatise on the nature and definition of law. [109] These ideas were taken up by one of Bentham's followers, John Austin (1790-1859) who developed then into a systematic analytical jurisprudence of law. [110]

2.5.2   John Austin and legal positivism

Austin's legal philosophy is contained in his lectures on jurisprudence, first delivered at University College, London, in 1828, where he held the Chair of Jurisprudence from 1827-1832. [111] Austin followed Bentham in drawing a sharp distinction between law and morality, or, put differently, between what law is definitionally, and what law ought to be. Austin affirmed that: "The existence of law is one thing; its merit or demerit another." [112] Thus, the laws of nature, which Austin called divine law, had to be distinguished from "positive" law, that is, laws existing not by nature, but by position.

Austin defined law as a species of command. A command, he wrote, has three elements:

"1. A wish or desire conceived by a rational being, that another rational being shall do or forbear. 2. An evil to proceed from the former, and to be incurred by the latter, in case the latter comply not with the wish. 3. An expression or intimation of the wish by words or other signs."

In Austin's view, not all commands are laws. Laws proceed from a sovereign:

"Every positive law, or every law simply and strictly so called, is set by a sovereign person, or a sovereign body of persons, to a member or members of the independent political society wherein that person or body is sovereign or supreme."[113]

The sovereign is one who has a habit of obedience to no one, and who receives the habitual obedience of at least the bulk of the population.[114] In the context of England, Austin located sovereignty in the will of the monarch, the House of Lords, and the House of Commons, although he noted that "speaking accurately, the members of the commons house are merely trustees for the body by which they are elected,"[115] that is, those entitled to vote. In other societies, a sovereign might be a totalitiarian ruler.

What further distinguishes a law from other species of command is its characteristic of generality. Laws impose obligations of a general nature on a class of people. By contrast, a sovereign may issue a specific command to a class to do something; or the sovereign may instruct a particular individual to act, or refrain from acting in a certain way. These, Austin classified as "occasional or particular" commands. Laws, by contrast, were those commands emanating from the sovereign which laid down general and continuing rules for the guidance of the conduct of subjects.

In Austin's theory, the simplest illustration of a law is an Act of Parliament, validly passed by the Commons, the Lords, and receiving the royal assent. Austin also saw a species of implied command in those laws which the sovereign chooses not to repeal or alter. Thus, in the common law countries such as England and Australia, in which much of the basic law was first laid down by judges (and originally derived from custom),[116] these judge-made rules have continuing authority because the sovereign has chosen to leave them unaltered.

The important contribution of Bentham and Austin to legal philosophy was in drawing a sharp distinction between law and morality. Nonetheless, Austin's picture of a legal system was too simplistic to fit with the complexity of a modern legal system. His notion of law as command, backed up with sanctions, fitted best the criminal law. It was less appropriate to the many other forms of law, for example, the law of wills and contracts in which various legal requirements are pre-conditions to the enforceability of such arrangements. Much of the law regulates relations between citizens, and confers rights, including, especially in the 20th century, rights against the government. Furthermore, even in relation to the criminal law, Austin's model seemed to imply that the motive for obedience to law is fear of punishment, which is not the only reason, and may not be at all the most important reason why most people habitually keep to most laws. Austin's scheme also had a primitive explanation for the continuity of law through successive generations, and his notion of a sovereign was difficult to maintain as an explanation for legal authority in a democratic society. The difficulties are the greater in relation to countries such as the United States and Australia which have federal systems.

2.5.3   *Hart's concept of law*

A much more sophisticated version of legal positivism was put forward by Professor H L A Hart in, *The Concept of Law*, first published in 1961. [117] In this work, Hart exposed all the weaknesses of Austin's account of law, and used these deficiencies as a starting point to construct a new analytical model. Hart's approach to jurisprudence was greatly influenced by a school of philosophy in Oxford which saw it as important to elucidate the meaning of words and concepts as they are used in everyday speech. Hart, therefore, began his analysis of the concept of "law" by discussing forms of social obligation generally, and noting their common characteristics. He observed that all rules and forms of obligation, whether moral rules, the rules of a game, the rules of etiquette, or legal rules, have the common features of habitual obedience and an internal attitude to that behaviour as a common standard. All such rules are, in this sense, species of social rules. In particular, he noted a necessary coincidence between law and morality, and accepted that there must be a minimum content of "natural law" since all societies have, and must have, rules restricting violence, some system of property in a world of limited resources, and some system of promises.

In identifying specifically the characteristics of legal rules, Hart noted two factors which set them apart from other rules. The first is a feature shared with moral rules, which is the notion of obligation. One is obligated to obey rules when the general demand for conformity is insistent, and the social pressure brought to bear upon those who deviate or threaten to deviate is great. Furthermore, the values promoted by these rules of obligation are seen as important to the maintenance of some social life in the community, or a highly prized aspect of social life, and there may be a conflict between the obligation and one's own desires. Rules of speech, and most rules of etiquette, are also social rules, but do not have this characteristic of a strong sense of obligation.

The second feature of legal rules, which sets them apart from all other species of rule, is that legal rules have a systematic quality about them which depends on primary and secondary rules. All legal systems identify a number of primary obligations, such as the basic rules of the criminal law. However, no sophisticated legal system can exist only with primary obligations. Secondary rules are necessary to confer powers upon officials to interpret the meaning and the ambit of the primary obligations, to adjudicate on whether the rule has been breached, and to enforce the obligations by punishment or otherwise.

Hart noted also that if laws are not to remain static, then there needs to be a means of changing the primary obligations so as to eliminate redundant laws and to create new obligations. This applies to primary obligations generally, but individuals also need means by which they may change their legal relationship with each other—rules for entering into contracts, rules for the disposition of property or the grant of interests in property, such as by lease, and other such rules which individuals may use to alter their legal relationships between each other and in relation to property.

In addition to rules of adjudication and rules of change, a legal system must also have rules of recognition. Such rules must determine what is, and is not, the law, by attributing law-making authority to a Parliament or some other such body. The rules must also determine which officials are given authority to interpret the law and to adjudicate in particular cases, and which have the power and responsibility of enforcement. In Hart's view, it is the rules of recognition which give to law its sense of legitimacy. In particular, the rule by which law-making authority is recognised by officials is the ultimate rule of a legal system, for from this, the status of all other laws is derived. In Hart's interpretation, therefore, the rule of recognition identifies the status of the constitutional documents, Acts of Parliament, the common law, and other sources of legal authority. Hart wrote that the rule of recognition "exists only as a complex, but normally concordant, practice of the courts, officials and private persons in identifying the law by reference to certain criteria."[118] Thus, in many legal systems, including that of Australia, the rule of recognition is not written down, or at least, not written down in totality. It rests on shared assumptions as to authority held by those who interpret and administer the law in particular, and may also be established by constitutional documents which are themselves recognised as foundational sources for the rule of recognition.

Hart's analysis of law as being a combination of primary and secondary rules, ultimately drawing its legitimacy from the rule of recognition, is not the only version of legal positivism, nor does it represent the only major starting point for modern analysis of the nature of law. In particular, the work of the Austrian jurist Hans Kelsen (1881-1973) has also been influential. Nonetheless, in Australia, it has been the work of Austin and Hart, as developed and modified by others, which has dominated discussion of legal positivism, and which has been most influential within the Australian legal system.[119]

2.5.4   Positivism, natural law and legitimacy

The positivist critique of natural law is, at its most fundamental, a criticism of the use of the word "law" to affirm or withhold affirmation of the moral quality of rules enforced by governments through the courts. The positivist creed is that bad law is still law, as long as it fulfils the criteria for formal recognition as law within a given political community.

Analytically, this may be so. It makes no sense to describe an immoral legal system as not being "law" because one disapproves of its content. Indeed, oppressive legal systems attract condemnation precisely because governments have used the force of law to achieve immoral ends. At the same time, while accepting the positivist analysis of the nature of law as descriptively much more accurate than natural law ideas, it is important to recognise that the questions of Bentham and Austin were not the same questions as those asked by the philosophers of previous generations. Primarily, the concern of the natural law philosophers was not with legality but with legitimacy. The concern to demarcate the authority of secular rulers in relation to the Church was a theme of the natural law theories of the middle ages. Later, the legitimacy of the governmental order was an issue which came to the fore in the 17th century in Britain, and in particular at the time of the Glorious Revolution of 1688. [120] By contrast, these issues had faded into the background by Bentham's time. The late 18th century and the early part of the 19th century in Britain was marked more by a fear of revolution among the ruling elite, than an intellectual concern to justify revolution.

The debate between natural law and positivism has continued in the 20th century, when questions about the legitimacy of oppressive regimes, such as existed in Nazi Germany and elsewhere, have been to the fore. Does the attribution of the description "law" to the commands of a ruling elite require that there be at least some conformity with minimum requirements of justice? Augustine expressed the issue when he described kingdoms without justice as "but robber-bands enlarged". [121] Is there a point when we must say of any given society that what is claimed to be "law" is nothing more than organised banditry? The argument is more than merely one about the correct usage of a word. For the word "law" carries with it, in the western legal tradition, inherent connotations of legitimacy, and the question is whether it is appropriate to apply this to any regime which proffers a rule of recognition supported by the barrel of a gun.

These questions were being asked in the aftermath of World War II. A German jurist, Gustav Radbruch (1878-1949) raised the issue in relation to the violations of human rights which occurred in the Nazi era. Radbruch was critical of positivism's insistence that law was whatever those in power decreed. He regarded this as rendering the German justice system helpless when confronted with cruelty and injustice dressed in the cloak of legal authority. [122] An issue which arose from the German experience is whether there can be law which is both higher than, and independent of, the laws of a nation state. This question had to be faced following the demise of the Nazi regime in Germany. In particular, it was an issue in the Nuremberg trials, when leading Nazis were charged with crimes against humanity. What right did the victorious nations have to put the leaders of the conquered nations on trial? By what law were they being tried? There were some answers given to this, of course. The Nuremberg trials were set up and authorised by agreement of the victors, so the tribunal had formal legal authority from those nations which held power in Germany by reason of conquest. However, the question must be raised whether people should be charged, convicted and condemned to die on the basis of offences which were only declared to be such retrospectively by the fiat of the conquering powers. Another basis for authority lay in "customary international law". However, this was an uncertain basis for jurisdiction. It was far from clear that such a customary international law was recognised at the time. The real basis, from a moral point of view, could best be provided by a theory of natural law which insists that there is a fundamental law of humanity which is superior to national law and to which, in conscience, the contrary provisions of a national law, or the orders of a superior authority, ought to provide no defence.

The same issue arose in two different periods in the domestic law of 20th century Germany. German courts have had to address the question of whether acts which were either lawful, or commanded, by the regime of the time, could afterwards be treated as contrary to law. The issue was addressed in relation to the conduct of people under the Nazi regime. [123] Radbruch argued that Nazi war criminals were not being punished by retroactive legislation because, although the post-war decrees of the conquering powers were not in existence at the time the offences were committed, the content of those laws was binding at the time, as being derived from the law of God, nature, or reason. [124] The issue was raised again by the collapse of the communist government of the German Democratic Republic in 1989, and the consequent reunification of Germany. When border guards who had shot would-be escapees were put on trial, the validity of their defence that they were only obeying orders was rejected.

Thus, in a century which has demonstrated in Auschwitz and the gulags, and in countless other regimes, how thin can be the veneer of civilisation which protects human liberties, old questions become new again. The questions of Augustine and Aquinas, of Locke and Rousseau, are not merely the questions of a bygone age. In the stable political society of Australia, questions about the legitimacy of the constitutional order rarely arise. In the broader international community, however, they recur continually.

2.6   History, Tradition and the Western Idea of Law

The western tradition of law, as it has developed gradually over the centuries, has had a profound impact upon every aspect of modern society. Such basic notions of modern legal and political discourse as the concept of human rights and of the rule of law are the result of that historic legacy. Indeed, all the characteristics of the western legal tradition described at the beginning of this chapter are explicable only by the context of the birth of that tradition and the history of its development over the subsequent centuries. The autonomy of law, which had been an aspect of the Roman tradition, was re-established when law began to be studied in its own right in the law school at Bologna and in other parts of Europe from the end of the 11th century onwards, and when it was gradually applied in the life of the emerging nation states. The medieval scholars took the laws of the late Roman empire and by dialectic analysis turned it into a system, renewed and reinterpreted to do service in the different context of medieval Europe.

Although, as will be seen in the next chapter, the development of the common law in England has a distinct history, the notion that law could be a coherent system, and that it was founded upon reason, passed into the thinking of English lawyers as well as their continental counterparts. The way in which law was studied and systematised by the scholastics and commentators of the 12th and 13th century laid the foundations for modern legal method.

The centrality of law may also be traced to the origins of the western legal tradition. The Church was governed by law. Indeed, it has been said that "it was the Church that first taught western man what a modern legal system is like."[125] The authority of rulers was limited by law, for law restrained the exercise of arbitrary power. Mercantile law allowed for the growth of trans-national commerce. International law emerged as a system of rules to govern relations between sovereign countries.

The moral authority of the law may also be traced to its history. The close relationship between law and theology in the formation of the western legal tradition, the belief in law as ultimately given by God, and the idea that there were natural laws which governed human relations meant that law was imbued with a certain aura of sacredness. The close relationship between law and faith meant that law was believed in; for law, in Caesar's kingdom, was an aspect of the will of God. The experience of harsh laws and oppressive rulers did not reduce this faith in the law. Rather, it strengthened it, for it was perceived that oppressive laws should not be dignified with the term "law" at all. Disobedience to rulers could be justified in the name of law when rulers refused to be bound by its foundational moral precepts.

In many respects, the concept of law which was inherited from the middle ages, and indeed even from the 19th century, is remote and distant from modern ideas of law and the concerns of modern legal theory. The 20th century has seen a prolific flowering of ideas concerning the nature of law, its role in society, and theories concerning legal reasoning and adjudication. In the 1990s, the ideas which are most fashionable in the law schools of the western world are critical theories such as critical legal studies and feminist theories of law. Yet even the critical theories are part of that complex organic growth of tradition. They presuppose the established understandings of law which have developed over centuries, seek to challenge aspects of the tradition, and correct its deficiencies. The tradition of law is constantly evolving, and it may sometimes do so with the benefit of insights from those who are most critical of it.

It is the western idea of law which was received in Australia. Australia's legal institutions reflect central precepts of that tradition; the language of political rhetoric is drawn from it; and the authority of law in Australia is derived from its connectedness to it. Yet Australia's tradition of law has a particular connection with the history of legal institutions in England; it is there that the detailed framework of Australian law found its origins, and it is to the development of law and political institutions in that country that we now turn.

NOTES

1. More extensive lists of such characteristics may be found in Berman, H, *Law and Revolution* (Harvard UP, Cambridge, Mass, 1983); Sawer, G, "The Western Conception of Law", *International Encyclopedia of Comparative Law* (Mouton, The Hague and Mohr, Tubingen, 1975), Vol II, pp 45-48.
2. The idea that law is autonomous is not universally accepted in contemporary western thought. Indeed, it is denied in radical critiques which see the apparent autonomy and "neutrality" of law as masking the real significance of law in reinforcing oppression. Thus, the notion of autonomy is challenged in marxist theory which sees law as reflecting the underlying economic relations in society, and in which power resides in the ownership of the means of production. The autonomy of law is similarly challenged by some feminist theorists.
3. Some theorists, applying Nicklas Luhmann's theories, regard law as an "autopoietic", self-referential system which is, in certain ways, closed off from other systems. See Teubner, G, *Law as an Autopoietic System* (Blackwell, Oxford, 1993); King, M, "The Truth about Autopoiesis" (1993) 20 *Journal of Law and Society* 218.
4. Berman, H, op cit, p 8.
5. See Australian Law Reform Commission, Report No 31, *The Recognition of Aboriginal Customary Laws* (AGPS, 1986), paras 98-127.
6. Kelly, J M, *A Short History of Western Legal Theory* (Clarendon, Oxford, 1992), p 68.
7. Bozeman, A, *The Future of Law in a Multicultural World* (Princeton UP, Princeton, 1971), p 38.
8. Sawer, G, op cit, p 47.
9. Quoted in Needham, J and Ronan, C, *The Shorter Science and Civilization in China* (Cambridge UP, Cambridge, 1970), Ch 16. See also Tay, A, *Law in China* (Sydney University, Sydney, 1986).
10. See generally, David, R and Brierley, J, *Major Legal Systems in the World Today* (3rd ed, Stevens, London, 1985), pp 534-546.
11. Obuchi, T, "Role of the Court in the Process of Informal Dispute Resolution in Japan: Traditional and Modern Aspects, with a Special Emphasis on In-court Compromise" (1987) 20 *Law in Japan* 74-101.
12. Berman, H, *The Interaction of Law and Religion* (SCM Press, London, 1974), p 29.
13. See above, 1.2.4.
14. For detailed histories of these developments see Berman, *Law and Revolution*, op cit; David, R, and Brierley, J, op cit; Clark, D, "The Medieval Origins of Modern Legal Education: Between Church and State" (1987) 35 American J of Comp Law 653.
15. Stromholm, S, *A Short History of Legal Thinking in the West* (Norstedts, Stockholm, 1985), p 57.
16. David, R and Brierley, J, op cit, pp 41-42.
17. Watson, A, *The Evolution of Law* (John Hopkins UP, Baltimore, 1985), Ch III.
18. Watson, A, *The Making of the Civil Law* (Harvard UP, Cambridge, Mass, 1981), pp 83-98.
19. The estimates of the numbers of students vary, but it is likely that during the 13th century there was an average of some 500-1500. At times, there may have been as many as 6,000. Clark, D, op cit, p 681.
20. For a comparison of the universities at Bologna and Paris, see Clark, D, op cit.
21. Stein, P, *The Character and Influence of the Roman Civil Law—Historical Essays*, (Hambledon, London, 1988), p 96.
22. The most influential work of Donnellus was his *Commentarii de iure Civili*, which offered an understanding of the civil law as a system of rights.
23. See below, 2.3.5.
24. For discussion of Grotius' account of national law, written in the vernacular, see Stein, P, op cit, pp 77-78.
25. Of the canon lawyers from about 1150-1500, Stromholm writes that "there has hardly been any other period in Occidental history when an intellectual *elite* has exercised such a continuous, massive and direct influence upon a great centre of political power; scholarship and power never worked so closely together for such a length of time; in fact, brilliant canon law scholarship *meant* power." Stromholm, S, op cit, p 130.

26. Bracton wrote his work, *On the Laws and Customs of England*, in the second half of the 12th century. He quoted extensively from Justinian's Digest, without attribution, and drew upon the work of Azo (1150-1230) who was one of the most influential of the early Roman law scholars. See "Select Passages from Bracton and Azo", 8 *Selden Society* (Maitland, F, ed, 1894).
27. Leslie, W, "Similarities in Lord Mansfield's and Joseph Story's View of Fundamental Law" (1957) 1 Am J of Legal Hist 278.
28. Berman, H, *Law and Revolution*, op cit, p 529.
29. Sigmund, P E, *Natural Law in Political Thought* (University Press of America, Washington DC, 1971), p ix.
30. Weinreb, L, *Natural Law and Justice* (Harvard UP, Cambridge, Mass, 1987), Ch 1.
31. Lloyd, D, *The Idea of Law* (Penguin, Harmondsworth, 1981).
32. *Digest*, Bk I i 1.
33. Plato, *Gorgias*, No 482.
34. See Sigmund, P E, op cit, 9-12; Finnis, J, *Natural Law and Natural Rights* (Clarendon, Oxford, 1980).
35. Aristotle, *The Politics*, Bk I.
36. Ibid.
37. Ibid. This is literally translated, "man is by nature a political animal." However, this rendering has attained a different colloquial meaning and may be misunderstood. See Kelly, J, op cit, p 13.
38. Ibid, pp 5-9, 19-20.
39. Sigmund, P E, op cit, p 11.
40. Cicero, *De Legibus*, 1.16.43-44, 2.5.11.
41. Cicero, *De Re Publica*, 3.22.33.
42. Cicero's invocation of God as the source of natural law in *De Re Publica* was not, of course, the God of Judaeo-Christianity. Roman thought did not recognise God as being personal and the creator of the universe. Rather, there were numerous localised deities. Cicero's invocation of God was, therefore, as an abstract force, about which no developed theology existed. Nonetheless, Cicero's ideas were influential for the development of natural law theory by the Church, since the concept of law originating in the divine will was married in Christian thought with a developed theology of a personal God with an active concern for the world. See Kelly, J M, op cit, p 102.
43. Cicero, *De Officiis*, Bk III 5.
44. Sir Henry Maine popularised the notion that the ius gentium was the law applied between Romans and foreigners, but this view has now been discredited: see Nicholas, B, *An Introduction to Roman Law* (Clarendon, Oxford, 1962), p 56.
45. *Digest*, I i 4.
46. Cicero, *De Legibus*, I 10.
47. See further, Kelly, J M, op cit, pp 104-108.
48. Seneca, *Ad Lucilium Epistulae Morales*, Ep 90.
49. In Christian theology, the world was created perfect by God, and God, nature and mankind were all in harmony with one another. The tranquillity of the Garden of Eden was broken by the rebellion of Mankind against God's laws, and from this "fall" came not only a change in people's relationship with God (Genesis 3: 21-24), but disorder in civil society (Genesis 4) and in the natural world (Genesis 3: 16-19; Romans 8: 18-25).
50. Augustine, *City of God*, XIX, 15.
51. Romans 2: 14-15.
52. The name Aquinas is derived from the town of Aquinum, near Naples, where he was born.
53. Weinreb, op cit, pp 54-55. For a critique of this attempt to synthesise grace with nature, and the intellectual consequences of it, see Schaeffer, F, *Escape from Reason* (Inter-Varsity Press, London, 1968).
54. Aquinas, *Summa Theologica* 1-2, qu 90, a 4.
55. Ibid, qu 91.
56. Ibid, qu 91, a 1.
57. Weinrib, op cit, p 56.
58. Ibid, qu 91, a 4 and 5.
59. Ibid, qu 95, a 2.

60. Aquinas, op cit 1-2, qu 91, a 2: "Therefore, since all things subject to divine providence are ruled and measured by the eternal law, it is evident that all things partake in some way in the eternal law, insofar as from its being imprinted on them, they derive their respective inclinations to their proper acts and ends. Now among all others, the rational creature is subject to divine providence in a most excellent way, insofar as it partakes of a share of providence, by being provident both for itself and for others. Therefore, it has a share of the eternal reason, whereby it has a natural inclination to its proper act and end; and this participation of the eternal law in the rational creature is called the natural law".

61. Aquinas, op cit, qu 94, a 4.

62. Aquinas acknowledged therefore that "human laws cannot have the inerrancy that marks conclusions of demonstrative science." Ibid, qu 91, a 3.

63. Aquinas, op cit 1-2, qu 94, a 2.

64. Ibid.

65. Sigmund, P E, op cit, p 40.

66. Socrates, in submitting to an unjust sentence of death, spoke of the need for obedience to the laws of the city-state in which he had lived, as an absolute obligation, for to flout those laws would be to destroy them, and to renege upon his solemn agreement as a member of that community. See Plato's account of the death of Socrates (c 398 BC) in *Crito*.

67. For discussion by modern jurists on this issue, see Rawls, J, *A Theory of Justice*, (Oxford UP, Oxford, 1971), pp 342-368; Rostow, E, "The Rightful Limits of Freedom in a Liberal Democratic State: Of Civil Disobedience" in Rostow, E (ed), *Is the Law Dead?* (Simon and Schuster, New York, 1971).

68. Aquinas, op cit, qu 95, a 2.

69. Ibid, qu 96, a 4.

70. Ibid.

71. Romans 13: 1-3 (NIV).

72. Christ taught his followers to "render unto Caesar that which is Caesar's" (Mark 12:17). See also John 19:11.

73. Origen, *Contra Celsum*, 5.37.

74. Aquinas, op cit, qu 96, a 5.

75. See below, Chapter 4.

76. Kelly, J M, op cit, pp 186-189.

77. Hooker, R, *Laws of Ecclesiastical Polity*, 1.8.

78. D'Entreves, A P, *Natural Law* (Hutchinson, London, 1951), pp 50-54; Sabine, G H, *A History of Political Theory* (4th ed, Dryden, Hinsdale, Ill), pp 390-395.

79. For example, Alberico Gentili (1552-1608) and Francisco de Suarez (1548-1617).

80. *De Jure Belli ac Pacis*, Prologemena, para 11.

81. Sigmund, P E, op cit, p 62.

82. See further, Stein, P, *Legal Evolution: The Story of an Idea* (Cambridge, UP, Cambridge, 1980).

83. See below, Chapter 4.

84. Weinreb, L, op cit, pp 68-76. While Hobbes made reference to God, and assumed a divine providence in ordering the affairs of humankind, his ideas were not premised upon belief in God in the same way as for Aquinas and other theorists.

85. "Whatsoever is the object of any man's appetite or desire, that is it which he for his part calleth good; and the object of his hate or aversion, evil . . . For these words of good, [and] evil . . . are ever used with relation to the person that useth them: there being nothing simply and absolutely so; nor any common rule of good and evil, to be taken from the nature of objects themselves." Hobbes, *Leviathan*, Part 1, Ch 6.

86. Ibid, p 82.

87. Ibid, Ch 15, p 103.

88. Kelly, J M, op cit, p 214.

89. Sigmund, P E, op cit, p 81.

90. Weinreb, L, op cit, p 77.

91. Locke, J, *Essays on the Law of Nature* (1660).

92. Locke, J, *Essay Concerning Human Understanding* (1690). In this work, Locke denied that natural law was innate, but he did affirm that it was something which could be discovered and understood by reason.

93. Ibid, Ch 2.

94. Ibid, 2.11.

95. Ibid, 2.5.

96. Kelly, J M, op cit, pp 292-293.

97. See below, Chapter 4.

98. Although there were numerous other writers who were influential in the development of the revolutionary ideas in America, it was Locke's ideas which were substantially restated in the American Declaration of Independence of 1776, which read: "We hold these truths to be self-evident: that all men are created equal; that they are endowed by their Creator with certain inalienable rights; that among these are life, liberty and the pursuit of happiness. That to secure these rights, governments are instituted among men, deriving their just powers from the consent of the governed; that whenever any form of government becomes destructive of these ends it is the right of the people to alter or to abolish it, and to institute a new government, laying its foundations on such principles, and organising its powers in such form, as to them shall seem most likely to effect their safety and happiness". Although this declaration referred to the third great right as one to the pursuit of happiness, and not a right of property, Locke's trilogy of fundamental rights—to life, liberty and property—became enshrined in the fifth and 14th amendments to the United States Constitution.

99. See below, Chapter 4.

100. *The Social Contract*, 1.6.

101. Ibid, Bk II, Ch 6: "when we have defined a law of nature, we shall be no nearer the definition of a law of the state."

102. Montesquieu, C, *The Spirit of Laws*, 1.3.

103. It has been questioned whether, in fact, Hume should be attributed with the fundamental logical attack which is associated with him. See Finnis, J, *Natural Law and Natural Rights* (Clarendon Press, Oxford, 1980), pp 36-42. See also Stein, P, op cit.

104. MacIntyre, A, *After Virtue* (2nd ed, Duckworths, London, 1985), pp 51-61.

105. Finnis, J, op cit, p 34.

106. Bentham, J, *An Introduction to the Principles of Morals and Legislation* (Burns, J H and Hart, H L A, (eds) Methuen, London, 1982), II.14, n 6.

107. Bentham, J, *Anarchical Fallacies*, Art II. Bentham also criticised the concept of natural rights for its potential as a tool of coercive demagogy. In the same work, he wrote: "When a man is bent upon having things his own way and can give no reason for it, he says: I have a right to have them so. When a man has a political caprice to gratify . . . he sets up a cry of rights." Bentham's criticisms proved prophetic of the way in which the rhetoric of rights is used in the modern era, transplanted from its original context within the philosophical, political and religious worldviews of the era from which the concept of natural rights emerged.

108. Hart, H L A, Introduction to Bentham's *Principles of Morals and Legislation*, op cit, p xxxviii.

109. This was entitled *Of Laws in General*. The manuscript was only discovered in 1945. It was among Bentham's papers at London University.

110. For a discussion of Austin's life and work, see Morison, W L, *John Austin* (Arnold, London, 1982).

111. Austin's writings are collected in *The Province of Jurisprudence Determined and the Uses of the Study of Jurisprudence* (Hart, H L A (ed), Weidenfeld and Nicolson, London, 1954).

112. Ibid, 184-185.

113. Ibid, 193.

114. Ibid, 194.

115. Ibid, pp 230-231.

116. See below, Chapter 3.

117. Hart, H L A, *The Concept of Law* (Clarendon, Oxford, 1961).

118. Ibid, p 107.

119. See Morison, W L, op cit.

120. See below, Chapter 4.

121. Augustine, *City of God Against the Pagans*, Bk XIX 13.

122. Radbruch, *Vorschule der Rechtsphilosophie* (1947) cited in Kelly, J M, op cit, p 379.

123. In particular, the cases of grudge informers. These cases led to a celebrated debate between Professor H L A Hart and Professor Lon Fuller in the *Harvard Law Review*. Hart, H L A, "Positivism and the Separation of Law and Morals" (1958) 71 Harvard LR 616-620; Fuller, L, "Positivism and Fidelity to Law—A Reply to Professor Hart" (1958) 71 Harvard LR 648-657.

124. Radbruch, op cit.

125. Berman, H, *The Interaction of Law and Religion*, op cit, p 59.

Part Two

The Legacy of English History

Chapter 3

THE DEVELOPMENT OF COMMON LAW, EQUITY AND STATUTE

3.1 The Significance of English History

It took a number of years for the early colonists of Australia to develop more than a rudimentary legal system. The early years of the colony were marked by military rule and dictatorial power. The governors had supreme authority in the colony, subject only to the limitation that it was authority delegated from London, and that they themselves were men under orders. Only gradually did recognised institutions of law emerge, and later still, did the new colonies which emerged in Australia gain a form of representative government. However, for the reasons given above, in Chapter 1, when they did develop legal and political institutions of their own, it was the English system which was largely copied with all its strengths and weaknesses.

The system which, in this manner, was transplanted to Australian soil, was itself the product of a curious historic evolution. It had been born in a feudal era, and its distinctive form had evolved through several centuries of English history as a result of bureaucratic process, statutory reform and judicial decision making. Like so many other evolved systems, the English legal system was reasonably well attuned for its purpose, but carried with it many accretions which were explicable only by tradition and which had outlasted the reasons for their existence.

An understanding of the Australian legal tradition requires an awareness of the origins of these various sources of law within England, for Australian law still bears the imprint of that process of development, and many of the terms used to describe legal institutions and officers today originated in medieval English history. Familiar features of Australian law such as the use of juries, the patterns of legal reasoning, the importance of procedure and of pleading, the distinction between law and equity, and many aspects of property ownership, all owe their origins to the development of English law in the seven centuries following the Norman Conquest of 1066.

While in its substance, and in the manner of its formation, the common law is quite distinct from the civil law of continental Europe, an emphasis upon the separateness of the development of the common law can obscure the extent to which the common law was shaped by the same philosophical, political and religious influences as the civil law of Europe. Many aspects of English history which affected its legal system were currents within a broader stream of European history. In matters of law, the British Isles were not as separate from the rest of the continent as some British legal historians have seemed to suggest.[1]

3.2   The Birth of the Common Law

3.2.1   Origins

The formative period of the common law was between the 12th and 14th centuries. It has been said that the "common law is the by-product of an administrative triumph, the way in which the government of England came to be centralised and specialised during the centuries after the Conquest".[2] This is not to suggest that the English common law was in some way planned. It was not the product of any grand design at all. The substantive common law evolved from the procedures by which cases came to be resolved in the royal courts. Rights emerged from the opportunities available to litigants to bring various grievances before the king's courts, and the extent to which cases could be brought before royal courts came to depend in turn upon the extent to which local power-brokers had conceded authority to the central government for the administration of justice.

3.2.2   Customary law before the Conquest

The administration of justice which emerged from the centralisation of government after the Norman Conquest may best be understood in contrast to what had existed before. In England at this stage, as in much of Europe, proprietary rights were ordered, disputes resolved and transgressions punished primarily at the local level according to the customs of the village or region. Decisions were made by local assemblies. In the period preceding the Conquest, law was largely undifferentiated from other aspects of the life of local communities. Indeed, the first stage in the process of the development of law as we know it was the recognition that the resolution of disputes and the righting of wrongs came to be seen as a community responsibility. Only gradually did this become the case. As Baker notes: "the suppression of private force by investing the community at large with a greater force required a degree of social organisation which it must have taken countless dark and forgotten centuries to achieve".[3] In societies without such organisation, basic justice may only be achieved through self-help, reprisals and family feuds. There was a need, however, to discourage such private warfare and to offer a more peaceful means of resolving disputes. The influence of the church was partly responsible for the changes. The church taught that it was honourable to show mercy and to accept monetary compensation for wrongs instead of resorting to blood feuds.[4] Gradually, the resolution of disputes came to be seen as a matter for community involvement. Disputes were thus brought to the local assembly.

It was at the level of local government that society was fundamentally organised. At least a dozen kingdoms existed at one stage in the area of land which came to be called England. Even within these kingdoms, the extent of control exercised by the monarch varied. By about the tenth century, however, a single and effective monarchy had been established in England, and with it, an organised and homogenous system of local government. There were "shires", or counties, into which the whole country was divided, and which played a role in military organisation and the collection of taxes. In rural areas, shires were divided into "hundreds" under a hundredman, and within each "hundred", there were "tithings", consisting of ten families each. The hundreds met monthly, and it was in these meetings that the business of the community was conducted, including its work of dispute resolution. There were also boroughs, which were the urban equivalents of the hundreds, and which held similar assemblies. Shire (or county) meetings, known as shire moots, were also held, but these were much less regular and rather more formal. They were attended by the military commander (known as the ealdorman), and the local bishop, and discussed the more important matters affecting the shire.[5] These assemblies were convened by the shire reeve, or "sheriff", who held the major power in the shire as a delegate of the king.

These assemblies, whether at the level of the boroughs and hundreds, or in the counties, were not merely, or even mainly, legal institutions. They were administrative in nature, and the resolution of disputes was only a part of that business. Justice was communal, in the sense that the decision-making power was not vested in an individual, but in the gathered assembly. Nor was justice administered according to law in the modern usage of that word. A system of law requires that similar disputes be resolved in the same way over a period of time, thus establishing some sort of right in a plaintiff to have the matter adjudicated in her or his favour in similar circumstances. There was no such system of precedent in these assemblies. They did, however, apply local customs, such as the custom, which developed in most parts of England (though not all), that land should devolve to the eldest son.[6]

Thus, to the extent that these assemblies applied rules, they were the customary rules of the community, and these might vary from one community to another. There was a small body of law which did not have this origin. In limited spheres, kings issued specific instructions about how to deal with certain matters. Written legislation survives in England from the reign of King Aethelberht of Kent in about 600 AD.[7] King Alfred of Wessex (d 899 AD) in particular, sought to make laws on a variety of matters, although much of this "legislation" repeated passages of the Holy Scriptures and the laws of the church.[8] There was at that time no distinction to be drawn between sacred and secular authority within the kingdom. A further influence, in some parts of Eastern England, was "danelaw" which resulted from the Danish invasions of the ninth century.

The resolution of disputes also required the invocation of the deity, as it did throughout Europe where Germanic kings reigned. It was not until the 12th and 13th centuries in England that juries emerged. Until then, God was seen as the judge. Traditions for proving matters which had been handed down from the pre-Christian era survived for many years after the church gained ascendance, and became melded with Christian theology. A "trial" was initiated by an oath. The plaintiff established a prima facie case by bringing a group of followers who were willing to support the claim by swearing an oath. This then put the defendant to the test. In less serious matters, it might be sufficient for a denial to be supported by sufficient "oath-helpers" to back up the defendant's word. This came to be known as trial by wager of law. More serious accusations led to trial by ordeal. These were forms of appeal to God to reveal the truth, and required priestly involvement.

A number of types of ordeal were available, of which the most commonly used were the ordeals of fire and water. The ordeal of fire involved placing a hot piece of iron into the hand of the defendant, and then binding it up. If, several days later, the burn had festered, then God was seen to have decided against the defendant. Trial by water was no more pleasant. The defendant was bound, and lowered into a pond. Sinking was taken as a sign of innocence. All being well, that innocence was established before he or she drowned. The Normans did not bring with them any more sophisticated methods of proof. They did, however, add to the available list the ordeal of trial by battle. The truth of the matter was to be resolved by single combat. The severity of this means of proof was mitigated by the fact that the parties need not fight personally. They could choose a "champion" to fight for them. Indeed, the demandant had to find a champion since no one was allowed to be a "witness" to their own cause. The champion had to be someone who had a knowledge of the relevant facts and swore to the truth of the demandant's claim.[9] Trial by battle was initiated by throwing down a gauntlet.[10]

3.2.3   Centralisation in the Norman period

The great contribution of the Norman and Angevin kings to the development of the common law lay in their flair for administration, and their efforts at centralisation. With their arrival, they inherited a system of law and of government which was reasonably well developed and which provided a cohesive system of control throughout the country by means of the shires (or counties) and the hundreds. William the Conqueror affirmed the existing order; he assured the English that they could keep their old laws, and in no sense did the new order seek to replace existing customs by a series of royal decrees. There were accretions to the body of the law, such as the "forest law" to protect the royal hunt, but there was no fundamental reform.[11]

The new rulers did, however, have an interest in consolidating their hold on the country, and the existing system gave them the means to do so. When they arrived, the system of counties and hundreds provided a governmental framework for England which was answerable to the king. Since the sheriff was a royal official, and directly responsible to the monarch, effective control of the whole country was possible through the counties and their institutions. The power of the sheriff within the county was at the same time a source of potential threat to the king. There was good reason to keep the sheriffs in check.

The maintenance of law and order was a natural part of this process of consolidating power, not only because the Norman monarchs understood it to be a first duty of government, but also because it was profitable. The criminal justice system bore much fruit in fines and forfeitures. More than one military campaign was financed from the profits of justice. The Crown thus had incentives for the proper administration of criminal law in the realm, [12] and the proper administration of criminal justice according to law was a particular concern of Henry II (1154-1189). [13]

3.2.4   Itinerant justice and the general eyre

One of the means by which the Norman and Angevin kings maintained their central control was through the general eyre. [14] This was established during the reign of Henry II (1154-1189), and lasted over 150 years. Leading members of the king's court were given commissions to visit a county and to conduct a general audit of the county on behalf of the king. The eyre could be a cataclysmic event for the county. All normal activities ceased; leading people of the county gathered in the appropriate place, and the justices took over from the sheriff for the time in which they were there. The eyre was a complete review of local government, to ensure that the royal commands had been heeded. The books were inspected to make certain that the proper sum due to the king was accounted for. Other matters of concern to the Crown were dealt with. Amongst these matters was the hearing of cases.

There were two sorts of cases brought before the royal judges. First, there were matters of direct relevance to the revenue of the Crown. The justices investigated crimes for which part of the punishment was the forfeiture of property to the king. Unexplained deaths were looked into for this reason. Other matters which were of concern to the treasury included wrecks and finds of treasure. Secondly, there were the "common pleas"—ordinary litigation between people. It was at the eyre that first the royal judges dispensed justice as a matter of routine. There were good reasons why litigants might want royal justice for private disputes. Chief among the benefits of having one's dispute adjudicated by the king was that the judgment was more likely to be enforced than in the shire moot or the manorial court of a local lord, especially where the defendant was a local power broker or had friends in high places. In deciding cases between private litigants, the judges applied the laws and customs of the realm, and where relevant local customs existed, these would have been applied by the judges.

The general eyre was, however, infrequent. Years might pass between visits. Not that the local officials would have wanted them more often; they were occasions to be avoided if at all possible. It remained the case, however, that the demands of justice required some means of dealing with cases between eyres. This need was met by the appointment of "justices of assize" who, as the system became established, went on circuit twice a year to hear cases.

A further development at the local level was the appointment of justices of the peace. The maintenance of law and order required not only an efficient system of royal justice, but trusted officers who could investigate crimes and bring the matters before the judges. Originally, this had been a communal responsibility. The hundreds were responsible for presenting crimes, and could be punished for failing to do so. This developed into the institution called the grand jury,[15] which still plays a role in the criminal justice system in the United States. This system was unreliable, however, and as early as 1200, the practice began of appointing various knights in each county to "keep the peace". This involved a policing function initially, but by the 14th century it had developed into a judicial role; justices of the peace were appointed increasingly to exercise judicial functions in some of the less serious criminal cases.[16] These justices of the peace were the forerunners of the modern magistracy. While in Australia this role has been substantially professionalised, English law still relies heavily on the lay, part time justices of the peace to deal with less serious criminal and civil cases.[17]

3.2.5   The establishment of central courts

Royal authority was not only maintained through itinerant justice. Ultimate power rested with the king's court (the curia regis), and it was from this body of royal advisers that the itinerant justices were sent out. When their duties were fulfilled, they returned to the king's side. The Norman kings were, themselves, itinerant. It was not safe to remain constantly in the one place. Nonetheless, a practice grew up that some judges would remain at the palace of Westminster in London even when the king was elsewhere. Eventually, during the reign of Henry II in the 12th century, a central royal court, known as "the Bench" was established at Westminster. King John (1199-1216) abolished it for a while: but he was compelled to restore it in 1214 by popular demand. The Magna Carta (or Great Charter) of the following year recorded the agreement between the king and his subjects that "common pleas shall not follow our court but shall be held in some fixed place."[18] By the beginning of the 14th century, three courts were in operation at Westminster: the Court of the Exchequer,[19] which was ostensibly only concerned with matters of relevance to the treasury, the Court of Common Pleas, and the Court of King's Bench.

It was with the establishment of these central royal courts, that the common law began to take shape. Many features of the modern system have their origins in the procedures which were adopted then. The establishment of courts at Westminster had both advantages and disadvantages. The advantages included the ready availability of these courts in a given place, combined with all the other advantages of appealing to the king's authority rather than to a local court. The disadvantages arose from the long distances which might exist between the suitors and the court. How could courts sitting at Westminster ensure that the defendant was submitted to the jurisdiction of the court? And how could it determine the facts in issue? Ensuring the personal attendance of the defendant proved not to be a problem. By about 1200, a class of professional attorneys developed, and they were given the authority to represent their absent clients throughout the litigation. Determining the facts was a greater difficulty, due to the need for a jury.

It quickly became a feature of royal justice that matters should be resolved by jury. This change from the old method of trial by ordeal was hastened by the decision of the western church in 1215 to forbid the clergy to participate in ordeals.[20] This left only trial by battle as a traditional means of deciding issues of fact. The jury of the medieval period was not the same as the present day jury. It is of the essence of the modern system that jurors should be neutral parties with, as far as possible, no pre-conception concerning the matters of fact to be tried. The medieval jurors, however, were not merely the passive recipients of the evidence presented to them by the parties. They were 12 or more men from the locality, unrelated to the parties, who were required to report concerning what they knew of the events in question; if they did not have personal knowledge, then they were expected to look into the matter.[21] For this reason it was essential that the jury was drawn from the county in which the matter had arisen. Trial by jury could not take place unless a way was found to combine central justice with local knowledge.

These problems were overcome not by bringing the parties and the witnesses to London, but by utilising the network of royal officers. A writ would issue from Westminster which was addressed not to the defendant but to the sheriff of the county requiring him to bring the defendant to answer.[22] This writ was purchased from the Chancery. The Chancery was a department of state, presided over by the Chancellor. If trial was by jury, then a jury was empanelled, and summoned to appear before the king, or the court at Westminster, "unless before then the king's justices should have come" to the county.[23] The expectation was that the judges would come to the county. It was part of the work of the judges on circuit to receive verdicts from juries and to convey them to the relevant court at Westminster.

In this way, justice from the courts at Westminster, although expensive, was made possible. By the early 13th century, justice was made available to the people in a number of forums. The court system formed a complex mosaic. Matters could be taken to the local courts, or to the county court.[24] It could be heard by the justices in eyre, or between eyres by the justices of assize. It might also be heard by a justice of the peace. If one of these means were used, then the matter could be initiated merely by complaint to the relevant court. The Westminster courts provided an exceptional means of relief. Justice as of right was in the locality. Justice from the Court of Common Pleas or the King's Bench had to be specially authorised by the issue of a writ. However, the exceptional became normal in the course of time. It is a curious accident of history that it was from this exceptional procedure that the common law derived. Most of what happened in the county courts and in the assizes is lost to record and had little lasting impact upon the future development of the law. The customary law of the realm has all but disappeared. But the learning which developed around the exceptional procedure of the writ was to have a lasting influence. Indeed, it produced the common law.

3.2.6   The writ system

Beginning legal proceedings by writ was no easy task, and it required professional assistance from people who were learned in the writ system. A writ could take a number of different forms, but essentially it was a letter specifying the nature of the complaint and demanding certain action from the defendant.[25] A writ seeking to enforce a right typically demanded that the defendant should do what the plaintiff required, or come to the court to explain why this should not be done. A writ alleging a wrong required the defendant to come before the justices to answer for a specific alleged misdeed. The type of claim was, therefore, necessarily expressed in the writ itself. The writ was not merely a general summons to attend the court.

These writs formed precedents which were then used subsequently. It followed that a potential litigant needed to select the correct writ to deal with the matter in issue, or else persuade the Chancery to issue a new form of writ. Before the middle of the 13th century it proved relatively easy to establish a new form of writ. However, there were political pressures to constrain this free expansion. The issuance of a new writ was, in essence, the making of a new law, at least in one sense. It allowed for a cause of action which had hitherto been pursued, if at all, only before local courts or itinerant justices, to be heard through the exceptional procedure of a case at Westminster. This increased the trend towards centralisation, which was resisted by some members of the nobility. Furthermore, it was recognised that the royal courts could not deal with all the disputes of the realm, and thus certain of the more minor cases were confined to the county courts.[26] Certain novel writs were also opposed because they were considered to be contrary to justice, as interpreted by clerical learning, reason and custom.

By 1258, action was taken to curtail the issuance of new writs. The *Provisions of Oxford* of that year required that the chancellor "shall seal no writs, other than routine writs" without an order of the king's council. The king's sole command was insufficient.[27] This constituted almost a complete prohibition on the creation of new writs. The *Second Statute of Westminster* 1285 (13 Edw I) did modify this somewhat, by allowing for writs to be issued in like cases (in consimili casu) to existing writs. However, this was not a licence to create completely new forms of action. Thus, after these developments, there were only a limited number of available writs, and the plaintiff's case had to be brought within one of them, unless some new writ were allowed. Necessity is the mother of invention, and ways were found in subsequent centuries to overcome these limitations.[28] Nonetheless, the limitation on the issuing of new writs was an important constraint upon the development of the common law, and it was those forms of action which were allowed, which gave outline to the law, and from within which the substantive law developed.[29]

3.2.7 Pleadings and the emergence of substantive law

After the writ was issued, the next stage of the litigation was the "count". This was the formal statement of claim, and was essential to the legal process. It was this which formed the basis of the trial, and the correct words had to be used exactly, for this was the question being put to the Almighty, or later to the jury, and about which an answer was sought. In the early forms of trial, the defendant would issue a general denial, which followed exactly the terms of the complaint. This was known as the process of pleading, and was highly formalised. The terms of the statement and denial were confirmed by oath.

When God was in charge of settling the issue, nothing more than the oath and denial was needed. If the plaintiff sought the return of his land on the basis that the defendant was now in possession of land which had belonged to his father and grandfather, it was scarcely necessary for the defendant to justify his possession by recounting that the land had been granted to his father legitimately.[30] God would know all the details, and decide according to the true justice of the case.[31]

Juries, however, were not quite as trustworthy. A precise question had to be put to the jury to which a positive or negative answer was required. It would be insufficient for the defendant merely to issue a general denial that the land which he possessed had belonged to the plaintiff's father and grandfather, for that was indeed true. He needed instead to put in a defence that although the plaintiff's claim was true, he had lawful posse' reason of the grant to his father. Allowing the defendant to plea' facts by way of defence ensured that the jury was being asked t' question. While some such defences would be uncontroversi might be taken whether other defences provided a valid answe' grant of the land had been procured through taking advantage of the original owner's insanity? The plaintiff's "counter", or "serjeant-at-law" as he later became known, would issue the reply that the grant was invalid because the owner was not of sound mind, and the defendant would then have to decide whether to challenge the validity of that reply. If there was no challenge to the reply, then the question of law would be resolved by default, and the matter would go to the jury to determine whether the original grant was made by a man who was insane.

However, the defendant's serjeant might instead challenge the legal validity of the reply. If one party to the proceedings considered that a plea made by the other was not valid, then he would make a demurrer. He was not denying the facts which were pleaded, but rather, submitting that even if those facts were true, they should not affect the outcome of the case. The facts asserted were not relevant, and so should not form any part of the question which was being framed for the jury. In the 14th century, the records suggest that the judges were quite reluctant to decide demurrers.[32] The matters were resolved informally among the legal practitioners, who might withdraw a plea which was challenged, or change it so that it was more acceptable. Sometimes, the judges of the court would discuss the issue collectively. The tendency, if a particular plea was in doubt, was for it to be withdrawn, and the defendant would simply plead "the general issue", denying all the facts and leaving it up to the jury to do substantial justice. The records, contained in the "year books" of the time, did not consist of judgments of the court in the manner of modern law reports, but would record whether or not a particular plea had been accepted. The process of pleading, therefore, revealed issues which called for a ruling on the substantive law; but the issues were decided through the process of pre-trial procedure, in settling the questions which should go to the jury.

It was through this process of plea and defence that detailed legal rules began to develop. The nature of the writ merely established that the royal courts would provide a remedy for wrongful dispossession of land. The process of pleading gave substance to that form of action, and new fact situations threw up for decision different questions. The refined learning about the writs and pleading was handed down from one generation to the next through apprenticeship schools. Learning about procedures—what were the forms of action, and what would be acceptable as pleas—was what was meant by learning the law.[33]

3.2.8   Subsequent development of the common law

By the end of the 16th century, much of this manner of doing things had changed. Pleading, instead of being oral, was done on paper. Judges were willing to make authoritative pronouncements on the law, given a set of admitted facts. Issues of law could be stated for the court after the jury had given its verdict. These matters of law were settled "in banc", that is by a "full court" of judges deciding together, rather than a ruling by an individual judge. An early form of appellate structure could be observed in outline.

In this way, the law was adapted to changing values and needs. Another means of bringing about legal change was the widespread use of "fictions". A fiction is a way of making changes to the law while pretending not to. They were used widely by the various courts of common law in order to gain jurisdiction over certain kinds of cases. The motivation for this competition between the courts was financial. Essentially, the more cases which might be heard by the Court of Exchequer, or King's Bench, as the case may be, the better off were its judges and officials. Consequently, competition occurred at various stages to attract jurisdiction from the Court of Common Pleas which had the broadest jurisdiction. For example, the King's Bench, which did not have jurisdiction in cases of debt, allowed a fictitious allegation of trespass to be brought which was sufficient to place the defendant within the court's jurisdiction. [34] To this, the allegation of debt might be added, and the claim of trespass quietly dropped. Procedural advantages and lower costs made such devices attractive to litigants.

Fictions also affected the substance of the law. Thus parts of what is now known as the law of restitution began life as fictions. An example is the action of quantum meruit. If someone ordered services without agreeing on the sum to be paid for them, then an action could be brought for payment of as much as the plaintiff deserved. The form of action used for this purpose was one which alleged that the defendant had assumed the debt. It was based on an implied promise to pay the reasonable sum fixed by the court. These were "quasi-contracts". The matter was treated as if there was a contract, although the failure to fix an agreed sum for the work prevented an actual contract from coming into existence. It is often the case that traditions long survive the reasons for their existence. It was only in 1987 that the High Court of Australia repudiated implied contract as the basis for this doctrine. [35]

3.2.9   Reform of common law procedures

Essentially, the writ system, with its attendant pleadings to determine the issue to be tried, continued without major reform until the 19th century. The technicalities of the system, in particular the need to frame one's case in terms of a particular form of action, observing some highly refined distinctions, made it cumbersome and arbitrary. [36]

Nonetheless, further major change was slow in coming. In the course of the 19th century in Britain, a series of reforms made the system simpler, and less formal. Most of the old forms of action were swept away by statutory reforms in 1832 and 1833. [37] Further reforms were made to the writ system in 1852. [38] With the *Judicature Acts* of 1873-1875, (see below, 3.3.6), the writ itself was replaced by a statement of claim as a means of starting a civil suit. This involved stating briefly the facts on which reliance was placed, and the relief sought. These reforms were copied in Australia, and essentially this remains the system today. Pleadings remain important in major civil actions, but only as a way of defining the issues to be resolved at trial. Their substance is the important issue, not their form.

This, however, is to jump ahead several centuries. By this stage, two other prominent sources of law had developed and were playing a vital role. The first was equity, a form of judge-made law which operated alongside the common law system and which developed in order to overcome some of the common law's limitations. The second source of law was statute. This, of course, had been a source of law for much longer than the common law, but it developed into a major source of law largely as a result of the need for Parliamentary reform of the common law. Thus, equity and statute were both sources of law reform, but in different ways. Had the common law been less restricted in its development, equity would not have been necessary; and Parliament would have had less work to do in reforming the law.

3.3   The Development of Equity

3.3.1   The need for equity

A major factor in the growth of the common law was the demands of litigants who, for a variety of reasons, could not find the justice they wanted from the local courts of the district and county. Equity developed also as a direct result of popular demands for justice; but it was not the deficiencies of the local courts which led to this development, so much as the limitations of the common law courts. As early as the 14th century, it was common for petitions to be made to the king to exercise an overriding residual power to do justice in a given case. The reasons were various: in some cases, complaint was made about misconduct by litigants or officials. In other cases, the cause for complaint was that the common law would work a hardship by not taking into account various facts which affected the justice of the case. Initially, these petitions were heard by the king's council. Later, however, they were delegated to individual officials, including the Chancellor.

3.3.2   The Chancellor's jurisdiction

The Chancellor was the head of a great department of state. The origins of the Chancery were as the royal secretariat, and it was from there that writs were issued, along with a variety of other royal documents. Commonly, the Chancellors were archbishops or senior bishops and many of them exercised functions akin to a prime minister, but they were not without legal knowledge. Many of them were learned in canon law or Roman law, and their supervision over the issuance of writs ensured that they had a working knowledge of the common law. However, when cases were referred to them for decision, it was not their legal knowledge which was applied to these "hard cases", but conscience. Conscience was the ultimate court of appeal for the medieval lawyer, and no insistence upon the need for certainty and predictability could prevent justice being done according to the merits of the case, if otherwise an unconscionable result would prevail. [39]

By the end of the 14th century, this jurisdiction of the Chancellor had developed into its own court, which came to be known as the Court of Chancery. It operated in a quite different manner from the common law courts. Proceedings were conducted in the vernacular English rather than in Latin or Norman French; there was an air of informality in the way evidence was given; there was no jury; and the Chancellor saw his role as inquiring into the merits of the case free from the technicality of common law pleadings and rules of evidence. Decrees were made in personam, that is, against the litigants personally. Thus, it was possible that the Chancellor could acknowledge the right at common law of the defendant to have title to certain land, and yet order that the defendant should hold that land for the use of the petitioner. This might occur, for example, where the defendant received title to the land on the basis that he would hold it for the petitioner's benefit. The general rule about the validity of the legal title was not abrogated; it was merely qualified in its application to a given set of facts, by considerations of equity and good conscience which justified a different order against the defendant.

In the earliest period of the Court of Chancery, the court's jurisdiction was quite wide. It administered justice swiftly and without great expense, and it was a source of refuge for the poor and for those who could not get justice in any other way. The Chancellor was much less open to corruption or duress than a local sheriff or jury. In this way, the Chancery was an answer to corrupt practices which might occur in the common law system. It also relieved litigants from some of the rigours of the common law. Rules, such as those which required written evidence for certain transactions, were necessary to maintain certainty in the common law, but could also work injustice in various cases. A famous work, St German's *Doctor and Student* (1531), having noted that it is not possible for legislators to make general laws which cover every particular case, stated:

> "[T]herefore to follow words of the law is in some cases both against justice and the Commonwealth, thus in some cases it is good and even necessary to leave the words of the law and to follow what reason and justice requires and to that intent equity is ordained, that is to say, to temper and mitigate the rigour of the law." [40]

Echoing Christopher St German, Lord Chancellor Ellesmere argued in the *Earl of Oxford's Case* (1615) that the Court of Chancery was necessary because "men's actions are so diverse and infinite that it is impossible to make a general law which may aptly meet with every particular and not fail in some circumstances". He went on to state that the "office of the chancellor is to correct men's consciences for frauds, breaches of trust, wrongs and oppressions of what nature soever they may be, and to soften and mollify the extremity of the law".[41]

There was nothing especially new in this idea. Aristotle had put forward the need for such a form of justice about two thousand years earlier,[42] and the idea was also familiar to the Roman lawyers.[43] Aquinas explained the role of equity in these terms:

"Law is written down in order to manifest the lawgiver's meaning and intention. Yet sometimes it happens that, were he present, he would judge differently . . . Laws that are rightly enacted prove deficient where to observe them would be to offend against natural right. In such cases, judgment should be delivered, not according to the letter of the law, but by recourse to equity, this being what the lawgiver aimed at."[44]

The innovation of English law was that this "equitable" jurisdiction was exercised in a different court, and developed, in the course of time, according to a discrete set of principles.[45] A distinct jurisdiction in equity was necessary because of the rigidity of the common law. Had the common law been more flexible, more ready to develop new remedies and new defences, then there would have been no need to have a separate court with different rules to the common law.

3.3.3   The relationship between equity and the common law

The relationship between common law courts and the Chancery was a complex one in cases where they both exercised jurisdiction in a matter. It was not uncommon for one party in litigation to seek relief in Chancery from a judgment of the Court of Common Pleas, or the King's Bench. The petitioner's case in such circumstances would be that although justice had been done according to legal right, it had not been done according to conscience. Such a challenge to the common law judgment could be offensive to the justices of that court. The Chancellors always accepted the validity of common law judgments, but sometimes found it necessary to restrain a party from executing them. They did this by issuing a "common injunction". This was an injunction restraining the litigant, on pain of imprisonment, from proceeding at common law. The common law judges accepted this jurisdiction for as long as it was exercised wisely. However, tensions began to emerge in the 16th century, in particular during the tenure of Cardinal Wolsey as Chancellor (1515-1529). Later, a major dispute developed in the early 17th century as a result of conflicts between Lord Chancellor Ellesmere and the chief justice of the Court of King's Bench, Sir Edward Coke.[46] Coke challenged the authority of the Chancellor by releasing from prison those whom the Chancellor had incarcerated for breach of the common injunction. The dispute between the two courts was finally settled by James I, who ruled in favour of the Lord Chancellor.

Although his decision was later regarded as illegal,[47] the position became established that in any conflict of the rules of common law and the rules of Chancery, the equitable rule should prevail.

Nonetheless, Equity always was, and remains, a supplementary jurisdiction. It presupposes the validity of the common law. Maitland expressed it in this way:

> "We ought not to think of common law and equity as two rival systems. Equity was not a self-sufficient system, at every point it presupposed the existence of a common law. Common law was a self-sufficient system. I mean this: that if the legislature had passed a short Act saying 'Equity is hereby abolished', we might have got on fairly well; in some respects, our law would have been barbarous, unjust, absurd, but still the great elementary rights, the right to immunity from violence, the right to one's good name, the rights of ownership and of possession would have been decently protected and contract would have been enforced. On the other hand, had the legislature said, 'Common law is hereby abolished' this decree if obeyed would have meant anarchy. At every point equity presupposed the existence of the common law".[48]

3.3.4   The development of equitable principles

It was the nature of the early jurisdiction of the chancellors that they exercised justice in an ad hoc manner. Their prescriptions were intended to be cures for the ills of particular cases, and any concept that they were creating a body of law separate from the common law would have been quite incomprehensible to them. As Maitland put it: "Equity had come not to abolish the law, but to fulfil it".[49] In particular, they saw an important role in preventing fraud. This was given a wide meaning, but in particular the courts were concerned to prevent an unconscionable reliance upon common law rights.

One of the earliest developments from this concern to prevent fraud was the "trust".[50] In the medieval period, there arose a number of situations in which it was necessary for land to be given to one person for the benefit of another. An example of this was a gift to a community of Franciscan monks. Because of their rule of poverty, they were not allowed to own land. They were, however, allowed to accept the use of land from others. Thus, permanent arrangements were made in which land would be given to nominees to hold it for the benefit of the monks. There were also less noble reasons for transferring land to others. It proved to be a means by which certain feudal dues could be avoided. Many of these were owed when land passed by inheritance. An owner of land could ensure that property was passed to a particular beneficiary without it passing as a result of his death, by granting it to friends to hold it for him during his lifetime, and then after his death, for the beneficiary. Like the holding of lands for religious orders, this was done initially as a matter of trust. However, the obligations of those to whom the land had been granted came to be enforced by the Court of Chancery, since the grantees were bound in conscience to carry out the wishes of the grantor. The routine enforcement of these "uses" in Chancery turned them into an institution. Enforced originally to prevent the fraudulent denial of a moral obligation, they became merely another way of owning property. From this enforcement of "uses", the modern trust developed.

The recognition of uses is an early illustration of how the Chancery jurisdiction had the consequence of creating a set of rules which paralleled the common law. The use, or trust, allowed for two different entitlements to property simultaneously. The one who had accepted the obligation of trust[51] owned the land in the eyes of the common law courts. Yet, in equity, the beneficiary[52] was regarded as the true owner. Other rules developed similarly. Once certain entitlements became recognised by the Chancellors independently of common law rights, they passed into the currency of legal practice.

In this way, the Court of Chancery became the source of new rights; but not all of its jurisdiction was exercised according to settled principles. Indeed, the amount of consistency in decisions varied greatly between one chancellor and another. This was a common source of complaint as late as the 17th century. There were chancellors like Wolsey, who had no legal training, and who preferred their version of common sense to the learning of the common lawyers. There were also reasons why certain Lord Chancellors were quite reluctant to be governed by settled principles. It was the nature of Equity after all, that it had a role to play where the provisions of general laws failed.[53] The problem of unbridled equitable discretion was put by lawyer and parliamentarian, John Selden (1584-1654) in a famous gibe:

> "Equity is a roguish thing: for law we have a measure, know what to trust to; equity is according to the conscience of him that is chancellor, and as that is larger or narrower, so is equity. 'Tis all one as if they should make the standard for the measure we call a foot, a chancellor's foot; what an uncertain measure would this be? One chancellor has a long foot, another a short foot, a third an indifferent foot: 'tis the same thing in the chancellor's conscience."[54]

The Chancellors, at least from the time of Lord Nottingham, who took up office in 1673, recognised the need for consistency. The sheer extent of equity's power to intervene in modifying the effects of certain statutes, in setting aside contracts and gifts, in offering powerful remedies in its discretion, meant that care had to be taken in the application of equity's rules.[55] Between about 1673 and 1827, equitable principles were systematised and formalised.

By this time, however, the Court of Chancery had reached an advanced stage of decay. A jurisdiction which had been a source of speedy and effective justice for the disadvantaged in its infancy, had become a slow, cumbersome and expensive court in which to litigate.[56] This in itself, was a sufficient reason to consider reform. A greater impetus still, was the recognition that the division in the court structure between common law and equity could no longer be sustained.

3.3.5   *The fusion of the administration of law and equity*

By the middle of the 19th century, it was widely recognised that the system of having two separate jurisdictions, one applying the common law, the other administering equity, was a source of inefficiency in the legal system. Where litigation involved both common law and equitable rules, the effect of the divided jurisdiction was that the same matter had to be heard in two different courts. Typically, a plaintiff might begin a case at common law, and be met with an equitable defence. The defendant, instead of being able to plead that defence at common law, had to go to the Court of Chancery to obtain a common injunction preventing the plaintiff from pursuing the claim at common law. The validity of the equitable defence might then be decided in the Court of Chancery. Similarly, if a litigant wished to discover evidence from an opponent in a common law suit, application had to be made to the Chancery for an order of "discovery", since this was an order which was only available in equity. There was also an ever present danger that mistakes could be made, and a litigant who initiated a case in the wrong court would have to be sent to the other court to begin again.

Certain reforms were carried out in the mid-19th century to overcome the most obvious of the deficiencies, but major reform in England waited until 1873. The *Judicature Act* 1873 effected a restructuring of the English court system. Further reform was made by the *Judicature Act* 1875. After the *Judicature Acts* 1873-1875, there was to be one High Court of Justice which had a number of divisions. While the names "Chancery" and "Queen's Bench" (or "King's Bench") survived, they did so merely as the names of divisions of the High Court.[57] They ceased to be separate courts. In the new High Court, the principle of specialisation was retained. It was expected that matters such as trusts, which had hitherto been the special province of Chancery, would continue to be heard in the Chancery Division. Similarly, common law claims would normally be initiated in the Queen's Bench Division. However, there was no need for litigants to do so. All doctrines and remedies, whatever their origin, could be administered in any division of the High Court. There would be no question of having to begin litigation again because of a mistake as to jurisdiction, nor of having to go to two different courts in relation to the same matter.

The reform was not without its opponents. Indeed, serious concerns were expressed by Chancery practitioners. They feared that the existing equitable principles would be administered by judges trained only in common law rules, and that this threatened the very existence of a distinct equity jurisprudence.[58] The opposition of some equity practitioners to the fusion of the courts is one explanation for the reluctance of some Australian jurisdictions to adopt similar reforms. Indeed, as will be seen below, in Chapter 7, New South Wales maintained a separate court of equity until 1972.[59]

Fusion was intended only to affect the administration of law and equity. It was not to make changes to the substance of the law. In a famous metaphor, Ashburner, a writer on equity, explained that "the two streams of jurisdiction, though they run in the same channel, run side by side, and do not mingle their waters."[60] While there has been a certain amount of fusion of common law and equitable principles in the last 100 years,[61] there remain good reasons for keeping clearly in mind that a given rule is a common law rule or an equitable rule. Despite the fusion of the courts, there remains a separate body of legal principle which has a distinctive character, and which operates on distinctive principles. This is not to say that there remain two bodies of rules which are unchanged in their substance since the 19th century when fusion first occurred in England. Equity has developed in the 100 or so years since 1873 just as it developed substantially in the 100 years before 1873. In the hands of the judges—some conservative, some radical, some cautious, some creative—all law is continually evolving and developing. Equity is no exception.

3.4   The Doctrine of Precedent

By the 19th century, the common law system began to develop for the first time a rigid doctrine of precedent. The doctrine of precedent or in Latin, stare decisis,[62] provides that judges should stand by previous decisions, certainly when that decision was made by a court which is superior in the hierarchy of the courts, and generally when the previous decision was given by a bench of the same court. Underlying the doctrine of precedent is the notion that like cases should be treated as like.

This doctrine, at least in an embryonic way, developed early in the history of the common law. For centuries, English judges typically followed the rules of law which had previously been laid down, and legal reasoning proceeded on the basis of a consideration of past precedents or the records of the year books. The traditional nature of the law, and the belief that the common law had existed from time immemorial, ensured that a reverence for the past and a commitment to precedent was inherent in the nature of common law reasoning. There was not a rigid system of precedent, however, for there did not need to be. Cohesion within the common law was achieved not through the attribution of a special authority to particular courts or judges, but through the informal mechanisms by which traditions are so often handed down. The law was the possession of a small, and tightly-knit group of practitioners and judges. Power and authority within that group resided with a gerontocracy, and advancement of younger practitioners depended upon the approval of these senior members of the profession.[63] Naturally, in such a close-knit group, the common law tradition could be transmitted as a form of custom without the need to establish hierarchical patterns of authority. From early on, it was accepted wisdom that issues about the law once settled should not be re-opened, especially in relation to land titles. The importance of following precedent was never elevated to dogma, however, and it was considered that reason, rather than precedent, must ultimately guide the courts. Thus, Chief Justice Vaughan could say in 1673, that judges who considered a previous decision to be wrong need not follow it, since they were sworn to do justice according to the law. It was not a sufficient reason for giving an unjust decision in the case before the court, that the same injustice had been done before.[64]

The importance of adherence to previous decisions was also recognised in the Court of Chancery. From the late 17th century onwards, when the doctrines of equity began to be systematised, judges looked to precedent and decided cases by the application of previous decisions in much the same way as the common law courts.[65]

Eventually, the doctrine of stare decisis emerged. Lower courts considered themselves bound by the decisions of higher courts, and customarily would give effect to previous decisions of their own or of courts of co-ordinate jurisdiction for the sake of consistency.[66] Nonetheless, it was only in the 19th century that the doctrine achieved considerable rigidity and that it was expounded in a sophisticated way. The emergence of a stricter doctrine of precedent finds expression in a statement of the English judge Baron Parke in a case in 1833:[67]

> "Our common law system consists in the applying to new combinations and circumstances those rules of law which we derive from legal principles and judicial precedents; and for the sake of obtaining uniformity, consistency and certainty we must apply those rules where they are not plainly unreasonable and inconvenient, to all cases which arise; and we are not at liberty to reject them, and to abandon all analogy to them, in those to which they have not been judicially applied, because we think that the rules are not as convenient and reasonable as we ourselves could have devised."

Even this statement contains within it some room for flexibility in its condition that the rules will be applied unless "plainly unreasonable and inconvenient".

It was not until the second half of the 19th century, that the doctrine of precedent became firmly established as a rule to be followed without question by the courts. In *Beamish v Beamish* (1861), Lord Campbell, speaking in the House of Lords, expressed his disapproval of the decision in a previous case, pointing out that the decision had been made hurriedly, and the judges were equally divided, resulting in the order of the lower court being upheld. Nonetheless, he considered himself bound by the previous decision, and stated that only an Act of Parliament could alter it.[68] This almost superstitious reverence for precedent was characteristic of the latter half of the 19th century.

The possibility of strict adherence to precedent was aided by a developed system of law reporting. Until the 1860s, all law reporting was unofficial. Judges, barristers and others would collect the arguments and judgments in decided cases, and publish them, usually under the name or names of the reporters. These nominate reports published in England, are now collected in the English Reports. Similar unofficial reports were made in colonial New South Wales.[69] Depending on the reputation of the reporter, they were deemed more or less reliable as accounts of what transpired in the course of the trial. In 1865, for the first time, an official series of reports was published in England. This meant that the text of the judgment was published with the authority of the courts, and thus subsequent courts had an account of the precedent which had been established, and the arguments which had led to it, which could be treated as entirely reliable.

The doctrine of precedent reached its high point in England at the end of the 19th century when it was determined beyond doubt in 1898 that the House of Lords should regard itself as unequivocally bound by its own prior decisions.[70] Lord Halsbury declared that "a decision of this House once given on a point of law is conclusive on this House afterwards." This doctrine applied in the United Kingdom until 1966, when the House of Lords announced in a Practice Direction that it would no longer consider itself bound by its own prior decisions, although it would treat these decisions as "normally binding".

The doctrine of precedent which was so firmly established in English law during the course of the 19th century was, naturally, adopted in Australia, but was never applied as rigidly. As will be seen below, in Chapter 8, the High Court has traditionally been very reluctant to depart from its own prior decisions,[71] although the doctrine has been relaxed in recent years.[72]

The doctrine of precedent, in the form which it developed in the 19th and 20th centuries, turned on an important distinction between the ratio decidendi and obiter dicta. When it is said that judges are bound by previous decisions this is really only a convenient shorthand. What is binding on future courts is the ratio—the reason, or reasons, given for the decision. The ratio decidendi has been defined by Sir Rupert Cross as being "any rule of law expressly or impliedly treated by the judge as a necessary step in reaching his conclusion having regard to the line of reasoning adopted by him, or a necessary part of his direction to the jury".[73] Judges, in expressing their reasons for coming to a particular decision on a point of law, often make statements about the law which go beyond that which is necessary to decide the issue. Sometimes, they consider what the legal position would be if the facts were a little different. Such commentaries are described as obiter dicta—statements made "by the way". Depending on the status of the judge, and the cogency of the views expressed, these dicta may have more or less persuasive authority.

3.5   Statute Law

Statutes played a part in the formation of English law from the beginning of the development of the common law. Both the common law and modern statute law trace their origins to the powers of the monarch to make laws and to decide cases. Just as the common law developed from requests made to the king to do justice in a given case, and these cases were initially dealt with by the royal advisers, so the origins of Parliament lie in the same authority. It is questionable when a distinct Parliament first became the source of legislative authority in England. The early statutes sometimes were issued in the name of the king alone, and sometimes recited that they were made with the consent of the royal court or the nobles. *The Statute of Westminster* I (1275) was said to have been made at the first Parliament of King Edward I "by his council, and by the assent of the archbishops, bishops, abbots, priors, earls, barons and the commonality of the land", all of whom met at Westminster. This appears to be the origins of a distinction between the "lords" and "commons".[74]

From the time of Edward I, the supremacy of Parliament over the common law became established. In the House of Lords sat the king's officials, councillors and judges, the leading magnates (or "peers") of the realm, and the most senior bishops and abbots. In the House of Commons, sat the representatives of the various local communities—representing both town and country constituencies. Parliament was treated as the highest court, and one which had the power of law making, which was not entrusted to the judges of the common law.

Statutes in this period were not carefully considered written enactments as came to be the pattern by the 15th century. Rather, they were often forms of judgment given in response to particular complaints or petitions, having supreme authority as deriving from the highest court in the land, but usually not written down until after the matter was agreed and assent given. It was during this period nonetheless, that the distinction between the law-making function, and the adjudicatory function was first clearly drawn as a matter of political theory. Hitherto, the boundary lines had been blurred by the coincidence of both functions in the king and his advisers, his council or "court". Chief Justice Herle could say in 1334 that judges had no power to change a particular rule, but that a litigant "could sue in Parliament to make a new law".[75] The reality was, of course, more complex than this. The judges made new law in a variety of ways through the use of elaborate "fictions" and the development of certain new causes of action.[76]

The importance of Parliament as a law-making body did not develop significantly until the reign of the House of Tudor.[77] As will be seen below, in Chapter 4, Parliament gained a new authority in the reign of Henry VIII (1509-1547), who needed its support and legitimising authority to achieve the break with the Papacy. Through the support of Parliament, Henry was able to make himself head of the Church in England. Parliament also played an important role in law reform in other respects during his reign. 677 statutes were passed in his 38 year reign, which almost doubled the size of the collection of statutes.[78]

The reign of James I (1603-1625) brought new consideration of the need for law reform, but the use of statute law to achieve this was caught up with the constitutional conflicts of that century and the battle for authority between the common law courts, the Crown, and Parliament. One particular advocate of a complete restatement of the law was Sir Francis Bacon, an eminent lawyer who was a Lord Chancellor during the reign of James I. Bacon was much influenced by the civil law tradition of continental Europe, based upon Roman law. In contrast to the apparent clarity of that law, the common law seemed chaotic. He advocated a rationalisation of all the common law and the statutes, for the "heaping up of laws without digesting them maketh but a chaos and confusion and turneth the laws many times to become but snares for the people."[79] James I went further. He wanted a fundamental review of the law, with Parliament playing a role through statute. As he stated it: "I desire not the abolishing of our laws, but only the cleansing and the sweeping off the rust of them, and that by Parliament our laws might be cleared and made known to all the subjects."[80]

However, nothing came of these proposals for fundamental review. To many others in the same period, the common law represented a bulwark of liberty against the power of royal prerogative. It was only in the 19th century that statute law was used as a means of significant reform of the common law. It was in general a century which saw major social and political reform, and the reform of both the common law and the court system were aspects of this. In particular, this movement was influenced by Jeremy Bentham,[81] who offered his principles of utilitarianism as the basis for a science of legislation.[82] The reform of the common law in this period occurred in the context of a movement, influenced by the civil law tradition of Europe, to see law as a science and to legislate clearly and systematically.[83] It was in the 19th and 20th centuries, that legislation took over from the common law as the primary source of law in England. Inevitably, these developments were replicated in Australia.

3.6   Other Courts and Systems of Law

Other courts and systems of law require brief mention because of their significance for the development of English (and by derivation, Australian) law, or for their importance in constitutional history.

3.6.1   The ecclesiastical courts and canon law

Separate from the common law courts and the Chancery, the church had its own courts,[84] and its own jurisdiction in matters which affected its government and property and also in various other matters which were considered particularly the subject of religious rules and principles.[85] The law applied in these courts was canon law, the law of the church, and, as was noted in the last chapter, this had a quite different basis to the common law. It was not confined at all to England. The law of the church was applied wherever the western church was established. Furthermore, the canon law was much influenced by Roman law.

Amongst the matters in which the ecclesiastical courts had jurisdiction was the law of marriage. In the medieval period, the law of marriage was complicated by the legal validity of clandestine marriages. Although the church strongly encouraged marriages to take place in public by holding them at the door of the church in the presence of a priest and with witnesses, marriages which did not occur in this way could still be valid. Marriages could be contracted in private through the giving of consents or the exchange of promises. The parties might give their consent to become husband and wife from thenceforward (sponsalia per verba de praesenti), or they might promise to marry in the future (sponsalia per verba de futuro); the latter promise could become binding as a marriage by consummation (the occurrence of sexual intercourse). An apparently valid marriage could also be declared a nullity on a number of grounds, such as that the parties were within ties of kinship or affinity, or because one of the parties had not freely consented, or for a variety of other reasons. Thus difficult evidentiary questions were often dealt with by church courts. They also exercised a criminal jurisdiction in relation to mortal sins such as adultery, fornication and gluttony. It is, perhaps, not surprising that these courts became known as the "bawdy courts".[86] The law of succession to personal property, by will or on intestacy, also was within the ecclesiastical courts' jurisdiction.

In the mid 19th century, these matters came to be dealt with in secular courts,[87] but many of the principles of the canon law continued to be the basis of the secular jurisdiction, and historically, canon law has been an important formative influence in the development of English, and thus Australian, law.

3.6.2   Prerogative courts

The ancient notion that the fountain of justice was the monarch, continued to be a source of innovation and additional jurisdiction until the 17th century. It was only in that century that, through violent conflict and revolution, the scope and limits of the authority of the common law, Parliament and the royal prerogative came to be settled in a way which made law independent of the person of the monarch and her or his royal council. It left the legislative power with Parliament (subject to the royal assent to Acts of Parliament) and left the adjudicative function with the established courts of the land, which had an existence independent of the person of the king.

Most controversy was aroused by the Court of Star Chamber. Like the Court of Chancery, it originated from petitions for justice which were made directly to the royal council, by-passing the existing courts. When this council met in a judicial capacity, it did so in a chamber with gilded stars on its ceiling, which was a part of the palace of Westminster. The judicial work of the royal council, meeting in the Star Chamber, may be traced to the mid 14th century, but the Star Chamber did not gain a distinct identity as a court until much later. It was only in 1540, when the Privy Council emerged as a separate body in which the main executive business of government was discussed, that the Star Chamber took on an entity distinct from the general work of a royal council. However, the personnel of the Privy Council and Star Chamber remained almost identical.[88]

Although, in the 16th century, the Star Chamber exercised mainly a civil jurisdiction, it was with its criminal jurisdiction that it both made its contribution to the law, and through which it achieved its notoriety. Offences such as forgery, perjury, conspiracy and attempts to commit crimes were developed there, and passed into the usage of the common law courts. It was through the Star Chamber that offenders against the monarchy could be brought to justice without fear that a jury would refuse to convict. The procedure was simple for the Crown to initiate, and trial was by summary process—no jury took part. Only where capital punishment was sought did the defendant have a right to jury trial at common law. The Star Chamber was thus a place for unpopular prosecutions. It also devised its own forms of cruel physical punishment.

The existence of a court which exercised a criminal jurisdiction, and which was closely associated with the royal government, was a source of considerable tension in the 17th century. Its overt use for political purposes ensured its abolition in 1641, as the conflicts between Crown and Parliament were reaching a high point. In the constitutional settlement which resulted from the ensuing civil war and temporary republic, criminal courts existing by royal prerogative and tied closely to the Crown, could find no place. However, the Privy Council continued to have a minor role as a prerogative court. It exercised an appellate jurisdiction in relation to cases from the colonies, and in a few other contexts, but this was the limit of its adjudicatory function. It was in this role, that until the 1970s and 1980s, it acted as a final court of appeal for Australia.[89]

3.7   The Sources of Law in Australia

English legal history thus provides the background to the sources of law which were received into Australia. Discussion of the sources of law applicable in Australia is complicated by the Federal structure which creates two sources of written constitutional law—State and federal—and two sources of general statute law, with the federal Constitution usually deciding the validity of State and federal statutes in cases where the two jurisdictions might conflict. Until quite recently, a third source of statute law, beyond that of State and federal law, also existed. This was statutes passed by the English Parliament applicable to Australia. It is possible that some such provisions remain applicable to the Australian States. An account of the reception of English law, the development of Australian constitutions, and the long path towards the legislative independence of Australia, is to be found below, in Chapters 5 and 6. Before that, more must be said of the constitutional legacy of English history.

NOTES

1. For a discussion of the development of the common law within the broader context of European developments, see Berman, H, *Law and Revolution* (Harvard UP, Cambridge, Mass, 1983), pp 404-481.
2. Milsom, S F C, *Historical Foundations of the Common Law* (2nd ed, Butterworths, London, 1981), p 11.
3. Baker, J H, *An Introduction to English Legal History* (3rd ed, Butterworths, London, 1990), p 4.
4. Ibid, p 3.
5. Ibid, pp 7-8.
6. Kent was an exception. In this county, the sons took the land in equal shares. Milsom, S F C, op cit, p 11.
7. Baker, J H, op cit, p 2. Aethelberht was the first Christian monarch in England. The introduction of written laws was related to his conversion, for it was the Christian emperors who followed the tradition of the Romans in having written law books. Aethelberht's laws bore some resemblance to the laws of other Catholic kings in Europe. See Wallace-Hadrill, J M, *Early Germanic Kingship in England and on the Continent* (Clarendon, Oxford, 1971), pp 29-39.
8. The laws began with the Ten Commandments and a restatement of the law of Moses, summarised the Acts of the Apostles, and then referred to various monastic and other church rules. Berman, H, op cit, p 65.
9. Glanvill, R, *Treatise on the Law and Customs of England*, Bk II, c 3, reproduced in Evans, M, and Jack, I, *Sources of English Legal and Constitutional History* (Butterworths, Sydney, 1984), pp 23-24.
10. See, eg, the last such case, *Ashford v Thornton* (1818) 1 B & Ald 405 at 409; 106 ER 149.
11. For an extensive discussion of the impact of the Normans on early English law, see Van Caenagem, R C, *The Birth of the English Common Law* (Cambridge UP, Cambridge, 1973), Ch 1.
12. It is only with hindsight that this can be described as a system of criminal law. The distinction between crimes and other wrongs would not have been quite as clear to the 12th century mind. Certain wrongs, however, were of concern to the king, notably murders and other "breaches of the king's peace", and these formed the basis of the criminal law. They were known as "Pleas of the Crown".
13. Berman, H, op cit, pp 438-457.
14. The word "eyre" comes from the Latin "iter" which means "journey". Justices in eyre were itinerant judges who were sent on circuit by the king.
15. See further, Baker, J H, op cit, pp 576-577.
16. For example, the *Statute for Justices of the Peace* 1361 provided: "in each county of England there shall be assigned for the keeping of the peace, one lord, and with him three or four of the most worthy in the county, together with some learned in the law and they shall have the power to restrain malefactors, rioters and all other barrators and to pursue, arrest, take and punish them according to their trespass or offence; and to have them imprisoned and duly punished according to the law and customs of the realm . . . and also to hear and determine at the king's suit all manner of trespasses done in the same county, according to the laws and customs aforesaid." Evans, M, and Jack, I, op cit, pp 184-185.

17. For the English system see Smith, P F, and Bailey, S H, *The Modern English Legal System* (Sweet & Maxwell, London, 1984), pp 132-149; Walker, R J, *The English Legal System* (6th ed, Sweet & Maxwell, London, 1985), Ch 9.

18. Magna Carta went through a number of versions. The re-enactment of 1297 became authoritative. The provision quoted was cl 11 of the text of 1297. See Evans, M, and Jack, I, op cit, p 50.

19. The Exchequer was the Treasury Department of the monarchy, so named because it originally functioned in a room which had a chequered table. Since many matters of justice involved feudal dues owed to the Crown, the Exchequer necessarily required a court to hear cases. While jurisdiction of this court was limited to matters involving the Crown by the *Magna Carta* 1215, the court proved popular to litigants, and by the 16th century its jurisdiction had expanded to hear certain private disputes. The fiction was adopted that money owed to the monarch could not be paid because of the failure of the defendant to pay money which was owing.

20. Berman, H, op cit, p 251.

21. Initially, the jurors were interviewed individually as witnesses, but by the 14th century, they came to consider their verdict collectively, and in secret. See further, Mitnick, J, "From Neighbour-Witness to Judge of Proofs: The Transformation of the English Civil Juror" (1988) 32 Am J of Legal Hist 201. For a comparison with legal process in civil law countries see Stein, P, *The Character and Influence of the Roman Law* (Hambledon, London, 1988), pp 101-113.

22. For examples of early writs see Baker, J H, op cit, pp 612ff; Evans, M, and Jack, I, op cit, pp 39-43.

23. Baker, J H, op cit, p 24.

24. The local courts which pre-dated the development of royal justice were not entirely displaced by it. Indeed the itinerant royal justices did work within the normal county court calendar. *Magna Carta* 1215, cll 18-19 required the justices of assize to sit on the day and at the place of the county court.

25. The term "writ" was originally used in reference to any brief, official document which ordered, forbade, or notified something. Its origins are in the Anglo-Saxon period. See Van Caenagem, R C, op cit, pp 30-31.

26. *The Statute of Gloucester* 1278, 6 Edw I c 8 provided that "sheriffs shall hold pleas of trespass in their counties, as they have been accustomed to do before. And that no one hereafter shall have a writ of trespass before justices unless he swears on oath that the goods taken away were worth at least 40 shillings". Reproduced in Evans, M, and Jack, I, op cit, p 101.

27. Reproduced in Evans, M, and Jack, I, op cit, p 128.

28. The most significant of these new developments was the emergence of "actions on the case". See Kiralfy, A K R, *The English Legal System* (7th ed, Sweet & Maxwell, London, 1984), pp 33-44. The in consimili casu clause has been seen as the legal basis for these developments, but it is apparent that they did not happen immediately. See Watkin, T, "The Significance of 'In Consimili Casu' " (1979) 23 Am J of Legal Hist 283.

29. Maitland, F W, *The Forms of Action at Common Law* 1909 (repr eds, A H Chaytor, and W J Whittaker, Cambridge UP, Cambridge, 1963).

30. This example is taken from Milsom, S F C, op cit, p 42.

31. As Milsom puts it, "Law, like fact, had hitherto been comfortably wrapped in the judgment of God". Milsom, S F C, op cit, p 43. See also Milsom, S F C, "Law and Fact in Legal Development" (1967) 17 Univ of Toronto LJ 1.

32. Baker, J H, op cit, p 94.

33. See above, Baker, J H, op cit, pp 90-96.

34. The court had jurisdiction if the defendant was personally within the County of Middlesex. A warrant for arrest would issue, on the basis of the alleged trespass, to bring the defendant there. Eventually, the fiction became even bolder, alleging that an imaginary trespass had occurred in Middlesex. It was thus known as the Bill of Middlesex.

35. *Pavey & Matthews Pty Ltd v Paul* (1987) 162 CLR 221 especially at 252-259, per Deane J.

36. For an example of a cause failing because the wrong form of action was chosen, see *Reynolds v Clarke* (1725) B & M 354.

37. *Uniformity of Process Act* 1832, 2 & 3 Will IV c 39; *Real Property Limitation Act* 1833, 3 & 4 Will IV c 27, s 36.

38. *Common Law Procedure Act* 1852, s 41.

39. Thus Fortescue, C J, invited to attend a Chancery case to advise on the common law, stated: "We are to argue conscience here, not law". Mich 31 Hen VI, Fitz Abr, *Subpena*, pl 23. (Cited in Baker, J H, op cit, p 124.)

40. Plucknett, T F T, and Barton, J L (eds), "St German's Doctor and Student", 91 *Selden Society* (1974), p 97, reproduced in Evans, M, and Jack, I, op cit, pp 217-218.

41. *Earl of Oxford's Case* (1615) 1 Rep Ch 1 at 6; 21 ER 485 at 486.

42. Aristotle, *Nicomachean Ethics*, translation, D Ross (Oxford UP, Oxford, 1980), pp 133-134.

43. Kelly, J M, *A Short History of Western Legal Theory* (Clarendon, Oxford, 1992), pp 53-55.

44. Aquinas, *Summa Theologica* 2a 2ae 60.5.

45. It need not have been this way. Sir Thomas More, who was Lord Chancellor from 1529-1533, dealt with the complaints of common law judges concerning the Chancery jurisdiction by urging them to "mitigate and reform the rigor of the law". The plea fell on deaf ears. Roper, W, *The Lyfe of Sir Thomas Moore* (E V Hitchcock, ed, 1935), pp 44-45, cited in Baker, J H, op cit, p 124.

46. See further, Dawson, J, "Coke and Ellesmere Disinterred: The Attack on the Chancery in 1616" (1941) 36 Illinois L Rev 127.

47. See Baker, J H, *The Legal Profession and the Common Law—Historical Essays* (Hambledon, London, 1986), p 438.

48. Maitland, F W, *Equity—A Course of Lectures* (Brunyate, J, ed, 2nd ed, Cambridge UP, Cambridge, 1936), p 19.

49. Ibid, p 17.

50. For a historical introduction see Martin, J (ed), *Hanbury & Maudsley's Modern Equity* (13th ed, Stevens, London, 1989), pp 7-11.

51. These were known as the feoffees que use.

52. Known as the cestui que use.

53. An example of this is in the reluctance to define "fraud". Lord Hardwicke, who was Lord Chancellor between 1737 and 1756 wrote to Lord Kames that "as to relief against frauds, no invariable rules can be established. Fraud is infinite, and were a Court of Equity once to lay down rules, how far they would go and no farther, in extending their relief against it, or to define strictly the species of evidence of it, the jurisdiction would be cramped, and perpetually eluded by new schemes, which the fertility of man's invention would contrive." Cited by Sheridan, L, *Fraud in Equity* (Pitman, London, 1957), p 2.

54. Evans, M, and Jack, I, op cit, pp 223-224. See also, *Table Talk of John Selden* (Pollock, F, ed, Selden Society, London, 1927), p 43.

55. See, eg, the judgment of Lord Nottingham in *Cook v Fountain* (1672) 3 Swanst 600; 26 ER 984: "I hold it necessary to lay down some rules and distinctions touching trusts, which I must keep to, and by which I must govern myself in all cases whatsoever."

56. Baker, J H, op cit, pp 128-131.

57. The courts of Common Pleas and Exchequer initially survived as divisions of the High Court also. However, they were abolished in 1880.

58. Meagher, R, Gummow, W, and Lehane, J, *Equity: Doctrines and Remedies* (3rd ed, Butterworths, Sydney, 1992), pp 38-39.

59. See below, 7.2.2.

60. *Ashburner's Principles of Equity* (Browne, D, ed, 2nd ed, Legal Books, Sydney, 1983), p 18.

61. See further, Meagher, R, Gummow, W, and Lehane, J, op cit, pp 46-59; Perell, P, *The Fusion of Law and Equity* (Butterworths, Toronto, 1990).

62. This may be translated: "It stands decided."

63. Simpson, B, "The Common Law and Legal Theory" in Twining, W (ed), *Legal Theory and Common Law* (Blackwell, Oxford, 1986), p 21.

64. *Bole v Horton* (1673) Vaugh 360; 124 ER 1113.

65. For the attitude of Lord Chancellor Hardwicke to precedent, see Croft, C, "Lord Hardwicke's Use of Precedent in Equity" (1989) 5 *Australian Bar Review* 29.

66. This development is described by Brett, M R, in *Vera Cruz No 2* (1884) 9 PD 96 at 98.

67. *Mirehouse v Rennell* (1833) 1 Cl & F 527 at 546; 6 ER 1015 at 1023.

68. *Beamish v Beamish* (1861) 9 HLC 274 at 338; 11 ER 735 at 760 per Lord Campbell.

69. The most important early decisions in New South Wales were collected in Legge's Reports.

70. *London Street Tramways Co v London County Council* [1898] AC 375.

71. See below, 8.3.2. *Perpetual Executors and Trustees Association of Australia Ltd v FCT* (1949) 77 CLR 493. In this case the court set out some of the factors involved in considering whether it would overrule a previous decision. It said that departures from prior decisions should only occur in "very exceptional cases". Changes to the personnel of the court should not be sufficient, nor the fact that the earlier decision was only made by a majority. The court said that the strongest argument for overruling a prior decision was that it was manifestly wrong and its maintenance was injurious to the public interest.

72. *John v Commissioner of Taxation* (1989) 166 CLR 417. See further, below, Chapter 8, 8.4.

73. Cross, R, *Precedent in English Law* (3rd ed, Clarendon, Oxford, 1977), p 76.

74. Baker, J H, op cit, p 235.

75. Baker, J H, op cit, p 239. In this idea of Parliament as the highest court lies the continuing adjudicatory role of the House of Lords in Britain. The House of Lords represents the final court of appeal in English law, and is also the upper house of Parliament, exercising a role in the making of laws. The adjudicatory functions of the House of Lords have long since been entrusted to a "Judicial Committee" of the House, comprising the country's most senior judges. These judges are also members of the House of Lords when it exercises its legislative function.

76. For a discussion of these changes in the medieval period, see Milsom, S F C, op cit, Ch 3.

77. The House of Tudor began with Henry VII (1485-1509) and ended with Elizabeth I (1558-1603).

78. Baker, J H, op cit, p 237. Major statutes include the *Statute of Uses* 1536 and the *Statute of Wills* 1540. For the significance of the legislation of the Reformation Parliament, see McIlwain, C, "Book Review" (1942) 56 Harvard LR 148.

79. Veall, D, *The Popular Movement for Law Reform 1640-1660* (Clarendon, Oxford, 1970), p 70.

80. Ibid, p 71.

81. See above, 2.5.1.

82. See Bentham, J, *An Introduction to the Principles of Morals and Legislation* (1789).

83. See below, Chapter 8.

84. These courts date from 1072 when William the Conqueror decreed that the canon law of the church should be dealt with in separate courts.

85. For a brief history, see Baker, J H, op cit, Ch 8. See also, Helmholz, R H, *Canon Law and the Law of England* (Hambledon, London, 1987).

86. Stone, O, *Family Law* (Macmillan, London, 1977), p 27, n 33.

87. *Probates and Letters of Administration Act* 1857, 20 & 21 Vict c 77; *Divorce and Matrimonial Causes Act* 1857, 20 & 21 Vict c 85.

88. Baker, J H, op cit, p 136.

89. The Privy Council still operates within the English constitution as a formal advisory body to the monarch. It has only a few functions within the modern political order, although, it is frequently by "Order-in-Council" that the British government makes regulations under the authority of an Act of Parliament. The Privy Council also has a Judicial Committee consisting of senior appellate judges in the same way as there is a Judicial Committee of the House of Lords. Although, it is usual to refer to these courts as the Privy Council and the House of Lords respectively, it is only the members of the Judicial Committee, the most senior judges in the country, who hear appeals. Usually, the same British judges sit on Privy Council appeals as on appeals to the House of Lords, although, occasionally senior judges from Commonwealth courts are invited to sit on Privy Council appeals.

Chapter 4

CONSTITUTIONAL LAW AND THE WESTMINSTER SYSTEM OF GOVERNMENT

Australia inherited from England, not only a system of law derived from common law, equity and statute, but also the constitutional principles of government which had been forged through centuries—at times through peaceful evolution, at other times through violent conflict or expedient compromise. These constitutional principles were themselves influenced by the ideas of law and government which were current throughout Europe, and which derived from Roman, Greek and Judaeo-Christian thought.[1] The system of government which resulted, known as the Westminster system, is essentially the system which has constitutional force in Australia today, modified as it is by Australian conditions, and various terms and ideas borrowed in particular from the United States. Those constitutional ideas, with their relative strengths and weaknesses, cannot be understood without an awareness of the history which produced them, and the experiences of government which made various features of that system seem necessary.

4.1   Royal Authority in the Feudal Era

It was characteristic of the state of government in the years following the Norman Conquest, that royal authority was limited both as a matter of political practice and of constitutional theory. The feudal monarchs were not totalitarian rulers. Nor was there such a strong centre of government that control could be exercised throughout the kingdom at the behest of the monarchy. It was the Norman and Angevin rulers who sought to build up such central power, but they were, from the beginning, dependent upon the co-operation of other members of the ruling elite. There was no standing army. William the Conqueror effectively leased the kingdom to his tenants-in-chief in return for the provision of knights, and they in turn had subtenants who provided the knight service. Power was, therefore, diffused through the realm, and the king's power depended on feudal loyalties.

For the Norman and Angevin rulers, power was also diffused through a variety of bodies. As has been seen, the development of a system of administrative control through the general eyre was a means by which power was exercised by the monarchy over the hundreds and counties where community affairs were ordered. The monarchy did not create local government; rather it subsumed local means of organisation in a national system of control. The church represented another power centre. William

95

the Conqueror resisted the claims of the Pope to supremacy over church affairs, and insisted on his right to appoint bishops. However, eventually, his successors were forced to concede a considerable degree of autonomy to the church.[2] The church and the monarchy thus represented two different power centres, with overlapping claims of jurisdiction which were sometimes in conflict. Mostly, however, they succeeded in living together in co-operation and compromise.

Monarchical power was also limited in theory. Broadly, two theories of the authority of rulers were prevalent in the middle ages. The first, which predominated for most of that long period, has been called the "descending" theory of government. This view was derived from the Roman empire and adopted, with modifications, in Christian thought. The second has been termed the "ascending" theory of government, and reflects the view that prevailed in the Germanic tribes which dominated Europe after the decline and fall of the Roman empire.[3]

In the "descending" theory, power was seen as being centred in the ruler, who was not beholden to any other human authority for his power. Christian thought modified this in a significant way: the ruler's authority was entrusted to him by God, and a ruler was a minister of the Almighty for the benefit of Christian people.[4] Among some early Christian writers, that authority was regarded as being unchallengeable. Just rulers were God's gift, while tyrannical rulers were God's punishment.[5] However, later writers saw the authority of rulers as a sacred trust for the benefit of the people. For example, a work of political theory, the *Policratus*, written by John of Salisbury in 1159, held two conflicting ideas in tension together. On the one hand, kings held office by God's will. Even tyrants did so, since they were means by which God chastened his people, and oppressive rulers would eventually be overthrown. At the same time as stating this, John of Salisbury also affirmed the right, and even the duty of civil disobedience. No ruler could be justified in commanding a subject to disobey precepts of the Christian faith, and those who did so should not be obeyed. John even went as far as to say that subjects might need to uphold the law by killing tyrants who violated it.[6]

The "ascending" theory of government also placed limitations on monarchical power. On this view, power derived ultimately from the people, and was entrusted to the ruler. This Germanic view, for which support could also be found in some Roman texts, found favour with the Roman law scholars of the 12th century onwards. While some argued, with respect to the Roman emperors, that the people had conferred authority on their rulers irrevocably at some point in the past, others argued that the people had never finally abdicated their power, and this authority was demonstrated by the ongoing force of customary law. Christian thought produced another version of this idea. Towards the end of the 11th century, it was argued by a German monk, Manegold of Lautenbach, that although the ruler's authority was given by God, the relationship between ruler and ruled could be seen as a form of contract, with obligations owed by the ruler to govern justly. It followed from this that if the ruler broke his agreement by disrupting the things which he was appointed to keep in order, then the people were released from their obligation of obedience.[7] Later, Aquinas also expressed a similar view. He wrote:

> "If it is a people's right to provide itself with a king, and if that king tyrannically abuses the royal power, there is no injustice if the community deposes or checks him whom they have raised to the kingship . . . because, by not faithfully conducting himself in government as the royal office demands, he has brought it on himself if his subjects renounce their bargain with him."[8]

One particular idea which survived from the germanic origins of the "ascending" theory was that the ruler was bound to respect the people's laws which were antecedent to him, and this idea gained support especially in England. This meant that the monarch should be under the law which was established, unless and until that law was changed. There was no place for arbitrary power, nor for rulership only by military force. Thus, Bracton's *Treatise on the Law and Customs of England*, a great 13th century work, stated that the king had a duty to obey the law, since the king is under God and the law and it is the law which makes the king. Bracton wrote:

> "Let the king accord to the law what the law accords to him, namely sovereign power; for where will and not law is sovereign, there no king can be said to be."[9]

Elsewhere, Bracton wrote that law "is the bridle of power".[10]

The *Magna Carta* of 1215 laid down various such limitations on monarchical power. In this treaty between King John and his rebellious nobles lie the origins of the principle that only with the consent of the "general council of the realm" (later Parliament) could the king impose extraordinary taxation on his subjects. It stated also that no one should be put on trial upon an accusation which was not supported by credible witnesses, that no free man should be imprisoned, dispossessed of property, outlawed, exiled or otherwise destroyed "except by the lawful judgment of his peers or the law of the land", that justice should not be sold, refused or delayed, and that people should be assured freedom of movement.

Thus, the constitutional position of monarchs in the feudal era was limited by the need to preserve certain fundamental principles of "due process" of law, by the need for taxation to be consented to by Parliament (over and above certain established feudal dues) and by various practical constraints upon autocratic power. The position of the monarch in England was expounded at the end of the 15th century by Sir John Fortescue, a Chief Justice of the King's Bench, who wrote in his book, *The Governance of England* (c 1470) that the form of government which existed in England was not one of royal absolutism but a mixed form of government, dominium politicum et regale. In this system "the King may not rule his people by other laws than such as they assent unto. And, therefore, he may set upon them no impositions without their own assent". [11] While he acknowledged that the monarch had exceptional discretionary and prerogative powers by which he could act without Parliament, these were nonetheless seen as admitted exceptions to the general rule. [12] However, Parliament was still a body which was ancillary to the main organ of government, which was the king. It was not a permanent institution, but rather was summoned from time to time as the need for it arose.

4.2   The Growth of Parliamentary Authority

The accession of Henry VII to the throne in 1485 marked a turning point in English history. Henry inherited a government which was weakened by prolonged conflicts both within the nation and through foreign wars; these had diminished the authority of the Crown in relation to other power brokers in English society. Henry VII's reign saw a dramatic strengthening of royal authority, and the creation of a highly efficient central administration which permeated every area of national life. None of this could have been achieved without the co-operation of the middle class of property holders. The king had no standing professional army, nor a salaried bureaucracy amenable to his direction and command. [13] In this, lay the seeds of the growth of Parliamentary authority. While Henry VII did not need to rely on Parliament very much in his 24 year reign—he only had to ask for extraordinary taxation six times—his son proved more dependent upon parliamentary support.

It was in the reign of Henry VIII (1509-1547) that the importance of Parliament in the governance of the country was significantly elevated. The early part of Henry's reign was marked by foreign wars which obliged him to go to Parliament for financial supply. His reliance upon Parliamentary support was greater still in his conflicts with the papacy. Henry sought the annulment of his first marriage to Catherine of Aragon, in order that he could marry Ann Boleyn. Even monarchs could not bend the rules of the church on the sanctity of marriage to suit their whims, and there were political ramifications of a decree of nullity in terms of the Pope's relationship with Spain. Inevitably, the main opposition to his plans to marry Ann Boleyn from within the country came from the church, which was under the authority of the Pope. Consequently, Henry needed Parliamentary support to counterbalance the power of the Church and to legitimate actions (and children) which the ultimate spiritual authorities regarded as illegitimate. It was the Reformation Parliament (1529-1536) which fulfilled this role. Legislation, notably the *Act in Restraint of Appeals to Rome* (1533) [14] and the *Act in Absolute Restraint of Annates* (1534) [15] secured for Henry the rulership of both church and state within England. [16] These Acts, which effectively stripped the Pope of his power and authority in the English Church, were completed by the *Act of Supremacy* 1534 which made Henry VIII the "Supreme Head in Earth of the Church of England".

The effect of this break with Rome was far more than to legitimise a second marriage. It effected the conquest of the church which hitherto had represented an independent source of authority in the country, and in so doing it brought about a constitutional revolution. In Henry was vested the ultimate authority both of church and state. It was, in this sense, a reversal of that separation of church and state which had been accomplished by the Papal Revolution of 1075. Prior to that time, church and state had been governed together by monarchy. The attitude of Charlemagne, who ruled the Franks between 768 and 814, and who was crowned Holy Roman emperor in 800, typifies the relationship between church and state in that period. He regarded the Pope as his chaplain, and had told him that it was the Emperor's business to govern and defend the church and the Pope's duty to pray for it.[17] Pope Gregory VII had put an end to such ideas in 1075 by asserting his ultimate authority over the church.[18] Henry VIII was no Charlemagne, anymore than his country could have been described as a holy empire; nonetheless, he had concentrated in the monarchy a power which was unprecedented in the feudal order of things.

Henry VIII's action not only concentrated power in the hands of the monarchy; it also placed the monarch personally at the very centre of the religious debates and conflicts which were to dominate the following 150 years. In a situation where the civil government was stipulating for the nation what it should believe and how it should worship, there was the potential that the overthrow of the government should be seen by citizens as a necessary duty of obedience to God.[19] The break with the Roman Church had required parliamentary backing, however, and the Parliament continued to play a significant role in enforcing conformity to various formulations of Christian doctrine[20] and in settling the complex matters of the royal succession.[21]

The reign of Henry VIII effected a change in the political and constitutional order which was of immense significance. It has been said that the religious revolution which was wrought by the king in Parliament:

> "was the most notable chapter which had ever been inscribed in the history of Parliament, since it involved the rejection of a limit to parliamentary competence which had hitherto been unquestioningly accepted. Panoplied in parliamentary authority, the Crown triumphantly met and overthrew every force which denied its supremacy within the domain hitherto monopolised by the ecclesiastical power."[22]

In this revolution, continued notably by the reign of Elizabeth I (1559-1603), lay the beginnings of the notion of the absolute sovereignty of the monarch "in Parliament"—that is, the overriding supremacy of laws made by Parliament and receiving the royal assent.

4.3   The Constitutional Conflicts of the 17th Century

It was in the reign of James I (1603-1625) that the tensions between the various branches of government first surfaced strongly. His reign proved to be the start of a period of considerable constitutional turbulence as Britain began its painful transition from a feudal order in which the king had an overriding supremacy, to a parliamentary democracy in which ultimate authority lay in the elected representatives of the people (or at least a few of the people, for until the 19th and 20th centuries the franchise remained very limited). There were three aspects of this constitutional struggle. First, the relationship between the common law courts and Parliament; secondly, the relationship between the common law courts and the Crown; thirdly, the relationship between the Crown and Parliament.

4.3.1   The common law and Parliament

Although the principle of parliamentary authority appeared to have been established, courts in the 16th century took a reasonably free approach to interpretation; so free, in fact, that they thought it appropriate to ignore the text of statutes which were deemed unreasonable or unjust. For example, in *Fulmerston v Steward* (c 1554)[23] Bromley J declared:

> "It is most reasonable to expound the words which seem contrary to reason according to good reason and equity. And so the judges who were our predecessors have sometimes expounded the words quite contrary to the text, and have sometimes taken things by equity contrary to the text, in order to make them agree with reason and equity".

One of the greatest of the common law judges, Chief Justice Coke, took this one stage further, and claimed that the courts had a residual power to declare invalid an Act of Parliament if it was "contrary to reason". Coke saw in the common law a level of perfection which more impartial observers found difficult to understand. He described the common law as "the golden metwand whereby all men's causes are justly and evenly measured",[24] and wrote in his report of *Dr Bonham's Case* (1610)[25] that:

> "It appears in our books that in many cases the common law will control acts of Parliament and sometimes adjudge them to be utterly void; for when an act of Parliament is against common right and reason, or repugnant, or impossible to be performed, the common law will control it and adjudge such an act to be void."

Although Coke gained some support from his successor as Chief Justice of the Common Pleas,[26] this statement appears to reflect the dying embers of a belief that the courts could disregard statutes, rather than an opinion which was widely held at the time.[27] It may indeed have been a statement which gained far more importance for its utility in later political controversies than for the significance which it merited in its original context. In any event, such a view was severely criticised by his contemporary, Lord Chancellor Ellesmere, and appears to have been repudiated by Coke later.[28] Yet Coke had raised a concern which still reverberates through to the present time. What constraints are there upon the tyranny of the majority? If Parliament has an absolute power to make laws, what protection do citizens have from the violation of fundamental human rights? It was an issue which was to exercise the minds of 17th and 18th century thinkers, and which led to the enactment of a Bill of Rights as a restraint upon legislative authority in the American Constitution.[29]

4.3.2 The common law and the Crown

A further issue that surfaced in the reign of James I was the relationship between the common law and the personal authority of the monarch to do justice between his subjects. The common law had, after all, emanated from the king's role as the fount of justice. To what extent had it now taken over from the king personally as the arbiter of people's rights? The issue arose clearly in the *Case of Prohibitions* (1607)[30] at a meeting summoned by the king in Whitehall in which Coke clashed openly with King James I on the extent of the royal power to decide cases in person. Coke reported of their discussion:

> "Then the King said that he thought the law was founded upon reason, and that he and others had reason as well as the Judges: to which it was answered by me that true it was, that God had endowed His Majesty with excellent science, and great endowments of nature; but His Majesty was not learned in the laws of his realm of England, and causes which concern the life, or inheritance, or goods or fortunes of his subjects, are not to be decided by natural reason but by the artificial reason and judgment of law, which law is an art which requires long study and experience, before that a man can attain to the cognisance of it".[31]

Coke went on to cite the statement of the 13th century writer Bracton, that "the King should not be under man, but under God and the Laws." To James I, such a statement was treasonable. Coke reported that the King was "greatly offended". The reports of others indicate how offended he was. According to one observer, the king flew into a rage, "looking and speaking fiercely with bended fist, offering to strike him". Coke had to plead for forgiveness, falling on all fours. The king was only pacified by the intervention of Coke's uncle, Sir Robert Cecil.[32] Nonetheless, Coke's assertion of the independence of the courts was to point the way for the future. The claim that the law was characterised by "artificial reason", and that it could only be understood through long study and experience, marked out law as an autonomous discipline which was clearly separated from the personal authority of the monarch. The independence of the common law was something which Coke insisted upon. This was only one of a number of occasions when Coke stood up to the king's claims of prerogative powers. In the *Case of Proclamations* (1611),[33] Coke and his fellow judges rejected the notion that criminal offences could be created by royal proclamation. They said that "the King by his proclamation cannot create any offence which was not an offence before, for then he may alter the law of the land by his proclamation in a high point . . . the King hath no prerogative but that which the law of the land allows him."

In these ways, Coke, and certain of the other judges, showed their independence from the Crown, and their insistence that the king himself must rule by law, and in accordance with the established laws. In the years which followed, the courts would often be the arbiters of the extent of royal prerogative power, although generally, they held in favour of the Crown.[34] In this process was the beginnings of the constitutional separation of powers which was to be a hallmark of the English constitutional system.

4.3.3   Crown and Parliament

Of all the constitutional issues which arose in the 17th century, the most critical question was the relationship between the Crown and Parliament, and in particular, where the ultimate law-making authority in the kingdom resided. It was an issue on which a civil war would be fought, and which resulted in the temporary abolition of the monarchy in Britain.

James I succeeded to the throne of England in 1603, having been King of Scotland for many years prior to that. In so doing, he united the thrones of England and Scotland, but at the same time brought to the English throne an idea of monarchy which was one of enlightened absolutism, derived from a quite extreme view of the "descending" theory of government. James was not isolated in his views; he reflected a current of thought in many parts of Europe.[35] His ideas of kingship had been expounded at length in his work *True Law of Free Monarchies* (1598).[36] For James, monarchy was a divine right; his fundamental position is stated in his view that "the Kings were the authors and makers of the laws and not the laws of the kings."[37] It followed that the monarch was above the law, although a just king would only rule by it. Legislatively, he operated together with Parliament, but that was nothing else than the "head court of the King".[38] After taking the English throne, James continued to express similar views. This is exemplified by his speech to an assembled gathering of the Lords and the Commons in 1610:

"The state of monarchy is the supremest thing upon earth. For Kings are not only God's lieutenants upon earth and sit upon God's throne, but even by God himself they are called gods . . . for that they exercise a manner or resemblance of divine power upon earth. For if you will consider the attributes of God, you shall see how they agree in the person of a King. God hath power to create or destroy, make or unmake at his pleasure, to give life or send death, to judge all and to be judged nor accountable to none. Kings make and unmake their subjects; they have power of raising and casting down; of life and death . . . and make of their subjects like men at the chess."[39]

In James' view, executive authority rested with the king alone, although in practice, this authority was exercised by him through his various departments of state, and especially through the Privy Council, a body of his most senior advisers. The Council constituted the executive branch of government, but it also exercised the royal prerogative in regard to defence of the realm, foreign relations and trade.

By contrast with James' views about the divine right of kings, the "ascending" theory of government was gaining acceptance in other parts of Europe. The idea that the authority of government rested on a compact between the people was the basis of the agreement for the establishment of a new body politic by those who sailed on the Mayflower to begin a new life in America in 1620. The notion that government was based upon a contract between government and the governed also was to be found in Catholic Spain. Thus, the oath taken to the Crown by members of the Parliament of Aragon recited simply:

"We, who are as good as you are, take an oath to you who are no better than we, as prince and heir of our kingdom, on condition that you preserve our traditional constitutional rights and liberties, and, if you do not, we do not."[40]

Parliament continued the role it had had in the reign of Elizabeth. It remained a body which was summoned and dismissed at the king's pleasure, and the king might well seek to do without it for as long as he could manage without its exceptional money-raising authority or the necessity for its power to legislate. Indeed, the sitting of Parliament was an exceptional, rather than a routine, feature of Stuart government. The total number of parliamentary sessions between 1603 and 1640 amounted to less than four and a half years.[41] Parliament nonetheless had grown in authority and confidence during the Tudor monarchy. Elizabeth I had found it far from compliant to her will in the latter years of her reign. In the reign of James I, it was populated by members who had gained in wealth and independence in the age of peace and prosperity which had been the legacy of Tudor rule.

Those members who made up Parliament were unwilling to accept a passive role in the government of the nation, and they asserted their authority and independence from Crown control soon after the accession of James I. This was expressed notably in the *Form of Apology and Satisfaction* of 1604,[42] in which Parliament asserted that its privileges and liberties were not a matter of grace, given by the king, but "are our right and due inheritance, no less than our very lands and goods" and that "they cannot be withheld from us, denied, or impaired, but with apparent wrong to the whole state of the realm."[43] They went further, to assert a divine authority of their own. The king should listen to Parliament because "the voice of the people, in the things of their knowledge, is said to be as the voice of God".[44]

The potential for conflict between Crown and subjects was accentuated by religious differences. There were observable tendencies in James I towards the abandonment of a strict protestantism, and a growing friendliness towards Rome. These tensions were played out primarily over the issue of money supply for the Crown, although the grievances held by Parliament against the Crown were not primarily economic. James I had a substantial budget deficit, and could not run the government without a vote of supply from Parliament. The amount which he needed, however, was not usually forthcoming. The 1621 Parliament, asked to vote extra money for military action to assist James' son-in-law in Germany, allied this with an unprecedented bid for control over foreign policy matters which hitherto had always been in the prerogative of the Crown alone. The other weapon they used in this period was the ancient power of impeachment, by which ministers could be removed from office and punished for wrongdoing. It had lain dormant in the Tudor years, but it proved an effective means of harassing government ministers.

The conflicts continued, and increased, in the reign of James' son, Charles I (1625-1649). Continuing conflict with the Parliament in 1629 led to its dissolution, and no Parliament was summoned again for 11 years. In the meantime, Charles I sought to rule through the Privy Council, relying on such prerogative powers to raise money as were still available to him. A number of issues concerning the discretionary powers of the government fell to be decided by the courts. One of the most hotly contested matters concerned the demand for ship-money. European conflicts which threatened British security made it imperative that Charles I should have a strong navy. There had been an established practice that the king could demand ships, or money to build them, from the maritime towns and districts, and writs were sent levying this in 1634. In 1635 they were extended to the kingdom at large, and were issued annually thereafter until 1639. The extension of this levy to the inland counties created much opposition, and was challenged by John Hampden, a property owner in one inland county. The resulting case, the *Case of Ship-Money* (1637)[45] was heard by the judges of the Exchequer Chamber, who by a majority of seven to five found in favour of the Crown.

4.3.4   The Long Parliament and the English civil war

By 1640, Charles I was unable to do without Parliamentary supply. There was rebellion in Scotland, which was over religious issues. The Scots wanted a presbyterian form of church government, rather than the episcopal authority on which Charles I insisted. Charles had to respond to the threat of invasion by the Scottish rebels into northern England. He summoned Parliament again in order to raise an army. At this Parliament, which was to last just three weeks, all the grievances concerning fiscal abuses and other invasions of liberties spilled out in a sustained and strong protest. The new

Parliament voted not to give any money to the king until its grievances were dealt with. The Parliament was dissolved without supply being granted. An invasion by the Scots forced Charles I to summon Parliament once again, however, and it was in this Parliament, which came to be known as the Long Parliament, that the battle lines were clearly drawn. It sought to reinforce its own position by making the king agree to regular Parliamentary terms,[46] and secured itself against arbitrary dissolution by requiring that the king gain Parliament's own assent before dissolving it.[47] Other restraints were placed upon the king in regard to fiscal powers. The Prerogative Courts, such as the Star Chamber, were abolished,[48] and in this way the final supremacy of the common law courts was established.

By 1642, the position had declined into a civil war. The king, surrounded by his loyal supporters, based himself initially at York, and later at Oxford. Amongst his supporters were about half the members of the House of Lords and 175 members of the House of Commons. The remaining 300 members of the House of Commons remained at Westminster.[49] This remainder of Parliament established a rival centre of government. Although the royalists had some early successes, it proved to be an uneven struggle. After the possibilities of voluntary donations had been exhausted, the Royalists were unable to secure sufficient financial resources. Their power to raise either loans or taxes was very limited, and the ability to recruit soldiers was similarly handicapped by the weakness of royal authority.

A much stronger power developed at Westminster. By contrast to the royalists, the Parliamentary forces had control of the major sources of customs revenue.[50] Militarily, they strengthened their position by an alliance with the Scottish rebels.[51] Parliament also asserted its authority through Ordinances which became law without the need for royal assent. It raised a professional army, known as the New Model Army, with officers commissioned by the Commander in Chief and from which posts members of Parliament eventually excluded themselves,[52] leaving the army in the hands of military, rather than political leaders. The war lasted just four years, and led to the defeat of the Royalists by 1646.

The triumph for Parliament was not without constitutional cost. The creation of a professional army produced a powerful body which was independent of direct parliamentary control. Uncertainty about the future structure of government in the wake of the king's defeat divided the victors further, between those who were in favour of a limited constitutional monarchy, and those who preferred republicanism. There were not only political differences, but religious ones, between those who wished to impose a rigid presbyterian form of church government, who constituted a majority in Parliament, and those who would not accept an enforced conformity of any kind. The latter had a power base in the army. The divisions between those who had defeated him allowed Charles I an extension to his natural and political life. However, it was to be limited. In January 1649 a tribunal established by Parliament sentenced him to death.

The monarchy and the House of Lords were both abolished, and a Commonwealth put in its place in which the House of Commons was supreme.

4.3.5   Constitutional experimentation in the Commonwealth

Following the abolition of the monarchy, effective control of the country rested with the army, led by Oliver Cromwell. For some three years, the House of Commons exercised a vigorous leadership of the country, and gained control over every aspect of executive government. However, it proved as capable of totalitarianism as the monarchy it had replaced. Its undoing was its inability to relinquish voluntarily its own power. The statute passed during the conflicts with Charles I had established that Parliament could not be dissolved without its own consent. Yet if it was willing to call fresh elections, it wanted the existing members to be returned automatically, and to have some power over who would become new members. As a result, parliamentary government, which had apparently been the victor in the Civil War, itself experienced a temporary demise. In April 1653, the Army took over and disbanded the Parliament. The end result of all these upheavals had been the successive removal of the king, the Lords, and finally the Commons.

A series of experiments followed. The Instrument of Government of 1653 established a form of executive authority controlled by a Protector and Council, with a regular income for civil and military expenditure. The Protector and Council also had power to legislate by ordinance. They were subject, nonetheless, to some control from Parliament. Its approval was required for nominations to the highest administrative and judicial posts. The Parliaments which were set up under the Instrument continued to press for greater powers, however, and the constitutional debate continued through the rest of the Cromwellian period of rulership.

No particular form of government managed to last. As long as Oliver Cromwell was alive, the army remained loyal and the government survived. By the time of Cromwell's death, dissatisfaction with the Protectorate was rife, and a yearning for the restoration of the monarchy was being heard. In 1659, Cromwell's son Richard was ousted from the Protectorship by the army, and what emerged from the successive failures of republicanism was the restoration of a limited monarchy with the accession of Charles II (the son of Charles I) to the throne in 1660.

The 20 year period of turmoil had not been without its fruits. It had at least demonstrated that there were aspects of the old constitutional order which were indispensable to stable government. It was as dangerous to vest absolute power in a single house of Parliament as in the person of the monarch. The constitution required checks and balances between the different branches of government and the various constituencies of power.

The Restoration period heralded the emergence of a new constitutional order.

The failure of the Cromwellian period had been a failure to establish legitimacy. Those who overthrew the monarchy discovered that it was easier to tear down than to build. If the deficiencies of monarchical rule justified the overthrow of the existing order, there remained the necessity to gain popular acceptance of whatever was put in its place. Cromwell never gained that legitimacy, and in the ultimate analysis, all power during those years belonged with the army. In the absence of an accepted constitutional order which had the recognition and acquiescence of the populace, power could only be maintained by the barrel of a gun.

4.3.6   Constitutional monarchy after the Restoration

The restoration of the monarchy was the restoration of a sense of legitimacy. It was a return to an order of government which had history and tradition behind it, and in which the various roles of monarch, Parliament and the courts were, at least substantially, understood. Clearly though, much remained to be worked out in terms of this balance of power. The civil war of 1642-1646 had increased the constitutional standing of Parliament; the personal, prerogative power of the monarchy had been diminished, and thenceforward it was established that the king could not rule without the co-operation of Parliament.

At the same time, the validity of the Crown's role as head of the government was accepted. Charles II was not a mere figurehead. He had personal charge of his government, and he selected and dismissed his ministers at will. At this stage, Parliament had not developed in the way in which it was later to develop; it did not have political parties of any established kind, nor was there any tradition that ministers should be elected from within the ranks of Parliament. It was only over the next 50 years that the shape of the new order emerged; and this was a time of continuing turbulence and upheaval which only came to an end at the death of the last Stuart monarch, Queen Anne, in 1714. During this period of 50 years, the relationship between Crown and Parliament was settled; political parties emerged; and Britain saw in embryo, the formation of cabinet government headed by a prime minister.

None of this, however, was settled in 1660. The accession of Charles II to the throne in that year saw the return of a monarch who was a wiser political manager than his father, but who held a similar belief that monarchy was given to him by divine right. In his eyes, executive government continued to be the preserve of the king, advised by his Privy Council, and Parliament remained a body which was summoned and dissolved at his command. Yet, any prospect that Parliament would accept a passive role was an illusion. It had exercised too much authority since 1640 to retreat back to an advisory function. Its independence was first demonstrated in relation to the Church. The "Cavalier" Parliament, elected in 1661, was a conservative and royalist body which acted swiftly to establish the Anglican church by parliamentary authority and to punish religious non-conformity. It enacted persecutory laws against the expressed wishes of the king. Charles II wanted a more tolerant religious policy in which Catholics could find a place. Nonetheless, he had to bow to the political realities of the post-Restoration period. He could not refuse the Royal Assent to the legislation in the face of such a clear demonstration of the Parliamentary will. It was clear that if this Parliament was fiercely loyal to the restored monarchy, it was not Charles II's pawn.

The intolerance of the royalist, Anglican power-brokers had various consequences. It ensured the development, within the following 20 years, of two distinct parties. The "Tories" represented an alliance of the royalist, landed aristocracy with the Anglican church; it was to be a party associated with the old order based on ownership of land, loyal to the principle of monarchy, and out of sympathy with the revolutionaries who had caused the overthrow of that monarchy in 1649. Those who adhered to a less conformist tradition found themselves in opposition to this conservative political regime. Puritan faith, and its democratic political tradition, was not destroyed in the Restoration. Rather, it continued, albeit cautiously, in the new "Whig" party which was to provide the major political opposition to the Tories. The basis of the Whig party was a combination of aristocratic leadership descended, in the main, from those who had asserted Parliamentary authority against Charles I, and religious dissentients who were powerless within the established Tory order. It was a party with greater notions of democracy, and with a view of monarchy which saw its legitimacy not in terms of divine right but in the assent of the people. Such people had voted for the restoration of the monarchy, but remained committed to the gains for parliamentary authority achieved since 1640.

The turbulence of English politics continued after 1660 while the political relationship between Crown and Parliament was being worked out. Financial matters and religious policy continued to be the main grounds of conflict and compromise. Money continued to be a serious problem for Charles II. On his accession, he was voted an annual sum to pay for the work of government; but it was based only on a rough estimate of need, not on a detailed budget. Furthermore, it was only enough for peace-time. Yet, war appeared to be a regular activity for the Tudor and Stuart monarchs, and Charles II proved no exception. A war with the Dutch between 1665 and 1667 placed new and substantial demands on the public purse. Parliamentary provision of additional funds was conditional upon a proper system of accounting for the revenue spent. Subsequently, Parliament sought to exercise a much more direct control over foreign policy generally—a matter which hitherto had been seen as a prerogative of the Crown.

Much of Parliament's concern with foreign policy revolved around religious issues. Charles II was inclined towards Catholicism, and his brother James was openly a Catholic. In contrast, Parliament had a strong adherence to Protestantism and was greatly concerned by the prospect that James would succeed to the throne, as he was the heir apparent of Charles II. Attempts were made in Parliament to pass a law excluding James from the succession. Charles II blocked this by successively suspending Parliament, and then dissolving it. Eventually, on Charles II's death in 1685, James did accede to the throne as James II. His reign was to be brief, however, and his overt support for Catholicism led to his downfall and exile.

4.3.7   The revolution of 1688

James' brief reign as king saw renewed conflict between the Crown and the leading power-brokers of the realm over religion. Had James II been content merely to pursue his faith privately, it would have been accommodated. However, his campaign was more vigorous than this. He sought, by exercise of his prerogative powers, to suspend or remove the restrictions which existed on Catholics holding office. This involved a claimed power to dispense with or suspend a law of the realm, and it challenged Parliamentary authority. The greater concern was a religious one. In the turbulent 17th century the prospect that major political power in the nation could shift from Anglicans to Catholics represented a major crisis. The crisis was made more acute by the birth in 1688 of a son to James. This meant a new heir apparent who would be brought up in the Catholic faith. James had two daughters, both of them protestants. The eldest, Mary, was married to Prince William of Orange, a Dutchman. While she was the heir apparent, there was no prospect that a Catholic dynasty would prevail, but the new prince displaced her from the right of succession.

The result was the overthrow of a reigning king for the second time in 40 years. A group of leading peers issued an invitation to Prince William of Orange to intervene. In November 1688, William landed on the Devonshire coast with an invading army. James II, realising the weakness of his military and political position, fled the country. He was deemed to have abdicated the throne, and although his infant son was his legitimate heir, it was William and Mary who were invited to accede to the throne jointly. This was not achieved by any formal constitutional mechanism. Initially an informal assembly of members of the Lords and Commons invited Prince William to issue writs summoning a Constitutional Convention. This body, which had no recognised constitutional standing, declared the throne vacant and invited William and Mary to become king and queen. The Convention then declared itself a Parliament.

Constitutionally, the significance of this was in the shift of power which it entailed. All pretence of constitutional legitimacy was abandoned in favour of a political expedient.[53] William and Mary could not claim the throne by divine right as their predecessors had done; rather, they were monarchs by popular assent. A "practical and largely secular notion of monarchy"[54] had prevailed. The resolution of the Convention Parliament of 1689 was in terms that "King James the Second, having endeavoured to subvert the constitution of the kingdom, by breaking the original contract between king and people" had abdicated by fleeing the country.[55] The idea that the relationship between the monarchy and the people was contractual was, of course, quite contrary to the Stuart idea of monarchy being a divine right. However, the notion was consistent with the "ascending" theory of government which had continued for centuries as a subsidiary strand of thought within the western political tradition, and at the end of the 17th century, this contractual theory of government was given new life with its influential exposition by John Locke.

4.4   The New Constitutional Order

4.4.1   The Bill of Rights and the Act of Settlement

If James II had broken his contract with the people, then those who orchestrated the Revolution of 1688 took the opportunity to rewrite that contract between government and governed. In the *Bill of Rights* 1689, that new contract was more fully spelt out.[56] It declared illegal any pretended royal power to dispense with, or suspend laws. It reasserted that the power of taxation always required parliamentary consent; that the raising or keeping of a standing army within the kingdom in time of peace was illegal, unless it had Parliament's consent; that "the freedom of speech and debates or proceedings in Parliament ought not to be impeached or questioned in any court or place out of Parliament"; that "excessive bail ought not to be required, nor excessive fines imposed, nor cruel and unusual punishments inflicted"; and that "for redress of all grievances, and for the amending, strengthening and preserving of the laws, Parliaments ought to be held frequently."[57] These may still be considered fundamental constitutional principles in England and Australia today, subject to contrary provisions in subsequent enactments. Other provisions of the *Bill of Rights* were of more transitory significance.

Further matters of constitutional importance were addressed by the *Act of Settlement* 1701. The main purpose of this Act was to resolve the question of the protestant succession. The Act was made necessary by the death of the last surviving child of Princess Anne, who was the late Queen Mary's younger sister, and who would succeed to the throne on the death of William III. It provided that in the absence of direct heirs of William III or Anne, the throne should pass to the protestant House of Hanover, descended from Elizabeth, daughter of James I. So it was that, having provided for a Dutchman to accede to the throne, Parliament now prepared the way for the throne to pass to a German speaking Elector of Hanover, who eventually became king as George I in 1714. Thus, the revolution in the constitutional position continued. The monarchs who acceded to the throne did so only on the basis of a Parliamentary title.

The *Act of Settlement* also gave security of tenure to the judiciary. It provided that judges should hold office during good behaviour and that they should only be removed on an address of both houses of Parliament. It was also provided that their salaries should be "ascertained and established". In practice, this has been taken to mean that their salaries should not be reduced during their tenure of office, although they may be increased. This is to prevent salary levels being used as a form of political pressure upon the judiciary. The security of tenure of the judiciary has passed into Australian constitutional law as a fundamental principle which needs to be safeguarded.

4.4.2   Executive and legislature

After 1688, the relationship between Crown and Parliament became closer by necessity. The *Triennial Act* of 1694 stipulated that Parliaments should be called at least every three years, and that no Parliament should last longer than three years. However, sessions of Parliament proved to be annual events. The new closeness was once again motivated by financial considerations. War proved to be a major feature of the new reign as it had been for the previous regimes. This required additional taxation.

It became clear that the legislature and executive needed a close relationship. Government ministers could not merely be able administrators; they needed to be politicians who could defend government policy and explain its revenue needs to Parliament. Given the divided political composition of Parliament, favour had to be shown to both Whigs and Tories. After some experiments with having mixed ministries, containing members of both parties, it became increasingly clear that such a system was fraught with difficulty. During the reign of Queen Anne (1702-1714), the Crown's prerogative to choose as ministers whoever should be deemed suitable was maintained, as it was to be for many years to come. Yet it was seen to be desirable that ministers should be chosen from among the leaders of the political parties, and that the composition of the ministry should bear at least some relation to the relative strengths of the parties in Parliament. The development of party political government was, however, slow in coming, and as will be seen, it was only in the 19th century that the monarchy withdrew substantially from involvement in governmental affairs.

4.4.3   The emergence of Cabinet

A further innovation of the post-1688 period was the development of cabinet government, which had begun with Charles II. Officially, the executive power of the Crown was meant to be exercised through the Privy Council. It was in this forum that the leaders of the state expressed their

views on major issues of government, and through which the monarch
made administrative orders. The Privy Council was, however, ill suited to
its purpose. It was too large; at the Restoration, it had 27 members, but it
later grew as large as 50.[58] Charles II preferred the real decision making to
be done more informally, and confidentially by a "cabinet" of trusted
advisers; the Privy Council continued to fulfil those roles which belonged
to it by tradition (which included hearing appeals from courts overseas, in
addition to its administrative functions), but it was not the powerful
executive body which it had been before. This use of an informal cabinet
continued with the monarchs who followed Charles II. In the *Act of
Settlement* 1701, it was required that "all matters and things relating to the
well governing of this kingdom which are properly cognisable in the privy
council by the laws and customs of this realm shall be transacted there."[59]
This was implicitly a censure of cabinet government, but the cabinet
survived. Parliament retreated from its earlier censure in the *Regency Act*
1705, and the cabinet became an established feature of government in the
18th century.

4.5   The Emergence of Party Political Government

Through the rest of the 18th century, English government continued its
progress from a monarchical system wielding direct governmental
authority, to a system of parliamentary democracy. The evolution was a
slow one. Throughout most of the century, the monarchs retained a
personal involvement in government in the sense that ministers were in
office by royal choice and owed their position to that link with the Crown,
rather than with each other or with their political party. George I
(1714-1727) and George II (1727-1760) chose ministers from the Whig party
throughout their reigns, and managed to secure compliant Parliaments.
This favouritism towards the Whigs was because they had supported the
Hanoverian succession. The power and influence of royal ministers
increased with the succession of the Hanovers. George I knew as little about
his new kingdom as he did of its language and, therefore, was content to
leave decisions to his ministers. George II was similarly uninvolved in the
day to day work of government, and both of them rarely attended cabinet
meetings.

George III, who came to the throne in 1760, took a more active role in
government, but continued the practice of his predecessors in leaving
cabinet meetings to his ministers. The Privy Council continued to decline
in practical significance, and by the middle of the century it was possible
to identify one minister, usually, but not always, the First Lord of the
Treasury, who was the leader of the government. At the same time, the
practical power of the king to choose his own ministers declined. Ministers
needed to have the support of Parliament in order to govern effectively, and
there were times when the king was forced to accept ministers whom he
disliked, because their political position was so strong in the country.

From this, in due course, the system of party political government emerged. However, it needed a fundamental reform of the franchise before the personal power of the monarch was displaced. Under the 18th century political system, in which the right to vote was strictly limited and the size of electorates in each constituency varied markedly, royal patronage and influence could usually ensure that elections brought about a desirable composition of Parliament. It was in this way that the Whigs were able to dominate between 1714 and 1760, and the Tories for a half century thereafter.

In 1832, a *Reform Act* was passed which effected the abolition of various constituencies which no longer had sizeable populations to support them, and which created new constituencies, especially in London and the north of England. The franchise was also enlarged. Further reform took place by the *Reform Act* 1867. While these enlarged the franchise, it did so only for men. Universal adult suffrage of both men and women had to wait until the 20th century.

Nonetheless, the effect of these reforms was to make it impossible for the Crown to retain its influence over the Parliament in quite the way it had done hitherto. The power of the monarch to choose her or his own ministry, which had waned throughout the 18th century, was extinguished by 1867. Thenceforward, Parliamentarians had to be responsive to electorates in a way which had not been true of the 18th century. In order to govern, ministers needed the confidence of Parliament, and from that time on, party political government was firmly established. Furthermore, it was clear that the monarch had a very limited role constitutionally. Walter Bagehot, in his famous work, *The English Constitution* (1867) wrote:[60]

> "To state the matter shortly, the sovereign has, under a constitutional monarchy such as ours, three rights—the right to be consulted, the right to encourage, the right to warn."

The system of executive government which developed in England provided a model for Australia. It is a remarkable testimony to the triumph of form over substance that both the *Constitution of the Commonwealth of Australia* (1900), and the various State constitutions, drew upon the formal position of the Crown and executive in English law, and not upon the substantive position. By the time the Australian constitution was enacted, the position of the monarchy had long since become essentially ceremonial. Yet, the Australian constitution reads as if it was modelled upon the governmental system at the beginning of the 18th century or earlier. Executive power rests with a Governor-General who exercises authority through an Executive Council. Thus, the formal position of the Crown and Privy Council was replicated in the modern constitution. There is no mention of the Cabinet, nor of the Prime Minister. Until 1977, the constitution did not mention political parties. Ministers, according to the Federal Constitution hold office at the pleasure of the Governor-General, rather than through maintaining the confidence of Parliament. The Governor-General is in charge of the armed forces, and summons and dismisses Parliament.[61] Thus, while Australia has a written constitution, some of the most important constitutional law is unwritten. It exists as a matter of tacit understandings (or "conventions" as they are otherwise known). It was this adherence to formalism which contributed to Australia's most serious constitutional crisis—the dismissal of the Prime Minister by the Governor-General in 1975.[62] Furthermore, the formalistic nature of Australia's constitution raises serious complications for the proposed transition to a republic.

4.6   Constitutional Principles of the Westminster System

Australia inherited far more from the constitutional conflicts of the 17th century than merely the structures of government which, substantially, were reproduced in this country. More than this, out of the history of conflict and compromise had emerged principles of constitutionality which were regarded as fundamental, such as the principles of limited monarchy, the rule of law, the independence of the judiciary, and the sovereignty of Parliament. These constitutional principles became articles of faith, principles which people believed in, because they had been forged through the painful experience of arbitrary power and through hard fought battles to ensure basic liberties. Had they been mere abstractions of political philosophy, it is doubtful that they would have been so enduring.

To say that these principles were forged through British history is not, however, to suggest that they are British in origin, nor that they were only adopted in Britain. As will be seen, the idea of the rule of law originated with Aristotle; and another important constitutional principle, the separation of powers, was first expressed in its classic form by the 18th century French writer, Montesquieu. These ideas form aspects of both the common law and the civil law traditions. Yet, it is from the British experience that Australia derives its foundational constitutional principles. Thus, it is the particular form in which these principles of constitutionality were given concrete expression in Britain which influenced Australia.

4.6.1   The rule of law

A central principle of constitutionality is the necessity for the rule of law. The notion of the rule of law was one which had been a part of English political theory since the time of Bracton or earlier, although, the term itself did not gain great currency until the 19th century. It has meant different things at different times, and in modern political discourse, it has a range of meanings, many of them inconsistent with one another.[63] However, as a historical concept, it has meant essentially that government should be through law, as opposed to the exercise of arbitrary power.

The notion of the rule of law may be traced back to Aristotle, who was concerned to rebut Plato's theory that government was best in the hands of a learned elite of philosopher kings. Aristotle saw dangers in giving such power to men, and posited instead, government based upon the rule of law. In Book III of *Politics* he wrote that:

> "He who bids law to rule seems to bid God and intelligence alone to rule, but he who bids that man rule puts forward a beast as well; for that is the sort of thing desire is, and spiritedness twists rulers even when they are the best of men. Accordingly, law is intelligence without appetite". [64]

Aristotle's conception of the rule of law was one in which reason should rule, as opposed to "appetite", that is, people's own desires. It postulated for law an objective and neutral existence which acts as a check upon the will and whims of individual rulers.

In the area of private civil rights especially, Aristotle's conception of the rule of law has been played out in English political history. The protection by the common law of property rights and the respect which those rights were given by the political leaders of the nation, ensured that disputes would be adjudicated by law rather than "appetite", at least for those who had property rights to protect. The rule of law meant that adjudication should as far as possible be in accordance with the pre-existing law of the land. Of course, there was often an element of discretion in the way in which general rules were applied to particular fact situations, and sometimes new questions of law had to be decided by the courts. Nonetheless, even where judges did have to exercise discretion, the rule of law meant that the determination should be governed by reason rather than whim, prejudice or ad hoc decision making. The application of general rules to specific circumstances and the resolution of novel questions of law proceeded by logical examination of the existing law and, where necessary, the reasoned extension of the existing rules. For Coke, the common law was the "perfection of reason". [65] It was, of course, an "artificial" reason. Legal rationality meant an examination of the issues by attention to precedents and using the particular forms of argument and notions of authority which prevailed within the legal tradition. For the English lawyer, the legal rationality of the common law was in itself a brake upon arbitrary power. While the common law said nothing about distributive justice in terms of the way property was divided among members of society, the reasoned application of general rules relating to private rights was a source of protection from those for whom might alone made right. [66]

A further aspect of the rule of law is the principle of equality before the law. It was a corollary of the principle that adjudication should proceed by the reasoned application of general rules that the wealth or status of the parties should be irrelevant to the outcome of a case. Although reality often fell short of the law's ideals—and still does—the principle of equality before the law was an important aspect of the law's claim to fairness and impartiality even in a society dominated by the landed aristocracy. [67] Furthermore, monarchs were bound by the law. This was one of the central issues in dispute between the Stuart kings and Parliament in the 17th century. Its important legacy in the modern law is that the executive government may do only what it is authorised to do by the law of the land. It has no authority other than that given to it by Parliament and the constitution, and it is answerable for its exercise of governmental authority to an independent legal system.

This idea of the rule of law as a guard against arbitary power received its classic exposition in the writings of the famous 19th century English constitutional lawyer, A V Dicey. He wrote in his *Introduction to the Study of the Law of the Constitution* (first published in 1885) that the rule of law means first "the absolute supremacy of regular law as opposed to the influence of arbitrary power, and excludes the existence of arbitrariness, of prerogative, or even wide discretionary authority, on the part of the government . . . a man may with us be punished for a breach of law, but he can be punished for nothing else."[68]

This did not mean, for Dicey, that the substance of the law was necessarily just or virtuous. In this sense, the rule of law says nothing about the substantive fairness of the law's content.[69] Of 18th century England, Dicey could write that its singularity "was not so much the goodness or the leniency as the legality of the English system of government . . . [it was] a land where the laws might be harsh, but where men were ruled by law and not by caprice."[70]

The 18th century period demonstrates well how the law, which according to some critiques is merely an instrumental means of reinforcing and legitimising existing class relations, could also have an independent existence which qualified the domination of the ruling class, and could act as a restraint upon those in power. The left-wing historian E P Thompson thus criticised philosophers who reduced law to a simple equation with class power:

"It is inherent in the especial character of law, as a body of rules and procedures, that it shall apply logical criteria with reference to standards of universality and equity. It is true that certain categories of person may be excluded from this logic (as children or slaves), that other categories may be debarred from access to parts of the logic (as women or, for many forms of 18th century law, those without property), and that the poor may often be excluded, through penury, from the law's costly procedures. All this, and more, is true. But if too much of this is true, then the consequences are plainly counterproductive. Most men have a strong sense of justice, at least with regard to their own interests. If the law is evidently partial and unjust, then it will mask nothing, legitimise nothing, contribute nothing to any class's hegemony".[71]

Thompson concluded that "the rule of law itself, the imposing of effective inhibitions upon power and the defence of the citizen from power's all-intrusive claims, seems to me to be an unqualified human good."[72]

4.6.2   Due process of law

Another aspect of government through law which was initially established by Magna Carta, was the importance of "due process". The rule of law demands that the punishment of a person, or the deprivation of a person's liberty or property should only occur in accordance with proper legal process. This is a fundamental principle of all western legal systems. Important aspects of "due process" in the criminal law are the presumption of innocence, the right to trial by jury for serious offences, and various procedural requirements of the criminal law. Internment without trial is an obvious breach of the principle of due process.

Trial by jury and the presumption of innocence both have a very long history, but other aspects of due process took longer to establish as inviolable principles of English law. For example, Coke's common law was less protective of citizens' liberties than it was of their property. Coke's insistence in the *Case of Proclamations* (1611)[73] that "the King hath no prerogative but that which the law of the land allows him" was an expression of the supremacy of the common law over arbitrary government, but it still left a considerable degree of power in the Crown. As long as the courts recognised a broad prerogative power in the Crown (which, during the 16th century they certainly did) individuals could be subjected to arbitrary arrest and imprisonment.[74] It was only through the course of the 17th century, when these prerogative powers were curtailed, that civil liberties gained significant protection. These liberties had to be safeguarded again by judicial decisions in the mid-18th century.[75]

4.6.3   The separation of powers

The other cardinal constitutional principle which emerged from the 17th century struggles was the importance of the separation of powers, although it was imperfectly expressed in the English constitution. It was the French philosopher, Montesquieu, who first expounded this as a political principle. In *The Spirit of the Laws* published in 1748, Montesquieu posited that the protection of liberties depended upon confining individual power within limits, since there was an inherent tendency for power to be abused, and for those who held power to push their authority to its limits. This could best be achieved by a clear separation of legislative, executive and judicial authority.

The essence of this principle is that the power to make laws should be in separate hands from those who carry into effect the executive work of government administration and from those who apply those laws through judicial office.[76] It was this principle which had been fought for in the 17th century conflicts. The struggle for the abolition of the Court of Star Chamber had been a struggle to ensure that the monarch, through the Privy Council, should not have any involvement in punishing criminal offenders:

the work of adjudicating on breaches of the law must lie with the judges of the realm. For as long as the judges only held office at the pleasure of the Crown, they were vulnerable to executive pressure. It was for this reason that the principle of the security of tenure of the judiciary, established by the *Act of Settlement* 1701 (see above, 4.4.1), was seen as a fundamental constitutional principle to ensure their independence. The principle that executive authority should also be separated from the power to make laws was also a principle fought for in the 17th century. The curtailment of the prerogative power to suspend laws, and to impose taxation by proclamation, was seen as essential to the protection of liberty.

Montesquieu may have exaggerated the extent to which the principle of a separation of powers was to be seen in the English system. While, undoubtedly, the dispersal of power in 18th century Britain could readily be contrasted with the existence of autocratic power in France, it was still the case that during much of the 18th century, royal patronage in England proved sufficient to ensure a compliant Parliament. In broader terms, legislative, executive and judicial power was all concentrated in an oligarchy of aristocracy and landed gentry. It took reform of the franchise to secure a wider degree of representation.

The doctrine of the separation of powers does not necessarily imply a separation of personnel. It is the powers which are separate. Individuals may have responsibilities in more than one branch of government. Thus, in the Westminster system, the Prime Minister and her or his ministers of state are also, by convention, members of Parliament. However, they are not the only members, and before an Act can be passed, it must receive the scrutiny of the members of Parliament, and be passed by a majority of those members in each House. Similarly, in the British parliamentary system, the judges who comprise the Judicial Committee of the House of Lords (which acts as the final court of appeal for the United Kingdom) are also members of the House of Lords when it operates in its legislative capacity as a chamber of review for Bills which have received the assent of the House of Commons. The Law Lords do, on occasion, speak in debates, especially when they consider that their legal expertise is of assistance to the House. In the American system, there is much more of a separation of powers. Neither the President nor the various secretaries of state are members of Congress. Even so, the separation of personnel is not total. The Vice-President does have certain duties in the Senate.

4.7   The Australian Constitutional Inheritance

The ideas of the rule of law, due process of law and of the separation of powers became central components of Australian constitutional theory, as well as that of Britain. Indeed, as will be seen, the constitutional structures which had been developed in Britain over the centuries were largely replicated in Australia, subject to necessary modifications, since there could be no equivalent in the Australian colonies of the House of Lords, drawn from the hereditary peers, in the British Parliament. There were some borrowings from the United States, in devising the structure of the federal Parliament, but in most respects, Australia inherited the political tradition which had developed in England through the centuries. The way in which that tradition developed in the Australian context is the subject of the next chapters.

NOTES

1. See above, Chapter 2.
2. Berman, H, *Law and Revolution* (Harvard UP, Cambridge, Mass, 1983), pp 435-438.
3. For an explanation of these competing views, see Kelly, J, *A Short History of Western Legal Theory* (Clarendon Press, Oxford, 1992), pp 90-102.
4. Sedulius, *On Christian Rulers*, c 850 AD, cited in Kelly, J, op cit, p 94.
5. These views were expressed for example, by Isodore of Seville.
6. Berman, H, op cit, pp 281-282.
7. See Kelly, J, op cit, p 98.
8. Aquinas, *De Regimine Principum* 1.6, cited in Kelly, J, op cit, pp 129-130.
9. Bracton, Henry, De, *On the Law and Customs of England* (translator, S Thorne, Belknap Press, Cambridge, Mass, 1968), Vol 2, 3.9.3.
10. Ibid, p 305.
11. Fortescue, J, *The Governance of England* (C Plummer ed, Clarendon Press, Oxford, 1885), p 109.
12. Elton, G R, *The Tudor Constitution* (2nd ed, Methuen, London, 1974), p 13.
13. Keir, D L, *The Constitutional History of Modern Britain Since 1485* (9th ed, Adam & Charles Black, London, 1969), Ch 1.
14. This Act prevented appeals being made to Rome which challenged the validity of decisions in English courts. The move was made necessary to deal with an appeal to the Pope by Catherine of Aragon, whose marriage to Henry had been nullified by a court's decision in England.
15. This Act restrained the payment of monetary dues from the English Church to Rome.
16. Keir, D L, op cit, p 63.
17. Berman, H, op cit, p 66. King Alfred (871-900) was similarly head of the Church in England.
18. Ibid, pp 94-113.
19. England was not the only country where the monarch was at the centre of religious disputes. In the same vein, the Scottish reformer, John Knox, told Queen Mary Stuart that subjects are not "bound to frame their religion according to the appetites of their princes . . . If princes exceed their bounds, it is no doubt but that they may be resisted, even by power". Knox, J, *The History of the Reformation in Scotland* (1566), extracted in Hughes, P L, and Fries, R F (eds), *Crown and Parliament in Tudor-Stuart England* (Putnam, New York, 1959), p 149.
20. For example, the *Heresy Act* 1534, and the *Act of Six Articles* 1539.
21. *Succession Act* 1544.
22. Keir, D L, op cit, p 135.
23. 1 Plowden 102; 75 ER 160. See further Gough, J W, *Fundamental Law in English Constitutional History* (Clarendon Press, Oxford, 1955), pp 19-20.
24. Coke, E, *Institutes of the Laws of England*, Pt 4, s 240.
25. (1610) 8 Co Rep 107a at 118a; 77 ER 638. For the background to the case, and the context of Coke's pronouncements, see Cook, H, "Against Common Right and Reason: The College of Physicians v Dr Thomas Bonham" (1985) 29 Am J of Legal Hist 301.
26. Sir Henry Hobart echoed Coke's view in two cases, *Day v Savadge* (1614) Hobart 85; 80 ER 235 and *Lord Sheffield v Ratcliffe* (1615) Hobart 334 at 346; 80 ER 475 at 486-487.
27. Coke appeared to gain some support from judges later. See the statements by Holt CJ in *City of London v Wood* (1701) 12 Mod 669 at 687-688; 88 ER 1592.
28. Baker, J H, *An Introduction to English Legal History* (3rd ed, Butterworths, London, 1990), pp 241-242. See further, Gough, J, op cit, Ch 3.

29. For a discussion of the impact of Coke's ideas upon American courts before the Revolution see Plucknett, T, "Bonham's Case and Judicial Review" (1926) 40 Harvard LR 30, at 61-70. The activist tradition represented by Coke's views continues to be a strong one in the United States. It has even been suggested by a leading scholar that courts ought to be able to declare statutes obsolete or revise them if they have become outdated. See Calabresi, G, *A Common Law for the Age of Statutes* (Harvard UP, Cambridge, Mass, 1982).
30. (1607) 12 Co Rep 63; 77 ER 1342.
31. Ibid, at 64-65.
32. Bowen, C D, *The Lion and the Throne* (Hamish Hamilton, London, 1957), pp 261-264.
33. (1611) 12 Co Rep 74 at 76; 77 ER 1352.
34. For example, *Five Knights' Case* (1627) 3 Howell's St Tr 51; *The Case of Ship-Money* (1637) 3 Howell's St Tr 825; *Godden v Hales* (1686) 11 Howell's St Tr 1165.
35. The most influential exponent of an absolutist theory of monarchy was a French lawyer, Jean Bodin (1530-96) in *De la Republique* (1576). See further, Kelly, J, op cit, p 175.
36. Extracted in Tanner, J R, *Constitutional Documents of the Reign of James I* (Cambridge UP, Cambridge, 1952), p 9.
37. Ibid.
38. Ibid.
39. Bowen, C D, op cit, p 270. See also, Tanner, J R, op cit, p 15.
40. Cited in Kelly, J, op cit, p 211.
41. Keir, D L, op cit, p 163.
42. Reproduced in Tanner, J R, op cit, pp 217-230; Hughes, P L and Fries, R F, op cit, pp 156-163.
43. Hughes, P L, and Fries, R F, op cit, pp 158-159.
44. Ibid, p 163.
45. (1637) 3 Howell's St Tr 825.
46. *The Triennial Act* 1641.
47. *Act to Continue the Existing Parliament* 1641.
48. *Act Abolishing the Prerogative Courts* 1641.
49. Tanner, J R, *English Constitutional Conflicts of the Seventeenth Century 1603-1689* (Cambridge UP, Cambridge, 1962), p 119.
50. Ibid.
51. *The Solemn League and Covenant* 1643.
52. *The Self-Denying Ordinance* 1645.
53. See further, Nenner, H, "The Convention of 1689: A Triumph of Constitutional Form" (1966) 10 Am J of Legal Hist 282.
54. Keir, D L, op cit, p 271.
55. Evans, M and Jack, I, *Sources of English Legal and Constitutional History*, (Butterworths, Sydney, 1984), p 349.
56. Ibid, pp 352-357.
57. Ibid.
58. Keir, D L, op cit, p 244.
59. Evans, M and Jack, I, op cit, p 360.
60. Bagehot, W, *The English Constitution* (2nd ed, Henry S King, London, 1872, reprinted Garland Publishing, New York, 1978), p 57.
61. See below, Chapter 6.
62. See below, Chapter 6.
63. For discussions of this range of meanings, and critical analysis, see Hutchinson, A and Monahan, P (eds), *The Rule of Law—Ideal or Ideology* (Carswell, Toronto, 1987). See also Walker, G de Q, *The Rule of Law* (Melbourne UP, Carlton, 1988).
64. For discussion of Aristotle's interpretation of the rule of law in the light of contemporary debates see Weinrib, E, "The Intelligibility of the Rule of Law" in Hutchinson, A and Monahan, P (eds), op cit, p 59.
65. Coke, E, *Institutes of the Laws of England*, Pt 1, s 138.
66. Weinrib, E, op cit.
67. See Hay, D, "Property, Authority and the Criminal Law" in Hay, D, Linebaugh, P and Thompson, E P (eds), *Albion's Fatal Tree: Crime and Society in Eighteenth Century England* (Pantheon, New York, 1975), Ch 1.
68. Dicey, A V, *Introduction to the Study of the Law of the Constitution* (10th ed, E C S Wade, Macmillan, London, 1964), p 202.

69. Cf Raz, J, *The Authority of Law: Essays on Law and Morality* (Clarendon, Oxford, 1979), p 211: "[T]he rule of law is just one of the virtues which a legal system may possess and by which it is to be judged. It is not to be confused with democracy, justice, equality (before the law or otherwise) human rights of any kind or respect for persons or for the dignity of man. A non-democratic legal system, based on the denial of human rights, or extensive poverty, on racial segregation, sexual inequalities, and religious persecution may, in principle, conform to the requirements of the rule of law better than any of the legal systems of the more enlightened western democracies."

70. Dicey, A V, op cit, pp 189-190.

71. Thompson, E P, *Whigs and Hunters: The Origin of the Black Act* (Pantheon Books, New York, 1975), pp 262-263.

72. Ibid, p 266.

73. (1611) 12 Co Rep 74 at 76; 77 ER 1352.

74. See, eg, *Five Knights' Case* (1627) 3 Howell's St Tr 51.

75. The most famous of these was *Entick v Carrington* (1765) 19 St Tr 1030. In this case the court treated as invalid a general warrant issued by the Secretary of State which authorised entrance to the plaintiff's property for the purposes of search and seizure of books and papers. Such a warrant could only be issued by the courts on demonstration of cause, and thus the officers' entry constituted a trespass. See further, Heuston, R F V, *Essays in Constitutional Law* (2nd ed, Stevens, London, 1964), pp 32ff.

76. For a critique of the political purpose of the doctrine of the separation of powers, see Nonet, P and Selznick, P, *Law and Society in Transition* (Harper and Row, New York, 1978), pp 55-60.

Part Three

Colonisation, Federation and Independence

Chapter 5

GOVERNMENT AND LAW IN COLONIAL AUSTRALIA

5.1 The Colonisation of Australia

5.1.1 The establishment of a penal colony in New South Wales

It was an inauspicious beginning to the development of the legal tradition in Australia, that its earliest European inhabitants should have been those considered least fit to remain members of civil society. A parliamentary report on transportation in 1838 described New South Wales as a community "composed of the very dregs of society; and men proved by experience to be unfit to be at large in any society, and who were sent from the British gaols, and turned loose to mix with one another in the desert, together with a few taskmasters, who were to set them to work in the open wilderness; and with the military who were to keep them from revolt."[1]

From the perspective of the late 20th century, the convicts who were transported to New South Wales were not so incorrigible, (and nor were they only men). Eighteenth century criminal law in England was barbaric and oppressive. Without a coherent theory of punishment, it was a blunt and bloody instrument by which the property-owning classes of the day maintained power and suppressed the threat of riot and revolt.[2] It was heavily reliant upon capital punishment as the indiscriminate response to offences great and small. Indeed, one statute, the *Waltham Black Act* of 1723,[3] identified more than 200 capital offences.[4] If the criminal law was severe, it was at least tempered with mercy to a certain extent. Increasingly, as the century went on, capital sentences were commuted, and this mercy exercised by judges or by the royal prerogative went hand in hand with that unofficial mercy extended by jurors who would regularly convict offenders of stealing goods valued at 39 shillings (since stealing 40 shillings or more carried the death penalty).[5]

The government was short of alternatives to hanging, however. There were jails, such as Newgate in London, but they were few. Indeed, many were private jails. Owners made their money by extorting money from the prisoners.[6] One answer to the problem of the "criminal classes" was seen to lie in their export. Transportation as a punishment dated back to a statute of 1597,[7] and for many years therafter, the American colonies provided a suitable dumping ground. Indeed, the American landowners welcomed it since it provided a workforce of manual labourers. Other convicts were sent to the West Indies. The major destination for transportation was closed following the American Declaration of Independence in 1776, and this created a necessity to find new places for transportation. As a temporary expedient, the authorities took to housing criminals in old hulks—disused ships moored in rivers or at ports—which acted as jails until such time as transportation could be commenced again. This situation could not continue indefinitely, and it was against this background that the decision was taken to develop a new penal settlement at Botany Bay. Thus, in 1786, Captain Arthur Phillip received his commission to establish the colony of New South Wales.

Many of the offenders who were thus exiled to New South Wales through the policy of transportation were sentenced for crimes which today would be deemed trivial. The offences of which they were convicted were basically property offences. On the First Fleet, there was no one who had been convicted for murder or rape, although over 100 out of 736 had been convicted of thefts involving violence, or the threat of it. Among the convicts were the pitiful who were convicted of the theft of food, and a few children, the youngest of whom was nine.[8] The most trivial crimes were sufficient to secure a place on the First Fleet. It was in 1787 that the first convicts began their voyage to Australia, to be followed by some 163,000 others, before transportation finally ceased in 1868.[9]

Yet, New South Wales was not merely a penal settlement. The British intended to establish a new colony, and the principles of domestic and international law concerning the formation of new colonies were applied in its foundation.[10] The simple ceremony which took place on 26 January 1788 asserted for the British Crown the right to control New South Wales, and followed the traditional form for claiming a new territory. A more elaborate ceremony was held on 7 February 1788, in which the commission of Governor Phillip was read out, along with the Act of Parliament establishing the new colony, and the First Charter of Justice, which was given by Letters Patent of 2 April 1787. The land thus claimed for Britain was much more extensive than would have been needed only for a penal settlement. It extended from Cape York to the southern tip of Van Diemen's Land, and west to the 135th degree of longitude, approximately half the continent.

5.1.2   The Aboriginal peoples and the myth of the empty continent

The British chose to treat New Holland as a continent which was open to settlement as being "uninhabited", or in Latin terminology, terra nullius. Of course, they were aware of the Aboriginal inhabitants, but did not see them as proprietors of the land who needed to be dispossessed by conquest, or with whom they needed to make a treaty. In regarding New Holland as uninhabited, they were encouraged by contemporary ideas of international law.

One of the most influential writers on the law of nations was a Swiss-born jurist, Emmerich de Vattel. His book, *The Law of Nations*, was first published in 1758 and translated into English soon after.[11] Vattel argued that as a principle of natural law, wandering tribes could only be treated as owning property when they appropriated certain portions of the earth to render them fertile, and to derive subsistence from them. It followed that no country could lay claim to more of the land than it could use. Vattel raised the question whether "a Nation may lawfully occupy any part of a vast territory in which are to be found only wandering tribes whose small numbers can not populate the whole country." To this, he answered that:

"These tribes can not take to themselves more land than they have need of or can inhabit and cultivate. Their uncertain occupancy of these vast regions can not be held as a real and lawful taking of possession; and when the Nations of Europe, which are too confined at home, come upon lands which the savages have no special need of and are making no present and continuous use of, they may lawfully take possession of them and establish colonies in them."[12]

Vattel's ideas reflected within the sphere of international law, the ideas of men such as John Locke on the justification for the private ownership of property.[13] It followed from his concept of the right to settlement, that the Aboriginal tribes would not be treated as having lawful possession of the entire continent by 18th century English people.[14] Captain Cook wrote of his impressions of the Aborigines, that they had "no fix'd habitation but move on from place to place" and that they lived "wholly by fishing and hunting, but mostly by the former for we never saw one Inch of Cultivated Land in the Whole Country."[15] A further reason for regarding the Aborigines as not possessing a legal title to the land was that, to 18th century European eyes, their culture did not have a political organisation or legal system which gave to them a defined structure of property ownership. Thus, although there were inhabitants, the land was treated as essentially an empty continent belonging to no one who claimed a proprietary right in defined parcels of land.

Governor Phillip's instructions of 25 April 1787 required him to "endeavour by every possible means to open an intercourse with the natives and to conciliate their affections, enjoining all our subjects to live in amity and kindness with them,"[16] but no greater recognition of their rights was afforded than a right to mutual co-existence. The subsequent history of colonial New South Wales was scarcely marked by "amity and kindness". If, at first, Captain Phillip sought a positive relationship with the Aboriginal people, this attitude was not widespread among those who subsequently populated the fledgling colony. Especially on the frontiers of white settlement, warfare between settlers and Aboriginal people was widespread, and resulted in loss of life in both communities. However, the power of the gun habitually prevailed, and the slaughter of Aborigines was very much greater than any losses incurred by whites. Nor was warfare the only cause of death among Aborigines. The ravages of disease introduced by the British settlers resulted in considerable loss of life, and as the colonial settlers spread across New South Wales and beyond it, Aboriginal communities were more and more displaced from their traditional lands. One settler, writing to the London-based Methodist Missionary Society in 1826, concluded from his travels through the colony that:

"Civilisation has been the scourge of the natives; Disease, Crime, Misery and Death, have hitherto been the sure attendants of our intercourse with them. Wherever we trace the steps of white population we discover the introduction of evil, the diminution of numbers, the marks of disease, the pressure of want, the physical and moral ruin of this people. If we inquire where are the tribes that once inhabited the places where Sydney, Parramatta, Windsor and other Towns now flourish, what will be the answer? Their existence is but a name . . . it is a sad truth to assert that our prosperity has hitherto been their ruin, our increase their destruction. The history of nearly 40 years seals the veracity of this declaration." [17]

After white settlement, Aborigines were treated as British subjects, and subjected, however, incongruously, to British law. Aborigines could be subject to punishment under the criminal law of the colony, even for offences committed against another Aborigine. [18] More often, they were ignored by the white man's law, and certainly were not protected by it. It was the beginning of a tragic period in the history of the Aboriginal peoples, with lasting damage to their population and culture.

The idea that Australia should be treated as a settled territory, rather than being obtained through treaty or conquest, was significant not only for the purposes of legitimising English rule in international law, but also for its consequences in English law. In 1722, the Privy Council had recognised a distinction between conquered and settled territories in terms of the law which governed the new possession. In *Case 15—Anonymous* (1722) [19] it was held that "if there be a new and uninhabited country found out by English subjects, as the law is the birthright of every subject, so, wherever they go, they carry their laws with them, and therefore such new-found country is to be governed by the laws of England." However, a different position prevailed if a country was conquered rather than settled. If so, the governance of that country was within the royal prerogative, and the king could impose upon them whatever law he chose to make. Until such times as the king did make new law, however, the laws and customs of the conquered country would remain in force: "unless where these are contrary to our religion, or enact any thing that is malum in se, or are silent."

The identification of the new Australian colonies as being settled, rather than conquered, meant that there was no place for Aboriginal native title to land, [20] nor for the recognition of Aboriginal custom or law. [21] This identification of New South Wales as a settled territory was confirmed by the Privy Council in *Cooper v Stuart* (1889). [22] Lord Watson, speaking for their Lordships in that case, said:

"There is a very great difference between the case of a Colony acquired by conquest or cession, in which there is an established system of law, and that of a Colony which consisted of a tract or territory practically unoccupied, without settled inhabitants or settled law, at the time when it was peacefully annexed to the British dominions. The Colony of New South Wales belongs to the latter class."

This was in stark contrast to other British colonies which were not treated as settled and in which recognition of local customary law continued after English rule came.

5.1.3   The abolition of the doctrine of terra nullius

The failure of Australian law to recognise the possibility of Aboriginal native title lasted until 1992, when the doctrine of terra nullius was swept away in a landmark decision of the High Court of Australia, *Mabo v Queensland (No 2)*.[23] Long before then, the doctrine had come under attack. For even if the doctrine of terra nullius were accepted on its own terms, there was abundant evidence that the European settlers had failed to see the political organisation and legal system at work in Aboriginal communities. It was quite incorrect to say that Aboriginal societies had no sense of ownership of the land, although they would have disavowed the common law association of ownership with the power of alienation. It was also quite incorrect to say that they were without organisation or laws. As Deane and Gaudron JJ said in *Mabo*[24] of the Aboriginal peoples at the time of the European settlement:

"Under the laws or customs of the relevant locality, particular tribes or clans were, either on their own or with others, custodians of the areas of land from which they derived their sustenance and from which they often took their tribal names. Their laws or customs were elaborate and obligatory. The boundaries of their traditional lands were likely to be long-standing and defined. The special relationship between a particular tribe or clan and its land was recognised by other tribes or groups within the relevant local native system and was reflected in differences in dialect over relatively short distances. In different ways and to varying degrees of intensity, they used their homelands for all the purposes of their lives: social, ritual, economic. They identified with them in a way which transcended common law notions of property or possession."

An important difference, which is common to other societies where native title is recognised, is that Aboriginal societies ordinarily saw their claim to land as being vested in the group, and not in individuals. The fact that their relationship with the land was different to prevailing notions of property in the western legal tradition should not obscure the fact that their sense of association with particular territory was as strongly felt as those who claim ownership of land in European societies.

This was finally recognised in *Mabo*, and the notion that Australia was "practically unoccupied, without settled inhabitants or settled law" was discarded.[25] The case concerned the title to their native lands of the Meriam people. They had lived on the Murray Islands in the Torres Strait long before the arrival of the Europeans, and had been in occupation of their land continuously after the islands were formally annexed by the Crown and added to the territory of Queensland in 1878. Although portions of land had been dedicated to administrative purposes, and certain land had been leased by the Crown for a sardine factory, substantially the use and enjoyment of these islands by the Meriam people had continued with little disturbance from the governing authorities after annexation. Nor did the islands have an influx of settlers from elsewhere. Indeed, many who did try to settle were expelled by the authorities.

The High Court declared that the Meriam people should be recognised as having native title to the lands on the basis of historic and continuous possession. This native title may be a communal title which rests in the community as a whole, and not necessarily with particular individuals. As Brennan J said:

> "Whether or not land is owned by individual members of a community, a community which asserts and asserts effectively that none but its members has any right to occupy or use the land has an interest in the land that must be proprietary in nature: there is no other proprietor. It would be wrong, in my opinion, to point to the inalienability of land by that community and, by importing definitions of 'property' which require alienability under the municipal laws of our society, to deny that the indigenous people owned their land."[26]

The High Court held that this native title was recognised by the common law and protected by it subject only to the ultimate title which vested in the Crown as the sovereign power in the nation. Thus, the native title might be lost if the community ceased to be associated with the land, or if the Crown had acted inconsistently with the recognition of native title, as where it alienated the land to others. This occurred with respect to some areas of land on the islands. Subject to this, however, native title survived the acquisition of Australia and its neighbouring islands by the Crown, and continued to be held by native peoples unless lawfully extinguished by sale, cession or by the clear intention of the Crown in its sovereign role.

The *Mabo* case was a historic acknowledgment of the injustices which had been done to the Aboriginal people and of the dispossession of their lands which had occurred. Indeed, Deane and Gaudron JJ referred to this dispossession as "the darkest aspect of the history of this nation".[27] Although it had taken two centuries, Aboriginal claims were finally vindicated by recourse to the courts. However, it took the political process to make further progress in achieving some reconciliation between Aboriginal claims and the established rights and claims of non-Aboriginal Australians. *Mabo* had raised the possibility that Aboriginal communities on the mainland of Australia would be able to lodge similar claims in relation to Crown land. It also created some uncertainty concerning the status in particular of mining leases on Crown land which might be subject to native title claims. The result of more than a year of discussion and debate concerning *Mabo* was that comprehensive legislation was passed by the federal Parliament just before Christmas in 1993 following extensive negotiations with Aboriginal leaders and with those parts of the white community which were most affected by claims to native title. The *Native Title Act* 1993 (Cth) places on a statutory basis the recognition of native title, and provides for a Native Title Tribunal to evaluate claims. In certain circumstances, compensation may be paid to Aboriginal communities which have been dispossessed from traditional land.

5.2   From Autocratic Rule to Responsible Government

5.2.1   The convict colony

In the early years of the colony, the priorities were first and foremost survival in the harsh conditions of the country, and the establishment of New South Wales as a working convict settlement. In this early period, the colony was essentially under the personal rule of the Governor with the assistance of the army. If it was not a colony under martial law—and for the most part it was not—in its earliest years it was a colony under military command, in which the major institutions were dominated by the Governor and his corps of soldiers.

Despite this, thought had been given in the establishment of New South Wales to the development of a colony which had some of the central features of civil rule, notably the application, so far as it was possible, of English law, and the provision of a civil and criminal court system. It was to be a colony established by proper legal authority, and one in which some semblance of the rule of law prevailed. The first Charter of Justice for New South Wales, established by Letters Patent of 2 April 1787,[28] provided for a court of civil jurisdiction consisting of the Judge-Advocate and two other "fit and proper persons". This had the authority to determine all pleas of a civil nature, such as disputes arising out of contracts, debts, trespasses or cases concerning land. It also had jurisdiction in relation to wills and intestate estates. This court was created by the royal prerogative. There was also a court of criminal jurisdiction, which was established by the same Letters Patent, but also had a statutory basis in the *Act Constituting a Court of Criminal Judicature in New South Wales* (1787).[29] The Letters Patent provided for the court to consist of the Judge-Advocate and six military officers. The Governor also had the power of declaring martial law in times of invasion or at other times when it might lawfully be declared according to English law, and martial law was indeed declared on several occasions in the first few years of the colony.[30]

In addition to the rudimentary courts, the Letters Patent of 1787 provided for justices of the peace to exercise a similar authority to those in England. The Governor, Lieutenant-Governor and Judge-Advocate were all ex-officio justices, and other officials were appointed as justices. It was an honorary position, as in England, but justices nevertheless played a vital role not only in the administration of justice but also in the government of the colony as a whole, especially in more remote districts. They dealt with minor criminal offences, and also disciplinary offences by convicts. Governor Macquarie entrusted them with the responsibility for dealing with matters concerning the wages of free men and apprentices.

The court system was established from the beginning of the colony's existence. This criminal court first sat on 11 February 1788. It was clear from the beginning that before punishment could be meted out to convicts for infringements of the law, there had to be a proper criminal trial.

The criminal court differed in numerous respects from criminal courts in England. There was, of course, no jury, only a panel of military officers. Indictments were drawn up by the Judge-Advocate who thus fulfilled a role associated with the prosecution, as well as being a member of the panel which decided the case. Furthermore, nobody was in the position of a judge giving instructions to the jury on matters of law. The Judge-Advocate voted on matters of guilt and innocence along with the other members of the panel. Ellis Bent, the first legally qualified Judge-Advocate, drew attention to these anomalies in a letter sent to London in 1811:

> "The Judge-Advocate is president of the court; and it is his duty to examine the depositions taken (perhaps by himself) upon the committal of offenders, to prepare the informations upon which they are to be tried, to cause the necessary witnesses to be summoned, to exhibit those informations to the court, to conduct and make minutes of the trial, to take down the evidence, to make such observations thereon to the other members of the court, as he may deem expedient, to pronounce the judgment of the court, to make up the record of the conviction or acquittal of the prisoners, and to take charge of all the records of the court . . . The Judge-Advocate is thus at once, the Committing Magistrate, Public Prosecutor and Judge; and he is called upon to decide the legality of the informations drawn up and exhibited by himself."[31]

Despite these important differences between the criminal law process in an English court and the structure of the criminal court in New South Wales, the 1787 legislation did at least require the court to apply most other aspects of English criminal procedure.[32]

The civil court also sat within a few months of the establishment of the colony. Indeed, the first civil case shows the extent to which even convicts were treated as having legal rights and could seek to vindicate those rights before the courts. This case was brought in July 1788 by two convicts, Henry and Susannah Kable, against Captain Sinclair, the captain of one of the ships of the First Fleet. They claimed the loss of a parcel of clothes and other items worth 15 pounds. It was proved that the parcel was loaded on board the ship Alexander before they set sail in 1787, but the parcel was missing when they landed in New South Wales. Damages of 15 pounds were awarded to them against the ship's captain. [33] The case is remarkable since the doctrine of attainder in English law provided that as convicted felons, they had lost all civil rights and were not entitled to the protection of the courts. By overlooking this problem, the court established early in the life of the new colony that convicts would be able to use the civil law in their favour. Inasmuch as the case was brought by convicts against as powerful a man as a ship's captain, it also showed that the principle of equality before the law was taken seriously even in a new penal settlement 12,000 miles from Britain.

Nonetheless, despite these signs of a rudimentary legal system, the colony remained in essence one which was under military control, especially in the first few years of its existence. Indeed, for nearly three years, between the departure of Governor Phillip and the arrival of Governor Hunter in 1795, the colony was administered by the New South Wales Corps, which dispensed largely with the niceties of civil justice and created conditions conducive to its own prosperity.

Certain reforms of the civil jurisdiction were made by Letters Patent in 1814, [34] following recommendations by Ellis Bent, the Judge-Advocate, which were endorsed by Governor Macquarie. [35] A Supreme Court was established, but it differed in significant respects from the superior courts in England. The government did not take the opportunity to introduce juries even for civil cases. Furthermore, and by contrast to England, the judge was required to sit with two magistrates appointed by the Governor. The court was also given a jurisdiction in equity for the first time.

5.2.2   The Governor's authority and the rule of law

In many respects, government by prerogative rule was a necessity in the early years of the colony. The Governor needed to have broad powers in what was for all intents and purposes an open prison. There was no body with which the Governor shared responsibility, such as an Executive Council, nor a legislature. However, this did not mean that the Governor was in the same position as an autocratic ruler. The Governor's powers were limited by his commission, and by the existence of the courts. Especially after the first legally qualified judge arrived in the colony in 1810, the courts acted as a check upon arbitrary and autocratic rule. If a direct and public challenge to the authority of the Governor was likely to be an uncommon event in the political circumstances of early New South Wales, and the Governor was immune from civil suit in the colony, governors were also mindful of the fact that they could be sued in the English courts after their return to Britain. [36]

One particular limitation on the Governor's authority was that he had no legislative powers. This in itself caused numerous difficulties in circumstances where what needed to be done for the practical governance of the colony did not fall within the powers which were conferred on the Governor. Communications with London were too slow to make referral to England a viable option on a regular basis. In practice, governors did legislate, although they did not term their actions as being legislative. By orders and proclamations, governors created new offences. For example, treating Aboriginals with "inhumanity or injustice" was made an offence.[37]

This practice did not pass without criticism. Although successive governments connived at the orders and proclamations emanating from the Governor, Ellis Bent, who became Judge-Advocate of the colony in 1810 when Lachlan Macquarie became Governor, was critical of the de facto legislative power which the Governor exercised, and found that not infrequently, there was a conflict between his duty to administer the law, and his duty to obey the Governor.[38] If there was doubt about the legal validity of many of the Governor's edicts, there was especially reason to doubt that he had power to impose taxation on the importation of spirits and tobacco, for the cry of "no taxation without representation" evoked memories of the important constitutional conflicts of Britain in the 17th century,[39] and was reminiscent of some of the complaints of the American colonies. The disputes between Governor Macquarie and the courts continued when Ellis's brother Jeffery arrived as a judge in the colony in 1814. The conflict between Macquarie's perceived need to legislate for the proper administration of the colony, and the Bents' strict adherence to the requirements for lawful authority, reached such a level of intensity that it could only be resolved with the dismissal of the two judges by the Colonial Secretary in London.[40] While Macquarie won this battle, he in turn was rebuked by the Colonial Secretary and reminded that the law was the only true foundation of authority.[41]

The problems encountered by Governor Macquarie, combined with influential voices in England such as Jeremy Bentham,[42] led to a review of the constitutional situation. As the colony increased in size, wealth and complexity, it became increasingly apparent that the colony had outgrown the constitutional structures which had seemed appropriate to the establishment of a convict settlement. By 1819, the first generation of children born to the English settlers had reached adulthood, and less than 40 per cent of the population of the colony were convicts.[43] Furthermore, the civil and criminal courts which were established by the Letters Patent and the Act of 1787, were quite inadequate for the needs of a growing colony, and indeed defective from the point of view of a fair trial in numerous fundamental aspects. There was no right to a jury trial, although Hunter, Bligh, King and Macquarie, as Governors, had all recommended the introduction of civilian juries, rather than having the court staffed by military officers. There was ample evidence, especially during the years when the colony was dominated by the Rum Corps, that a criminal court staffed by military personnel was open to bias and manipulation.

Pressure for change came particularly from the emancipists, those who had come to New South Wales as convicts, but who had stayed on in the colony after their terms of sentence had expired. Involvement in trade and commerce, together with the opportunities for the ownership of land which the colony's expansion provided, allowed a small number of emancipists to achieve considerable wealth, and Governor Macquarie, at least, allowed them to aspire to positions of influence in the colony. Increasingly, they campaigned for change to bring New South Wales more into line with the rights and freedoms which citizens enjoyed in England. A petition by the Emancipists to the Prince Regent in England for trial by jury in 1819, likened the criminal courts in New South Wales to a court-martial rather than a court of law. [44] One of their leaders was William Charles Wentworth. He was not himself an emancipist, although he readily associated with them. He was the son of a convict mother and a father who had been tried for highway robbery in England, but acquitted. Wentworth, who was born in New South Wales, read for the bar in London, and in 1819 published a book advocating constitutional reforms including the right to jury trial and the establishment of a bicameral legislature with an elected lower house. [45]

In their campaigns for change, the emancipists and their supporters appealed to the moral values and political principles of the English legal tradition. Even those who had suffered most at the hands of an often brutal criminal justice system, saw the legal tradition as something to be believed in, and claimed it as a birthright. As David Neal observes:

"While new and unusual circumstances called for some reorientation of the rule of law model, they drew upon this heritage when confronted by the problems of establishing a new political order. Like their 17th century forebears, they summoned up the ancient constitution, their birthright and inheritance, rather than adopting the revolutionary road and philosophical schemes of the French or American revolutions . . . When the Emancipists came to assert their political claims, they did not plead the rights of man. Rather they pleaded that the terms of their pardons restored them to all their British rights and liberties, and the Magna Carta's guarantee of trial by jury." [46]

Apart from the invocation of the Magna Carta, the emancipists also appealed to the constitutional position in England established by the 17th century conflicts in support of government by representation. In his book, Wentworth went as far as to threaten that New South Wales might make overtures to the United States or might declare independence if the British government did not implement reforms, but, in the main, his book was couched in positive terms as an appeal for the same rights and liberties as existed in other colonies. [47]

In opposition to the emancipists were the exclusives, those who had come to New South Wales as free settlers, and who opposed changes which would give to former convicts a greater degree of influence in the government of the colony.

In 1818, following agitation within the English Parliament concerning the affairs of the colony, the British government appointed John Bigge, a former Chief Justice of Trinidad, to report on the situation in New South Wales. Commissioner Bigge visited New South Wales for 18 months, and produced substantial reports on the colony in 1822 and 1823 which, among other things, recommended reforms to give the Governor some lawmaking authority. He also recommended a restructuring of the courts. The result was the passing of an Act in 1823 "for the better administration of justice in New South Wales and Van Diemen's Land, and for the more effectual government thereof".[48] This came to be known as the "New South Wales Act". As its long title indicated, the Act introduced reforms both to the court system and to the governance of the colony. The reforms were modest, but they set New South Wales and Van Diemen's Land on a path towards representation in government, and the establishment of legal institutions which reflected those existing in England.

5.2.3   The reforms of 1823

The 1823 Act had a number of effects. First, it authorised the establishment of Van Diemen's Land as a separate colony, which occurred in 1825. Secondly, it established a court system which reflected much more closely the English model than had been the case hitherto, and gave to the Supreme Court the same status and authority as was enjoyed by the superior courts at Westminster. In this respect, the Act was only intended as an interim measure, but its provisions in relation to the courts were essentially confirmed by the *Australian Courts Act* of 1828.

The 1823 Act abolished the Criminal Court and the First Supreme Court which was established in 1814. It authorised instead, the creation of two new Supreme Courts, one in New South Wales and one in Van Diemen's Land. Section 2 of the 1823 Act declared that the courts "shall have cognizance of all pleas, civil, criminal and mixed, and jurisdiction in all cases whatsoever, as fully and amply . . . as His Majesty's Court of King's Bench, Common Pleas and Exchequer at Westminster." Additionally, the Act authorised the creation of other inferior courts based upon English models, as the need arose.

The creation of a Supreme Court with all the powers of the courts at Westminster was an important step forward in the normalisation of the legal system in the colony. Nonetheless, even after 1823, the legal system in New South Wales did not afford to its citizens the same protections as existed in the English system. In particular, the colonial authorities were reluctant to grant general trial by jury, in part because of tensions between the exclusives and emancipists. Bigge had recommended that jury trials should not be introduced until the distinctions between free settlers and emancipists had faded away. There was a concern that law suits and criminal trials would assume the character of a party quarrel.[49] There was also a question of whether emancipists should be allowed to serve on juries.

The 1823 Act did allow for the use of civilian juries in civil cases if the parties together agreed to this, but for criminal cases, the jury was to consist of seven military officers. The *Australian Courts Act* of 1828 went further than the 1823 Act, by empowering a judge to order a jury trial in civil cases on the application of either party. Further, it authorised the King in Council to authorise the Governor and his Council to introduce trial by jury generally. In 1833 Governor Bourke established general use of civilian juries in criminal trials. He did so, however, only against considerable opposition from the exclusives, who had for a long time fought to keep emancipists off the jury rolls, and the option of a military jury was retained for a time to appease those who feared that a civilian jury would be affected by the tensions between the different factions in New South Wales society. [50]

A third major effect of the 1823 Act was that it established a Legislative Council on the advice of which the Governor was empowered to make laws for the colony provided that they were not inconsistent with the laws of England. A Legislative Council was also to be established in Van Diemen's Land once it became a separate colony. This was far from a concession towards representative government. There were only five to seven members on the Council, and they were appointed by the Secretary of State. In New South Wales, the first five appointees were officials [51] who could be relied upon no doubt to endorse the proposals of the Governor. Furthermore, legislative proposals could only be initiated by the Governor. In certain circumstances he was authorised to act with the concurrence of only one other member, and the Governor had an emergency power to make laws without the consent of the Council, if necessary to deal with a rebellion or insurrection. The establishment of the Council brought more formality to the process of lawmaking than had existed when governors acted independently, but the Council did not act as a serious restriction upon the authority of the Governor. The most significant limitation was that no law could be passed by the Council unless the Chief Justice first certified that it was not repugnant to the laws of England.

Despite the lack of representation on the Legislative Council introduced by the 1823 Act, its establishment was nonetheless, the beginning of a process of reform. In 1825, the Governor's personal rule was further limited by the creation of an Executive Council composed of certain officials. Governor Darling's commission gave instructions that: "You do in all things consult and advise with [the] Council, and that you do not exercise the powers and authorities [committed to you] except by and with the concurrence of Our . . . Council." There were exceptions for certain matters, and provision was made for the Governor to act without the Executive Council in emergencies. [52] Despite the expectation that the Governor would normally act with the concurrence of the Executive Council, he did not necessarily have to act in accordance with the Council's opinion. However, he was responsible to explain to the authorities in London why he had departed from this advice. [53] The Executive Council thus was given the same kind of constitutional role within the fledgling colony as the Privy Council had in Britain. In practice, until 1856, the members of the Executive Council were generally the same men as were the Governor's official nominees in the Legislative Council, and this coincidence of membership laid the foundations for the emergence of cabinet government in New South Wales.[54]

5.2.4   *The development of popular representation*

An expansion of the Legislative Council occurred with the passing of the *Australian Courts Act* in 1828.[55] The numbers were increased to include between ten and 15 members, and the Governor ceased to have the power to pass laws without the concurrence of the Council. Although the members continued to be nominated, and in no sense represented a cross-section of the free population of the colony, the Council was intended to have a more representative function than hitherto. Those who were not officials were expected to canvass opinions on legislative proposals, and this public discussion was encouraged by a procedure which required the Governor to publish legislative proposals at least eight days in advance of their presentation to the Council.[56] The legislation of the Council no longer needed to have the approval of the Supreme Court, but s 22 provided that if the Supreme Court declared an Act to be repugnant to the laws of England, then the Act had to be suspended and resubmitted to the Council. If it was once again passed, then it remained in force until its status was resolved by the Crown. Similar changes to those in New South Wales occurred in Van Diemen's Land.

The 1828 legislation, however, could only be an interim stage. Agitation within the colony for greater representation continued after 1828, and this pressure came in particular from the emancipists, who were challenging the control of the colony by the Governor and the exclusives. Under a system of appointment to the Legislative Council, positions which were not allocated to officials went almost invariably to the exclusives, and a Council composed in this way proved to be a brake even upon a reformist Governor such as Bourke, who was Governor of New South Wales from 1831-1838. The free settlers in the colony had everything to lose from the establishment of an elected body in which emancipists would have a decisive voice.

Of course, even among those who advocated an elected body, it was not contemplated that there should be universal suffrage, even for adult males. Voting would be restricted, as in England, to free men who satisfied certain property qualifications. On its own, however, this did not ensure that the emancipist influence in such an assembly would be limited. Many emancipists had done very well in the new colony, and if property holdings were to be the criterion for eligibility to vote, then the emancipists were not at a disadvantage. A further restriction on the development of representative government in the colony was that it scarcely existed in England. It was only after the *Great Reform Act* of 1832 in England, that the old electoral system which was so prone to manipulation and "influence" from the Crown, was swept away in a manner which required the government of the day to be responsive, in a broad sense, to its electorate. Thus, if representative government came slowly to New South Wales and the Australian colonies, this partially reflected the fact that England was only in the early stages of its own reform of the franchise.

Despite these factors which slowed the pace of change, further reform occurred in 1842, with the passing of the *Australian Constitutions Act (No 1)*.[57] This established that two thirds of the Legislative Council should be elected from amongst those men who satisfied certain property requirements. There were to be 24 elected members and 12 nominees. The Act also omitted the provisions in the 1828 Act for the Supreme Court to be able to declare an Act to be repugnant to the laws of England. However, it was assumed by the courts that an Act might still be declared to be invalid as repugnant to English law if its validity was called into question in the course of litigation.

With the passing of the 1842 Act, the Governor was, for the first time, subject to the wishes of a body over which he had little control. This body was also given some fiscal responsibility. While certain sums of money had to be allocated for the salaries of the Governor and officials, the Council nonetheless had the responsibility for the disbursement of the revenue from taxation. The provision of real fiscal responsibility to the Council gave it considerable power. The Council which came into existence after 1842 had a relationship with the Governor which replicated in some respects that between Parliament and the Stuart monarchy. By refusing to pass important financial bills, the Council was able to extract concessions from the Governor.[58] Control over the purse, even if, under the 1842 Act, it was not total, proved to be an important source of political power, and members such as Wentworth and Windeyer, who were leaders of the de facto opposition to the Governor in the Council, used it to good effect. However, the tension between Governor and Council came to be such that further reform, of one kind or another, seemed inevitable.

The 1842 legislation only applied to New South Wales, and not to Van Diemen's Land. The willingness of the British authorities to grant representation to the colonists in New South Wales was influenced in part by the fact that transportation of convicts to the colony had ceased in 1840. No such cessation applied to Van Diemen's Land, which therefore continued to have a nominated Council. Transportation to Van Diemen's Land finally ceased in 1853.[59]

In the years after 1842, the British government was aware of the need to keep the constitutional position of the various colonies under review. Not only was there Van Diemen's Land, but also the new colony of South Australia which had been established formally in 1836. In the west of the country, the Swan River Colony, established in 1829, was growing and expanding its geographical reach, while in Port Phillip, dissatisfaction with government from distant Sydney was intense. The Port Phillip community had been promised its separation from New South Wales, and to the north of Sydney as well, a new colony could be expected to come into being in the course of time.

The needs of the various colonies led to new legislation in 1850, the *Australian Constitutions Act (No 2)* (Imp).[60] This provided Van Diemen's Land, South Australia and the new colony of Victoria,[61] based on Port Phillip, with Councils on the same basis as New South Wales, having two thirds of its members elected. It also gave the various legislative councils the power to pass legislation setting up a bicameral legislature, subject to the royal assent. Thus, to a certain extent, they were given the power to devise their own constitutional arrangements for the future. It did not, however, give to the colonial legislatures all that the New South Wales colonists had wanted. In particular, it continued the system of fixed appropriations for the civil service, subject to some limited powers of alteration, and gave them no power over the revenue from Crown lands. They were thus not in full control of the revenues of the colony, and to that extent did not have fully responsible government.

As the Bill was first drafted, it provided for a federal structure, in which the colonies would elect delegates from their Legislative Councils to represent the colony at a General Assembly. This would have responsibility, in particular, for a uniform tariff. Whatever the merits of this proposal, it was years ahead of its time. The concerns of the colonists were too parochial, and their desire for autonomy for their communities too strong, to allow for them to submit the autonomy which they did have, to a federal body. As a result of this widespread opposition, the federal clauses in the Bill were withdrawn.

5.2.5   The emergence of responsible government

Full responsibility for the fiscal control of the established Australian colonies, and the management of their lands, was conceded in principle by the British government soon after the *Australian Constitutions Act (No 2)* of 1850. A change of minister at the Colonial Office brought a new willingness to cede authority to the colonies, and they were encouraged to submit draft constitutions to London for consideration. The Legislative Councils passed Acts to establish constitutions, which varied from each other in a number of ways, and these were sent on to London. In all the colonies, there was to be a bicameral legislature, but New South Wales decided upon a nominated Legislative Council as the upper house, while Victoria, South Australia and Van Diemen's Land, which became Tasmania, all had some form of elected upper house, albeit with a more limited franchise than was allowed in the lower house. Substantially, the British government was willing to approve the constitutions in accordance with the wishes of each colony, although it removed clauses which limited the powers of the Crown to veto legislation coming from colonial Parliaments. While in principle, the British authorities were willing to cede local autonomy, they were concerned to ensure that the Australian

Parliaments did not pass laws which might affect adversely the interests of the British Empire as a whole. Thus, a limitation upon the sovereignty and autonomy of the colonial legislatures was that the Governor's instructions required certain Acts to be reserved to the Crown in England for assent.[62]

The relevant Acts for New South Wales and Victoria were passed in London in 1855.[63] They needed this subsequent enactment because they went beyond the scope of legislative power conferred by the imperial legislation of 1850. The New South Wales Constitution reserved to the Crown a right to separate a northern region from New South Wales. The boundaries of the colony of Queensland were established in 1859, and it was granted a bicameral legislature in 1860. Tasmania[64] and South Australia[65] also had constitutions approved. Western Australia was eventually granted a similar constitution with a bicameral legislature in 1890.[66]

With the enactment of local constitutions, a considerable measure of autonomy was given to the local legislatures. The British government still remained as a mother Parliament, however, and retained a residual governance over the affairs of the colonies, in its imperial capacity. Control over the internal affairs of the colonies did not necessarily mean that the content of law in Australia thenceforward differed markedly from England. The Supreme Court judges followed English precedent without dissension in interpreting the common law. Furthermore, some Acts of Parliament which were passed at Westminster were adopted or copied without significant change in Australia, although the decision whether or not to adopt them might be a source of considerable debate.[67] Nonetheless, the new autonomy did allow the colonial legislatures to develop structures of government which were suitable to the conditions of Australia. There was extensive innovation in matters of colonial administration where the central government in each colony played a far more active role, especially in the economic life of the colony, than central government did in England. By contrast, in England there was a much more developed system of local government, enjoying a considerable measure of autonomy from the government at Westminster.[68]

Colonial Parliaments also introduced certain reforms which were not to occur in Britain until many years later. Foremost among these were electoral reforms. South Australia adopted universal manhood suffrage from the inception of responsible government. Victoria and New South Wales followed this lead soon afterwards, although the other colonies were slower to adopt this. The Australian colonies also introduced secret ballots. South Australia was in the vanguard of reform in terms of women's voting rights. It granted female suffrage in 1894, and all the Australian colonies, and the Commonwealth, had granted women the vote in relation to Lower Houses by the end of the first decade of the 20th century.

The emergence of responsible government in the 1850s allowed for the development of the cabinet system of government which is a central feature of executive government today. In New South Wales, for example, the Constitution cemented the role of the Governor-in-Council as the central repository of executive authority. While nothing in the formal constitutional documents required this, the emerging constitutional practice both in England and Australia dictated that the Executive Council should comprise the ministers of the Crown, and that they should also be members of Parliament. The Executive Council had the responsibility to advise the Governor, and in turn, the expectation was that the Governor would act on their advice. In the early years of the new constitutional order, the practice developed that the ministers would meet at some stage prior to the formal meetings of the Executive Council to determine what advice would be given to the Governor.[69] This reduced the practical significance of meetings of the Executive Council, largely, but not entirely, to being formal proceedings which ratified the decisions of the ministry made elsewhere. A similar pattern may be seen in the other colonies.[70] In this, the stage was set for a divergence between the formal repository of authority under the Constitution, and the practical repository of power in the day to day management of the affairs of the colony. This divergence between the letter of the Constitution, and the way in which the executive government operates in practice, continues to be a feature of Australian government both at State and federal levels.

5.3   English Law in Australia

5.3.1   The reception of English law

When New South Wales emerged from being a penal colony under military leadership to being a nascent civil society, questions remained about the status of English law in Australia. In theory, the designation of the Australian colonies as "settled" should have meant that English law applied from the beginning of the new colony. However, the colony was unlike others which were founded by free settlers, or gained by conquest. Its character as a penal settlement raised doubts as to the extent to which English law applied in the colony. The *Australian Courts Act* 1828 therefore endeavoured to clarify the situation.

Section 24 of the Act provided that all laws and statutes in force in England at the date of the enactment of the legislation should be applied in the courts of New South Wales and Van Diemen's Land so far as they were applicable.[71] From that date, 28 July 1828, the two colonies were placed on the same footing as any other settled colony. Since Queensland and Victoria were originally part of New South Wales, the same date applies in those States for the reception of English law. South Australia adopted a different date for reception. English law was taken to have been received as at the date of the settlement of the colony, which was designated as 28 December 1836.[72] In Western Australia, the relevant date is 1 June 1829.[73]

The significance of these dates for the future of Australian law was that all the common law and statute law which existed in England as at the relevant date was treated as being the law of the colony without the need for further enactment by the local legislature. Thus, various central constitutional laws, passed over the centuries, became part of Australian law insofar as they were still in existence in 1828,[74] as did many other important statutes, including the reforms of the criminal law initiated by Sir Robert Peel in the 1820s. The only qualification on this, and a source of some doubt, was that statutes were only received insofar as they were applicable to the situation of the colony. There were some statutes which the Supreme Court of New South Wales adjudged were not applicable in the colony as being unsuited to its conditions.[75] In one case, concerning the applicability of the English *Marriage Act* 1823 to New South Wales, Forbes CJ said:[76]

> "[To] hold that Parliament intended to force the whole mass of English laws—the laws of an old and settled society, which have grown out of occasions, during a long course of years, and are become more refined and complicated than the laws of any other country in the world—to apply all these laws at once to an infant community, without limitation or restraint, 'is a proposition much too inconvenient in its consequences to be perfectly just in its principle'."

In establishing that the common law of England, as it was established prior to 1828, was also part of the law of New South Wales and Van Diemen's Land, the 1828 legislation might be taken as meaning that new doctrines of the common law which were announced after that date by English courts should not be treated as representing the common law of Australia since they did not exist at the time that English law was received. This position, however, was never maintained. Even when apparently new doctrines were promulgated by English courts, as, for example, occurred in 1932 with the famous case of *Donoghue v Stevenson*[77] from which the modern law of negligence is derived, they were treated as being latent already within the common law at the time of reception. Thus, in *State Government Insurance Commission (SA) v Trigwell* (1979),[78] Gibbs J could say in relation to the common law of South Australia:

> "[T]he common law which was adopted is not frozen in the form which it assumed in 1836. It is the common law rules as expounded from time to time that are to be applied . . . if it is not right to say that the principle of *Donoghue v Stevenson* [1932] AC 562 became part of the law of South Australia in 1836, it is at least true to say that a body of principles, including those that developed into the rule subsequently expressed in that case, formed part of the law of South Australia from 1836 onwards."

5.3.2   The relationship between colonial and English legislation

In the 35 years which followed the passing of the *Australian Courts Act*, the relationship between colonial legislation and English law was shrouded in some uncertainty. A major reason for this was that it was not at all clear that the authority of the legislatures extended so far as to pass laws which were contrary, or "repugnant" to the principles of English law. Section 22 of the *Australian Courts Act* had seemed to imply that the validity of colonial laws rested upon their broad consistency with English law, and even though this section was not repeated subsequently, some judges struck down legislation which they regarded as repugnant to the fundamental principles of the common law, or English legislation.

A further question arose as to the status of English legislation passed after 1828. It was acknowledged, even after the first Legislative Council was set up in New South Wales, that the Westminster Parliament could still pass whatever laws it chose concerning the colony. As has been seen, even once the colonies gained their own representative Parliaments, they were still subordinate bodies, subject to governance from Westminster. It was clear that Acts of the English Parliament in its imperial role could override contrary local legislation and would apply by "paramount force". It remained to be determined nonetheless, which Acts of the Westminster Parliament did have this paramount force.

The uncertainty of the position, and in particular, problems in South Australia where the Chief Justice was prepared to strike down a considerable amount of local legislation,[79] led to the enactment of imperial legislation to clarify the position, not only for South Australia, but for all colonial legislatures. The *Colonial Laws Validity Act* 1865 (Imp), s 2, declared that colonial legislatures were only bound by statutes of the Westminster Parliament which extended to them, and which consequently applied by paramount force. Section 3 of the Act declared that no colonial law was to be regarded as void because it was repugnant to English law unless it was in relation to legislation (or regulations or orders pursuant to such legislation) which applied to the colony by paramount force. The Act thus made it clear that no colonial law was to be invalidated merely because it appeared to be inconsistent with basic principles of English law. The Act also stated that colonial legislatures had the power to amend their own constitutions, provided only that such laws were passed in accordance with the manner and form laid down by existing law.

When would an Act of the British Parliament be treated as "extending to" a colony? In *Phillips v Eyre* (1870),[80] Willes J stated that the repugnancy which makes a colonial Act void "means repugnancy to an Imperial Statute or order made by the authority of such statute, applicable to the colony by express words or necessary intendment". The possibility that an Act might apply by "necessary intendment" made the application of the *Colonial Laws Validity Act* less certain than it would otherwise have been. However, there were English statutes, notably concerning maritime law, which had for many years regulated shipping throughout the empire, and it was Acts such as these which were deemed to apply by necessary intendment.[81]

The *Colonial Laws Validity Act* was welcomed in the colonies at the time as a clarification of the legal position and a confirmation of the broad scope of autonomy conferred upon colonial legislatures. It was clear that English legislation enacted after 1828 would need to be adopted specifically in each Australian colony unless it applied by paramount force. Equally, it meant that repeals of existing English law would not apply in the Australian colonies unless replicated in the colonies. Thus, the conferral of legislative autonomy meant that anachronistic laws could survive in the colonies, by intention or by oversight, long after their sensible repeal in the United Kingdom.

The position of English statutory laws as part of the law of Australia has been clarified in certain States by legislation which re-enacts those English statutes, or parts thereof, which are still relevant in Australia, while repealing all other English statutes. For example, the *Imperial Acts Application Act* 1969 (NSW) confirmed some pre-1828 English Acts as applying in their entirety in New South Wales, re-enacts various other ancient legislation, and repeals everything else which would otherwise form part of the law of the State, as being inherited from Britain. These English laws therefore remain part of the law of New South Wales by re-enactment of the New South Wales Parliament, and not merely because they were received as part of the law of the colony in 1828.

NOTES

1. *Report from the Select Committee of the House of Commons on Transportation* (London, 1838), extracted in Bennett, J M and Castles, A C, *A Sourcebook of Australian Legal History* (Law Book Co, Sydney, 1979), p 2.
2. See Hay, D, Linebaugh, P and Thompson, E P (eds), *Albion's Fatal Tree: Crime and Society in 18th Century England* (Allen Lane, London, 1976).
3. 9 Geo 1 c 22.
4. Thompson, E P, *Whigs and Hunters: The Origin of the Black Act* (Allen Lane, London, 1975).
5. Hughes, R, *The Fatal Shore* (Pan Books, London, 1988), pp 35-36.
6. Ibid, p 37.
7. 39 Eliz c 4.
8. Hughes, R, op cit, pp 71-74.
9. Castles, A C, *An Australian Legal History* (Law Book Co, Sydney, 1982), p 32.
10. Ibid, p 24.
11. Its full title was *The Law of Nations or the Principles of the Natural Law Applied to the Conduct and Affairs of Nations and Sovereigns*, reflecting the influence of natural law ideas upon international law. See further, above, Chapter 2.
12. Vattel, E, *The Law of Nations*, Bk 1, Ch 18 in Bennett, J M and Castles, A C, op cit, pp 250-252. See also McRae, H, Nettheim, G and Beacroft, L, *Aboriginal Legal Issues* (Law Book Co, Sydney, 1991), pp 76-78.
13. See above, Chapter 2.

14. Vattel's writings offered a justification for colonising part of the continent, but they did not justify the expropriation of the whole continent. See Reynolds, H, *The Law of the Land* (Penguin, Ringwood, 1987), p 18.
15. Castles, A, op cit, p 22.
16. Ibid, p 23.
17. Extracted in Reynolds, H, *Dispossession* (Allen and Unwin, Sydney, 1989), p 2.
18. *R v Jack Congo Murrell* (1836) Legge 72. See further, Bridges, B, "The Extension of English Law to the Aborigines for Offences Committed Inter-se, 1829-1842" (1973) 59 *Journal of the Royal Australian Historical Society* 264 at 267.
19. (1722) 2 Peer William's Reports 75; 24 ER 646.
20. *Millirpum v Nabalco Pty Ltd* (1971) 17 FLR 141.
21. The explorer, Edward Eyre, acknowledged the failure to recognise Aboriginal customs and laws as one of the reasons for frontier conflict with settlers, when he wrote in his journals of expeditions of discovery in 1845 that: "as we ourselves have laws, customs, or prejudices, to which we attach considerable importance, and the infringement of which we consider either criminal or offensive, so have the natives theirs, equally perhaps, dear to them, but which, from our ignorance or heedlessness, we may be continually violating, and can we wonder that they should sometimes exact the penalty of infraction? Do we not do the same?" Extracted in Reynolds, H, *Dispossession*, op cit, p 27.
22. (1889) 14 App Cas 286 at 291.
23. (1992) 175 CLR 1.
24. Ibid at 99-100.
25. *Cooper v Stuart* (1889) 14 App Cas 286 at 291. For a discussion of the meaning of terra nullius, and the abandonment of this doctrine in *Mabo* see Simpson, G, "Mabo, International Law, Terra Nullius and the Stories of Settlement: An Unresolved Jurisprudence" (1993) 19 Melbourne ULR 195.
26. (1992) 175 CLR 1 at 51.
27. Ibid at 109.
28. Extracted in Bennett, J and Castles, A, op cit, pp 19-22.
29. 27 Geo III c 2 (1787).
30. Castles, A, op cit, pp 40ff.
31. Cited in Melbourne, A C V, *Early Constitutional Development in Australia* (2nd ed, Joyce, R B, ed, University of Queensland Press, St Lucia, 1963), pp 37-38.
32. See Neal, D, *The Rule of Law in a Penal Colony* (Cambridge UP, Cambridge, 1991), pp 89-90.
33. This account is taken from Neal, D, op cit. The case was remarkable in many other respects, including the fact that the couple were sent to New South Wales together, and the parcel was the fruit of donations by members of the public who had learned of their plight. See further, Neal, D, op cit, Ch 1.
34. This came to be known as *The Second Charter of Justice for New South Wales*. For extracts, see Bennett, J and Castles, A, op cit, pp 31-37.
35. Melbourne, A C V, op cit, pp 41-45.
36. Only a few years before the establishment of New South Wales, the Governor of Minorca had been ordered to pay a substantial sum in damages in a suit for wrongful imprisonment brought after he returned to England. *Mostyn v Fabrigas* (1773) Cowp 161; 98 ER 1021. See Neal, D, op cit, p 76.
37. Castles, A, op cit, p 35.
38. McMinn, W G, *A Constitutional History of Australia* (Oxford UP, Melbourne, 1979), pp 5-6.
39. See above, Chapter 4.
40. The issue which brought matters to a head was whether emancipist lawyers were entitled to practice before the Supreme Court. Emancipist lawyers had been practising for a number of years in the absence of freemen who were legally qualified. However, when two solicitors were sent out to New South Wales, Justice Jeffery Bent held out against the admission of the emancipists to practice in the court.
41. See Neal, D, op cit, pp 95-105.
42. Bentham published a pamphlet in 1803 entitled *A Plea for a Constitution* in which he detailed many of the constitutional defects in New South Wales.
43. McMinn, W, op cit, pp 12-13.
44. Neal, D, op cit, pp 166ff.
45. The book, entitled *A Statistical, Historical and Political Description of the Colony of New South Wales*, was published while Wentworth was in London reading for the bar.

46. Neal, D, op cit, pp 76-77.
47. Melbourne, A C V, op cit, pp 65-72.
48. (1823) 4 Geo IV c 96.
49. McMinn, W, op cit, p 25.
50. See further Neal, D, op cit, Ch 7.
51. Ibid, p 21.
52. Finn, P, *Law and Government in Colonial Australia* (Oxford UP, Melbourne, 1987), p 35.
53. Lumb, R, *The Constitutions of the Australian States* (5th ed, University of Queensland Press, St Lucia, 1991), pp 10-11. In fact, Governor Darling ignored these Instructions to a considerable extent, and failed to consult with the Executive Council, when he should have done, on numerous occasions. Melbourne, A C V, op cit, pp 109-110.
54. Finn, P, op cit, p 35.
55. "An Act to Provide for the Administration of Justice in New South Wales and Van Diemen's Land", 9 Geo IV c 83.
56. McMinn, W, op cit, p 26.
57. 5 and 6 Vic c 76.
58. See further, McMinn, W, op cit, pp 36-39.
59. The last convict ship sailed in November 1852, and in 1853, the British government rescinded its orders which had made Van Diemen's Land a convict repository. By this stage Western Australia had been opened up as a new repository for convicts, to supply much needed labour there. Transportation to all parts of Australia only ceased in 1868 with the arrival of the last convicts to be sent to Western Australia.
60. 13 and 14 Vic c 59. This is also known as the *Australian Colonies Government Act*.
61. The colony formally came into existence as being separate from New South Wales in 1851.
62. For a discussion of the relations between the colonial legislatures and the imperial Parliament, see Lucy, R, "The Division of Powers Between the British Empire and Its Self-governing Colonies, 1855-1900" (1990) 6 Aust J of L & Soc 83.
63. *Constitution Act* 1855 (NSW); *Constitution Act* 1855 (Vic).
64. *Constitution Act* 1854 (Tas).
65. *Constitution Act* 1855 (SA).
66. *Constitution Act* 1890 (WA).
67. See, eg, the enactment of divorce legislation, following the passage of the *Matrimonial Causes Act* 1857 in England. While some States enacted legislation in the same terms soon after the Act was passed in England, New South Wales took another 15 years to pass similar legislation. See Parker, S, Parkinson, P and Behrens, J, *Australian Family Law in Context* (Sydney, Law Book Co, 1994), Ch 3.
68. See Finn, P, op cit.
69. Ibid, pp 45-46.
70. Ibid, pp 81, 86ff, 120ff.
71. 9 Geo IV c 83, s 24.
72. *Acts Interpretation Act* 1915 (SA), s 48.
73. *Interpretation Act* 1918 (WA), s 43.
74. For example, the *Act of Settlement* 1701, 12 & 13 Will III c 2. See further, above, Chapter 4.
75. *Macdonald v Levy* (1833) 1 Legge 39; *R v Maloney* (1836) 1 Legge 74; *R v Schofield* (1838) 1 Legge 97; *Ryan v Howell* (1848) 1 Legge 470.
76. *R v Maloney* (1836) 1 Legge 74 at 77.
77. [1932] AC 562.
78. (1979) 142 CLR 617 at 625. See also *Dugan v Mirror Newspapers Ltd* (1978) 142 CLR 583.
79. Benjamin Boothby was appointed to be the Chief Justice of South Australia by the British government in 1853. For a discussion of the conflicts between him and the South Australian Parliament, see Castles, A, op cit, pp 406-408.
80. (1870) LR 6 QB 1 at 20-21.
81. A particular difficulty arose in cases where an Act of the Westminster Parliament was intended to apply to the colonies, but the repeal of the same Act, or a clause within it, did not apparently have an imperial reach. For example, in *Bistricic v Rokov* (1976) 135 CLR 552, the High Court held that a shipowner was entitled to the benefit of a clause in the *Merchant Shipping Act* 1894 (Imp) which placed a limitation on damages recoverable by an injured crew member, because the repeal of that limitation in an 1858 Act of the British Parliament showed no intention of extending to New South Wales. See also *China Ocean Shipping Co v South Australia* (1979) 145 CLR 172.

Chapter 6

AUSTRALIAN FEDERATION AND THE PATH TO LEGAL INDEPENDENCE

6.1 The Movement Towards Federation

6.1.1 The beginnings of the federal idea

From 1788-1855, the development of constitutional law in Australia had progressed to a stage where out of the original penal colony of New South Wales, there had emerged a number of colonies each of which had a bicameral legislature and responsible government. Additionally, in Western Australia, another colony was developing, centred upon the area of the Swan River. Already, by 1847, there was some discussion of a federal structure, but the impetus for this came from Britain rather than the Australian colonies. Earl Grey, as Colonial Secretary, had tried to introduce such a structure in the Bill which later became the *Australian Constitutions Act* 1850, in order to promote inter-colonial co-operation, especially over such matters as tariffs. However, 1850 was too early for the colonies to consider federation. Port Phillip had only then been conceded a separate existence as its own colony of Victoria. South Australia prided itself on its differences as a colony with only free settlers, and Western Australia was just beginning to become a place for transportation of convicts at the very time when this was ceasing in Van Diemen's Land, and had already ceased in New South Wales.

It was another 50 years before the Australian colonies were to become a federation. For much of this period, the various colonies were consumed by internal political problems such as land policy and electoral reform. There were, however, numerous issues on which inter-colonial co-operation was necessary or desirable. Chief amongst the problems was that of customs tariffs at colony borders. These were resolved to a certain extent by compacts and compromises, but they were likely to continue as a source of friction between the colonies for as long as protectionist ideas flourished in other parts of the world—as they did in the late 19th century. Victoria, in particular, adopted a protectionist policy from the middle of the 1860s, in order to protect its local industries which were suffering from a severe downturn following the end of the gold-mining boom. By contrast, there was a strong ideological commitment in New South Wales to free trade. The problem of customs duties, thus represented both a reason for federation, and an obstacle to it. Federation had the potential to ensure that throughout the continent, trade and commerce would be unaffected by customs tariffs

148

imposed between the colonies. However, a federated Commonwealth would need to determine whether its tariff policy with regard to imports from overseas would be protectionist or free trade. Complicating the picture was the fact that customs tariffs were not only a means of protecting local industry, but also the main source of income for the colonial governments. Thus, while Victoria and New South Wales were opposed to one another in their philosophy about trade, both in fact had tariffs; one was designed to protect local industry, while in the other, customs duties were fixed as a source of governmental revenue. [1]

These were not the only tensions which inhibited federation. The colonies also had to be persuaded that federation was in their interests. For those colonies which were smaller in population, there was the potential for losing their identity in the larger mass, and being dominated by New South Wales. For the larger colonies there was the possibility that they could be required to subsidise the struggling economies of Tasmania and South Australia, and, if it joined, Western Australia. Furthermore, the experience of other federations in the second half of the 19th century was less than inspiring. In particular, the United States had experienced a traumatic civil war.

If there were reasons to be cautious about federation, there were other factors which drew the colonies closer together. Fear of common enemies was one cause of co-operation between the rival colonies. The expansion of German interests in the South Pacific, and the activities of the French, led to the formation of a body to represent the affairs of the Australasian colonies in their relations with the South Pacific islands. Formally established in 1885, the founding members of the Federal Council of Australasia were Victoria, Tasmania, Queensland, Western Australia and Fiji. South Australia joined later, for a short period, but New South Wales and New Zealand were not involved. The Federal Council had the power to pass Bills in relation to such matters as the exclusion of criminals, extradition, the enforcement of judgments beyond the borders of a colony and the regulation of fisheries. It was the first major form of inter-colonial co-operation, and a movement towards closer ties was encouraged by an increasing nationalism amongst Australians, the great majority of whom were native born. However, for as long as New South Wales remained outside of the Council, it could not be an effective federal voice; New South Wales preferred to deal with its problems alone and was large enough to do so.

6.1.2   *The constitutional conventions*

It was in the course of the 1890s that serious proposals were developed for a federation. [2] Henry Parkes, the Premier of New South Wales, was instrumental in encouraging this further discussion. He involved leaders of the other colonies in attending a conference in Melbourne in 1890, which led to the National Australasian Convention, meeting in Sydney in 1891.

New Zealand was represented at both the conference and the Convention, although there was no great likelihood that it would want to enter into the proposed federation, and its delegates realised that their participation was mainly as interested observers.

A basic question for the delegates to these assemblies was how to structure a federation within the Westminster tradition of government. Britain, of course, could provide no experience with federation, since the Scots, the Welsh and the Irish were part of a United Kingdom, not a federated one. The prospect of federation created both the opportunity and the necessity for Australians to fashion their own political order without reliance upon British models, and to adopt forms of government which were most suitable for Australian circumstances. Canada did offer an example of federation within a Westminster system of government. The *British North America Act* 1867, which had formed the Canadian provinces into a federation, provided a model with respect to the relations between the federation and the Crown within the context of the Empire. However, there was less enthusiasm for other aspects of the Canadian approach. In particular, it was considered by the smaller Australian colonies that the Canadian Constitution gave far too much power to the central government. In its division of legislative powers between the provinces and the federal government, it had enumerated a list of powers given to the centre and a list of powers retained by the provinces. All other powers were to be exercised centrally. Parkes put forward as a central proposition at Sydney that "the powers and privileges and territorial rights of the several existing Colonies shall remain intact, except in respect to such surrenders as may be agreed upon as necessary and incidental to the power and authority of the National Federal government."[3]

Although Switzerland provided another example of a federation, it was inevitable that the delegates should look to the Constitution of the United States as the other major model of a federation within the English-speaking world. The American Constitution provided an example for the protection of States' rights. It gave just a few powers to the federal government and left the majority of matters within the legislative competence of the States. It also provided that the Senate should consist of an equal number of members from each State while the House of Representatives should reflect the national distribution of population. It was early perceived that a suitable constitution for Australia would marry the American concept of a Senate representing each State equally, with the Westminster system of government by which the government of the day, with its ministers drawn from the ranks of the Parliament, would be required to maintain the confidence of a popularly elected lower House.

Proposals on these lines were submitted to the 1891 Convention. Parkes, as Chairman, moved various resolutions which had resulted from an informal gathering of almost all the premiers and other leading figures who were to be involved in the Convention. Trade between the federated colonies would be absolutely free. Customs duties would be levied exclusively by the federal government, and the revenue which was not required by the Commonwealth would be distributed to the States. It was assumed that the Commonwealth would require comparatively little money, and taxation was not seen at the time as a significant source of government revenue. It was proposed that specified powers should be given to the federal legislature, including defence, while all other powers should remain with the federated colonies. There was to be a bicameral Parliament, with a House of Representatives and a Senate. Thus, the proposed bicameral Parliament was to adopt the nomenclature of the American Congress. The House was to be elected by districts drawn up on the basis of population, while in the Senate there was to be equal representation for each "province". There was also to be a Federal Supreme Court which would act as a final court of appeal for Australia. The executive government should consist of the Governor-General, "and such persons as may from time to time be appointed as his advisers, such persons sitting in Parliament" and whose term of office would depend upon their maintaining the confidence of the House of Representatives.[4] Thus, the assumption was that the Australian federation would adopt the Westminster system, in which the Prime Minister and the other ministers would be appointed by the representative of the Crown from among the members of the political party holding a majority in the lower House.

In these proposals, put to the Convention, can be seen the broad outline of the Constitution which was to emerge from the ensuing years of negotiation. However, there was much in the way of detail which had to be resolved before the various colonies could agree to enter into a federation. There would be strong resistance to the federation in New South Wales unless its politicians could be satisfied that the federation's tariff policy would not be protectionist. One former Victorian premier described this as "the lion in the way" of federation.[5] A further fundamental issue was how to distribute the excess customs duties from the central government to the States. Sir Samuel Griffith, sometime premier of Queensland, and later the first Chief Justice of the High Court of Australia, identified with great clarity at the Sydney Convention perhaps the greatest problem of all: how to structure the relationship between the lower and upper houses within the federal Parliament. How were they to reconcile government by a majority of the people with government by a majority of the States? If the latter consideration was important, then the Senate must be given a power of veto over bills emanating from the lower house, including money bills. Otherwise, the most populated States, Victoria and New South Wales, with their dominance in the lower house, would have effective control over the country. The smaller colonies, by and large, thus favoured a powerful Senate. In Victoria and New South Wales, however, there was great nervousness about the potential which this would create for serious conflict between the upper and lower houses. Victoria, in particular, had experienced a succession of intractable conflicts between the lower and upper houses and its delegates were extremely wary of establishing a federal constitution which would replicate the potential for similar conflicts and constitutional crises.

The 1891 Convention attempted answers to some of these questions. It produced a draft Constitution, under the guidance of Griffith, which, inter alia, enumerated a substantial list of powers which would be given to the federal government, some derived from the *British North America Act* 1867, some from the American Constitution, some from the powers of the Federal Council of Australasia, and others still which were deemed necessary by delegates. It left open the question of whether the federation would adopt the principle of responsible government since doubts were expressed about this. The draft said that ministers might sit in Parliament, but not that they needed to do so. The draft also said that the members of the Senate should be elected by State Parliaments. Further, it imposed certain restrictions on appeals to the Privy Council in London. This was a compromise position. There was considerable support for the view that appeals to the Privy Council should be abolished entirely.

The Convention agreed that this draft constitution should be submitted to the colonial Parliaments. However, the enthusiasm of some of its proponents was not matched by widespread support in the various colonies. The Convention had been attended only by parliamentary representatives. It had not galvanised popular support. Furthermore, opponents pointed out the areas in which the draft Constitution had avoided the difficult issues. The Bill lapsed in New South Wales, and the other colonies were unwilling to proceed unless and until New South Wales signalled its commitment. With the failure of the Bill in New South Wales, the Convention's work could be taken no further.

It was not until 1895 that the federation movement gained a major fresh impetus. A proposal was accepted by the premiers of the six Australian colonies to establish a new Convention by popular vote, with the resulting draft of the constitution being submitted to the electors in each colony in a referendum. The enabling Bill was to be submitted to the New South Wales Parliament first, to ensure that the largest colony was committed to the process. The Convention finally met in 1897. Internal political disputes in Queensland meant that it was not represented, and the Western Australian delegation was appointed by the State Parliament rather than elected by popular vote, since it did not pass an enabling Bill in the same terms as the other colonies. New Zealand, which had shown no interest in federation since 1891, was not involved.

The Convention held meetings over the course of a year, beginning first in Adelaide in 1897, later meeting in Sydney and culminating in Melbourne in March 1898. After the Adelaide meeting, the colonial Parliaments took the opportunity to debate the emerging Bill and to suggest changes. The draft Constitution Bill which emerged from this process was in many respects quite similar to the Bill of 1891. The basic principles which had been agreed upon in 1891 were once again adopted in 1898. Additionally, the principle of responsible government—that ministers should be drawn from Parliament and resign if they lost its confidence—was adopted without the reservations which had influenced the final wording of the 1891 draft. There was also a consensus for more democracy in the constitutional structure. It was agreed that the Senate should be chosen by popular vote with the voters in each State acting as one electorate.

However, the problem of the extent of the powers of the Senate, which had been debated extensively in 1891, continued to be a source of division in 1897-1898. Eventually, the compromise was reached that proposed laws appropriating revenue, or imposing taxation, should originate in the House of Representatives. The Senate should have no power to amend a Bill imposing taxation or appropriating revenues for the ordinary annual services of government, but it could request the House of Representatives to make changes. It could also reject such a Bill outright. In the event of any deadlock between the Houses (whether over money bills or otherwise) there should be a dissolution of both, so that the matter could be submitted to the electorate. In the event of continuing deadlock, a Bill could be passed if it achieved a three-fifths majority in a joint sitting of both Houses.

A further issue which aroused considerable debate was the question of appeals from the High Court to the Privy Council. A degree of lobbying between the Adelaide and Melbourne sessions, together with indications from London that it wished to retain the possibility of Privy Council appeals in all cases, led to the adoption of a provision that the High Court should be the final court of appeal in matters of constitutional interpretation unless the public interests of another part of Her Majesty's Dominions were involved. While allowing for other appeals from the High Court to the Privy Council, it empowered the federal Parliament to limit the matters upon which such an appeal might lie.

In the Convention, the larger colonies (Victoria and New South Wales) were outnumbered by the smaller ones, since each delegation had an equal number of members. However, before being submitted to London, the draft constitution needed to be ratified by the electorate in each colony, and this referendum allowed the opportunity for these issues to be debated afresh in the public arena. Although the 1898 Bill was a great improvement on its predecessor, still it had features about it which were disturbing to New South Wales in particular. One area of concern was about customs duties. At the insistence of the smaller colonies, a section had been inserted into the draft Constitution which provided that three quarters of the customs dues would be paid to the States. This was acceptable to New South Wales as an interim measure in order to help the smaller States put their budgets on a sound financial basis, but it was unacceptable in the longer term because a high tariff would be necessary to meet the growing financial needs of the federal government as it expanded. A second area of concern, not surprisingly, was the question of the powers of the upper house and the way in which deadlocks should be resolved. By allowing deadlocks to be resolved by a three fifths majority in a joint sitting of the Houses, it was realised that this gave disproportionate power to the smaller States to assert their will over that of the House of Representatives, which was taken to reflect the will of a majority of the population.

The referendum in June 1898 saw large majorities in favour of the Bill in Victoria, South Australia and Tasmania. In Western Australia, no referendum was held, although the Bill was considered again by Parliament. Queensland remained outside the process. In New South Wales, the Bill was passed by a small majority of those who voted, but the affirmative vote did not reach the minimum number of those eligible to vote which had been specified by the New South Wales Parliament in its enabling legislation.

The result was that further negotiations took place between the premiers, including the premier of Queensland. They agreed to amend the deadlock provision so that, following a dissolution of both Houses, only an overall majority in a joint sitting of the Houses was required to resolve the deadlock. Further, they agreed that the provision which stipulated that three quarters of the customs revenues would be given back to the States should be limited to the first ten years of federation, unless federal Parliament provided for its continuance. They added to this a seemingly innocuous proviso that the Parliament might grant financial assistance to any State on such terms and conditions as it saw fit. This was to assume a degree of constitutional importance which the premiers could never have anticipated. Other difficulties were also resolved by the premiers' conference, including the location of the seat of government within the territory of New South Wales, at least 100 miles from Sydney.

In its amended form, the draft constitution was submitted afresh to a referendum in every colony except Western Australia. This included Queensland, despite its absence from the Convention. It secured the approval of the electors, and the legislatures of each colony formally passed an Address requesting the Queen to enact the Bill in the Westminster Parliament. This was necessary, for only by an Act of the imperial Parliament could there be any legal basis for the federation of a group of colonies. Western Australia held back at that stage. The Bill as accepted by the five colonies went to Britain where a final opportunity presented itself for those who were dissatisfied with any aspect of the Bill to seek changes by lobbying the Colonial Office. The instructions given to the delegates from the Australian colonies by their governments were that they should endeavour to maintain the text as it had been put to the electors, and that they should oppose any changes suggested by the government in Britain. Nonetheless, they were reliant on the Westminster Parliament to pass the relevant legislation, and eventually, changes were forced on them.

The issue was the question of Privy Council appeals. There was disquiet among the Chief Justices of some of the colonies at the prospect that the federal Parliament could pass legislation severely curtailing the right to appeal from the High Court to the Privy Council. The result of this lobbying was that the imperial government insisted upon alterations to the relevant clause. It provided, as enacted, that on constitutional matters concerning the limits of the powers of the Commonwealth or States, no appeal should be taken to the Privy Council unless the High Court first certified that the matter should be determined by the Council. The power of the federal Parliament to curtail appeals from the High Court in other matters was retained, but any such Bills should be reserved by the Governor-General for "Her Majesty's Pleasure".[6]

Finally, the *Commonwealth of Australia Constitution Act* was passed by the British Parliament in 1900. Western Australia agreed to join the Commonwealth in time for it to be an original member at the beginning of the Federation on January 1st 1901. The Commonwealth of Australia thus came into being nearly ten years after the Convention meeting in Sydney had approved for the first time, a draft Bill for a federal constitution.

6.2   The Federal Constitution

6.2.1   *The Commonwealth of Australia Constitution Act 1900*

The *Commonwealth of Australia Constitution Act* 1900, as an Act of the British Parliament, consists of just nine sections. The first eight sections are essentially preliminary to the ninth section which contains the Constitution itself. The Constitution consists of 128 sections and is divided into eight chapters. Chapter I concerns the Parliament. Section 1 provides for the legislative power of the Commonwealth to be vested in a federal Parliament which consists of the Queen, a Senate and a House of Representatives. The role of the Queen in the legislative process lies in her responsibility to assent to legislation passed by Parliament. The power to grant the Royal Assent is normally exercised on the Queen's behalf by the Governor-General.

Section 7 provides that the senators shall be elected by popular vote, with all the people in the State voting as one electorate. Currently there are 12 senators for each State, and two senators each from the Australian Capital Territory and the Northern Territory, making a total of 76. The present system of election by proportional representation for the Senate does give much greater opportunities for smaller parties to be represented than does the "first-past-the-post" system in the House of Representatives. Section 7 also provides that the senators shall be chosen for a term of six years.

Section 24 provides that the House of Representatives should be directly elected, and should contain approximately twice the number of senators. Although constituency boundaries are drawn up to divide the population into roughly equivalent units, a minimum of five members of the House should be elected from each original State.[7] At present, there are 147 members, of which 88 come from either New South Wales or Victoria. In accordance with s 28, the House of Representatives sits for a maximum of three years.

Part V of Ch I concerns the powers of the federal Parliament. These may either be exclusive or concurrent with the States. Section 51 lists those specific matters on which the Commonwealth has the power to legislate together with the States. It is possible to have State and federal laws on the same subject, which operate without conflict with one another.[8] In the case of a conflict, s 109 provides that the law of the Commonwealth should prevail and the State law is invalid to the extent of the inconsistency. There are currently 40 "placita" in s 51. The section enumerates 36 specific powers given to the federal Parliament. In addition, there are four other placita which are more general in character. Placitum (xxxvii) allows the Parliament of the Commonwealth to legislate on matters referred to it by the Parliament of one or more States. This has made possible uniform legislation on matters such as the law concerning the custody and guardianship of children. There is also a power to legislate on matters which are "incidental" to a Commonwealth power (placitum xxxix). Section 52 specifies certain matters on which necessarily only the Commonwealth could legislate. These include laws concerning the seat of government of the Commonwealth, and matters concerning the control of the Commonwealth's public service. Other matters are made exclusive to the Commonwealth by virtue of other sections of the Constitution. For example, s 90 gives it exclusive power to impose duties of customs and excise, while ss 114 and 115 prohibit the States from raising or maintaining any military force without the consent of the Commonwealth, or coining money.

Other provisions in Pt V of Ch I concern the powers of the Senate and House of Representatives respectively. Section 53 provides that proposed laws appropriating revenue or moneys, or imposing taxation, shall not originate in the Senate. Furthermore, the Senate "may not amend proposed laws concerning taxation, or proposed laws appropriating revenue or moneys for the ordinary annual services of the Government". It may, however, at any stage return such a law to the House of Representatives "requesting, by message, the omission or amendment of any items or provisions therein." Section 57 provides for what should happen in the event of a disagreement between the Houses. The Governor-General has the power to dissolve both Houses of Parliament simultaneously if the Senate has rejected a proposed law or failed to pass it in terms acceptable to the House of Representatives, and it is submitted again after an interval of three months and rejected a second time. If after a dissolution of both Houses, the Senate once more rejects a proposed law or passes it only with amendments which are unacceptable to the House of Representatives, the Governor-General may convene a joint sitting of the Houses. The Bill will then pass if it achieves an absolute majority of the votes of the combined Houses.

Chapter II of the Constitution concerns the powers of the executive. Section 61 provides:

> **61. Executive power** The executive power of the Commonwealth is vested in the Queen and is exercisable by the Governor-General as the Queen's representative, and extends to the execution and maintenance of this Constitution, and of the laws of the Commonwealth."

Section 62 provides for a Federal Executive Council "to advise the Governor-General in the government of the Commonwealth". The Governor-General may also appoint Ministers of State to administer the departments of State of the Commonwealth. They must be members of one or other House of Parliament, or become so within a period of three months. The Governor-General is also commander-in-chief of the armed forces.

Chapter III of the Constitution concerns the Judicature. Section 71 provides, in part:

> "The judicial power of the Commonwealth shall be vested in a Federal Supreme Court, to be called the High Court of Australia, and in such other federal courts as the Parliament creates, and in such other courts as it invests with federal jurisdiction."

This allowed for the creation of a High Court, and either the establishment of other federal courts, or the vesting of federal jurisdiction in State courts, whichever was more appropriate for the jurisdiction concerned. The modern system consists of a mixture of these two approaches. There are federal courts with a jurisdiction which is defined by legislation, and there are also certain matters concerning which State courts may exercise jurisdiction under federal law.[9]

Section 74 provides:

> "No appeal shall be permitted to the Queen in Council from a decision of the High Court upon any question, howsoever arising, as to the limits inter se of the Constitutional powers of the Commonwealth and those of any State or States, or as to the limits inter se of the Constitutional powers of any two or more States, unless the High Court shall certify that the question is one which ought to be determined by Her Majesty in Council."

The section (which was the result of the negotiations in London in 1900), thus ensured that the High Court had the final say over the interpretation of the Federal Constitution unless it permitted an appeal to the Privy Council. The wording of s 74 also ensured that on other matters, the right of appeal from the High Court to the Privy Council was unimpaired, but it allowed for the federal Parliament to pass laws limiting the matters on which leave to appeal might be sought, as long as such Bills were reserved by the Governor-General for the personal assent of the Queen. It was nearly 70 years before the federal Parliament passed legislation limiting appeals to London. First, by the *Privy Council (Limitation of Appeals) Act* 1968 (Cth) the right of appeal in matters of federal law was abolished. Then in 1975, the Commonwealth Parliament passed another Act, the *Privy Council (Appeals from the High Court) Act* 1975 which prevented appeals being taken from the High Court to the Privy Council. However, the Constitution, and these federal laws passed pursuant to it, did nothing to interfere with a litigant's right to appeal to the Privy Council on matters of State law, by-passing the High Court, since it was still open to them to appeal directly from the appeals court of a State to the Privy Council. The right of appeal to the Privy Council from State courts was only abolished in 1986.[10]

Other chapters of the Constitution concern finance and trade, the States, and other matters. There are few guarantees in the Constitution of human rights—there is no equivalent of the Bill of Rights in the American Constitution. There is an implicit guarantee in s 51(xxxi) which allows the Commonwealth to acquire property "on just terms" from a State or a person. Section 80 provides for a right of jury trial for indictable offences under Commonwealth law. A further guarantee is given in s 116 which provides that the "Commonwealth shall not make any law for establishing any religion, or for imposing any religious observance, or for prohibiting the free exercise of any religion." Despite the similarity between the wording of this section and the words of the First Amendment in the American Constitution, it has not been interpreted in the draconian way it has been in the United States to limit religious freedom in the name of a complete separation between church and state.[11] Other rights have been declared by the High Court as a matter of interpretation. A guarantee of freedom of political speech was found by the High Court to be implied in ss 7 and 24 of the Constitution concerning direct elections to Parliament, and consequently the court struck down legislation which prohibited political advertising during elections.[12] The High Court has also decided that there is a constitutional right to the recognition of interstate professional qualifications.[13]

The final chapter of the Constitution, s 128, provides for its amendment. For a constitutional amendment to pass, it must normally first gain a majority in each House of Parliament. However, there is a provision for the Governor-General to resolve a deadlock where the two Houses of Parliament cannot agree. The second stage is for the proposed alteration to be submitted to a referendum. It will pass if it receives the approval not only of a majority of the voters overall, but also majorities in a majority of the States. The Constitution has proved difficult to amend. The referendum record is that only eight out of 42 proposed amendments have passed through the referendum process.[14] The last successful amendments were in 1977.

6.2.2   *The 19th century Constitution*

The Constitution which was finally enacted in 1900, and which came into force on 1 January 1901, was the product of nearly ten years of debate, discussion and negotiation. Even after the broad outlines of the Constitution had emerged, there was much argument over the details. Without those details being resolved to the sufficient satisfaction of each colony, the federation would never have come into being. Yet many of the issues which divided the conventions so deeply reflected little more than the politics of the moment. As La Nauze observes of the 1897-1898 Convention: [15]

> "Within the lifetimes of many of the delegates it would be evident that the great matters of debate in the Convention were much less significant in the polity of the Commonwealth than many sentences, clauses, phrases and even single words on which they had spent little or no time."

However much the drafters of a constitution have their eyes upon eternity, it is inevitable that the result of their efforts will reflect the preoccupations of their own time. So it was with the federal constitution. To a significant extent, it is a colonial document, albeit that many of the framers were nationalists who were seeking a greater degree of independence for Australia within the Empire. It assumed the primacy of the imperial government[16]—full independence was not on the agenda—and reserved certain matters for the Queen's pleasure, rather than leaving the matter to the Governor-General.

That the Constitution is a product of its time may be seen in many of its sections. One of the longest debates of the 1897-1898 Convention concerned the Murray-Darling river system. New South Wales wanted to use the waters for irrigation. South Australia was concerned to preserve the water levels for the use of its paddle-wheel steamers. The resulting debate led to the enactment of s 100 of the Constitution. Within another decade, the South Australian steamboat trade was headed for extinction.[17] The provisions concerning financial matters, with their emphasis upon the distribution of customs and excise duties (ss 86-95), similarly reflect the period in which the Constitution was drafted. Customs dues are only of limited relevance to modern government, for which direct taxation is the primary source of revenue.

The issue of the powers of the Senate, and the way in which deadlocks between the Houses were to be resolved, proved to be of great importance. However, the powers of the Senate have proved important for reasons quite different to those which occupied the minds of convention delegates in the 1890s. The issue has not been the balance of power between the larger and smaller States as the Convention debates supposed. A few of the delegates could foresee this. Alfred Deakin of Victoria, one of the most influential of the participants in the Conventions, observed in the course of the Convention debates that the real issue was not where the population is, but how the population will be politically divided. Deakin foresaw, as only a few others did, that quickly the members of the federal Parliament would divide into political parties representing the traditional differences between progressives and conservatives, and that these would be the real sources of conflict both in the House of Representatives and the Senate. This has proved to be the case. In no meaningful sense does the Senate act as a States' house, although small groups representing regional or sectional interests may sometimes hold the balance of power.

Perhaps most anachronistic of all, for they were outdated long before they were enacted, are the provisions concerning the Executive. There is no mention within the Constitution of the office of Prime Minister, nor is there any reference to the Cabinet. Meetings of the Executive Council are usually perfunctory affairs in which the Governor-General meets with a couple of ministers to adopt, formally, the decisions which have been made by the government. Until an amendment in 1977, the Constitution made no reference to political parties. [18]

In nominating the Governor-General as the head of the executive, the Constitution mirrors the purely formal position of the Crown within the British Constitution, and the practical role which the Governor of New South Wales had fulfilled in the formative years of the colony. That by the 1890s, the substance of the distribution of power within the executive bore little relation to its form did not seem to matter. The executive government was to operate within the proposed federation in accordance with the same unwritten conventions and gentlemen's agreements as had marked the operation of British and colonial government hitherto. A number of reasons have been given for the approach which the drafters of the Constitution took. One is that they wanted to create a flexible structure in which the system of government could evolve and develop as was appropriate for Australian conditions. Another argument was that the well established conventions concerning the use of vice-regal powers would circumscribe their exercise sufficiently. A third reason was that a dominion Governor, unlike the monarch, would need the scope for independent judgment and initiative in order to preserve British interests or to protect the constitutional framework. [19]

That reliance upon unwritten conventions is dangerous was shown in the constitutional crisis of 1975. In that year, the Senate refused to pass the budget, thus blocking supply to the government and creating the possibility that the government would be unable to meet the wages of its employees and its other financial obligations. The Governor-General sought to resolve this constitutional crisis by dismissing the Labor government (headed by Gough Whitlam), and dissolving both Houses of Parliament. The consequence of this was that the resolution of the deadlock between the Houses was left to the electorate. In doing so, the Governor-General ignored the convention that he should act only on the advice of the Prime Minister. Literally, of course, he was within his constitutional powers. The Governor-General has the unqualified power to appoint and dismiss ministers, and the power to dissolve both Houses of Parliament. [20] Whether or not the Governor-General was within his powers as limited by unwritten convention was another matter. Conventions have an uncertain status in constitutional law. They exist in the twilight zone between political and legal obligation. The legality of the dismissal of the Whitlam government has been a source of disagreement between politicians and constitutional lawyers ever since.

6.2.3   The federal-State balance

If one of the major concerns of the framers of the Constitution was to work out a suitable balance between government by a majority of the people and government by a majority of the States, another was to ensure that the States only surrendered such powers to the Commonwealth as were necessary for its effective functioning. In the convention debates it had been axiomatic that the delegates did not want to go down the Canadian path which they saw as one in which the provinces had surrendered much of their power to the federal government.

A concern to preserve States' rights was a marked feature of the first few years of federation. [21] This was evidenced by the High Court's interpretation of the Constitution which restricted its general words so as not to limit the powers of the States. Powers were "reserved" for the States unless specifically allocated to the Commonwealth, and in case of doubt, the High Court's interpretation erred in favour of the States. Furthermore, the High Court, led by Sir Samuel Griffith, developed a doctrine of inter-governmental immunities by which the Commonwealth and the States were each treated as sovereign governments within their own spheres. The States could not legislate to burden the Commonwealth, for example, by imposing State income tax on Commonwealth employees, [22] nor could the Commonwealth legislate to burden the States, except as provided in the Constitution. The doctrine of inter-governmental immunities was abandoned in 1920, with the decision in the *Engineers Case*. [23] With its demise, implicitly the doctrine of reserve powers was abandoned as well. Instead, the view which prevailed was that the words of the Constitution should be interpreted literally. Literal interpretation has generally favoured the expansion of federal legislative power. For example, the power to legislate with respect to "external affairs" has been given a broad interpretation by the High Court, thereby enabling the federal Parliament to legislate not only concerning matters external to Australia, [24] but also in areas which would otherwise be reserved exclusively to the States. The external affairs power may be used to regulate areas which would otherwise be matters for State law as long as the legislation gives effect to an international treaty made in good faith and not for the purposes of achieving such legislative power. [25] With the growth in the number of international conventions, such as those concerning human rights, this has brought a great range of matters within the potential or actual legislative authority of the Commonwealth.

A second factor in the growth of federal power at the expense of the States was that the Constitution gave to it considerable power over the distribution of government revenues. Initially, the major source of income was customs and excise revenue which was to be levied and collected by the Commonwealth. For the first ten years, three quarters of it was to be distributed to the States, but no provision was made in the Constitution for what should happen after ten years, other than that revenue which was surplus to the requirements of the Commonwealth should be paid to the States "on such basis as [the Parliament] deems fair" (s 94). Furthermore, there was the provision in s 96 which had resulted from the premiers' agreement in 1899. It provided that "the Parliament may grant financial assistance to any State on such terms and conditions as the Parliament deems fit." Alfred Deakin saw the potential of this for control by the Commonwealth. In a letter in 1902, he wrote:

"As the power of the purse in Great Britain established by degrees the authority of the Commons, it will ultimately establish in Australia the authority of the Commonwealth. The rights of self-government of the States have been fondly supposed to be safeguarded by the Constitution. It left them legally free, but financially bound to the chariot wheels of the Central Government. Their need will be its opportunity."[26]

It was not many years before this prophecy came to pass. After the first ten years, the Commonwealth abandoned the practice of returning three quarters of the revenues to the States. Instead, it made block grants to the States on the basis of a formula. Eventually, the practice developed that the Commonwealth would also make special grants for specific purposes. Its right under s 96 to impose conditions on the use of the money gave it power to influence the way in which the money was expended. As long as the States had their own sources of revenue and were not seriously reliant on grants from the Commonwealth, this power over the purse did not matter so much. Until World War II, the States did have their own income taxes, as well as other sources of income. However, in the emergency of the war, in 1942, the Commonwealth took over the collection of income tax in spite of the resistance of the States. It did so by increasing the Commonwealth tax to a level which would produce from the taxpaying public the same amount of money as had previously been produced from the Commonwealth and State taxes combined. It encouraged the States to refrain from imposing their own taxes by assuring them that they would receive the same amount of tax income as they had been receiving before, by a block grant from the Commonwealth. It took the States' income tax departments into the Commonwealth public service. Finally, it enacted a requirement that taxpayers should pay their Commonwealth taxes before their State taxes. This scheme survived constitutional challenge in 1942,[27] and although it was initially intended to last only for the duration of the war and a short time thereafter, it was continued by subsequent governments. A further constitutional challenge occurred in 1957, and the requirement that taxpayers pay their Commonwealth tax first was struck down.[28] However, the other elements were sufficient to maintain the scheme.

The result was that the Commonwealth was left as the only collector of governments' primary source of revenue—taxation. Approximately 80 per cent of national income is collected by the Commonwealth.[29] States could have their own supplementary income taxes, but it is not politic to do so. Their revenue-raising powers are limited to such means as petrol taxes and stamp duties. In practice, the States are heavily dependent upon the amount of money they receive from Canberra each year, and are in a weak bargaining position with respect to it. One of the consequences of this is that the States experience an enormous disparity between their capacity to raise revenue and their needs.

Increasingly after World War II, the Commonwealth used its power, under s 96, to make grants on such conditions as it saw fit, in order to make extensive incursions into areas of government which the Constitution had hitherto left to the States. It did so with the support of the High Court which took the wording of the section entirely literally. In *Deputy Federal Commissioner of Taxation v Moran*,[30] decided in 1939, Latham CJ said: "The remedy for any abuse of the power conferred by s 96 is political, and not legal in character."[31] He repeated these views in the *First Uniform Tax Case* (1942) which upheld the Commonwealth's takeover of national taxation. He said that "the controversy before the court is a legal controversy, not a political controversy. It is not for this or any court to prescribe policy or to seek to give effect to any views or opinions upon policy. We have nothing to do with the wisdom or expediency of legislation."[32] The Chief Justice also acknowledged that by its control over taxation and its use of s 96, the Commonwealth could bring about a situation where all State powers were controlled by the Commonwealth, resulting in the end of the States' political independence. Nonetheless, this "cannot be prevented by any legal decision".[33]

An illustration of the reach of federal power by the use of specific grants is the area of education. The Constitution of the Commonwealth gives no power to the federal government in the area of education, but it has assumed almost complete control over universities, and also plays an important role in the funding of the school system. It does this by the use of specific purpose grants. In a case brought in 1981,[34] a challenge was made to the Commonwealth's use of specific purpose grants to the States to pass on to non-government schools. The form of the legislation left no discretion with the State governments about how the money should be distributed. All the amounts were fixed by the Commonwealth which laid down the conditions for the use of the money. The legislation was upheld as constitutionally valid by the High Court.

Thus, the Constitution has proved a relatively ineffective means of preserving States' rights. However, this is not the important issue it was in the 1890s. In some instances, the States have referred legislative power to the Commonwealth where this was in the interests of orderly government.[35] In other instances, they have co-operated with the Commonwealth to establish national schemes, such as for the cross-vesting of jurisdiction between the Supreme Courts of the States and federal courts.[36] The expansion of central government is perhaps an inevitable progression. While the framers of the Constitution of Australia had looked to the American Constitution as an example of the preservation of State powers within a federal system, the same pattern may be seen there. In particular, creative constitutional interpretation by the Supreme Court of the United States, notably of the power with respect to interstate commerce, has led to a considerable expansion in the reach of federal law. In Europe, far more diverse societies than existed in the various Australian colonies, have voluntarily surrendered individual sovereignty for the sake of the European Union.

The expansion of federal power in Australia has certainly been aided and abetted by the High Court. However, had the court been overly concerned with the intentions of the framers of the Constitution, had it been more protective of States' rights, it would have bound Australia to a 19th century worldview, and handicapped its capacity to compete in the very different conditions of the world at the end of the 20th century. The virtue of the Commonwealth constitution has been that, partly by design, but to a large extent by accident, it has allowed enough flexibility for the High Court to allow significant changes in federal-state relations.

6.3   Establishing Legislative Independence from the United Kingdom

If the Constitution of the Commonwealth of Australia was born within the context of the British Empire, it was nonetheless an important step forward in the de facto independence of the country. With the advent of the 20th century, Britain's role in the government of Australia became increasingly nominal. Although the Constitution did provide for certain federal Acts to be reserved for the Royal Assent, which at that stage would have been given or withheld on the advice of the British government, no such legislation was disallowed by the Crown, and nor has state legislation been disallowed in the 20th century.[37] Furthermore, the *Australian States Constitution Act* 1907 (Imp) limited the State governors' powers to reserve Bills for the personal assent of the Crown. It was apparent that Australia, like other parts of the empire, had come of age. Apart from insisting on Governors and Governors-General being sent out from Britain in the first part of the century, the Colonial Office increasingly recognised the autonomous status of the former colonies, which came to be called "dominions".

6.3.1   The Commonwealth and the Statute of Westminster

The status of the dominions was expressed in the Balfour Declaration, made at the Imperial Conference of 1926, which said that Great Britain and the dominions were:

"autonomous communities within the British Empire, equal in status, in no way subordinate one to another in any aspect of their domestic or external affairs, though united by a common allegiance to the Crown, and freely associated as members of the British Commonwealth of Nations."

The Report of the Conference also observed that this involved a different role and position for the Governor-General in each dominion. The Governor-General was to be a representative of the Crown, holding, in all essential respects, the same position in relation to the administration of public affairs in the dominion as the king held in Great Britain. He was not to be the representative or agent of the British government. This had the practical consequence that in future, the Governor-General would act only on the advice of his Australian ministers, and would not be required to act on the advice of the imperial government in Westminster. A further consequence of the new arrangements was that foreign affairs would be the responsibility of each dominion, separate from the foreign policy of the government of Great Britain.

There was another Imperial Conference in 1930, and the result of the negotiations was the enactment of the *Statute of Westminster* 1931 (Imp). It provided by s 4 that no British Act passed after the commencement of the statute should be deemed to extend to the dominions unless the dominion expressly requested and consented to this. Furthermore, s 2 provided that the *Colonial Laws Validity Act* 1865 (Imp)[38] was not to apply to any law made by a dominion Parliament after the commencement of the statute, and nor was such a law to be deemed void as being repugnant to a law of the United Kingdom. Thus, the effect of the legislation was to free the dominion Parliaments which were covered by the statute from any fetters which had hitherto restricted their legislative competence, other than in relation to their constitutions, which could only be amended in the manner provided for in the constitution itself. No longer could an Act of the British Parliament apply by paramount force to override a provision of the dominion Parliament. The statute did not have the effect of making British legislation enacted in the past, inapplicable to the dominions. British legislation which hitherto had applied by paramount force continued to be part of the law of each dominion unless and until amended by an Act of the dominion Parliament.

The *Statute of Westminster* applied only to certain dominions which had participated in the conference leading to its enactment.[39] The constituent provinces of Canada were covered by the terms of the statute (s 7), but in contrast, it applied only to the Commonwealth of Australia and not to the

Australian States. The States had declined to be involved, and their constitutional position was protected in s 9 of the statute, which provided that nothing in the statute should be interpreted as giving to the Commonwealth the power to make laws within the authority of the States.

It may seem surprising that the States did not wish to be liberated from the fetters of the *Colonial Laws Validity Act*. There seemed, however, to be little desire to be freed from British authority, and the States could foresee the possibility in the future that they might want to request the Imperial Parliament to legislate for them again.[40] While the *Statute of Westminster* did not prevent this, on the other hand there seemed insufficient reason for the States to want to be freed from restrictions which they did not perceive to be chains, and the continuing independent relationship between the States and Westminster represented by their constitutional links was a possible counterbalance to the power of the Commonwealth. Furthermore, even the Commonwealth was not particularly keen to assert its independence from Britain. It was Canada and South Africa, rather than the Commonwealth of Australia, which had been behind the moves towards a more independent status. The Commonwealth was in no hurry to invoke the provisions of the statute. The statute provided that it would not apply to Australia unless the Commonwealth Parliament formally adopted it subsequently. As Attorney-General, Robert Menzies attempted to get a ratification Bill through Parliament three times between 1936 and 1938, all without success.[41] The statute finally became applicable to the Commonwealth of Australia, with the *Statute of Westminster Adoption Act* 1942 (Imp), which was passed after doubts were expressed about the validity of federal wartime regulations dealing with foreign shipping. It was backdated to the start of the war in 1939.

The effect of the *Statute of Westminster* was to leave Australia in a curious constitutional position. As Coper has written:[42]

> "Thus was created a bizarre situation, infinitely stranger than fiction: a federal system in which the central body had shaken off its colonial shackles and was fully sovereign within its own sphere of competence, but whose regional units were subjected to laws which were made by a foreign power and which the regional units were powerless to displace."

A further curious consequence of the position that the *Statute of Westminster* did not apply to the Australian States was that, formally at least, the British government continued to advise the Crown on the appointment of Australian State governors even though it was the federal ministers in Australia who advised the monarch on the appointment of the Governor-General. In practice, however, the Foreign and Commonwealth Office merely passed on the advice of the relevant State premier.[43]

6.3.2   The Australia Acts

The curious constitutional position of the States was finally resolved by the Australia Acts of 1986, following agreement between the States and the

Commonwealth at the Premiers' Conferences of 1982 and 1984. These Acts established that as a matter of law, the Commonwealth of Australia and its constituent States and Territories were independent of the legislative authority of the British Parliament. The Australia Acts were passed variously in the States and by the federal Parliament, and also by the Parliament at Westminster at the request and by the consent of the Commonwealth Parliament. In so doing, the Commonwealth and the States sought to invoke s 51(xxxviii) of the federal Constitution which allowed the Commonwealth, together with the Parliaments of all the States, to exercise a power which at the commencement of the Constitution, could have been exercised only by the British Parliament. The scope of this provision was in doubt until the High Court gave it a broad interpretation in 1989,[44] and it was not clear that the Australia Acts would be legally valid by this means alone. Consequently, the request and consent provisions of the *Statute of Westminster* were used, along with request and consent legislation from all the States, to invite the Westminster Parliament to pass the Australia Acts and thereby to abdicate its remaining constitutional power to legislate for Australia.

The Acts provided that no Act of Parliament of the United Kingdom would extend or be deemed to extend to the Commonwealth or to a State or Territory. This went beyond the *Statute of Westminster* which had maintained the possibility of legislation being enacted at the consent and request of a dominion. Section 2 provides that the State legislatures might make laws with an extraterritorial operation. Section 3 provides that the *Colonial Laws Validity Act* 1865 shall not apply to the laws of the States made after the commencement of the Australia Acts, and that no State laws will be invalid on the grounds of inconsistency with existing or future English legislation. The Commonwealth Constitution and the *Statute of Westminster* were specifically preserved from being affected by the provisions of ss 2 and 3 of the Act, and by s 6, State constitutions may only be amended in accordance with the manner and form laid down for such amendment in the existing law. Thus, the Australia Acts did not authorise any means of amending the federal Constitution or State constitutions otherwise than had hitherto been provided.

A further provision of the Act concerned appeals to the Privy Council. Section 11 of the Act provided for the complete abolition of appeals to the Privy Council from any Australian court otherwise than as entrenched in the federal Constitution.[45] This completed the process of removing the Privy Council as the ultimate court of appeal for Australia. The effect of the Australia Acts was to remove the right of appeal to the Privy Council from State courts. The Federal Constitution still contains within s 74 a theoretical right of appeal with the leave of the High Court on matters involving the limits of constitutional power between the Commonwealth and the States (or between two States). The reason for this is no doubt that the Commonwealth and the States did not wish to effect an amendment to the Constitution otherwise than in accordance with s 128 of that

Constitution. In theory, the Act of the British Parliament (passed in accordance with the *Statute of Westminster*) could otherwise have achieved such amendment. In any event, it is clear that such leave to appeal will not be granted by the High Court.[46]

The Australia Acts thus represented an important symbolic break with Britain, emphasised by the Queen's visit to Australia to sign the legislation personally. Although British legislation remains important to Australian constitutional law, since the federal Constitution is a British Act of Parliament, the apron strings were finally, and formally untied with the Australia Acts, and Australian courts will not recognise any further legislation of the Westminster Parliament as affecting Australian law. It is, of course, inconceivable in any event that Britain would wish to pass any. Long after Australia's independence had become a political reality, the Australia Acts thus ensured that this was also a reality legally and constitutionally.

6.4   Australian Courts and English Precedents

A further feature of the last quarter of this century has been the growing divergence between the common law as it is interpreted in Australian courts, and the common law in England.[47] This has been a result of a gradual movement in Australian courts away from a loyal following of English precedent. This may be contrasted with the strong adherence to English precedent which had marked the first half of this century. The gradual movement towards independence from British precedent parallels historically, the movement towards legislative independence.

The reason for the historic deference of Australian courts to English authority lay in the view that there should be consistency in the interpretation of English law between England and other courts in the empire.[48] One very practical outworking of this was, of course, that there was one final court of appeal for all the colonies, the Judicial Committee of the Privy Council. The Privy Council acted as a unifying factor between English and Australian courts. Although Privy Council decisions were not formally authoritative for English courts, and the House of Lords' decisions were not formally authoritative for colonial courts, the common membership of both courts ensured in practice that colonial courts showed very great respect for decisions of the House of Lords. Thus, in *Piro v W Foster & Co* (1943),[49] the High Court overruled its earlier decision in *Bourke v Butterfield & Lewis Ltd* (1926)[50] in deference to a contrary decision of the House of Lords. Since this view was adopted by the High Court, it was said that lower courts should consider themselves bound by the House of Lords as well, and in the event of a conflict between High Court authority and that of the House of Lords, the House of Lords' authority should be followed.[51]

There was less certainty about the attitude Australian courts should adopt to decisions of the English Court of Appeal. Certainly, these were treated with considerable respect both by the High Court and lower courts. In *Saxton v Horton* (1926)[52] Knox CJ and Starke J said that the High Court rendered an "abiding service to the community" if it accepted decisions of the English Court of Appeal, "particularly in relation to such subjects as the law of property, the law of contract and the mercantile law". If the High Court chose not to follow a pertinent decision of the English Court of Appeal, at least it would feel a need to explain why it considered it to be incorrect.[53] Lower courts, however, including appellate courts in each State, made it a matter of practice to follow the English Court of Appeal.

Thus, there were parallel hierarchies of authority in the Australian legal system. Formally, the hierarchy of courts which could make authoritative pronouncements on the law in Australia was, in ascending order, the Supreme Court of a State, the appellate court of a State, the High Court of Australia and, at the pinnacle, the Privy Council. Alongside this was a parallel hierarchy of English decisions, decisions of the English High Court, of the English Court of Appeal and of the House of Lords, which were cited interchangeably with Australian decisions and given equal weight with, or usually greater weight than, the equivalent court within the Australian hierarchy.

It was only in 1963 that the High Court made it clear that it did not consider itself bound by the decisions of the House of Lords. Initially, this decision to depart from the House of Lords was made with considerable regret. It was provoked by the decision in *DPP v Smith* (1961),[54] a case concerned with issues of intent in the criminal law. In *R v Parker* (1963)[55] the High Court indicated its very strong disagreement with that decision, which was also much criticised in the United Kingdom. Dixon CJ stated:[56]

"Hitherto I have thought that we ought to follow decisions of the House of Lords, at the expense of our own opinions and cases decided here, but having carefully studied *Smith's Case* I think that we cannot adhere to that view or policy. There are propositions laid down in the judgment which I believe to be misconceived and wrong. They are fundamental and they are propositions which I could never bring myself to accept."

Since that time, in a number of subsequent decisions, the High Court had cause to differ from the House of Lords,[57] although, the decisions of the House of Lords were acknowledged as strongly persuasive.[58] Although the High Court indicated its own independence from English authority from 1963 onwards, surprisingly perhaps, it instructed lower courts to follow loyally decisions of the House of Lords and English Court of Appeal. In *Viro v The Queen* (1978),[59] Gibbs J said that decisions of these courts, while not technically binding, "should generally speaking be followed if they are applicable and not themselves in conflict with a decision of this Court or of the Privy Council." Similar views were expressed by

Barwick CJ and Gibbs J in *Public Transport Commission of New South Wales v J Murray-More (NSW) Pty Ltd* (1975).[60] Gibbs J said in that case that the appellate judges of the New South Wales Supreme Court should have considered themselves bound by a decision of the English Court of Appeal.[61] This statement was all the more remarkable because the issue in question in that case did not concern the common law but the interpretation of workers' compensation legislation in which similar words had been used in the English and New South Wales Acts.[62]

In subsequent years, the notion became established that the common law of Australia might differ from the common law of England,[63] but the freedom of the High Court to settle the law of Australia could not be complete while the possibility of appeal to the Privy Council remained. Thus, the final abolition of appeals to the Privy Council by the Australia Acts marked an important turning point for Australian law, since it finally severed a link in the curial hierarchy which had ensured the continuing importance of English precedents to Australian courts. Justice Kirby, the President of the New South Wales Court of Appeal, commented on the abolition of appeals to the Privy Council:[64]

"So long as the [Privy Council] appeals remained . . . Australian jurisprudence was inescapably hitched to the star of the English legal system. This was not, despite fashionable recent assertions to the contrary, an entirely inappropriate umbilical cord . . . the connection at least had the merit of linking the Australian system to one of the great world legal orders. Especially in earlier times, it was probably appropriately tuned to our colonial economic organisation. It may even sometimes have saved us from provincial mediocrity."

Whatever the merits of the retention of appeals in the colonial era, the final abolition of such appeals left the Australian courts entirely in charge of their own destiny, and able to the fullest extent, to chart a different path from that in the United Kingdom.[65] A decision of the High Court in 1986 confirmed the severance of a formal link in the chain of precedent between English and Australian courts. In *Cook v Cook*,[66] four members of the High Court in a joint judgment clearly signalled a new approach. Referring to the earlier statements of High Court judges that lower courts should follow the decisions of the English Court of Appeal and the House of Lords, the judges said:[67]

"Whatever may have been the justification for such statements in times when the Judicial Committee of the Privy Council was the ultimate court of appeal or one of the ultimate courts of appeal for this country, those statements should no longer be seen as binding on Australian courts. The history of this country and of the common law makes it inevitable and desirable that the courts of this country will continue to obtain assistance and guidance from the learning and reasoning of United Kingdom courts just as Australian courts benefit from the learning and reasoning of other great common law courts. Subject, perhaps, to the special position of decisions of the House of Lords given in the period in which appeals lay from this country to the Privy Council, the precedents of other legal systems are not binding and are useful only to the degree of the persuasiveness of their reasoning.''

It is only in the very recent past, since about 1980, that there has been a clear tendency for the High Court to develop indigenous Australian solutions to legal problems without any deference to the decisions of English judges. What is emerging now is a distinctive Australian version of the common law. Although this is sometimes explained as resulting from differences in English and Australian conditions,[68] many of the differences arise from sharp disagreements between the High Court and the English courts on matters of legal principle. It is thus only quite belatedly that Australian law has come of age and achieved a significant level of independence from its progenitor. English case law continues to be the major source of persuasive authority.[69]

It is likely that the divergences between English and Australian law will increase. As Australia has left behind its colonial origins and has established its legal, as well as political independence, so in turn, Britain has turned away from its orientation towards its former empire. As Australia's economic future is likely to focus increasingly upon the Asia-Pacific region, so Britain has tied its fortunes to its membership of the European Union. To the extent that the law is shaped by the economic and political needs of a country, the divergence between English and Australian law will become more marked. Conversely, Australian courts may find more and more points of comparison with the legal systems of other countries sharing common origins in English history, and dealing with similar legal problems. In this sense, Australian courts will continue to draw guidance from other member courts in the Commonwealth, while being formally subject to none, nor deferential to the courts which once exercised a supervisory jurisdiction over them.

6.5   Australia as a Republic?

In the 1990s, the major issue for debate in terms of Australia's constitutional arrangements is the future of the monarch as Australia's Head of State. To many, it seems increasingly anomalous that Australia should cling to the last vestiges of colonial status by retaining as Head of State a monarch whose primary loyalty is, and always will be, to Britain. Malcolm Turnbull, a leader of the Republican movement, has expressed well the essence of the Republican case for change: ''A nation defines itself by being different. Only colonies continue to borrow the monarchies of other lands''.[70] Against those who call for the monarch to be replaced by a president, are those who argue for the retention of the monarchy in the name of tradition and stability, and because it provides Australia with a Head of State who is above politics.

The idea that Australia should finally sever the ties with Britain by severing the link with the Crown is one which has only recently gained a great deal of support. A generation ago, the idea that Australia would want this degree of independence, and that it should stand alone as an entirely independent nation in the South Pacific, would have been incomprehensible to most Australians. It was intrinsic to the Australian identity that Australians were Britons living on a distant shore, standing for British values and traditions in the farthest reaches of the Empire. Robert Menzies, the longest serving Australian Prime Minister, regarded the boundaries of Britain as extending to Cape York and Invercargill, and, in 1953 said that "to us the Crown is the enduring symbol that wherever we are in the world we are one people".[71]

That assertion of British identity was especially important for a nation at times uncertain of itself. It gave an assurance that the prodigal sons, once banished and exiled to the farthest continent, were once more treated as full members of the British family. It also distinguished white Australians (and New Zealanders) from the citizens of other dominions and former colonies in Africa and the Indian subcontinent who had been "British" only by conquest. That Australians were just Britons living under different stars was always far more important to Australians than it was to the English. It also linked Australia, as a small population on the edge of a world politically and economically dominated by the United States and Europe, to a country which remained in the 1950s, a major world power.

Since World War II, however, the Australian population has changed markedly, and large numbers of immigrants have come from countries which were never under British rule, and have no particular affection for British traditions. Even amongst the white settlers who came to Australia many generations ago, there are a large number who came from countries which have since established independence from Britain, such as Ireland. This profile of the Australian population contrasts with Britain itself. Britain too, is a multicultural society, but the majority of its immigrants since World War II have come from countries which were once, or still remain, part of the Commonwealth. Britain's population now reflects its past empire which once extended to almost every corner of the globe. Australia's multicultural society does not represent the vestiges of former glory, but is the result of a conscious decision to open the country, subject to a controlled immigration policy, to people from all over the world.

Furthermore, Australia no longer has the economic ties to Britain which it once had. Britain's entry into the Common Market in 1973 initiated a change in its trading patterns which was of the utmost significance, orienting it towards Europe. Australia has had to find new markets in Asia and elsewhere, and is discovering a new identity as part of the Pacific Rim which has increased in global economic and political significance. It is inevitable that as the Australian population has changed, as Britain has declined as a world power and has focused upon its place in Europe, and as Australians have become more confident in their own identity and their own future, the severance of the monarchical link should be a real possibility.

In practice, the present constitutional arrangements may be termed a "crowned republic", since Australia has a republican system of government in every practical sense of the term, but still has the monarch as a ceremonial Head of State. Formal constitutional authority is vested in the Governor-General, not as the delegate of the Queen, but as her representative. This means that the Governor-General is not given instructions by the Queen concerning the exercise of his responsibilities and nor is he subject to being overruled by the Queen in any decisions which he makes. This is a matter of present constitutional practice rather than constitutional theory. Section 2 of the Constitution makes it clear that the Governor-General continues in office "during the Queen's pleasure", and subject to the Constitution, may exercise such powers as the Queen may please to assign to her or him. In practice, though, the Queen has made it clear that she will not intervene in Australian constitutional affairs. During the 1975 crisis, the Speaker of the House of Representatives wrote to the Queen asking her to intervene to restore Gough Whitlam as Prime Minister. Her private secretary replied: [72]

> "As we understand the situation here, the Australian Constitution firmly places the prerogative powers of the Crown in the hands of the Governor-General as the representative of the Queen of Australia. The only person competent to commission an Australian Prime Minister is the Governor-General, and the Queen has no part in the decisions which the Governor-General must take in accordance with the Constitution. Her Majesty, as Queen of Australia, is watching events in Canberra with close interest and attention, but it would not be proper for her to intervene in person in matters which are so clearly placed within the jurisdiction of the Governor-General by the Constitution Act."

The Constitution does specify in certain places that the Queen has a personal role to play in Australian constitutional affairs. Notably, s 59 provides:

> "**Disallowance by the Queen**. The Queen may disallow any law within one year from the Governor-General's assent, and such disallowance on being made known by the Governor-General by speech or message to each of the Houses of the Parliament, or by Proclamation, shall annul the law from the day when the disallowance is so made known."

While the power of disallowance exists, it is clear after the Imperial Conferences of 1926 and 1930 that such advice would never be tendered by the British government to the Queen, and it is unthinkable that such advice would be given to the Queen by an Australian Prime Minister.

Becoming a republic would involve the removal of the formal powers of the monarchy in relation to the Constitution of the Commonwealth and the constitutions of the Australian States, and removing the monarch as Australia's ceremonial Head of State. However, constitutional change could not be accomplished as easily as this implies. First, it would involve amendment of large parts of the Constitution. Forty five sections of the Constitution either recognise the monarchy in Australia, define the role and powers of the Governor-General, or contain monarchical assumptions such as references to the Crown. State constitutions would also need to be amended. Furthermore, if the Crown were to be removed as Head of State, and the Governor-General to be transformed into a President, the question would have to be resolved as to the constitutional powers which such a President should have. The conventional assumptions which informed the operation of monarchy as Britain emerged to be a parliamentary democracy can scarcely be assumed in a republic which has consciously cast off its colonial and monarchical clothes. Furthermore, a Governor-General with her or his own claim to popular acceptance, whether by popular election, or "indirect" election by Parliament, has a stronger claim to be entitled to exercise independent judgment than a Governor-General who has no claim to democratic support and is not responsible to the electorate. One of the features of the present system is that the Head of State does not have a claim to exercise substantive political authority, although, like the Queen in Britain, he or she has the "right to be consulted, to encourage and to warn".[73] He or she also has the constitutional authority to safeguard the constitution if the government embarks on a path of flagrant illegality.

Thus, one of the central questions which must be answered if Australia is to become a republic, is the form that such a republic should take. What powers should a president have? How should he or she be elected or chosen? What place should remain in the existing constitution for the unwritten conventions which have guided the Governor-General's exercise of his powers hitherto? If there was doubt about the existence and status of conventions under the existing system in 1975, it seems especially desirable if there is to be a republic, that important matters are not left to convention in the future.

The Republic Advisory Committee, which was established in 1993, considered the various options for a republican constitution,[74] but it was not its brief to make affirmative recommendations. Its terms of reference were to describe the minimum constitutional changes necessary to achieve a viable Federal Republic of Australia, maintaining the effect of our current conventions and principles of government. It considered that even a minimalist position on constitutional change would require the Constitution to determine the method of appointment of the Head of State, the length of her or his term of office and the circumstances in which the Head of State could be removed. There would also be a need to deal with the powers of the Head of State and to provide for the positions of the States in relation to the Crown. While canvassing a variety of options, the Committee appeared to favour the election of a President by a two thirds majority in Parliament, ensuring bipartisan support, and also favoured some form of written codification of the conventions circumscribing the exercise of those powers which the Head of State could only exercise alone, rather than on the advice of the prime minister. These are known as the "reserve powers". The report also canvassed a number of options for dealing with a recurrence of the situation which occurred in 1975 when the Senate "blocked supply" by failing to pass a Bill appropriating money for the ordinary services of government.

On all of the issues which would have to be decided for Australia to adopt even a minimalist approach to becoming a Republic, there is extensive room for disagreement and debate. Part of the reluctance to codify the written conventions which circumscribe the Governor-General's powers derives from a fear that it would be difficult to achieve a consensus on the circumstances in which a government should be dismissed from office. Difficult issues also arise at times on the choice of prime minister in situations where there is a hung Parliament.[75] Leaving it up to the discretion of the Head of State, however, creates as many problems as it evades.

If Australia does become a republic, it is important for the legitimacy of the new Constitution that it is "owned" by the people of Australia, and reflects a broad consensus of opinion. In determining whether Australia should become a republic, there are many issues to be decided. Can we agree on an alternative form of government, given the extent of constitutional change which becoming a republic would entail? Can we, indeed, continue into the 21st century with a Constitution which has been described as "the rule book for a colony"?[76] The choice to remain as we are needs to be as much a conscious choice as the decision to change. There are, perhaps more important issues concerning the future of Australia than the identity of its Head of State. Nonetheless, national symbols matter as much as traditions do. The question is whether the monarchy represents a tradition which is so intrinsic to Australian life, that it ought to be preserved as it is.

NOTES

1. See the discussion by the High Court in *Cole v Whitfield* (1988) 165 CLR 360 at 386ff.
2. For a detailed history, see La Nauze, J A, *The Making of the Australian Constitution* (Melbourne UP, Melbourne, 1972). See also McMinn, W G, *A Constitutional History of Australia* (Oxford UP, Melbourne, 1979); Coper, M, *Encounters With the Australian Constitution* (CCH, Sydney, 1987), Ch 2.
3. La Nauze, J A, op cit, p 37.
4. Ibid, pp 37-38.
5. Ibid, p 11.
6. *Commonwealth of Australia Constitution Act* 1900 (Imp), s 74 (hereafter, *Constitution*).

7. This provision has been of particular benefit to Tasmania. On the basis of population, it would currently be entitled to only four members of the House of Representatives. However, it receives five members by virtue of this provision.

8. For example, there are both State and federal laws concerning some forms of discrimination, and relief may be sought under either law.

9. See below, Chapter 7.

10. This was by a provision in the Australia Acts. See below, 6.3.2.

11. *Attorney-General for Victoria (ex rel Black) v Commonwealth* (1981) 146 CLR 559.

12. *Australian Capital Television Pty Ltd v Commonwealth* (1992) 177 CLR 106.

13. *Street v Queensland Bar Association* (1989) 168 CLR 461, applying *Constitution*, s 117.

14. *Constitution Alteration (Senate Elections)* 1906; *Constitution Alteration (State Debts)* 1909; *Constitution Alteration (State Debts)* 1928; *Constitution Alteration (Social Services)* 1946; *Constitution Alteration (Aboriginals)* 1967; *Constitution Alteration (Senate Casual Vacancies)* 1977; *Constitution Alteration (Retirement of Judges)* 1977; *Constitution Alteration (Referendums)* 1977.

15. La Nauze, J A, op cit, p 232.

16. This may be seen in Quick, J and Garran, R, *The Annotated Constitution of the Australian Commonwealth* (Angus and Robertson, Sydney, 1901), p 295. The authors wrote that it was the intention of the framers for Australia to remain "an integral part of the Empire presided over by the wearer of the Triple Crown of England, Ireland and Scotland".

17. Ibid, pp 208-211.

18. See *Constitution*, s 15.

19. McMillan, J, Evans, G and Storey, H, *Australia's Constitution: Time for Change?* (Law Foundation of New South Wales and Allen and Unwin, Sydney, 1983), p 194.

20. See ss 5, 28, 57, 64.

21. On the federal-state balance see further Zines, L, *The High Court and the Constitution* (3rd ed, Butterworths, Sydney, 1992), Ch 14; Galligan, B, *Judicial Activism in Australia* in K Holland (ed), *Judicial Activism in Comparative Perspective* (St Martin's Press, New York, 1991), p 70.

22. *Deakin v Webb* (1904) 1 CLR 585.

23. *Amalgamated Society of Engineers v Adelaide Steamship Co Ltd* (1920) 28 CLR 129.

24. *Polyukhovich v Commonwealth* (1991) 172 CLR 501.

25. See *Commonwealth v Tasmania* (1983) 158 CLR 1 (the *Franklin Dam Case*); *Richardson v The Forestry Commission (Tas)* (1988) 164 CLR 261. See generally, Rothwell, D, "The High Court and the External Affairs Power: A Consideration of Its Outer and Inner Limits" (1993) 15 Adel LR 209.

26. Letter to London's *Morning Post*, 1 April 1902, quoted in C Howard, *Australia's Constitution* (Revised ed, Penguin, Melbourne, 1985), p 86.

27. *South Australia v Commonwealth* (1942) 65 CLR 373 (the *First Uniform Tax Case*).

28. *Victoria v Commonwealth* (1957) 99 CLR 575 (the *Second Uniform Tax Case*).

29. McMillan, J, Evans, G and Storey, H, op cit, p 117.

30. (1939) 61 CLR 735.

31. Ibid at 764.

32. *South Australia v Commonwealth* (1942) 65 CLR 373 at 409.

33. Ibid at 429.

34. *Attorney-General for Victoria (ex rel Black) v Commonwealth* (1981) 146 CLR 559.

35. For example, the reference of powers over issues of custody, guardianship, maintenance and access in relation to ex-nuptial children, made in 1986 (NSW, Vic and SA), 1987 (Tas) and 1990 (Qld). Western Australia, which has a Family Court for both State and federal law, did not need to make a full reference of powers.

36. The *Jurisdiction of Courts (Cross-Vesting) Act* 1987 (Cth), and cognate legislation in each State: see below, Chapter 7.

37. This record may be contrasted with the legislation of the Australian colonies in the 19th century. Disallowance occurred on a number of occasions. The power to disallow legislation was in practice abandoned by the British government by an agreement with the dominions made at the Imperial Conference in 1930.

38. See above, 5.3.2.

39. These provinces are named in the preamble to the statute and in s 1 as being Canada, the Commonwealth of Australia, New Zealand, South Africa, the Irish Free State and Newfoundland.

40. Dixon, Sir Owen, *Jesting Pilate* (Woinarski ed, Law Book Co, Sydney, 1965), pp 86, 88.
41. McMinn, W, op cit, p 161.
42. Coper, M, op cit, p 6.
43. Winterton, G, "The Constitutional Position of Australian State Governors" in H P Lee and G Winterton (eds), *Australian Constitutional Perspectives* (Law Book Co, Sydney, 1992), pp 274-277.
44. *Port Macdonnell Professional Fishermen's Assoc Inc v South Australia* (1989) 168 CLR 340.
45. "Australian court" is defined for the purposes of s 11, as excluding the High Court (see s 16), thus retaining the right of appeal with leave under s 74 of the Constitution.
46. See *Kirmani v Captain Cook Cruises Pty Ltd (No 2); Ex parte Attorney-General (Queensland)* (1985) 159 CLR 461.
47. For analyses of this divergence see Mason, Sir Anthony, "Future Directions in Australian Law" (1987) 13 Monash Univ LR 149; Luntz, H, "Throwing Off the Chains: English Precedent and the Law of Torts in Australia", in M Ellinghaus, A Bradbrook and A Duggan (eds), *The Emergence of Australian Law* (Butterworths, Sydney, 1989), p 70.
48. *Trimble v Hill* (1879) 5 App Cas 342 at 345; *Waghorn v Waghorn* (1942) 65 CLR 289.
49. (1943) 68 CLR 313.
50. (1926) 38 CLR 354.
51. *Piro v W Foster & Co Ltd* (1943) 68 CLR 313 at 320, per Latham CJ.
52. (1926) 38 CLR 240 at 244.
53. See, eg, *Cowell v Rosehill Racecourse* (1937) 56 CLR 605, which refused to follow the English Court of Appeal's decision in *Hurst v Picture Theatres* [1915] 1 KB 1.
54. [1961] AC 290.
55. (1963) 111 CLR 610.
56. Ibid at 625.
57. See, eg, *Skelton v Collins* (1966) 115 CLR 94; *R v O'Connor* (1980) 146 CLR 64.
58. *Cooper v Southern Portland Cement Ltd* (1972) 128 CLR 427 at 438, per Barwick CJ.
59. (1978) 141 CLR 88 at 121.
60. (1975) 132 CLR 336 at 341, 349.
61. Ibid at 349.
62. These views of members of the High Court were reflected in statements of members of appellate courts. In *Brisbane v Cross* [1978] VR 49 at 51, Young CJ, in the Full Court of the Supreme Court of Victoria, took the view that where there was no contrary Australian authority, he should "unquestionably follow" a decision of the House of Lords. A similar view was taken in the New South Wales Court of Appeal. In *Life Savers (Australasia) Ltd v Frigmobile Pty Ltd* [1983] 1 NSWLR 431 at 433, Hutley JA, with whom Glass JA agreed, said that the court was bound by a certain decision of the House of Lords unless there were inconsistent decisions of the High Court or the Privy Council.
63. This was accepted by the Privy Council in appeals from Australia. *Australian Consolidated Press v Uren* [1969] 1 AC 590 at 644; *Geelong Harbour Trust Commissioners v Gibbs Bright & Co* [1974] AC 810 at 820-821.
64. Kirby, M, "Permanent Appellate Courts—the New South Wales Court of Appeal 20 Years On" (1987) 61 ALJ 391 at 392.
65. The last appeal was *Austin v Keele* (1987) 72 ALR 579.
66. (1987) 162 CLR 376.
67. Ibid at 390, per Mason, Wilson, Deane and Dawson JJ.
68. Mason, Sir Anthony, op cit, pp 153-154.
69. Between 1983 and 1987, the Australian Law Reports listed as "judicially considered" 397 English cases, but only 16 Canadian, 7 United States and 6 New Zealand cases. Crawford, J, "Australian Law After Two Centuries" (1988) 11 Syd L R 444 at 446. See also, Ellinghaus, M, "Towards an Australian Contract Law" in Ellinghaus, Bradbrook and Duggan (eds) *The Emergence of Australian Law* (Butterworths, Sydney, 1989), pp 44, 48-53. Ellinghaus studied 133 decisions of the High Court between 1975 and 1985 which involved substantial issues of contract law. Of 2037 cases cited in these judgments, 1103 (54 per cent) were English, 798 were Australian, and 136 came from other jurisdictions.
70. Turnbull, M, *The Reluctant Republic* (William Heinemann, Port Melbourne, 1993), p 4.
71. Cited in Turnbull, M, ibid, p 6.
72. Sawer, G, *Federation Under Strain: Australia 1972-1975* (Melbourne UP, Melbourne, 1977), p 211. See also Detmold, M, *The Australian Commonwealth* (Law Book Co, Sydney, 1985), Ch 12.

73. See above, 4.6.
74. The Republic Advisory Committee, *An Australian Republic: The Options* (AGPS, Canberra, 1993).
75. Consider, eg, the constitutional problem following the election in Tasmania in 1989. For a discussion, see Winterton, G, op cit, pp 304-331.
76. Turnbull, M, ibid, p 6.

Chapter 7

THE COURT SYSTEM IN THE AUSTRALIAN FEDERATION

7.1   The Mosaic of Courts in the Australian Federation

The establishment of an Australian federation brought both benefits, and new problems, to the court structure of Australia. One benefit was in providing an indigenous Australian court, the High Court, to act as a court of appeal for the country as a whole, and which would be a final court of appeal in most cases, even while there remained a right of appeal to the Privy Council in London. Apart from the convenience of having a national court of appeal in Australia which meant that appeals from State appellate courts did not need to be taken to London, the existence of such an Australian court made it more likely that the judges would be familiar with the context in which Australian legislation was originally enacted, and the particular needs and circumstances of each jurisdiction.

However, the development of the federation also made the court system all the more complex. Not only was there a new source of legislation, with the possibility of inconsistency between federal and State laws, but also the possibility that federal courts would be established, giving rise to jurisdictional conflict between State and federal courts. The federal Parliament was slow to create federal courts. It preferred instead to take another path envisaged by the Constitution, and to vest State courts with jurisdiction in a number of matters under federal law, while leaving other matters exclusively to the High Court. Nonetheless, federal courts of a specialist nature were created in the first 50 years after federation, notably the Commonwealth Court of Conciliation and Arbitration which was established in 1904, and which evolved over time into the Australian Industrial Court, and the Federal Court of Bankruptcy which was established in 1930.

Major developments in the federal court system occurred in the 1970s. In 1976, the Family Court of Australia came into existence. This is a specialist court exercising jurisdiction mainly under the *Family Law Act* 1975 (Cth). In addition, in 1977 the Federal Court of Australia came into being. This took over the work of the Industrial Court and the Court of Bankruptcy, and now exercises a general jurisdiction chiefly in matters of commercial, administrative and industrial law arising under federal legislation.

Thus, the move to federation led in time to the addition of a federal element to the court system. In Australia today, the court structure is a complex mosaic, in which courts may be characterised by whether they are State courts or federal courts, whether they are general or specialist courts, and whether they have a general, or limited jurisdiction. The complexity of the jurisdictional problems has led in turn to ways being devised to simplify the court structure. In 1987, legislation was passed in each State and Territory to vest the jurisdiction of State Supreme Courts in the Federal Court and the Family Court, and to give to State Supreme Courts federal jurisdiction additional to that which they have exercised since the beginnings of the federation. This is known as the cross-vesting scheme.[1] It also allows each State and Territory Supreme Court to exercise the jurisdiction of every other such court. Despite the cross-vesting scheme, the distinction between State and federal jurisdiction remains of importance.

7.2   The Hierarchy of Courts in the States and Territories

7.2.1   The dominance of the English model

As was seen above, in Chapter 5, the system of courts which was established in Australia in 1823 was modelled substantially on the system of courts which existed in England. The *New South Wales Act* of 1823 provided for the establishment of a Supreme Court in New South Wales and Van Diemen's Land with the power to deal with all criminal and civil matters "as fully and amply as Her Majesty's Court of King's Bench, Common Pleas and Exchequer at Westminster".[2] The conferral on the Supreme Court of all the powers vested in the different courts at Westminster was a shorthand for the grant of a number of inherent powers which the royal courts had exercised over the centuries. These included the power to punish for contempt of court, to award damages, and to grant injunctions ordering defendants to desist from violations of a plaintiff's rights. It also included what are known as the prerogative writs, mandamus, prohibition and certiorari. Mandamus and prohibition enable the court to make orders to government officials to act or refrain from acting in a certain way in accordance with their legal obligations, and certiorari enables the decision of a lower court, made without proper jurisdiction, to be quashed. Formally, this occurs by removal of the matter into the higher court. The Supreme Court, thus, was given a supervisory jurisdiction over the proceedings of courts lower in the curial hierarchy, and such writs are also used in relation to government officials and tribunals.

The 1823 Act gave power for the establishment of inferior courts, and thus, the Act provided the necessary legal foundation for a hierarchy of courts as existed in England. Specifically, the 1823 Act provided for the establishment of courts of General or Quarter Sessions. Historical features of the English court system deriving from the late middle ages thus were transposed without modification to Australia. These courts consisted of two or more justices of the peace, often presided over by a chairman with legal training. They met in four sessions per year (hence the name, Quarter Sessions). Meetings outside of such regular occasions were called General Sessions. General and Quarter Sessions had the power to deal with most crimes, with the assistance of a jury as the triers of fact. The most serious crimes were reserved for the Supreme Court. A law passed in 1825 filled a lacuna in the 1823 Act and gave to justices the power to sit in "Petty Sessions". This was, once again, modelled on the English position where one or two justices, sitting "out of sessions", could deal with minor matters summarily.

The 1823 Act also allowed for the creation of Courts of Requests, which existed in England and fulfilled a useful function in dealing with minor civil disputes without the normal formality and technicality of law and procedure. Courts of Requests no longer exist (although the name survived in Tasmania until 1989)[3] but the idea that certain bodies vested with adjudicatory authority should proceed without formality and legal technicality remains a very strong one. In Australia today, there are a number of tribunals exercising jurisdiction in relation to small claims. Other tribunals allow for appeals from decisions of government administrators, or have jurisdiction in discrete areas such as in landlord and tenant disputes or in relation to social security entitlements.

The system of courts which developed as a result of the 1823 legislation was replaced by courts with other names and structures in the supervening century or so, just as the court structure was changed in England. The present position is that all States and Territories have a Supreme Court which exercises plenary jurisdiction in relation to the law of the State, unless an area of law is specifically excluded by statute. All jurisdictions, apart from Tasmania, the Australian Capital Territory and the Northern Territory, have a three tier system of courts. The intermediate courts vary in nomenclature. In Victoria, the English name, "County Court", was adopted. In New South Wales, Queensland, South Australia and Western Australia they are known as District Courts. In addition to these courts, there are magistrates' courts which exercise a summary jurisdiction. The most common names for these courts are either Local Courts or Magistrates' Courts. In most States and Territories, the three levels of the courts exercise both criminal and civil jurisdiction, but there are exceptions to this. For example, the Local Courts of Western Australia and the Northern Territory formally exercise only civil jurisdiction, but they share personnel with the courts of Petty Sessions (WA) and the courts of Summary Jurisdiction (NT) which have a criminal jurisdiction.

In one respect, the court system in the Australian colonies did not follow closely the English model. This was in the use of paid justices of the peace, or magistrates as they were otherwise termed. Stipendiary magistrates were not unknown in England—there were a few in London, but they were few and far between in comparison to the honorary magistrates, and confined to the city. Governor Macquarie appointed D'Arcy Wentworth as the first stipendiary in 1810, and thereafter, there was an increasing tendency to rely on these full time appointees.[5] This was a result in part of the distances which needed to be traversed in Australia, which meant a considerable time commitment. The use of stipendiary magistrates remains the norm in Australia today, while in England it remains the exception. Honorary justices of the peace do exercise various functions in Australia such as witnessing documents, but judicial functions are almost entirely exercised by stipendiary magistrates.

7.2.2   The preservation of a distinct equity jurisdiction

Equity jurisdiction, which was originally given to the first Supreme Court of New South Wales by Letters Patent in 1814, was conferred on the new Supreme Courts of New South Wales and Van Diemen's Land by s 9 of the 1823 Act. This gave to the Supreme Courts the same equitable jurisdiction as was exercised by the Lord Chancellor in English law. The 1823 Act did not create separate courts to administer common law and equity, as existed at the time in England, nor did it require the Supreme Courts to divide itself into a Common Law Division and an Equity Division. Nonetheless, it was implicit in the 1823 legislation, and in subsequent amending Acts, that the common law and equity should be administered separately, since there were important differences in procedure. Issues in a common law trial were to be heard by a judge and jury.[6] By contrast, equitable jurisdiction was to be exercised by the court alone. Thus, it was a small step for the Supreme Court eventually to divide itself into divisions to apply common law and equity respectively.[7] Other colonies adopted a similar division between common law and equitable jurisdiction and so in the Australian colonies, as in England before the passing of the Judicature Acts of 1873-1875, common law and equity were administered in two separate courts. This meant that there were the same problems of divided jurisdiction as existed in England. This would not necessarily have been inconvenient if these claims were distinct. The inter-relationship between common law and equity was and is such, however, that claims of both kinds might arise in the same case, and in a divided system, there was the potential that issues arising in the course of the same matter might have to be heard in separate courts.

The effect of the Judicature Acts in England was that common law and equitable claims were capable of being heard in the one court, although there remained a separate Chancery Division of the High Court, along with a Queen's (or King's) Bench Division and a third Division (then known as the Probate, Divorce and Admiralty Division).[8] It was only gradually that Judicature Acts were passed in the various Australian States. Most States had adopted the *Judicature Act* system by 1883. Tasmania adopted a Judicature system in the first half of the 20th century,[9] but it was not until 1972 that the reform came into effect in New South Wales. It was not merely complacence or inactivity which delayed the implementation of the Judicature Acts throughout Australia. It was considered by many equity practitioners that the distinctiveness of equitable doctrine was most readily maintained by the retention of separate courts.[9] Most of the specific problems of having separate courts were addressed by legislation allowing for the Common Law Division of the Supreme Court to give equitable remedies and to adjudicate on equitable defences, while conversely the Equity Division could adjudicate on certain common law rights and award the common law remedy of damages.[10] Ultimately, however, administrative convenience prevailed.

The preservation of a distinct equity jurisdiction in New South Wales for almost a century after it had been abolished in the United Kingdom, seemed to many to be a curious anomaly when throughout the common law world, versions of the Judicature system had been adopted in the 19th century. Yet the preservation of a distinct equity court, with its own specialist practitioners, has had an important impact on the development of law in Australia in recent years. The depth of learning in matters of equity in Australia has led to the revival of equity as an important source of principle in the development and reform of common law doctrines. Many of the most important developments in the law of contract and property in recent years have resulted from the application of equitable principles.[11]

7.2.3   The modern jurisdiction of Supreme Courts

The Supreme Courts of the States today continue to have the full powers associated with the English superior courts without any need for a specific enumeration of judicial powers. In a number of States, this is achieved by the continuance of the original provision that the court is invested with the general powers of the Westminster courts (the English courts exercising jurisdiction at common law or in equity prior to 1875). New South Wales and Victoria have replaced this formula with a shorter one which expresses more clearly the extent of the State Supreme Court's jurisdiction. In New South Wales, the court is given "all jurisdiction which may be necessary for the administration of justice in New South Wales"[12] while the Victorian legislation simply confers on the Supreme Court "unlimited jurisdiction", although, it then refers back to the jurisdiction and power of the English courts.[13] Although the Supreme Court in each State is governed by a statute setting out its powers in some detail, this builds on rather than supercedes the understanding of the nature and function of a superior court and its inherent powers which was received from England as a result of colonisation. Even now, it is not unusual for Supreme Courts to refer to their inherent powers to justify a particular order in the absence of express statutory enactment.

The Supreme Courts have the status of being superior courts of record. This means that the decision of a superior court is regarded as valid and unimpeachable unless it is set aside on appeal. By contrast, the decisions of inferior courts are subject not only to appeal in the normal manner but to review as to whether the matter was within the jurisdiction of that court. Normally, this would be by a writ of certiorari to the lower court which has the effect of removing the matter into the superior court.

In general, State and Territory Supreme Courts have jurisdiction over every matter under State legislation, at common law and in equity, no matter how small in financial terms, unless its jurisdiction is specifically excluded by operation of statute in a particular matter. An example of such an exclusion exists in New South Wales where the Land and Environment Court, a specialist court dealing with environmental and planning matters, has exclusive jurisdiction in relation to particular planning legislation to the exclusion of the Supreme Court. While the Supreme Courts have a general jurisdiction, in some States the court is organised into a number of divisions for administrative convenience. In other States, there are fewer divisions or none at all.

That a case may be brought in the Magistrates' Court or District or County Courts is no barrier to initiating proceedings in the Supreme Court. However, the Supreme Courts of the various States have certain powers to remit cases to lower courts and conversely to remove cases which have been initiated in lower courts, into the Supreme Court. The provisions vary from State to State.[14] Furthermore, a litigant who begins a matter inappropriately in the Supreme Court might be punished by an adverse award of costs.

The normal procedure for the review of a decision of an intermediate court or a magistrates' court is by way of appeal. However, in certain States a power to review the decision in the exercise of the supervisory jurisdiction has survived alongside or even instead of an appeal procedure. In other States they have been superceded by statutory grounds for interfering with the decision of a lower court.[15]

7.2.4 The jurisdiction of intermediate courts and courts of summary jurisdiction

Intermediate courts and magistrates' courts deal with both civil and criminal matters. In those States with a three tier system of courts, only the most serious crimes are dealt with in the Supreme Courts. Most jury trials take place in the intermediate courts, while magistrates' courts exercise a "summary" jurisdiction, in which there is no jury.

In their civil jurisdiction, both the intermediate courts and the magistrates' courts operate within certain jurisdictional and monetary limits. These vary from State to State. As a generalisation, magistrates' courts are usually restricted to claims where the money sought is already quantified, such as a debt, in contrast to a motor accident case where the amount of damages is in the discretion of the judge or jury. The monetary limits of the lower and intermediate courts have increased substantially in recent years. This is due largely to the pressure of judicial work downwards to the courts lower in the hierarchy. The pressure is from two directions. First, litigants have an interest in minimising legal costs where the amount in dispute is not great, and justice is usually more speedy in the lower courts. The government also has an interest in increasing the jurisdictional thresholds of lower courts. The cost of running these courts, and in particular, magistrates' courts, is rather lower than the Supreme Court. The cost to legal aid funds where one or both parties is on legal aid is also lower.

A particular difficulty in the jurisdiction of intermediate and magistrates' courts has been the extent to which they may adjudicate on equitable rights and award equitable remedies. Historically, where equity was invoked, it was seen as a matter for the Supreme Courts to hear, since equitable matters were treated as being of greater difficulty than common law claims. However, the cost of bringing equitable claims in the Supreme Court is frequently so high that it is priced beyond the reach of the private individuals for whom some equitable doctrines were intended to provide relief. In an era when judges at every level of the court system have received an academic legal training, have years of practical experience and a wealth of published material to draw on, it is difficult to justify the exclusion of any one branch of the law as being too complex for the lower courts. The modern trend is to recognise this and to allow intermediate courts, and even magistrates' courts, to deal with all matters within their monetary limits, whether the principles of law derive from the common law or equity. [16]

7.2.5   The appellate system in State courts

In all the States and Territories there is an appellate court which hears appeals from the Supreme Court and from the District or County Court in those jurisdictions which have an intermediate court of first instance. In New South Wales there has been, since 1965, a specialist appellate court, the New South Wales Court of Appeal, consisting of the Chief Justice, a President of the Court of Appeal and other Justices of Appeal who only do appellate work. This specialist appellate court only hears civil matters. There is also a Court of Criminal Appeal which includes trial judges on the appellate panel. The court is headed by the Chief Justice.

It is not a qualification for appointment to the appellate bench or to the position of Chief Justice or President of the Court of Appeal that a person has had previous judicial experience. Indeed it is not uncommon for some of the most able and experienced members of the Bar to be offered an appointment directly to the Court of Appeal. Taking a judicial appointment may involve a significant drop in salary for a leading barrister. This is partly compensated by generous superannuation benefits and the prestige of appointment to the Bench. The offer of an appellate position is consequently seen as a necessary incentive to the most able members of the Bar to accept a judicial appointment.

In 1989, Victoria also moved in the direction of establishing a specialist appellate court, by creating an Appeal Division of the Supreme Court.[17] Consideration had been given by the State government to the development of a Court of Appeal along the New South Wales model, but another model was proposed by the judges of the Supreme Court and has been in operation since August 1989. The Chief Justice and three of the most senior judges sit nearly full time on appeals. Other judges, assigned mainly on the basis of seniority, sit in the Appeal Division for one or more terms per year. Queensland has also established a Court of Appeal.[18] In the other three States, and in the Northern Territory, appeals go to a Full Court, comprising three members of the court, although in the Northern Territory this is called the Court of Appeal.[19] While some judges are given a substantial amount of appellate work on the Full Court bench in these jurisdictions, the principle is maintained that judges who hear appeals shall continue to perform duties as judges at first instance. The Australian Capital Territory has a unique appellate structure. Appeals lie to the Federal Court of Australia from decisions of its Supreme Court.

The question of whether there should be a permanent appellate court or one staffed on a rotational basis or otherwise by trial judges is one which has attracted some debate.[20] There has been some opposition in the ranks of the judiciary to the creation of a hierarchy in which certain judges are regarded as senior to others on a basis other than length of judicial service, and in a manner which might adversely affect the collegiality of the court.[21] The advantage of a Full Court structure in which all judges have an opportunity to hear appeals, is that it adds variety to the judicial task and consequently may attract the most able members of the profession to accept judicial office more readily. However, there are advantages in a permanent court of appeal as well. The great majority of appellate work in Australia is done at a level below that of the High Court. The existence of a permanent court is likely to increase the consistency of these appellate decisions and to promote a greater efficiency in dealing with the court's workload.

7.3   The High Court of Australia

The High Court is established by the authority of s 71 of the Constitution which provides that there should be a "Federal Supreme Court to be called the High Court of Australia" and such other federal courts as the Parliament shall establish. The courts exercising jurisdiction under this section are often described as s 71 courts.

The jurisdiction of the High Court is defined by ss 73-76 of the Constitution, and by further enactments of Parliament passed under the authority of those sections. Unlike the House of Lords in England, which only acts as a final court of appeal, the Constitution gives to the High Court an original jurisdiction as well, and it is usual, where proceedings are begun at first instance in the High Court, that the matter is heard by a single member of the court. The major exception to this is when a State challenges the constitutionality of Commonwealth legislation in the High Court. In such cases a full bench of seven judges sits to determine the matter.

The original jurisdiction prescribed by the Constitution itself is given in s 75. It includes all matters arising under any treaty, or affecting consuls or other representatives of other countries; all matters in which the Commonwealth, or a person suing or being sued on behalf of the Commonwealth, is a party; all matters between States, or between residents of different States, or between a State and a resident of another State; and cases in which a writ of mandamus or prohibition or an injunction is sought against an officer of the Commonwealth. Since this jurisdiction is given by the Constitution itself, it cannot be removed by Act of Parliament, but only by constitutional amendment. There are other matters in which the High Court has been given original jurisdiction by the federal Parliament under s 76, the most important of which are matters arising under the Constitution, or involving its interpretation.[22]

In the early years after the formation of the Commonwealth, the sizeable original jurisdiction of the High Court presented no difficulty. The case load of the High Court was not so great as to necessitate the creation of other federal courts to share the court's jurisdiction. When the High Court was established by the *Judiciary Act* 1903, there was a Chief Justice and two other Justices. Four years later, the bench was increased to five members and in 1912 to seven members, the present number. However, the considerable increase in the workload of the High Court in recent years has necessitated restrictions being placed upon the invocation of the High Court's original jurisdiction, so that it can concentrate on appeals and matters of constitutional law.

Two aspects of the court's original jurisdiction are insignificant. While s 75 gives the court jurisdiction in a matter arising under any treaty, in the Australian context no matters arise directly under a treaty. Legislation must be passed to give effect to a treaty. By contrast, in the United States, from which this provision was copied, treaties with other countries, once ratified by the Senate, have the force of law. Subsection (ii) which provides that matters affecting diplomats should be heard in the High Court, is also not a significant aspect of the High Court's workload, especially given the principles of diplomatic immunity. Much more significant for the work of the High Court is the subsection which allows disputes between the governments of different States, or between a State and the Commonwealth, to be initiated in the High Court directly. This is regarded as appropriate for the High Court's original jurisdiction.

Other matters, which were once seen as worthy of being dealt with in the High Court, give rise to such a degree of litigation that it is impossible now for the High Court to handle all these cases. With the expansion of the federal government, there are numerous cases in which the Commonwealth, or one of its officers, is a party. The Commonwealth is a substantial employer, and hence may be liable for worker's compensation or unfair dismissal. It enters into contracts. It may be liable in tort. At common law, the Crown (of which constitutionally, the Commonwealth is a representative) was immune from being sued in civil litigation. This immunity was laid aside by ss 56 and 57 of the *Judiciary Act* 1903, acting under s 78 of the Constitution. Furthermore, s 75(iii) extends to persons or instrumentalities acting on behalf of the Commonwealth, such as individual ministers, government officials, or the Commonwealth such as the Commonwealth Bank. There are also numerous situations in which there may be conflicts between residents of different States. Few such disputes are of such significance as to justify being heard initially in the High Court. This jurisdiction between residents of different States is known as the "diversity jurisdiction". The dispute may not involve any issues of constitutional or federal law. In many cases, the High Court's jurisdiction has been invoked when a car accident has occurred which involved residents of different States. With the creation of other courts to share some or all of the original jurisdiction of the High Court, it is no longer necessary for the High Court to have a significant original jurisdiction.

Since the original jurisdiction cannot be removed because it is conferred by the Constitution, the problem has been addressed in two ways. First, other courts have been created to share the High Court's original jurisdiction. Secondly, certain State courts have been invested with federal jurisdiction. Going hand in hand with this, the High Court has certain powers under the *Judiciary Act* 1903 to control its caseload. It may remove into the court, cases from federal courts, Territory courts or State courts exercising federal jurisdiction, which are of importance. This may be requested by a party, in which case the court will exercise a discretion in the matter, or the Attorney-General of the Commonwealth or of a State may exercise a legal right to have a case removed.[23] Conversely, matters which are initiated in the High Court which are not of great importance may be remitted to a federal or Territory court, or to a State court exercising federal jurisdiction.[24] This may be on the application of a party, or on the High Court's own motion. This has allowed the High Court to remit all cases involving residents of different States to a State court to be heard there.[25]

Parliament has also limited the number of other matters in which it had conferred original jurisdiction under s 76(ii) of the Constitution. Reforming legislation between 1973 and 1979 removed many matters which hitherto could have been heard by a High Court judge sitting at first instance— income tax disputes, patent and trademark cases, and by the *Jurisdiction of Courts (Miscellaneous Amendments) Act* 1979, matters arising under some 30 other Acts. Some original jurisdiction under s 76(ii) remains. For example, the High Court, sitting as the Court of Disputed Returns, has original jurisdiction in certain matters arising under legislation governing federal elections.

Thus, although single justices continue to hear some matters, if only to affirm that the case should have been taken to the lower courts first, the major work of the High Court is in its appellate jurisdiction. Section 73 provides for the court to hear appeals from single justices of the High Court, from any other federal court or court exercising federal jurisdiction, and from State Supreme Courts. Additionally, the High Court has jurisdiction to hear appeals from any other court from which at the establishment of the Commonwealth, appeals lay to the Privy Council.

As with the court's original jurisdiction, it has proved necessary in recent years to limit appeals to the High Court in order for the court to be able to maintain a manageable workload and to ensure that it concentrates on important matters of legal principle and of constitutional law. The High Court's policy on appeals is that in all cases before a matter is heard in the court it should go through an intermediate court of appeal such as a State court of appeal or the Full Court of the Federal Court. All appeals from lower courts to the High Court are by special leave of the court, although, anomalously, the Family Court may also ensure that a matter is heard by the High Court without a grant of special leave if it certifies that an important question of law or of public interest is involved. [25] The decision to grant special leave is usually made at a preliminary hearing before three justices. There are facilities for having such hearings by video link between the advocates and the court in Canberra. In a further attempt to control its workload, the High Court has limited oral argument on special leave applications to 20 minutes for each side, with a further time allowed for a brief reply. [26]

Hearings of appeals are conducted by the advocates in person. It is usual for five judges to sit on appeals in all matters other than constitutional cases, in which all seven determine the matter. On other important issues of law, the Chief Justice may decide that a seven member court should sit. However, this does not always result in a clear determination of the legal principles involved. In some cases, where each judge has insisted on offering an individual opinion, it has left the law in a state of some confusion. [27] Judgment is almost always reserved by the High Court, and it may be many months between the hearing of an appeal and the date when opinions are delivered. Exceptionally, the High Court may declare the result and then give its reasons at a later date. [28]

7.4   The Federal Court of Australia

The Federal Court of Australia was established by the *Federal Court of Australia Act* 1976 and came into existence in February 1977. It was the product of years of debate on the appropriate forum for the resolution of disputes arising under federal law. Until this time, much of the work arising under federal law had been done by the State Supreme Courts, utilising the constitutional power given to the federal government to invest State courts with jurisdiction in regard to federal laws. Certain specialist federal courts had also been created, notably the Australian Industrial Court which had jurisdiction not only in industrial matters arising under the Commonwealth's *Conciliation and Arbitration Act* 1904, but in a miscellaneous collection of other federal statutes on matters quite unrelated to industrial law and policy.

The Federal Court was created to take over these matters so that while certain State courts still would exercise federal jurisdiction, in principle much of federal law would be administered in federal courts. With the creation of the new court, it was also possible to reduce further the original jurisdiction of the High Court. The jurisdiction of the Federal Court is not a general one in regard to all matters arising under federal law. The court has such jurisdiction as is conferred by other legislation. The court sits in two divisions, the Industrial Division and the General Division. Judges tend to sit the majority of the time in one Division or the other, but now all judges are assigned to both Divisions.

Appeals in the Federal Court are heard by a Full Court, consisting normally of three judges, although occasionally a five member court may be empanelled. The Full Court hears appeals not only from single judges of the Federal Court but also from the Supreme Courts of the Territories other than the Northern Territory. It is conventional for a majority of members of the Full Court to be specialists in matters arising in the Division from which the appeal is taken, however, this is not an inflexible rule.

7.4.1   The Industrial Division

The Industrial Division deals with matters arising under the Commonwealth's industrial relations legislation. The *Industrial Relations Act* 1988, which supercedes the *Conciliation and Arbitration Act* 1904 is the basis of the system at Commonwealth level by which awards of wages in various industries are decided, and provides a machinery by which industrial disputes can be resolved. Section 51(xxxv) of the Constitution provides that the Commonwealth has power to make laws with respect to "conciliation and arbitration for the prevention and settlement of industrial disputes extending beyond the limits of any one State." Similar legislation operates at State level in regard to industries which are beyond the reach of Commonwealth power.

Originally, all matters arising under this legislation were dealt with in the one court, the Commonwealth Court of Conciliation and Arbitration, but in *R v Kirby; Ex parte Boilermakers' Society of Australia* (1956),[30] the High Court held that under the Constitution, it is not permissible for a federal court to exercise both judicial and non-judicial powers. Clearly, the enforcement of industrial awards was a matter for the judiciary, interpreting and applying the terms of the relevant award. The making of such an award, however, was seen as an exercise of non-judicial power, close in kind to an act of legislation. The result was that the administration of the legislation had to be divided between two bodies, one making the award, the other interpreting and enforcing it. This is the present position. The resolution of disputes is the task in the first place of the Industrial Relations Commission which, by helping the parties in a dispute to reach their own settlement, or by arbitrating where this proves necessary, brings about the establishment of an award which may then be enforced between the parties.

The work of interpretation and enforcement of the Act and the enforcement of the awards made under it, falls to the Industrial Division of the Federal Court. It has powers to grant injunctions, to punish for contempt, and jurisdiction in a great variety of other matters which arise under the legislation. Questions of law may be referred to it by the Commission, as well as issues of inconsistency between State and federal awards.

7.4.2   The General Division

The General Division has been conferred with jurisdiction in a variety of other matters, the most important of which are in regard to bankruptcy, trade practices, administrative law, and questions of law arising out of the work of federal tribunals.

The administration of federal bankruptcy laws under the *Bankruptcy Act* 1924 was originally entrusted to State courts, although soon after this enactment, the government established a Federal Court of Bankruptcy which operated in New South Wales and Victoria. On its establishment, the Federal Court of Australia assumed the jurisdiction of this court, and gradually extended its reach into the other States. The current bankruptcy legislation[31] allows the court to assume the property of a debtor, and allocate her or his assets in appropriate proportions to creditors. The aim is to preserve equally the position of all creditors, once it is established that the debtor has insufficient funds to meet all the debts in full. Each creditor will then receive a proportion of the amount which is owed.

The Federal Court also exercises jurisdiction under the *Trade Practices Act* 1974, which regulates business in certain ways. Once again, this work is shared with other bodies. The *Trade Practices Act* established a Trade Practices Commission which has the task of scrutinising transactions which may result in a hindering of effective competition within a particular trade or industry. These include monopolies, mergers and price-fixing agreements. Section 45 of the *Trade Practices Act* makes certain transactions unenforceable or proscribed, but the Commission may give an authorisation that a certain transaction should be allowed. An appeal against an adverse decision of the Commission lies to the Trade Practices Tribunal. The Federal Court has the power to enforce the provisions of the

Act, and to impose sanctions for their breach. The court also has jurisdiction (concurrently with State courts) in matters relating to consumer protection under Pt V of the Act. This Pt makes misleading or deceptive conduct in the course of business illegal, and gives to aggrieved consumers certain remedies in relation to contracts which were procured by a variety of unfair means.

The third major area of jurisdiction is in relation to administrative law. The *Administrative Appeals Tribunal Act* 1975 established a means by which many decisions made by federal government officials can be reviewed on their merits by an independent panel. Questions of law which arise in the course of the work of the tribunal may be referred to the Federal Court, or an appeal may be taken from the tribunal to the court on a matter of law. The Federal Court is also given jurisdiction to review decisions as a matter of law under the *Administrative Decisions (Judicial Review) Act* 1977.

No decision by a government official can be legally valid if it was not made in accordance with the power given by the relevant legislation. Over many years, judges have developed a sophisticated set of principles governing the exercise of executive discretion which may lead to a decision of an official being invalidated as a matter of law, because it has not been made in a manner intended by the legislation and taking into account the factors contemplated by the legislation. Section 39B of the *Judiciary Act* 1903 gives this general supervisory jurisdiction to the Federal Court by conferring on it the power to hear a matter in which a writ of mandamus, or prohibition or injunction is sought against an officer or officers of the Commonwealth—a jurisdiction which is shared with the High Court (s 75(v) of the Constitution). The review of such decisions has now been placed on a statutory basis at federal level, by the Act of 1977, which provides a simplified application procedure. The prerogative writs still provide an alternative for those decisions which cannot be reviewed under the 1977 Act.

The Federal Court also has jurisdiction in a variety of other matters. It has a limited criminal jurisdiction, it is the venue for appeals on federal taxation, and has an important jurisdiction in regard to intellectual property. Since 1990, it has shared jurisdiction with the State and Territory courts in matters arising under the Corporations Law, which is a national law governing companies, established by co-operation between the States and the Commonwealth.

7.4.3   Associated and accrued jurisdiction

In addition to its jurisdiction given by various Acts of Parliament, the Federal Court also has an associated jurisdiction and an accrued jurisdiction, by which it may determine other matters which would otherwise not be within the jurisdiction of the court. The associated jurisdiction, given by s 32 of the *Federal Court of Australia Act* 1976, allows the Federal Court to determine other matters of federal law which are associated with a case being brought on a matter within the jurisdiction of the court. Thus, where a case involves two issues, one of which is within the court's jurisdiction, and the other of which concerns federal law but is not within the court's ordinary jurisdiction, the court is empowered to determine both matters. The accrued jurisdiction allows the Federal Court in the same way to determine matters of State law which arise together with matters under federal law. The State law matter will be capable of determination in the Federal Court if it is united to the federal matter by a single claim for relief or if the two matters arise from a common substratum of facts. [32] The accrued jurisdiction has been especially useful where a common law claim is pleaded along with a claim under a federal statute, since the Federal Court does not have a general common law jurisdiction. Common law claims would normally be heard in State courts.

7.5   The Family Court

The Family Court of Australia was established by the *Family Law Act* 1975 as a specialist court to deal with family law matters. For about 60 years after federation, family law was a matter which remained subject to legislation in each State. In 1959 the *Matrimonial Causes Act* 1959 (Cth) was passed, but this still gave jurisdiction in family law matters to the State Supreme Courts. It was only in 1975 that family law jurisdiction was entrusted to a specialist federal court. The Family Court and the Federal Court were both established within a few months of each other.

The Family Court of Australia, as it was originally established, represented a substantial break with tradition. The idea of a specialist court was itself not new, although Australia was one of the first countries in the world to have a specialist family court. What was new about the Family Court was its emphasis on conciliation as a means of resolving disputes, and that it was intended to be a "helping court" which did not adopt the same formality of procedure as traditional courts.

Alternative dispute resolution continues to have an important emphasis in the court. In regard to property disputes, the parties meet with a registrar or deputy registrar of the Family Court in what is known as an Order 24 conference. [33] These sessions vary in character depending upon the registrar. In some cases, the registrar gives to the parties an indication of how the court might resolve their dispute if the matter were to go to litigation, and encourages them to settle in the light of that information in order to avoid the expense and stress of litigation. Other registrars offer less guidance to the parties but endeavour to help the parties to reach agreement or to narrow the areas of difference between them. Where there are disputes concerning children, the court will order that before trial, the parties meet with a counsellor attached to the court and endeavour to resolve their dispute informally. [34] The Family Court Counselling Service is staffed by people trained in social work and the behavioural sciences. If conciliation fails to resolve the matter, the case may proceed to adjudication by a judge.

The conciliation conferences in the Family Court are confidential, and evidence is not admissible in court of what has been said during them. In addition to these established methods of dispute resolution, the Family Court is endeavouring to use other methods of alternative dispute resolution as well. In particular, it is increasingly using mediation, which differs from the existing forms of counselling and conciliation inasmuch as it is much more structured. The mediator controls the process through which the parties may negotiate face to face with one another concerning the issues in dispute between them. [35]

Since 1976, when the Family Court of Australia first came into being, it has undergone a number of changes. Despite the continuing emphasis on alternative dispute resolution, other aspects of the court have changed over the years. Until 1983, the court was closed to the public. It is now open, although publication of the names of parties is not permitted. The informal character of the court was also assisted by the fact that the lawyers and judges did not wear robes. In 1988, with an amendment to the *Family Law Act*, the judges and lawyers adopted the practice of other courts in wearing robes. It was considered that people would respect the court more, and accept its decisions, if it had the same trappings as other courts.

Appeals from a single judge of the Family Court go to a Full Court. The Full Court has a combination of permanent and temporary members. There is an Appeal Division and a General Division. The Appeal Division consists of the Chief Judge, the Deputy Chief Judge, and up to six other judges. [36] A majority of the members of the Full Court hearing a case must be members of the Appeal Division, but they are usually joined by a member from the General Division. Members of the Appeal Division also hear cases at first instance.

In recent years, there has been considerable debate about the future of the Family Court. In a speech in 1985, the then Chief Justice, Sir Harry Gibbs, suggested that it may have been a mistake for the Family Court to be separated from the judicial mainstream, and this view has been echoed by others. Part of the argument is that Family Court judges suffer from having an unrestricted diet of family law work, which can be emotionally draining, and that it would be easier to attract able practitioners if the work was varied. Another criticism of the court's separateness was that the Family Court lacks the status of the Federal Court in the minds of the legal profession. Subsequently, it was proposed that the Family Court should be made a division of the Federal Court. This would possibly lead to an increase in status for the Family Court and also break down the isolation of family law through the involvement of non-family law judges in the Full Court of the Federal Court. It was envisaged that while first instance hearings would continue to be heard by specialist family law judges, appeals would be to the Full Court of the Federal Court which would include judges from the General Division. This proposal has not yet been accepted. A different approach, enacted in 1988, was to give to the Family Court additional jurisdiction in matters which would otherwise normally be heard by the General Division of the Federal Court, such as bankruptcy and administrative law cases, if the matter is transferred to it by the Federal Court. [37] However, this has not in practice, led to any change in the nature of the Family Court as a specialist court, since there is little reason why such matters should be transferred to the Family Court when the waiting lists in the Federal Court are generally shorter, and the Federal Court has much greater expertise in those areas of law. As well as the jurisdiction added by the 1988 Act, the Family Court also has an associated jurisdiction like the Federal Court. Whether it may exercise an accrued jurisdiction is less certain. [38]

The aim of increasing the status of the Family Court, and of allowing judges a varied jurisdiction, may be in conflict with the original concept for a Family Court. Family Court judges have been appointed because of their interest in, and suitability for family law work, and this is a condition of their appointment in the *Family Law Act* itself. [39] It may be that the Family Court is better to remain a specialist court with unrivalled expertise in a particular area of dispute resolution without being overly concerned for its status in the wider profession.

7.6   Investing Federal Jurisdiction in State Courts

Section 77(iii) of the Federal Constitution provides that Parliament may make laws investing any court of a State with federal jurisdiction. The Commonwealth quickly acted to do this, by inserting into the *Judiciary Act* 1903 a general provision to this effect. Section 39(2) of the Act provides in part:

> "The several Courts of the States shall within the limits of their several jurisdictions, whether such limits are as to locality, subject-matter or otherwise, be invested with federal jurisdiction, in all matters in which the High Court has original jurisdiction or in which original jurisdiction can be conferred on it."

Certain exceptions are provided for in s 38, and the grant of federal jurisdiction is made subject to certain conditions, including limitations on those magistrates who may hear federal matters.

This general grant of power does not mean that all federal matters may be heard in State courts on the authority of this section. Certain matters at different stages of the history of the federation, have been made the exclusive province of the federal courts. An example of this now is the family law jurisdiction. The effect of the jurisdictional provisions in the

Family Law Act 1975 is that disputes between spouses over their property arising out of the marriage or concerning the children can only be heard in the Family Court or, with certain limitations, in the Magistrates' Court. Apart now from cross-vesting, the State Supreme Courts cannot hear these matters. Until 1987, certain *Trade Practices Act* cases were also exclusive to the Federal Court.

7.7   The Cross-vesting Scheme

The existence after 1976 of two federal courts (the Federal Court and the Family Court) hearing a large number of matters, created its own problems which the existence of accrued and associated jurisdiction could go only some way to resolving. Matters of State and federal law often arise together in ways which make it appropriate for all the matters to be resolved in one hearing. However, before the development of the cross-vesting scheme, it was often not possible to resolve all the issues together in a satisfactory manner. The problems were perhaps most acute in relation to family law but the problems were not confined to the entanglement of State and federal law. There were also situations where it might be desirable for State Supreme Courts to be able to deal with matters arising under the laws of another State.

The difficulties of jurisdiction experienced between federal and State courts in particular, led in the 1970s and early 1980s to a number of proposals for reform. The most radical of these was that there should be a unified national court system able to apply all the law of Australia, whether federal or existing in the various States. Another proposal was that there should be at least an Australian Court of Appeals which could provide some greater consistency in the interpretation of Australian law through appellate decision-making.

The cross-vesting scheme emerged as a compromise from this debate and was proposed by the Judicature Sub-Committee of the Australian Constitutional Convention[40] in a report in 1984. Legislation giving effect to it was passed by the Commonwealth and all the States in the course of 1987, and the scheme came into effect in 1988.[41] The aim of the scheme is to ensure that as far as possible all superior courts in Australia will be able to deal properly and effectively with cases brought before them, unencumbered by a lack of jurisdiction arising from the structure of courts within the Australian federation.

The effect of the cross-vesting scheme is to create a system whereby the power is given to each Supreme Court and the Federal and Family Courts to hear matters which are not otherwise in their jurisdiction. It builds on, without replacing, the jurisdiction already given to State courts to hear federal matters under the *Judiciary Act* 1903. It is also additional to the accrued jurisdiction of federal courts, although it has made accrued jurisdiction relatively unimportant now. The effect is achieved by vesting in the Supreme Court of each State and Territory all the jurisdiction of the Family Court and most of the civil jurisdiction of the Federal Court. Each Supreme Court also is given the jurisdiction of the Supreme Courts of all the other States and Territories.[42] Correspondingly, the Federal Court and the Family Court are given jurisdiction in State matters. In principle, therefore, each superior court may exercise the civil jurisdiction of any other superior court within Australia.

The Supreme Courts do not, however, have all the jurisdiction of the Federal Court. There are certain types of case which remain exclusively in the province of the Federal Court.[43] These are matters of industrial law and certain matters arising under the *Trade Practices Act* 1974 (Cth). Furthermore, s 6 of the Commonwealth Act says that "special federal matters"[44] which are initiated in a Supreme Court should be transferred to the Federal Court (or the Family Court)[45] unless the court finds "special reasons" which make it inappropriate for such a transfer to take place. Notice should be given to the Attorney-General of the Commonwealth and of the relevant State or Territory, inviting them to make submissions on the issue, before the court determines that such special reasons exist.

Apart from this reserved Federal Court jurisdiction, any matter capable of being heard in a superior court within Australia may be initiated in any such court. It is intended, however, that normally proceedings will be commenced in the court which would otherwise have jurisdiction but for the cross-vesting scheme, while allowing the possibility that cases involving the laws of more than one jurisdiction can be dealt with in the one court. This is apparent from the preamble to the Act which sets out the purpose of the Act as an aid to interpretation. It states that the aim is to establish a scheme which does not detract from the jurisdiction of any court. A further aim is to:

"structure the system in such a way as to ensure as far as practicable that proceedings concerning matters which, apart from this Act and any law of the Commonwealth or another State relating to cross-vesting of jurisdiction, would be entirely or substantially within the jurisdiction (other than any accrued jurisdiction) of the Federal Court of the Family Court or the jurisdiction of a Supreme Court of a State or Territory are instituted and determined in that court, whilst providing for the determination by one court of federal and State matters in appropriate cases."

This is achieved by a process of transferring cases which have been started in an inappropriate court. Prima facie, the court in which the proceedings have been commenced will have jurisdiction but it may refuse to exercise it and decide instead to transfer the case to the more appropriate court. The explanatory memorandum which accompanied the introduction of the Commonwealth Bill stated:

"The provisions relating to cross-vesting will need to be applied only in those exceptional cases where there are jurisdictional uncertainties and where there is a real need to have matters tried together in the one court. The successful operation of the cross-vesting scheme will depend very much on the courts approaching the legislation in accordance with its general purpose and intention as indicated in the preamble to the Commonwealth and State legislation. Courts will need to be ruthless in the exercise of their transferral powers to ensure that litigants do not engage in 'forum-shopping' by commencing proceedings in inappropriate courts."[46]

Section 5 of each Act sets down the basis for such a transfer, which may either be on the request of a party or at the court's own motion. There are three grounds for transfer although the second ground is to be exercised with regard to three other considerations. The first ground refers to a situation where related proceedings have been commenced in different courts. In such a case the matter should be transferred if the other court is more appropriate to hear the case, so that the related issues can be heard together in the one court. This assumes that the courts will co-operate with one another and that one will defer to the decision of the other in regard to whether the case should be heard in the first court or transferred.

The second ground for transfer arises where there are no related proceedings pending in different courts, but the court still considers that another court is more appropriate to hear the matter. The judge, in making this decision, must have regard to three considerations. First, whether, but for the cross-vesting scheme (or any accrued jurisdiction in the case of a federal court), the proceeding, or a substantial part of it, would have been incapable of being brought in that court but would have been brought in another court; secondly, whether the case involves the application, interpretation or validity of a law of another Australian jurisdiction; thirdly, whether it is in the interests of justice to order such a transfer.

The third ground for transfer is a residual one encompassing any circumstances which are not covered by the first two grounds. It simply provides for a transfer where it is otherwise in the interests of justice to do so. In regard to all three grounds, the court's discretion with regard to the transfer is unappealable.

If an appeal is taken from the trial judge on the substantive matters, then normally the appeal should be within the same court hierarchy as the original trial. Thus, a matter heard originally in the Federal Court must be appealed to the Full Court of the Federal Court even if the issues in the appeal concern the law of a State. Conversely, no appeal can be taken from a State Supreme Court normally to the Full Court of the Federal Court or Family Court. Section 7 of each Act does provide, however, that under certain federal Acts, the appeal should be taken to the Federal Court or the Family Court (as the case requires) notwithstanding that the original trial was in a State court. These Acts include the *Bankruptcy Act* 1966, the

Family Law Act 1975, the *Commonwealth Electoral Act* 1919 and Commonwealth intellectual property legislation.

When cross-vesting occurs, s 11 applies to the choice of law involved. Where the matter involves a right of action arising under the written law of another State or Territory, the court must apply the law of that State or Territory in determining the matter. Otherwise, the prima facie rule is that the law which is applied is the law in force in the State or Territory in which the court is sitting, while the rules of procedure and evidence may be drawn from any Australian jurisdiction. The choice is left to the discretion of the court, as it considers appropriate in the circumstances. Thus, the Supreme Court of Queensland may use its cross-vested jurisdiction to determine a matter of New South Wales statute law which arises in relation to another matter before it, and may choose in its discretion to apply a rule of procedure or evidence of New South Wales law in the interests of justice. This may alleviate any procedural disadvantage to a party who is having a matter heard in Queensland which would otherwise be heard in New South Wales.

The cross-vesting scheme only applies between the State and Territory Supreme Courts and the Federal Court and Family Court. It is not possible to transfer a case directly from the District Court of a State to the Federal Court or to another State Supreme Court. However, s 8 of each Act does provide a circuitous route for achieving the same result. The relevant Supreme Court may order that the matter be removed up to it from the lower court, and then the cross-vesting legislation will apply to the matter as if proceedings had been initiated in the Supreme Court originally. Thus, having received the case, the Supreme Court may wish to transfer it to the Federal Court or the Federal Court might transfer the matter pending there to the State Supreme Court. Section 10 of the Commonwealth Act provides that certain consumer protection matters under the *Trade Practices Act* may be transferred from a superior court, including the Federal Court, to a lower State court.

The cross-vesting scheme thus provides a means by which the variety of courts in the federation may operate together harmoniously. The question remains whether further reforms are needed. Cross-vesting between lower courts would be useful in some cases, and transfers of certain matters from the Children's Courts to the Family Court would facilitate the better handling of child abuse allegations within the family. A review of the cross-vesting scheme conducted on behalf of the Australian Institute of Judicial Administration concluded that the scheme had worked successfully in the first four years of its operation, and recommended that it be extended at least to the major trial courts in each State such as the District Court of New South Wales and the County Court of Victoria. This would be subject to appropriate appeal or review procedures to ensure the proper operation of the scheme in the lower courts.

In the first few years of the scheme's operation, it is apparent that jurisdictional jealousies have diminished, and a greater spirit of co-operation has developed between courts in different jurisdictions. The stage is thus set for the implementation of further reforms which will reduce the impediments to efficiency and effectiveness in the administration of justice within the federation.

NOTES

1. See below, 7.7.
2. 4 Geo IV c 96, s 2.
3. Crawford, J, *Australian Courts of Law* (3rd ed, Oxford UP, Melbourne, 1993), p 110.
4. Castles, A, *An Australian Legal History* (Law Book Co, Sydney, 1982), pp 67ff.
5. The 1823 Act initially provided for the Chief Justice to sit with either two magistrates or a jury. The section was subsequently amended.
6. Meagher, R, Gummow, W and Lehane, J, *Equity: Doctrines and Remedies* (3rd ed, Butterworths, Sydney, 1992), p 15.
7. See above, 3.3.5.
8. *Legal Procedure Act* 1903, extended by the *Supreme Court Civil Procedure Act* 1932.
9. See, eg, McLelland, C, "Fifty Years of Equity in New South Wales—A Short Survey" (1951) 25 ALJ 344 at 351-352. Meagher, R, Gummow, W and Lehane, J, op cit, pp 64-70 have a section on the Judicature System entitled "Was it a mistake?".
10. See further, ibid, pp 27-35.
11. See, eg, *Commercial Bank of Australia v Amadio* (1983) 151 CLR 447; *Muschinski v Dodds* (1985) 160 CLR 583; *Baumgartner v Baumgartner* (1987) 164 CLR 137; *Waltons Stores (Interstate) Ltd v Maher* (1988) 164 CLR 387; *Trident General Insurance Co v McNiece Bros* (1988) 165 CLR 107; *Stern v McArthur* (1988) 165 CLR 489.
12. *Supreme Court Act* 1970 (NSW), ss 22-23.
13. *Constitution Act* 1975 (Vic), s 85.
14. Crawford, J, op cit, pp 119-120.
15. Ibid, pp 95-97, 120-121.
16. Ibid, p 115.
17. See (1990) 64 ALJ 315.
18. *Supreme Court Act* 1991 (Qld). This followed a recommendation of the Queensland Law Reform Commission. Queensland Law Reform Commission, *Civil Proceedings in the Supreme Court* (Brisbane, 1982).
19. *Supreme Court Act* 1979 (NT), Pt III.
20. For a discussion of these issues see Kirby, M, "Permanent Appellate Courts—The New South Wales Court of Appeal 20 Years On" (1987) 61 ALJ 391.
21. See ibid at 402, and the letter from a former justice of the New South Wales Supreme Court, Else-Mitchell, R, ibid at 752-753.
22. Section 30(a) of the *Judiciary Act* 1903 provides: "In addition to the matters in which original jurisdiction is conferred on the High Court by the Constitution, the High Court shall have original jurisdiction . . . in all matters arising under the Constitution or involving its interpretation." Section 40(1) provides that causes which involve a matter of constitutional interpretation which are pending in a Federal Court or State or Territory court, may be removed into the High Court either by application of one of the parties, or as of right, on the application of the Attorney-General of the Commonwealth or of a State.
23. *Judiciary Act* 1903, Pt VII.
24. *Judiciary Act* 1903, s 44.
25. Barwick, Sir Garfield, "The State of the Australian Judicature" (1973) 52 ALJ 480, 488-489.
26. *Family Law Act* 1975 (Cth), s 95.
27. Mason, Sir Anthony, "The State of the Judicature" (1994) 68 ALJ 125 at 129.
28. See, eg, *Commonwealth v Verwayen* (1990) 170 CLR 394.

29. *Australian Capital Television Pty Ltd v Commonwealth* (1992) 177 CLR 106.

30. (1956) 94 CLR 254, affirmed by the Privy Council on appeal, (1957) 95 CLR 529.

31. *Bankruptcy Act* 1966.

32. *Philip Morris v Adam P Brown Male Fashions Pty Ltd*; *United States Surgical Corporation v Hospital Products International Pty Ltd* (1981) 148 CLR 457. See also *Burgundy Royal Investments Pty Ltd v Westpac Banking Corp* (1988) 18 FCR 212.

33. This is mandatory, prior to a contested hearing. *Family Law Act* 1975 (Cth), s 79(9).

34. *Family Law Act* 1975 (Cth), s 62.

35. See further, Astor, H, and Chinkin, C, *Dispute Resolution in Australia* (Butterworths, Sydney, 1992); Parker, S, Parkinson, P and Behrens, J, *Australian Family Law in Context* (Law Book Co, Sydney, 1994), Ch 7.

36. *Family Law Act* 1975 (Cth), ss 21A, 22(2AA), 22(2AB) as inserted and amended by the *Family Law Amendment Act* 1983 (Cth), ss 12, 13, and the *Family Court of Australia (Additional Jurisdiction and Exercise of Powers) Act* 1988 (Cth), s 12. Until the amending Act of 1988, it was possible for some judges to be appointed to the Appeal Division for a period of up to two years.

37. *The Family Court of Australia (Additional Jurisdiction and Exercise of Powers) Act* 1988.

38. *Smith v Smith* (1986) 161 CLR 217.

39. *Family Law Act* 1975 (Cth), s 22.

40. Australian Constitutional Convention Judicature Subcommittee, *Report to Standing Committee on an Integrated System of Courts* (Commonwealth of Australia, 1984).

41. Each Act is entitled the *Jurisdiction of Courts (Cross-Vesting) Act* 1987.

42. For discussion of the principles to be applied, see *Bankinvest AG v Seabrook* (1988) 14 NSWLR 711 (CA).

43. *Jurisdiction of Courts (Cross-Vesting) Act* 1987 (Cth), s 4(4).

44. A "special federal matter" is defined in s 3 of the *Jurisdiction of Courts (Cross-Vesting) Act* 1987 (Cth), as amended by the *Law and Justice Legislation Amendment Act (No 3)* 1992 (Cth).

45. In Western Australia, this is the Family Court of Western Australia. In the Northern Territory, the Supreme Court has jurisdiction in cases under the *Family Law Act* 1975 (Cth).

46. Jurisdiction of Courts (Cross-vesting) Bill 1986 (Cth)—Explanatory Memorandum, para 6.

Part Four

Legal Reasoning

Chapter 8

TRADITION AND CHANGE IN LEGAL REASONING

There are few aspects of modern law in Australia which are the subject of as much debate and controversy as the role of appellate judges in shaping the law. The traditional view of the judicial role has been that it is the task of judges to declare the law and the role of Parliaments to change it. This fundamental division of responsibilities between the courts and the legislature has its own roots in the constitutional struggles between the Crown, Parliament and the courts in the 17th century.[1] As a result of that century of conflict, the sovereignty of Parliament in law making became firmly established, and the notions that the Crown was free to make laws for the people without the approval of Parliament, or that the courts could declare a statute invalid because it was contrary to reason, passed into the mists of history.

That traditional view of the judicial role has in this century been subjected to a sustained critical challenge, on two counts. First, the objection has been made that courts do in fact make law through their existing processes of legal reasoning. This challenge is most strongly associated with the American legal realist movement, which emerged in the 1920s and 1930s. Now, the idea that judges do in fact have "leeways of choice" in declaring the law, and that they do develop and alter the law through their processes of reasoning, has become widely accepted throughout the common law world. The second challenge to the tradition has come from those who argue that the courts ought to make laws—that they have a responsibility to overturn even long-established doctrines which are indefensible or seriously inconvenient, if there is a lack of political will to achieve the same result through parliamentary enactment. In particular, those in the "activist" school argue that the law which has been made by the judges may, in principle, be unmade by them. This applies to the common law, which is the creation of the judges over the centuries, but it also applies to the body of case law which has developed on the interpretation of specific statutes, and the case law on the interpretation of the Constitution.

However, this acknowledgment of the law-making role of appellate judges rests uneasily with the traditional understanding of the role of the courts in a democracy. This is one reason why the High Court attracted so much criticism in some quarters for its 1992 decision in *Mabo v Queensland (No 2)*.[2] The result has been that in modern Australian law, as in other parts of the common law world, a tension exists between the principles of

205

adjudication which, by tradition, judges *ought* to follow, and the modern conception of the judicial role which sees judges of appellate courts as less fettered by established precedent than was the case hitherto.

To understand the debate concerning the proper function and limits of the judicial role in modern Australian law, it is necessary to examine how our traditional methods of legal reasoning developed from the notion that law was a science with a methodology analogous to the natural sciences. This view of law as a science has its origins, in turn, in the emergence of modern legal systems from the study of Roman law in the medieval period.

8.1   Law as Science: The Tradition of Legal Reasoning

As was seen, above, in Chapter 2, traditional approaches to legal reasoning may be traced to the development of legal thought from the middle ages onwards. The medieval idea of law, derived from the work of the scholastics in their study of Roman law, was that the law formed a coherent body of rules, which were based upon reason. The Roman law, as interpreted by the glossators and commentators, was "ratio scripta", written reason, and it was treated, within its sphere of influence, as having the same kind of authoritative status as the scriptures and teachings of the Church Fathers had for the life of the church.

With the work of the humanist scholars in the 16th century such as Donellus and Grotius, continental lawyers found a new freedom to rearrange the Roman law materials in a more coherent fashion, and to restate and systematise national laws in a way appropriate to the needs of their time.[3] This required a new paradigm for legal scholarship. In the medieval period, law was most similar to theology in terms of its philosophical premises and its method of scholastic reasoning. However, with the humanists, the study of law went beyond the elaboration of, and commentary upon, the old Roman law texts. The way was opened to fashion laws afresh for their own societies, building upon the existing body of rules developed from Roman law and local customs.

Eventually, the notion of law as a form of science emerged, with a method which paralleled the natural sciences. In England, Francis Bacon, who was for some time Lord Chancellor during the reign of James I, was an advocate of such an approach.[4] However, the main momentum for the new movement came on the European continent. The development of a scientific methodology of legal study has been traced to Gottfried Leibniz, one of the founders of modern mathematics, who, before becoming active as a mathematician, was the author of several legal treatises.[5] Leibniz developed the notion that law must be understood as a deductive, demonstrative science on the model of classical geometry. The analogy with geometry was taken up by other writers as well. Thus, Friedrich Carl von

Savigny, the founder of the historical school of jurisprudence in Germany,[6] wrote of his approach to legal method:

"In every triangle, namely, there are certain data from the relations of which all the rest are necessarily deducible: thus, given two sides and the included angle, the whole triangle is given. These may be termed the leading axioms. To distinguish these, and deduce from them the internal connection, and the precise degree of affinity which subsists between all juridical notions and rules, is amongst the most difficult problems of jurisprudence. Indeed, it is peculiarly this which gives our labours the scientific character."[7]

This method of legal reasoning was initially associated with natural law theory. The systematic treatises which emerged under the influence of this idea utilised processes of deduction. They reasoned from the general to the particular, deriving detailed rules from the first principles, as was occurring during the same period in philosophers' accounts of the principles of natural law. Lord Stair's *Institutions of the Law of Scotland* (1681) is an example of the genre. Stair began with the proposition that mankind is essentially free, except to the extent that obedience to God and voluntary agreement with others imposes various obligations. From this premise, a systematic treatment of obligations followed: obligations to family and to recompense others in various circumstances, such as damage resulting from delinquence, and then obligations which were assumed by agreements—"conventional obligations". He then went on to a discussion of rights, including rights in property and in succession.[8] Works such as Stair's treated law as representing natural truths discovered by this sort of deductive reason. However, "scientific" legal methodology was not dependent on belief in natural law, and in the 19th century, when the age of natural law had passed, this "scientific" method of legal reasoning still dominated the study of law on the European continent.

This perceived need for a systematic treatment of the law led in turn to the development of the great codes of law such as the French Civil Code. In France, Prussia, Austria and other continental European countries in the late 18th and 19th centuries, the law makers devised codes to order the legal relations of citizens with each other in the contexts of contract, tort, property law, succession, family law and in other areas. This did not involve a discarding of existing law. Rather, as Mary Ann Glendon has written, "the legal inheritance of customary and Roman law . . . was to be put through the sieve of reason. All that passed through it would be conserved, clarified, and systematised."[9] The drafting of these codes of law was regarded by people at the time as a development which had the greatest significance for continental European societies. The legal codes were seen to have an important educational role, and they contained many exhortations which went beyond the mere regulation of people's affairs and the resolution of their disputes. The codes pointed citizens towards the path of virtue.

8.2   Systematisation in the Common Law

By contrast, the common law systems were utterly pragmatic. Common lawyers preferred the practical reason of case by case development to the exposition of law in terms of general principles. For Sir Edward Coke, the great Chief Justice of the early 17th century, [10] law was the "perfection of reason", but it was not an abstract form of reasoning from first principles. For Coke, the law had emerged from the collective wisdom of many generations, "fined and refined" over centuries by long experience and by the contributions of "an infinite number of grave and learned men". [11]

The practical nature of the common law, based as it was on the intricacies of the writ system, and the case law which had accrued, meant that for many centuries the law was not seen as worthy of study in the universities. Law was seen solely as the province of practitioners, and taught only in the apprenticeship schools of the profession. Although the geographical distance between London and the continent was not great, the psychological distance between the Inns of Court and the legal ideas on the continent was much greater. Roman law influences entered in, to the extent they did, only through the back door, as judges drew upon Roman law learning in the universities and in the canon law. Generally, however, the baptism of young lawyers consisted of full immersion in the practical reason of the common law—its writs, its peculiar language and its arcane rituals of pleading. The legal scholar of the medieval and renaissance periods was little affected, in his profession at least, by movements within continental philosophy. As Goodrich observes:

> "To democratise or simply to open up the discipline of law entailed a move away from little England, its insular tradition, its myth of separateness. It required also that the continental basis of that tradition in the Hellenic and Latin classics, the history of their transplantation and translation, be recognised and rethought, that the faces of English scholarship turn again to those particular sources of their inspiration." [12]

However, English law could not be isolated from the influence of continental legal thought forever, and eventually, the notion of law as requiring a "scientific" form of analysis crossed over to England. The beginnings of an academic study of the common law occurred in the second half of the 18th century when Sir William Blackstone was appointed as the first professor of English Law at Oxford. His great work, *Commentaries on the Laws of England*, published from 1765-1769, attempted to expound the common law of England according to a set of logical categories. [13] But Blackstone could scarcely hide the disordered and inconsistent state of the common law. Its obvious disorder was the prelude to the 19th century attempts at codification and reform.

8.2.1   Legal science in the common law world

Jeremy Bentham, in particular, was a severe critic of the disordered condition of the common law. [14] Bentham saw little evidence for

Blackstone's proud assertions that the common law was founded on reason. He saw the common law as being full of fictions, outdated customs, and idiosyncracies. Bentham's answer, like his European counterparts in France and elsewhere, was to use legislation to systematise and to reform the law. Bentham's "science of legislation" was founded upon his utilitarian principles. However, there was little enthusiasm in England for major codification of the kind which was occurring in European countries.

Bentham's critique of the common law was nonetheless shared by others, and the first half of the 19th century saw the beginnings of systematisation in the common law. A part of the process of reform of the common law was to bring logical analysis to bear upon the accumulated mass of precedent. John Austin, who became the first Professor of Jurisprudence at the University of London in 1828, attempted a conceptual characterisation of the law in addition to his better known work of defining the nature of law as command.[15] In so doing, he borrowed freely the terminology and concepts of Roman law, although he adapted them creatively to his purposes.[16] Others undertook the work of systematic exposition in substantive areas of law, turning a chaotic body of specific legal rules into an ordered system of law expounded according to various legal categories and concepts.

Thus, it was only in the 19th century that the first great monographs of law began to appear in England, and similar texts were written in the United States. Before the 19th century there had, of course, been books written about the law. Generally, however, they were practitioners' texts on matters such as conveyancing, as well as collections of legal maxims, and other collections of the law. What was new in the 19th century was that areas of law were expounded systematically. In this work, the treatises of the civil lawyers of continental Europe provided a model. Monographs began with a definition, and then proceeded to expound the area of law logically from first premises. Thus, from the writ system, with its requirement for the correct choice of writ to cover the circumstances, emerged legal concepts such as "the contract" which had a life of their own as abstract entities. The mass of cases on these areas of law were rigorously analysed and synthesised by a process of inductive reasoning and from them a series of propositions, all apparently consistent with one another, were developed. In so doing, the textbook writers imposed a structure upon the common law which had a great influence upon its future development. It has been shown how contract law was systematised in this way by the treatise writers,[17] and the same is true of other branches of the law, such as the law of trusts.[18] The scholars' work was used by the judges in much the same way as the systematisations of scholars in continental Europe had influenced law in those countries. Judges' decisions increasingly conformed to the logical systems of the textbook writers. Much of the modern law still reflects this conceptualisation. Nonetheless, the interpretative grid which was developed by the textbook writers sat uneasily on the cases. Many were discarded because they did not fit the conceptual definitions and orderly exposition which the textbook writers provided.[19] Others were made to stand for propositions which would have surprised their originators.

8.2.2   The notion of legal correctness

One of the implications of this systematic exposition of legal subjects was that there was in place a framework by which the "correctness" of later decisions could be judged. A decision could be treated as wrongly decided if it did not follow from the fundamental precepts of that area of law or if it was inconsistent with the body of law already established. The ability to assess a particular decision by an external standard of correctness, using legal logic as the basis for assessment, gave to the academic study of law a legitimate role and purpose. It is no surprise, therefore, that the 19th century saw the development of law as an academic discipline, and in the common law world, its study focused on the cases which were selected for discussion as fitting within the frameworks of the textbook writers.[20]

Thus, the work of legal scholars became to analyse the authoritative materials, explaining cases and harmonising them with each other, extracting the reasons for the decision and interpreting the one case in the light of other cases within the same field. General principles were also extracted from particular cases and unifying features were found in disparate doctrines. This "legal science" had a number of underlying assumptions.[21] The first was that the law could be set out in the form of rules, principles, definitions and exceptions which would always yield a single correct answer to the problem in question. There was no such thing as a problem in which two alternative rules, or versions of a rule, were equally valid, giving to judges a choice between them. The correct answer was seen to lie in the correct analysis and interpretation of the existing legal materials. Secondly, it was considered that the law must always be consistent. The same rule was applicable whenever problems which raised the same issues of law arose, and distinctions between cases should be made only on differences in facts which made legal differentiation legitimate. Thirdly, legal science conceived of the rules as timeless, in the sense that they were not merely products of a particular time and place. They were treated as having a universal quality and continuing validity, whatever their particular historic origin. These beliefs about the law were not merely the assumptions of those who wrote treatises and taught the law to students. They were ideas which were foundational to the processes of reasoning and argument in the courts.

The academic work of analysis and synthesis continues amongst legal scholars today and is often termed "black-letter law". It is rule orientated. It takes as the explanation of what judges do what they say they do—the doctrinal utterances which are given as the reasons for decision. The assumption of much of this analysis is that the decisions although apparently divergent, are reconcilable—that there is an underlying principle which explains them even if it is not articulated in the case. Only when the decisions cannot be reconciled, must a choice be made between the conflicting rules, and that choice depends upon the status of the court from which the decision came, and perhaps the eminence of the judges involved.

Conventional legal reasoning, in which both practitioners and academic scholars engage, involves much the same kind of respect for the authoritative texts as the scholastics showed towards Roman law in the middle ages. Law is treated as a corpus, a coherent body of rules, and attempts are made to reconcile apparently conflicting texts in the same way as discordant scriptures and canons were reconciled hitherto. The echoes of a religious attitude to authoritative texts may still be heard in the courtrooms of today. The familiar patterns of legal argument require propositions to be supported by citations of cases and quotations from canonical judgments, and contrary arguments must similarly be supported by authority. In this way, the spirit of the scholastic jurists lives on in the traditions of the common law world.

8.3   Legal Formalism and the Declaratory Theory of Law

Traditionally, it was fundamental to judges' conception of their own role that they should declare the law, not make it. Implicit in this was the assumption that the legal materials contained the answer to the matter in dispute. Sir Matthew Hale, writing in the 17th century, expressed this view of the judicial role in stating that judges do not make law, since only the King and Parliament may do this; but the decisions of the courts "have a great weight and authority in expounding, declaring, and publishing what the law of the Kingdom is, especially when such decisions hold a consonancy and congruity with resolutions and decisions of former times." [22]

Thus, the traditional understanding of the judicial role was that if a dispute about the applicable law arose, it was for the judge to determine the correct answer after argument from the opposing counsel. That answer was to be found within the existing common law rules and statutes, and legal argument proceeded, as it still does, by reference to the decided cases and other sources of law. The appeal court judges engaged in a similar process to determine whether the conclusion which the trial judge had reached was founded upon a correct interpretation of the law. In deciding this, little reference could legitimately be made to matters of social policy or abstract notions of justice and equity, except to the extent that such ideas about public policy, or what was just and equitable in the circumstances, could be discerned in the previous case law. Thus, in deciding a disputed question of law, the judges' role was merely to declare what the law is; in no sense were they making law for the first time.

This approach to legal reasoning is often described as legal formalism, and it has been the hallmark of legal reasoning in Australia for most of the 20th century. The traditional role of the judges was expressed by Gibbs J in *Australian Conservation Foundation Inc v Commonwealth* (1980)[23] when he said:

> "If the law is settled, it is our duty to apply it, not to abrogate it. It is for the Parliament, whose members are the elected representatives of the people, to change the established rule if they consider it to be undesirable, and not for judges, unelected and unrepresentative, to determine not what is, but what ought to be the law."[24]

This view conforms to a traditional understanding of the separation of powers within a democracy. Parliament makes law, the executive has the function of putting the law into effect, and the role of judges is to apply the law in disputed cases. This traditional division of powers is so fundamental a principle of constitutional law that judges are usually reluctant to acknowledge that it is being abrogated by stealth through judicial law making.

8.3.1 Traditional legal reasoning and the process of change

This traditional approach to adjudication does allow for some development of the law through judicial decision making. However, the role of judges in making law is strictly circumscribed. Only Parliament may change the law if the law is settled, but the courts may nonetheless declare the law authoritatively where it is unsettled, and apply the existing law to new circumstances. Nonetheless, even where no precedent provides an authoritative answer to the matter in question, the decision of the court may be seen to be implicit in the existing sources of law. Thus, a former Chief Justice of the High Court, Sir Garfield Barwick, saw no difficulty in judges making new law when not so bound by precedent. In *Mutual Life & Citizens' Assurance Co v Evatt* (1968), which concerned the law of negligent misstatement first formulated in *Hedley Byrne v Heller & Partners*,[25] he said:[26]

> "the common law is what the court, so informed, decides that it should be . . . For where no authority binds or current of acceptance compels, it is not enough, nor indeed apposite, to say that the function of the court in general is to declare what the law is and not to decide what it ought to be . . . But of course the court is not to depart from what it realises the common law would provide in order to arrive at some idiosyncratic solution. So to do is to attempt to legislate and to tread forbidden ground."

The power to formulate rules afresh in a new situation has given rise to some considerable jurisprudential debate as to how this power of formulation should be exercised. Professor H L A Hart, formerly the

Professor of Jurisprudence at Oxford, endeavoured in the *Concept of Law* (1961)[27] to develop a model for how legal rules are different from other rules, and how sources of authority are identified within the legal system. He expressed the view that legal rules were not and could not be determinative of all cases which fell to be decided by the courts. Rules were open textured, inasmuch as there were situations which would give rise to doubts as to whether the rule applied, and others where there was no settled rule capable of application to the case at hand. Hart considered that in these situations, the judge exercised a discretion to develop the law in the most appropriate manner taking account of the competing interests involved in the case.

Professor Ronald Dworkin, who succeeded Professor Hart at Oxford, argued that in these "hard cases", far from exercising a discretion, judges may be guided, and are guided, by principles which are to be found within the legal order even if they are not, as yet, enshrined in a strict rule to govern the case at hand. The role of the judge, in Dworkin's view, is not to exercise a broad discretion based on economic, social or other criteria, but to look for a principle which is to be found within the existing law and which would be appropriate to the case at hand.

Where do these principles come from? To the late medieval writer, Dworkin's idea that hard cases should be decided by reference to principle would have been familiar. Between the 15th and 19th centuries, a large number of books were published which sought to elucidate the maxims and principles of the common law.[28] Professor Simpson describes the unique features of these principles:

> "First they were ultimate in that they could not be supported by any further arguments or logical demonstrations; hence it was idle to argue with anyone who doubted their validity, and equally idle to attempt to demonstrate a principle by arguments from authority. Secondly, they were thought to be self-evidently rational. Third, they had always been accepted, and thus they were timeless features of a timeless system. Finally, although only skilled lawyers could work out the detached application of principles, even a layman could, by knowing the principles, acquire a general knowledge and understanding of the law. With the belief in principles went the belief that there was always a right answer and in the 15th and 16th centuries disagreement among the judges was regarded not as a reason for voting, but as a reason for continuing the debate until answers appeared".[29]

Thus, the idea that hard cases could be decided by fundamental principles was deeply entwined with the idea of natural law—that there were principles to be discovered by human reason which were natural, universal and timeless. Many were rooted in moral reasoning. An example of such a principle, which is of some antiquity, is that "no man shall take a benefit from his owne wrong."[30] This example is used by Dworkin to illustrate how such a maxim might be applied to a hard case.[31] It has been applied in many contexts: to prevent a person receiving property under the will of someone whom he or she has murdered, and in construing statutes so as to prevent a murderer taking under his victim's intestacy,[32] to prevent a woman who had been found guilty of her husband's manslaughter from getting a widow's pension,[33] to deny a foreign national the right to citizenship on marriage where the marriage was procured by fraud, forgery and perjury,[34] and to prevent a man benefiting from the manslaughter of his wife in property proceedings under the *Family Law Act* 1975 (Cth).[35]

This illustration uses a maxim which is many centuries old. Other principles which might be used to resolve a hard case need not be of this antiquity. They might be discernible as principles underlying a number of lines of authority existing in the body of case law. Indeed, in deciding a hard case, the judge might have to consider the weight to be attached to two or more different principles which pull in opposite directions in the case at hand.[36]

The importance of Dworkin's theories has been to indicate that there are other sources of authority which are to be found within the settled law even when the case appears to be one of first impression on the particular facts before the court. This is an important corrective to the view that when one comes to the end of applicable rules there is a broad discretion. However, Dworkin, echoing somewhat the medieval view that law forms a coherent system, posited the view that all hard cases are determinable by such principles and that in any given case there is a right answer.[37] It is this aspect of Dworkin's theory which has been most controversial.[38]

The other traditional explanation for the growth of the common law, which is compatible with the declaratory theory, is that the law develops by a form of syllogistic reasoning in which the decision in one case may be applied to another even where the significant facts are not identical. This is an incremental theory of common law development in which later cases are seen as building on the groundwork of the earlier. The great American jurist, Judge Learned Hand, expressed this explanation of how judges make law by saying that "the whole structure of the common law . . . stands as a monument slowly raised, like a coral reef, from the minute accretions of past individuals of whom each built upon the relics which his predecessors left, and in his turn left a foundation upon which his successors might work."[39]

Syllogistic reasoning is a form of deductive reasoning which takes a major premise and a minor premise, and draws a conclusion from the application of one to the other. An example is: "All men are foolish. John is a man. Therefore, John is foolish." Lord Simon once explained common law reasoning in this way:[40]

> "A judicial decision will often be reached by a process of reasoning which can often be reduced into a sort of complex syllogism, with the major premise consisting of a pre-existing rule of law (either statutory or judge-made) and with the minor premise consisting of the material

facts of the case under immediate consideration. The conclusion is the decision of the case, which may or may not establish new law —in the vast majority of cases it will be merely the application of existing law to the facts judicially ascertained. Where the decision does constitute new law, this may or may not be expressly stated in a proposition of law: frequently the new law will appear only from subsequent comparison of, on the one hand, the material facts inherent in the major premise with on the other, the material facts which constitute the minor premise. As a result of this comparison it will often be apparent that a rule has been extended by analogy expressed or implied.''

According to this explanation, the law grows, not by the exercise of a free choice of the judge in the later case, but by logical processes of thought which makes the principle applied in the earlier case appropriate to be applied in the later case even though this may involve some broadening of the scope of that rule as hitherto understood. This form of syllogistic reasoning is a particular feature of the law of torts, and it is thus not surprising that so many writers, in expounding an incremental theory of common law development, draw examples from this area of the law.[41]

8.3.2   Legal formalism and the doctrine of precedent

By the end of the 19th century, as has been seen,[42] legal formalism was supported in England by a strict doctrine of precedent which bound judges to determine the law by reference only to the decided cases, and which ascribed differing levels of precedential authority to each case depending upon the status of the court in which the case was decided. The law, once declared by a final court of appeal, was immutable unless and until altered by an Act of Parliament. In 1898 it was established that the House of Lords should regard itself as unequivocally bound by its own prior decisions.[43] This doctrine applied in the United Kingdom until 1966, when the House of Lords announced in a Practice Direction that it would no longer consider itself bound by its own prior decisions, although it would treat these decisions as ''normally binding''.

Such a strict doctrine of precedent has never been applied in Australia, since the High Court was until the 1970s and 1980s, subject to the ultimate authority of the Judicial Committee of the Privy Council.[44] Nonetheless, the court has shown a strong reluctance in the past to depart from one of its previous decisions unless it was inconsistent with a decision of the Privy Council or the House of Lords.[45] One area of law where greater freedom to depart from precedent has been seen as desirable is in constitutional interpretation, since the court's interpretation of the Federal Constitution cannot be overturned by Act of Parliament. Judges have often said that the doctrine of precedent has less weight in constitutional matters.[46] A strong statement to this effect was made in the early years of the court by Isaacs J:

"Our sworn loyalty is to the law itself, and to the organic law of the
Constitution first of all. If, then, we find the law to be plainly in
conflict with what we or any of our predecessors erroneously thought
it to be, we have, as I conceive, no right to choose between giving effect
to the law, and maintaining an incorrect interpretation. It is not, in my
opinion, better that the court should be persistently wrong than that it
should be ultimately right."[47]

This statement assumes implicitly that in matters of constitutional
interpretation there is such a thing as a right and wrong answer. Isaacs J's
attitude to precedent in constitutional matters thus stands firmly within the
formalist tradition.

A strict approach to precedent has also characterised the lower courts
both in England and Australia. As a matter of authority, they are, of
course, bound by the decisions of the courts which are superior in the
hierarchy. Intermediate appellate courts have also taken the view, however,
that they are bound by their own previous decisions, unless clearly satisfied
that the previous decision was "wrong" in the sense that it was clearly an
incorrect declaration of the law.[48]

8.4   Legal Realism and the Challenge to Tradition

The first major challenge to the idea that the legal materials contain a
correct answer to legal problems, and that cases can be judged by an
external standard of correctness, came in the United States at the end of the
19th century. The reaction to the conception of law as a science of logical
analysis is associated most prominently with the great American judge
Oliver Wendell Holmes. He dismissed as "legal theology" the idea that
different propositions of law hang together in a logical system, and
criticised the notion that the only force at work in the development of the
law is logic. In a famous address, "The Path of the Law", delivered in
1897, he argued as a corrective to this that the scholar should instead take
the perspective of the bad man. Such a person is interested in knowing what
the courts will do in fact. He is scarcely interested that the decision of a
court of Massachusetts or England is wrongly decided when measured
against the plumbline of logical reasoning from previous decisions, if that
is nonetheless the decision which will be applied to him.[49]

Holmes focused attention on what judges actually do. He did not contend
that reason had no place. Far from it. He himself rose to be a judge of the
Supreme Court of the United States, and is identified as one of its greatest
judges. Holmes' point was that logic alone cannot explain the decided cases.
The "life of the law has not been logic", he wrote, "it has been
experience".[50]

8.4.1   The legal realist movement

Holmes' critique was taken up by others in the first half of the 20th century in what became known as the legal realist movement. Legal realism is a school of thought about judicial decision making which gained prominence in some of the great law schools of the eastern United States, such as Yale and Columbia, and gathered pace after World War I. The realist movement paid close attention to what judges do when deciding cases, and sought to undermine the notion that when deciding cases, judges reason towards a right answer which is to be located only in the authoritative texts. In this sense it represented a reaction to the traditional forms of legal scholarship.

The realist movement had many strands. One endeavoured to analyse the factors other than rules which may act as predictors of judicial decisions. This has led to a form of study known as jurimetrics, which is a study not of rules, but of judges. Particular appellate courts are studied. Predictions are made based on the other measurable factors which might affect the outcome of particular cases, such as viewpoints on policy, or more broadly, moral and political worldviews.[51] This attempt at scientific prediction assumes that rules are not the only factor in the equation. It also assumes that these other factors can in some way be measured.

Another important strand of realism was to analyse the way in which these extraneous factors may enter in. They could not do so if the law was a closed universe—if the decision in each case was logically determined by the ones which preceded it. The work of many realists, and perhaps their most lasting contribution, was to show that in deciding cases, judges have choices. They argued that judges are not compelled by logic and precedent to one decision. Logical arguments and authoritative statements may be amassed on either side. The authoritative materials delimit the choices, but do not necessarily constrain a particular result. Law, they argued, is to a greater or lesser extent indeterminate.

The realists were rule-sceptics. They varied greatly in the extent of that scepticism, and the extent to which they saw judges as having choices. One of their leaders, Karl Llewellyn, endeavoured to show the variety of techniques which judges use to interpret the authoritative materials. In large measure, the elements of choice in decision making generally derive from the availability of choice in the method of analysis of the previous cases. Llewellyn showed that there is a certain subjectivity in determining what are the relevant facts of a case and that it is often not possible to point to one clear statement of the law in a case which can be taken as the reason for the decision. Even if there is such a clear statement of the law, its application to later cases depends on the assessment of its scope and relevance to different fact situations.[52]

Nonetheless, in showing that judges have choices, Llewellyn did not wish to encourage the belief that appellate decisions are subjective and incapable of prediction. The fact that rules were not determinative did not mean that law was fundamentally irrational, only that the lawyer had to have an appreciation for the other factors of policy which may enter into judicial decisions. He referred to the law of leeways, and wrote that while an appellate court is free to make a shift in the content and direction of authorities, it must hold the degree of movement down to what is truly necessary to meet the need of the time.[53] In a work toward the end of his life, *The Common Law Tradition*, Llewellyn endeavoured to show how the law was reasonably predictable, and that there were stabilising factors in judicial decisions, even if the previous cases alone could not provide the basis for prediction.[54]

8.4.2   Legal realism in Australia

The fundamental contention of the realists that there are factors at work in the decisions of judges other than the application of foreordained rules, has passed into modern legal scholarship in America as a foundational truth. It has been slower to take root in England and Australia. Sir Owen Dixon in particular, was strongly critical of the contentions of the realists. In an address to American lawyers, Dixon responded to the realist critique by saying that the prediction of what judges will do by reference to their actions rather than their doctrine provided no assistance to judges in courts of last resort:

> "Predictability means nothing to a judge in that situation. His decision is final and a knowledge that what his court will say as to the rule of law is regarded by others as part of a general question of predictability does not help him to decide what to do. Such courts do in fact proceed upon the assumption that the law provides a body of doctrine which governs the decision in a particular case. It is taken for granted that the decision of the court will be 'correct' or 'incorrect', 'right' or 'wrong' as it conforms with ascertained legal principles and applies them according to a standard of reasoning which is not personal to the judges themselves. It is a tacit assumption. But it is basal. The court would feel that the function it performed had lost its meaning and purpose, if there were no external standard of legal correctness."[55]

Nonetheless, the realist critique did have able exponents in Australia. The most influential of them was Professor Julius Stone, who taught first at the University of Sydney and later at the University of New South Wales. Stone sought to show by exhaustive analysis of English and Australian law that judicial choice was as much a reality in these countries as in the United States. In one famous article,[56] Stone used the landmark case of *Donoghue v Stevenson*[57] to illustrate his view that it is impossible to say that there is only one ratio of a case, or that the ratio decidendi of a case can be determined from the case itself. Stone, as Llewellyn had done, pointed out that the "facts" of a case can be presented in many different ways. He criticised one well known formulation of how to find the ratio decidendi of a case which said that the ratio was the holding of the case in relation to the material facts. In *Donoghue v Stevenson*, the "facts" as alleged in the plaintiff's claim were that the plaintiff drank a bottle of ginger beer which was bought for her by a friend. Only after consuming some of the contents did she discover the remains of a decomposed snail at the bottom of the bottle. The bottle was opaque, and hence it was not possible to detect the remains through any intermediate examination by the retailer. The case proved to be a landmark because it removed what had hitherto appeared to be an insuperable obstacle to recovery. It was considered to be the position that where one person was in a contractual relationship with another, he or she could not be liable to a third person who was not a party to the contract for negligence in its performance. There was no contract between the manufacturer and the woman who drank the ginger beer. Nonetheless, the House of Lords held that the manufacturer could be liable in negligence. [58]

Stone showed that these facts could be characterised at several different levels of generality. For example, the agent of harm could be restricted to dead snails, or any noxious physical foreign body, or any noxious element. The vehicle of harm might be characterised as an opaque bottle, or any container of commodities for human consumption, or any containers of any chattels for human use, or any thing whatsoever. The potential defendants might be only manufacturers of goods nationally distributed through dispersed retailers, or any manufacturer, or any person working on the object for reward, or any person working on the object, or anyone dealing with the object. All the material facts could be characterised at these different levels of generality, and similarly, formulations of rules may be delimited at varying levels of abstraction.

It would be unreasonable to suggest that the rule derived from *Donoghue v Stevenson* could have been limited to manufacturers who allow dead snails to get into opaque ginger beer bottles thus causing physical illness to a person drinking the contents. The facts that the bottle contained first a dead snail, and secondly ginger beer, would not be seen as facts which circumscribe the operation of the rule since the result would no doubt have been the same if the bottle had contained orange juice and the noxious agent had been a dead cockroach. In any event, Lord Atkin did not confine his formulation of the rule in this way. [59] Nonetheless, much legal argument centres on the level of generality at which rules may be taken, or to which they may be extended. The scope of the rule in *Donoghue v Stevenson* on product liability was the subject of a series of appellate decisions in the ensuing years. [60] As Stone showed, it is often only with the benefit of hindsight after many years that it can be determined at what level of generality the ratio has been taken. Stone also pointed to a further reason for difficulty in determining the ratio of a case, that there may be competing formulations of the ratio within the case itself. Judges in appellate courts, who agree on the result of the case, may nonetheless formulate the rule in different and inconsistent ways.

Thus, a weakness of traditional accounts of legal reasoning lies in the assumption that individual cases lay down precedents which become binding for the future. It is more realistic to state that a succession of cases establishes a precedent than that one case in isolation does. No case stands as an island all alone. It is to be interpreted in the light of other cases which the judge or judges considered or which are otherwise relevant, other cases decided subsequently, and other areas of the law which may affect it. The result of the subsequent analysis of a case by later judges and academic commentators may well be that the case is made to stand for a proposition which cannot readily be found in the case itself. In this way precedents are shaped, refined and moulded through application, explanation and distinguishing. As Professor Schauer has written:

> "The passage of time compounds the difficulty of disentangling a precedent from its specific linguistic account, because the process of characterising a decision does not end with the first formulation. We necessarily and continuously reinterpret the past as we proceed into the future. People other than the initial decision makers use and talk about, and in the process recharacterise, the decisions of yesterday. The story of a decision changes as it passes from generation to generation, just as words whispered from child to child do in a game of 'telephone'. Past decisions thus come to the present encrusted with society's subsequent characterisations of, and commentary on those decisions."[61]

8.4.3   The demise of the declaratory theory

In recent years, it has come to be widely accepted both by academics and practitioners, that judges do have choices in deciding cases and that the judges do have a legitimate function even in a world where there is not always an external standard of legal correctness. There are few now, who would subscribe to the view that in deciding cases, judges simply declare what the law is. One of the most forthright denunciations of the declaratory theory was given by the great English judge Lord Reid, in an extra-judicial comment:[62]

> "There was a time when it was thought almost indecent to suggest that judges make law—they only declare it. Those with a taste for fairy tales seem to have thought that in some Aladdin's cave there is hidden the common law in all its splendour and that on a judge's appointment there descends on him knowledge of the magic words 'open sesame'. Bad decisions are given when the judges muddle the password and the wrong doors open. But we do not believe in fairy tales any more."

A similar view has been expressed by members of the High Court of Australia. Brennan J, regarded as one of the more conservative members of the High Court, commented in *O'Toole v Charles David Pty Ltd* (1991):[63]

"Nowadays, nobody accepts that judges simply declare the law; everybody knows that, within their area of competence and subject to the legislature, judges make law. Within the proper limits, judges seek to make the law an effective instrument of doing justice according to contemporary standards in contemporary conditions. And so the law is changed by judicial decision, especially by decision of the higher appellate courts."

The acknowledgment in the last few years that judges do make law, and that there are more considerations involved in adjudication than a declaration of the law on the basis of past precedents, has coincided with a greater willingness of courts to depart from longstanding precedents.[64] The High Court in particular has shown more readiness to depart from its previous decisions, and has encouraged a greater degree of flexibility by intermediate appellate courts.[65] Specific grounds on which the court would be prepared to overrule an earlier decision were spelt out in *John v Commissioner of Taxation* (1989).[66] In a joint judgment five members of the court referred with approval to the grounds for overruling given by Gibbs CJ in *Commonwealth v Hospital Contribution Fund* (1982).[67] These were that the earlier decisions did not rest upon a principle carefully worked out in a significant succession of cases, that there was a difference between the reasons given by the majority in an earlier case, that the earlier decisions had achieved no useful result but on the contrary had led to considerable inconvenience, and finally that the earlier decisions had not been acted upon in a manner which militated against reconsideration.

Even if courts are willing to acknowledge that there are grounds for overturning precedents other than that they were wrongly decided at the time, there are strong reasons why changing the law should still be left to Parliament. In particular, courts are mindful of the fact that the parties before the court may have ordered their affairs on the basis of the law as it was hitherto understood.[68] Since the reform may impact retrospectively on litigants it is more likely that judges will engage in active reform where there is a strong moral imperative revealed by the instant case. If it would be an affront to justice to allow the law to stand as it was understood hitherto, then the court will more readily make a decision which would amount to a clear change. Judges are also mindful of the tension between certainty and justice. While previous decisions should not be regarded as incapable of challenge, at the same time there is a danger in too liberal an attitude to previous authority. One judge of the American Supreme Court expressed this concern by saying that without a strong adherence to precedent, the decisions of the court might be treated "like a restricted railway ticket, good for this day and train only".[69]

8.5   Judicial Law Making and the Need for Legitimacy

The debate on the legitimacy of judicial law making is not entirely a new one. In a case in 1345 in the Court of Common Pleas, counsel raised the question of how courts should discharge their function in a society governed by law, since if they did not do what they had always done in the past, no one would know what the law was. To this, one judge responded that the law "is the will of the justices". Another judge, shocked at the first answer, responded: "Not at all; law is reason."[70]

A somewhat similar exchange occurred between the judges of the High Court in *Trident General Insurance Co v McNiece Bros* in 1988.[71] In this case, counsel sought to challenge a widely criticised, but entrenched doctrine of the common law, the doctrine of privity of contract, which holds that only those who are parties to a contract and who give value as part of the bargain, may sue on the contract. Mason CJ and Wilson J indicated their willingness to allow third parties generally to sue on contracts. They expressed the view that the court was entitled to review even basic and long established doctrines of the common law:[72]

> "Regardless of the layers of sediment which may have accumulated, we consider that it is the responsibility of this court to reconsider in appropriate cases common law rules which operate unsatisfactorily and unjustly."

By contrast, Deane J said that the disowning of established principle could only be justified by "precisely defined and compelling reasons advanced as part of a ˙ plainly identified process of legal reasoning".[73] However, Deane J agreed with Mason CJ and Wilson J in the result of the case, since he was able to reach a similar conclusion by application of the law of trusts. In the result, there was not a majority on the court which supported the abolition of the doctrine of privity entirely. Rather, they pointed out the ways in which by invocation of other legal doctrines, the doctrine of privity might be circumvented.

8.5.1 The method of legal change

Often, the debate between traditionalist judges and those of a more progressive disposition is not whether the law should change, but how. It is not unusual for judges to agree in the result but disagree very markedly in the way in which this should be achieved.

An illustration of this is the New South Wales Court of Appeal decision in *Halabi v Westpac Banking Corp* (1989).[74] In this case, it was alleged that a bank employee had defrauded his employer in the course of foreign exchange transactions. He was charged with a criminal offence and was also sued by the bank in the civil jurisdiction. He sought to stay the civil proceedings until the outcome of the criminal proceedings was determined, by invoking the felony-tort rule. This rule provides that a plaintiff against whom a felony has been committed by the defendant cannot make that felony the foundation of a course of action unless the defendant has been prosecuted or a reasonable excuse has been shown for the failure to prosecute.[75]

Historically, the rule originated at the time when the penalty for a felony was death and resulted in the forfeiture of the felon's property to the Crown. The rule thus protected the public interest in the prosecution of felonies and also the Crown's right of forfeiture. All three members of the New South Wales Court of Appeal agreed that the strict rule was no longer appropriate. Its historic rationale had long since gone and now criminal prosecutions were the task, not of private individuals, but of the police force and public prosecution authorities. However, unlike in other jurisdictions, the rule was still a part of the common law in New South Wales. The judges in *Halabi* held that the rule was inapplicable to the case, but differed strongly in their reasons.

Samuels JA considered that he had no power as a judge to strike down a settled rule of law. He did consider, however, that judges could "modify" rules in the light of changing circumstances. He proposed, therefore, that the rule be modified so as to require only that a complaint be made to the appropriate authorities. [76] Kirby P took a more robust approach, declaring that the rule was obsolete, since the legal reasons for it, and the social conditions upon which it depended, had changed so fundamentally that it was no longer apt to maintain the rule. [77] Furthermore, he was critical of Samuel JA's "modification". It was quite out of keeping with the historical sources and reasons for the rule, and inconsistent with past formulations of the rule. Kirby P thought it was more honest to say the rule is obsolete than to "develop or declare unhistorical exceptions and to 'add' spurious modern elaborations and 'modifications' ". [78]

McHugh JA took yet another approach. In a lengthy discourse on the role of the judge, McHugh JA argued that judges cannot invent new rules or declare settled rules of law obsolete. He accepted that it was legitimate on occasions to supercede a rule by incorporating it in a more general proposition by application of inductive logic. Further, a rule might be abandoned if it were logically inconsistent with other developments in the general body of doctrine. [79] However, with these exceptions, the judge's role was confined to modifying, varying or extending rules or principles of the common law. He said: [80]

> "The whole history of the common law demonstrates that it has been built by the judges modifying, extending and varying principles formulated by their predecessors. Many, indeed most, common law principles are still evolving. The contour of a principle changes as experience shows that it needs to be modified, varied or extended to deal with cases which were not foreseen when it was formulated. Its first formulation is rarely conclusive. When a principle is in a state of evolution, it is legitimate for a judge in dealing with an unforeseen case to take into account the justice, efficiency and reasonableness of the principle or rule in the light of the experience now gleaned from its application to cases of the class he is considering . . . But nevertheless the principle or rule as refined or extended must 'fit' with the existing corpus of law."

Rather than hold that the felony-tort rule was obsolete, McHugh J preferred to say it was "superseded" by the wider approach developed in *McMahon v Gould* (1982)[81] in which principles were formulated concerning the inherent jurisdiction of the court to order a stay of the civil proceedings where the conduct of those proceedings may interfere with the fair trial of the criminal proceedings.

At stake in this debate is the issue of legitimacy discussed above, in Chapter 1. Judges must not be seen to be legislators nor to let their personal opinions replace the authoritative materials as the source of legal decisions. Furthermore, too much judicial activism will upset the stability of the law. On the other hand, judges should not allow the law to remain archaic and inefficient for the sake of preserving the pretence of the declaratory theory. A former Chief Justice of California has commented aptly on the debate:[82]

> "The notion yet persists that the overruling of ill-conceived, or moribund, or obsolete precedents somehow menaces the stability of the law. It is as if we would not remove barriers on a highway because everyone had become accustomed to circumventing them, and hence traffic moved, however awkwardly. The implication is that one cannot render traffic conditions efficient without courting dangers from the disturbance of established patterns."

There is, nonetheless, a marked reluctance simply to discard, or to declare obsolete, doctrines which appear in modern circumstances to be inappropriate. The preference is for the approach which McHugh JA advocated in *Halabi*, to "reinterpret" the law in the light of more general principles. An example of this is the manner in which the High Court of Australia discarded the rule in *Rylands v Fletcher* (1868)[83] which for rather more than a century had been regarded as a distinct doctrine of tort law. In *Burnie Port Authority v General Jones Pty Ltd* (1994),[84] the High Court held that the rule in *Rylands v Fletcher* should be subsumed within the principles of negligence. They reached this result by a process of reinterpretation of the existing law. In *Rylands v Fletcher*, it was held that a landowner who stored water on his property was liable for the damage caused to a neighbouring landowner when that water escaped without any need for proof that the escape was caused by the landowner's negligence. The rule which was applied in that case was expressed by Blackburn J in the Court of Exchequer Chamber from which the unsuccessful appeal was taken. He said:

> "The person who for his own purposes brings on his land and collects or keeps there anything likely to do mischief if it escapes, must keep it in at his peril, and if he does not do so is prima facie answerable for all the damage that is the natural consequence of the escape."[85]

Although Blackburn J went on to state that the defendant could avoid liability by showing that the escape was the plaintiff's fault, or perhaps the result of an "act of God", the case was taken as imposing a form of strict liability for the escape of dangerous substances from one's land. The majority of the High Court, in *Burnie* considered that the rule had subsequently been subjected to so much explanation and qualification, and had given rise to so many exceptions, that Blackburn J's statement of the rule had been "all but obliterated". [86] They reconsidered the principles of liability for the escape of dangerous substances in the light of the subsequent development of the law of negligence, and concluded that the ordinary principles of negligence should be applied to such cases. The greater the risk of an accident happening, and the greater the potential seriousness of the damage if it did occur, the greater should be the degree of care taken to prevent such an accident.

8.5.2   The use of broad principles of law

The open abandonment of long-standing rules of law because they are no longer desirable, or the disappearance of well established doctrines by reinterpretation of the law, are rare events in Australia. More commonly, legal change is effected by other means. In recent years, the High Court has made great use of the "discovery" of broad principles which are said to underlie a number of related doctrines. The "discovery" of such an underlying principle can be the engine for new development in the law since the new principle is capable of application to many circumstances which were not encompassed by the existing and specific doctrines.

An example is the development of the law of estoppel in *Waltons Stores (Interstate) Ltd v Maher* (1988). [87] In this case, Waltons Stores had made it clear in the course of negotiations that, on the basis of an agreement for a lease, the Mahers should begin demolishing a building and erecting a new department store as a matter of great urgency. When the terms of the agreement had been settled between the solicitors, the solicitor for Waltons indicated that he would let the Mahers' solicitor know the following day if any of the amendments were not agreed to by his clients. When nothing more was heard from Waltons, the Mahers' solicitor sent the counterpart deed by way of exchange assuming that Waltons intended to proceed. In fact, Waltons changed its plans, without communicating this fact to the Mahers, and allowed the demolition and building work to continue after Waltons' officers had actual knowledge that this work had begun. In these circumstances, the High Court considered that it would be unconscionable for Waltons to be allowed to resile from the assumption which its conduct had induced.

The difficulty which was faced by the High Court was that although on the face of it the Mahers deserved a remedy, it was not clear on what basis this should be granted. A fundamental principle in a situation of this kind is that no one should be bound in law unless they have formed a valid contract. In this case the negotiations towards a binding contract had reached virtual completion. Yet no contract could come into existence until the draft contracts were actually signed and exchanged. The Mahers deserved some form of compensation because they had relied to their detriment on the assumption, induced by Waltons Stores, that the exchange of contracts was a formality.

However, as the law stood prior to *Waltons Stores v Maher* this in itself was not a ground for any remedy. In certain situations, people who relied to their detriment on the representations of others could gain a remedy. The doctrine of promissory estoppel applied to those already in a contractual relationship to prevent one party insisting on her or his strict legal rights under the contract where the other party was led to believe that these strict rights would not be insisted upon. The party making that representation would be *estopped* from going back on that representation. The High Court accepted this doctrine as the law of Australia in *Legione v Hateley* (1983)[88] but confined it at the time to those already in an existing contractual relationship.

There was also the doctrine of proprietary estoppel which applied in circumstances where one person encouraged another to build on land owned by the first. An example is *Morris and Morris* (1982)[89] in which a widower spent about $28,000 in building an extension to the house of his son and daughter-in-law in the expectation that they would live there together in the house on an enduring basis. When the marriage broke up, and he was forced to leave the home, it was held that he was entitled to recover his expenditure since he had relied to his detriment on the expectation created by the family arrangement. This doctrine has been applied variously to cases where a son built a house on his father's land with his father's encouragement,[90] where a man built a jetty on government land with its support,[91] and where a woman allowed builders mistakenly to build on her land rather than her neighbour's.[92] In each of these cases, the fact that the one who had expended money did not have legal title to the land concerned, was not a bar to a remedy. The legal owner was estopped by her or his conduct from asserting legal title against the one who had expended money.

Neither of these doctrines were of great assistance to the Mahers. There was no contractual relationship between them and nor did the Mahers spend money on land belonging to Waltons Stores. Rather, they expended money on their own land in anticipation of the contract by which Waltons would lease that land from them. Nonetheless, the High Court held that the Mahers were entitled to compensation for their expenditure. They held that promissory estoppel and proprietary estoppel as hitherto understood were manifestations of a broader principle of equitable estoppel which was explained by Mason CJ and Wilson J as: "the creation or encouragement by the party estopped in the other party of an assumption that a contract will come into existence or a promise will be performed and that the other party relied on that assumption to his detriment to the knowledge of the first party". Since Waltons had encouraged an assumption that the contract would come into existence and the Mahers relied on that to their detriment, they were entitled to a remedy. By defining estoppel in terms of a broad principle underlying the specific doctrines of promissory and proprietary estoppel, the court was able to extend the basic rationale of estoppel to the Mahers' case, and for the first time in Australian law, to allow recovery for detrimental reliance on an assumption that a contract would come into existence in the near future.[93] This idea that one broad legal doctrine may underlie a number of specific doctrines and lines of case law, is one which has great potential for judges who want to develop the law along particular paths.

8.5.3   Reconsideration from first principles

Another technique for creating legal change is by re-examining an issue on the basis of first principles. For example, in *Hungerfords v Walker* (1989),[94] the High Court overturned the long-established rule at common law that interest was not payable on the late payment of damages. That is, the damages must be assessed at the time when losses resulted from the breach of contract or negligence, and therefore, a right to sue accrued. Under this rule, the fact that the loss was not discovered for a period, or that subsequently, a further time elapsed before the right was vindicated in court, was not a reason to award further damages by way of interest. The rule had long since been modified by statute both in England and Australia, but the relevant South Australian statute in this case did not allow a full level of recovery since it provided for only simple interest from the date of commencement of proceedings, whereas the claim was for the losses since an amount was originally overpaid.

The common law rule was reaffirmed by the High Court as recently as 1984.[95] However, in *Hungerfords v Walker*, Mason CJ and Wilson J took a different approach by reconsidering the matter afresh in the light of the first principles of damages awards. The case concerned the losses suffered by a partnership through the negligent preparation of its tax returns by a firm of accountants. In the leading case of *Hadley v Baxendale* (1854)[96] it had been held that the level of damages should be assessed by reference to the losses which resulted as a natural consequence of the breach or those which were within the contemplation of the parties at the time they made the contract as the probable result of the breach. Mason CJ and Wilson J argued that the loss of the use of the money which had been wrongly overpaid in tax was a natural and foreseeable consequence of the accountants' negligence, and as such was recoverable in damages. Brennan and Deane JJ who had argued strongly against the open abandonment of a settled common law principle in *Trident General*, expressed their general agreement with the reasons given in the judgment of Mason CJ and Wilson J. They were able to concur "generally" in the abrogation of an unjust rule of the common law because it had been achieved through a process of reasoning from broader premises. In such ways considerable changes can occur in the common law without the need for specific overruling of contrary authorities.

8.6   Legal Reasoning and the Dialogue Between Past and Present

The acceptance that appellate courts in deciding cases often do have a choice whether to affirm the existing law or to reinterpret it, raises the question of the extent to which the past determines the present in legal reasoning. The realist challenge, in its most extreme form, suggests that at the heart of legal method is a flexibility which means that the law is indeterminate at its core. This is a view which has been taken up more recently by the critical legal studies movement. According to this view, on any given fact situation it would be possible to interpret the authoritative materials on either side of the issue quite plausibly. This is an extreme claim. It suggests that when judges apply the law they are in all cases exercising a choice to apply the law as hitherto settled, and could if they wished, decide the matter for either side.

The reality is, however, that lawyers and judges do treat most areas of law as settled. The legal system can cope with a penumbra of uncertainty in certain areas of the law, but it would cease to function if every rule were open to challenge and revision in every generation. The authority and legitimacy of the legal system depend at least in part on a sense of continuity between the past and the present. [97] Furthermore, judges do not wish to be accused of a naked usurpation of the legislative function. If judges do have choices in the application of legal rules, it remains the case that there are many reasons why they will opt for the accepted interpretation of the law unless compelling interests of justice necessitate its reconsideration.

Even where there are differing principles, cases and dicta which might be applicable to the issue before the court, not all carry equal weight and persuasive authority. Beyond the traditional distinctions between ratio decidendi and obiter dicta, and between binding and persuasive authority, lawyers and judges take account of other factors by which legal materials are accorded more or less weight. For example, the dicta of certain appellate judges, especially those who currently sit on the High Court, are likely to carry particular persuasive authority. Furthermore, there are certain propositions of law which might be advanced which are more consistent with general principle than others. Each rule forms part of a wider body of law, and its acceptability as a valid rule which should remain unmodified, depends not only on the internal coherence of the rule, but upon its compatibility with other doctrines and principles of law.

Furthermore, the fact that judges have choices in applying the law in many cases, does not mean necessarily that those choices are governed by extra-legal (or subjective) considerations alone. In determining what the law should be in an area where it is uncertain, or where traditional doctrines and interpretations have been subjected to challenge, judges reach their conclusion by an examination of the past, and perhaps a reinterpretation of the past. They refer to the decisions of previous cases, and the propositions of law advanced by previous judges, not as mere ritual, nor as an attempt to give their innovations an apparent legitimacy, but for the purposes of demonstrating both a degree of continuity with the past and of conformity with law's tradition. Reinterpretations and changes in the law occur not by reference to facts, ideas and principles derived from outside the law, although these may be introduced in support, but by reference to the concepts, principles, values and standards contained within the authoritative materials.[98] Thus, the tradition carries within it both the range of possible solutions to the legal problem, and the sources of authority which give legitimacy to the decisions of judges drawing upon that tradition.

This process of examining the legal tradition in reaching decisions about what the law should be is one of dialogue with the past. The past need not determine the present, but it is in the light of previous decisions, justifications for rules, and statements of principle that judges reach their conclusions in a given case. In this process previous decisions are reviewed in the light of their interpretation in later cases, and the decisions which have been made subsequently. Thus, it may be said that the past to which lawyers look for authority is the past as understood in the light of the present. The past is shaped by the very tradition which gives it authority and ensures its transmission. It is shaped by the values and understanding of those who interpret it. A particular case is read not merely as it stands alone but so as to be consistent with the whole corpus of law of which it is just a very small part. It ceases to be an island unto itself because subsequent interpreters insist on placing it into its context within that corpus. The writer and interpreter both have a part to play in giving legal precedents meaning and significance.

Change occurs through a reinterpretation of the legal tradition. The past is reviewed in the light of the priorities, needs and values of the present—sometimes consciously, often without a conscious recognition of the subtle changes which are being made. In this way, the old law continues to be shaped, modified, and where necessary, renewed.

NOTES

1. See above, Chapter 4.
2. (1992) 175 CLR 1.
3. See above, 2.4.
4. Shapiro, B, "Law and Science in 17th Century England" (1969) 21 Stanford L Rev 727.
5. Hoeflich, M, "Law and Geometry: Legal Science from Leibniz to Langdell" (1986) 30 Am J of Legal Hist 95.

6. This school taught that law needed to be understood in its historical context, as developed within a particular national society.

7. Quoted in Hoeflich, M, op cit.

8. Stein, P, *The Character and Influence of the Roman Civil Law—Historical Essays* (Hambledon, London, 1988), p 79.

9. Glendon, M A, *Abortion and Divorce in Western Law* (Harvard UP, Cambridge, Mass, 1987), p 129.

10. See above, Chapter 4.

11. Coke, *Institutes of the Lawes of England* (1628), 97b.

12. Goodrich, P, *Languages of Law* (Weidenfeld and Nicolson, London, 1990), p 48.

13. Professor Duncan Kennedy has seen, in this work of categorisation, a hidden socio-political agenda to legitimate the existing legal and social order. Kennedy, D, "The Structure of Blackstone's Commentaries" (1979) 28 Buffalo L Rev 205. For a contrary view, see Watson, A, "The Structure of Blackstone's Commentaries" (1988) 97 Yale LJ 795.

14. On Bentham, see above, 2.5.

15. See above, Chapter 2.

16. Hoeflich, M, "John Austin and Joseph Story: Two 19th Century Perspectives on the Utility of the Civil Law for the Common Lawyer" (1985) 29 Am J of Legal Hist 36.

17. Simpson, B, "Innovation in 19th Century Contract Law" (1975) 91 LQR 247.

18. Parkinson, P, "Chaos in the Law of Trusts" (1991) 13 Sydney L Rev 227. See also Alexander, G, "The Transformation of Trusts as a Legal Category, 1800-1914" (1987) 5 Law and History Rev 303.

19. As Sugarman writes, "the classical jurists . . . emphasised 'the best law', that is, they were highly selective in the cases they cited and and deliberately eschewed the enumeration of numerous authorities which was the hallmark of practitioner texts." Sugarman, D, "Legal Theory, the Common Law Mind and the Making of the Textbook Tradition" in W Twining (ed), *Legal Theory and Common Law* (Blackwell, Oxford, 1986), p 26 at 50.

20. See, eg, the discussion of Langdell's teaching of contract at Harvard in Gilmore, G, *The Death of Contract* (Ohio State UP, Columbus, 1974).

21. Simpson, B, *An Invitation to Law* (Basil Blackwell, Oxford, 1988), pp 186-188.

22. Quoted in Cross, R, and Harris, J, *Precedent in English Law* (4th ed, Clarendon Press, Oxford, 1991), pp 27-28.

23. (1980) 146 CLR 493 at 529.

24. A similar view was expressed by the former Chief Justice, Sir Garfield Barwick, in *Cullen v Trappell* (1980) 146 CLR 1 at 7: "[T]he court cannot alter the common law which it is satisfied has been correctly declared. Any such change must be left to the appropriate legislature. If, however, the court is convinced on its examination of the principle that the declaration already made is erroneous, then it seems to me the court is bound to declare the common law for Australia in that sense which the court thinks is correct." See also *Dugan v Mirror Newspapers* (1978) 142 CLR 583 at 586.

25. [1964] AC 465.

26. (1968) 122 CLR 556 at 563. It is not entirely true to say that in this case the issue was a new one. As hitherto understood, the law did not allow actions for negligent advice, but no decision of the Privy Council compelled that conclusion, and the House of Lords had in *Hedley Byrne & Co v Heller & Partners* [1964] AC 465, departed from it.

27. Hart, H, *The Concept of Law* (Clarendon, Oxford, 1961). See also, above, 2.5.3.

28. For example, Bacon, F, *A Collection of Some Principal Rules and Maximes of the Common Law of England* (London, 1630); Wingate, E, *Maximes of Reason* (London, 1658); Broom, H, *A Selection of Legal Maxims* (London, 1845).

29. Simpson, B, "The Rise and Fall of the Legal Treatise: Legal Principles and the Forms of Legal Literature" (1981) 48 Univ of Chicago LR 632 at 642-643.

30. Finch, H, *Law, or a Discourse Thereof* (London, 1627), pp 45-46, cited in Simpson, B, ibid at 649.

31. "The Model of Rules I" in *Taking Rights Seriously* (Duckworth, London, 1977), pp 23ff using the example of *Riggs v Palmer* (1889) 115 NY 506; 22 NE 188.

32. *Re Sigsworth* [1935] Ch 89; but see *Public Trustee v Evans* (1985) 2 NSWLR 188; *Re Keitley* [1992] 1 VR 583.

33. *R v National Insurance Commissioner; Ex parte Connor* [1981] 1 All ER 769.

34. *R v Secretary of State for the Home Department; Ex parte Puttick* [1981] 1 All ER 776.

35. *Homsy v Yassa and the Public Trustee* (1993) 17 Fam LR 299.

36. See further "Hard Cases" in Dworkin, R, *Taking Rights Seriously*, op cit. Dworkin posits a judge called Hercules of "superhuman skill, learning, patience and acumen" who is able to construct a theory drawing principles from the authoritative materials which will be sufficient to decide all hard cases. See also Dworkin, R, *Law's Empire* (Belknap, Cambridge, Mass, 1986).
37. Dworkin, R, "No Right Answer?" in P Hacker and J Raz (eds), *Law, Morality and Society* (Clarendon, Oxford, 1977); Dworkin, R, *Law's Empire* op cit, pp 225-276.
38. See, eg, Woozley, A, "No Right Answer" in M Cohen (ed), *Ronald Dworkin and Contemporary Jurisprudence* (Duckworth, London, 1984), pp 173-181.
39. Book Review (1922) 35 Harv L Rev 479.
40. *Lupton v FA & AB Ltd* [1972] AC 634 at 658-659.
41. See, eg, Maher, F K and Waller, P L, *Derham, Maher and Waller, Introduction to Law* (5th ed, Law Book Co, Sydney, 1986), pp 127-133.
42. See above, 3.4.
43. *London Street Tramways Co v London County Council* [1898] AC 375.
44. See above, 6.4.
45. *Attorney-General for New South Wales v Perpetual Trustee Co Ltd* (1952) 85 CLR 237 at 244, per Dixon J.
46. See, eg, *Queensland v Commonwealth* (1977) 139 CLR 585.
47. *Australian Agricultural Co v Federated Engine-Drivers and Firemen's Association of Australasia* (1913) 17 CLR 261 at 278. Other judges have been more cautious. For example, in *Damjanovic and Sons Pty Ltd v Commonwealth* (1968) 117 CLR 390 at 407-408, Windeyer J, after commenting that it was the text of the Constitution which is authoritative, remarked: "That does not mean that we are to ignore the authoritative expositions in earlier cases or disregard the facts in earlier cases, as illustrations of the operation of the section in the Constitution. These cases establish doctrine, expound principle, and by denotation, give a concrete content to the abstract and general words of the enactment. This restrains the predilections and idiosyncrasies of an individual judge from dominating his interpretation of the Constitution. It thus makes for a stable law and a stable economy". See also Gibbs J, in *Queensland v Commonwealth* (1977) 139 CLR 585 at 599.
48. See, eg, *Flanagan v HC Buckman & Son* [1972] 2 NSWLR 761 (a precedent should be adhered to unless it is "manifestly wrong"); *Raynal v Samuels* (1974) 9 SASR 264 (previous decision must be "clearly wrong"); *R v Chamberlain* (1983) 46 ALR 493. For criticism of the test that a previous decision must have been "manifestly wrong" see Aickin J in *Queensland v Commonwealth* (1977) 139 CLR 585 at 621-631.
49. Reprinted in Smith, P (ed), *The Nature and Process of Law* (Oxford UP, New York, 1993), pp 3-6. See also Twining, W, *Karl Llewellyn and the Realist Movement* (Weidenfeld and Nicolson, London, 1985), pp 10-20.
50. Holmes, O W, *The Common Law* (Little Brown, Boston, 1881), p 1.
51. For an Australian example see Blackshield, A, "Judges and the Court System" in Evans, G (ed), *Labor and the Constitution 1972-1975* (Heinemann, Melbourne, 1977), p 120.
52. See generally Llewellyn, K, *The Bramble Bush* (1930) (1960 ed, Oceana, New York) Chs 3, 4.
53. Ibid, Afterword 156, (1960 ed).
54. Twining, W, op cit, Ch 10.
55. Dixon, O, "Concerning Judicial Method" (1956) 29 ALJ 468 at 470.
56. Stone, J, "The Ratio of the Ratio Decidendi" (1959) 22 Mod LR 597.
57. [1932] AC 562.
58. The case is most famous for the statement by Lord Atkin that the command to "love your neighbour" becomes in law the rule that you must take reasonable care to avoid acts or omissions which you can reasonably foresee would be likely to injure your neighbour. To the question, "who is my neighbour?" he replied that the answer is persons who are so closely and directly affected by my act that I ought reasonably to have them in mind when considering the acts or omissions in question. This statement of the "neighbour principle" has influenced much of the development of the law of negligence.
59. "A manufacturer of products, which he sells in such a form as to show that he intends them to reach the ultimate consumer in the form in which they left him with no reasonable possibility of intermediate examination, and with the knowledge that the absence of reasonable care in the preparation or putting up of the products will result in an injury to the consumer's life or property, owes a duty to the consumer to take reasonable care." [1932] AC 562 at 599.

60. In *Stennett v Hancock* [1939] 2 All ER 578, *Donoghue v Stevenson* was applied to a case where a wheel on a lorry was negligently repaired. In *Haseldine v Daw* [1941] 2 KB 343, it was applied to a case where the negligent repair of a lift caused injury to a passenger. In both cases, the court found that no material distinction could be drawn between a manufacturer and a repairer, where the injury was the result of defective workmanship. Similarly, the principle was invoked where a company supplied to the plaintiff a reconditioned motor car in a defective condition: *Herschtal v Stewart and Ardern Ltd* [1940] 1 KB 155. The doctrine was also applied to distributors, who by their negligence, contribute to the harm caused to the ultimate consumer: *Watson v Buckley* [1940] 1 All ER 174.

61. Schauer, F, "Precedent", (1987) 39 Stanford L Rev 571 at 574.

62. Lord Reid, "The Judge as Lawmaker" (1972) 12 JSPTL 22 at 22.

63. (1991) 171 CLR 232 at 267. This may be contrasted with Justice Brennan's statement, made extra-judicially, in an article in 1978: "The judicial function is essentially syllogistic. The applicable principles—'the law as it is'—provide the major premise; 'the facts as they are' provide the minor premise; the judgment follows inexorably by applying 'the law as determined to the facts as determined'." Brennan, G, "Limits on the Use of Judges" (1978) 9 Fed L Rev 1 at 3.

64. The High Court has adopted a practice of requiring counsel to seek special leave to reconsider a High Court precedent. *Evda Nominees Pty Ltd v Victoria* (1984) 154 CLR 311.

65. *Nguyen v Nguyen* (1990) 169 CLR 245.

66. (1989) 166 CLR 417. See also *Street v Queensland Bar Association* (1989) 168 CLR 461.

67. (1982) 150 CLR 49 at 56-58.

68. See, eg, *Flanagan v H C Buckman & Son* [1972] 2 NSWLR 761 in which a majority of the Court of Appeal refused to depart from the decision in a previous case. Hutley AJA, with whom Moffitt JA agreed, said (at 781) that even if he were of the opinion that the decision was manifestly wrong he would not depart from it since it had stood for 12 years and had been acted upon in much litigation.

69. *Smith v Allwright* (1944) 321 US 649 at 669, per Roberts J.

70. Quoted in Simpson, B, *Invitation to Law*, op cit, p 189.

71. (1988) 165 CLR 107.

72. Ibid at 123.

73. Ibid at 143. Deane J has also put forward the view that if the court does change the law on the grounds, not of principle, but of policy, the adoption of that doctrine should be prospective only. *Oceanic Sun Line Special Shipping Co Inc v Fay* (1988) 165 CLR 197 at 257.

74. (1989) 17 NSWLR 26.

75. *Smith v Selwyn* [1914] 3 KB 98 at 106, per Phillimore LJ.

76. *Halabi v Westpac Banking Corp* (1989) 17 NSWLR 26 at 45-48.

77. Ibid at 38.

78. Ibid at 38-39.

79. Ibid at 51-52.

80. Ibid at 50.

81. (1982) 7 ACLR 202.

82. Traynor, R, "Reasoning in a Circle of Law" (1970) 56 Virginia L Rev 739.

83. (1868) LR 3 HL 330.

84. (1994) 120 ALR 42.

85. In *Fletcher v Rylands* (1865) 1 Ex 265 at 279.

86. *Burnie Port Authority v General Jones Pty Ltd* (1994) 120 ALR 42 at 51, per Mason CJ, Deane, Dawson, Toohey and Gaudron JJ.

87. (1988) 164 CLR 387.

88. (1983) 152 CLR 406.

89. [1982] 1 NSWLR 61.

90. *Dillwyn v Llewelyn* (1862) 4 De GF & J 517; 45 ER 1285. In this case, the father did not intend to deny his son's rights to the property. He signed a memorandum in which he indicated his desire for the son to have the land but this was insufficient in law to effect a transfer. He died subsequently. His estate was ordered to transfer the land to the son.

91. *Plimmer v Mayor of Wellington* (1884) LR 9 App Cas 699.

92. *Hamilton v Geraghty* (1901) SR 1 (NSW) 81.

93. The law of estoppel has since undergone further change as a result of the decision in *Commonwealth v Verwayen* (1990) 170 CLR 394. For a restatement of the law of estoppel in the light of these cases, see Parkinson, P, "Estoppel" in *Unfair Dealing, Laws of Australia* (Law Book Co, Melbourne, 1993), Vol 35.
94. (1989) 171 CLR 125.
95. *Norwest Refrigeration Services v Bain Dawes (WA) Pty Ltd* (1984) 157 CLR 149.
96. (1854) 9 Ex 341; 156 ER 145.
97. See above, 1.3.1 and Kronman, A, "Precedent and Tradition" (1990) Yale LJ 1029.
98. See also Krygier, M, "Julius Stone: Leeways of Choice, Legal Tradition and the Declaratory Theory of Law" (1986) 9 UNSWLJ 26; Krygier, M, "Thinking Like a Lawyer" in W Sadurski (ed), *Ethical Dimensions of Legal Theory* (Rodopi, Amsterdam, 1991), p 67.

Chapter 9

INTERPRETING STATUTES

The debates concerning legal reasoning generally, discussed above in Chapter 8, are as applicable to statutory interpretation as to common law reasoning. There are, however, differences between statutory interpretation and common law reasoning. In statutory interpretation, the judge is asked to interpret the exact words of a text which is authoritative,[1] whereas in common law interpretation the formulation of a rule by a judge in a previous case is not decisive of the scope and application of that rule. The common law also resides in a large number of judicial decisions which may have more or less bearing on the matter in hand. By contrast, the judge engaged in statutory interpretation has one text to construe. Furthermore, the specific nature of most statutes, and the precise context in which they apply, means that there is not the same flexibility in interpretation that there is in the common law. Yet even in statutes there is a certain level of indeterminacy due to the inherent imprecision of language.

9.1   The Need For Interpretation

9.1.1   *The imprecision of language*

Language is inherently an imprecise vehicle for communication, for communication is a process of interaction between the communicator and the person to whom that communication is made. What is said by one may not always be the same as what is understood by the other. People bring to what is communicated their own preconceptions of what the communicator meant. Furthermore, in both oral and written communication, people do not always take in every word. Rather they gain impressions from what is communicated which to a greater or lesser degree of accuracy reflect the essence of what the communicator intended to convey. Language is also frequently ambiguous. There may be an inherent ambiguity in what is said or written, since the words used are capable of more than one meaning. Thus, a listener or reader may in all good faith give one meaning to a word when another meaning was intended, or give to a generic word a broader or narrower scope than was intended by the one using it.

In daily life, the imprecision of communication is mitigated by many factors which reduce misunderstanding. In oral communication, it is usually possible for one person to seek clarification from the other if there

234

is an ambiguity in the words used. The person communicating may also realise from verbal or non-verbal signals that the other person has attached a meaning to the words which was unintended. A statement which is not fully understood may be explained more fully, with the communicator focusing on the area of difficulty in the recipient's understanding. If the speaker is addressing just one person, then he or she can use language which will most facilitate that person's understanding.

9.1.2   The problem of interpreting statutes

Legislation is different from other forms of communication in many respects. First, it is authoritative. It lays down a rule or standard which citizens, legal advisers and ultimately courts, must apply to given circumstances. Much may rest on a determination of what the words mean. Secondly, it is general. It is not addressed to an individual but to the population at large or to a segment of the population. Thirdly, the written text, and this alone, is determinative. There is no opportunity to ask the rule maker whether the rule was intended to encompass the given circumstances. The rule maker does not have a second chance to explain or clarify the meaning, or to consider how it might be applied to unforeseen circumstances or to subsequent technological innovations. At best, in most Australian jurisdictions, the courts may have recourse to speeches in Parliament or reports of committees which led to the introduction of the legislation in order to determine the general purpose of the statute. Fourthly, while in most oral or written communication, the person to whom the communication is made will endeavour to interpret it sympathetically, and to understand what was meant, statutes cannot be expected to be interpreted sympathetically. Indeed, the parties in opposition to each other in the process of litigation may have vested interests in giving different interpretations of the provision, motivated not by a desire to determine what the rule maker meant, but to advance the interpretation which is most beneficial to their case. In interpreting the law, therefore, litigants have an interest in finding ambiguity if the most obvious meaning is contrary to their interests, and the meanings which are presented to the court are those which benefit the litigants themselves.[2] Thus, the nature of legislation is that it must be interpreted in a very different context to other forms of communication, and with few of those factors which assist communication and clarification in oral discourse between individuals.

In order to seek to overcome the difficulties inherent in using statutes as a means of making and communicating rules, statutes have traditionally been drafted with a considerable degree of specificity in order to cover all conceivable circumstances and to reduce the possibility for misinterpretation. Such specificity has often been achieved at the expense of readability and simplicity. C K Allen once wrote that "a statute is probably the most repellant form of written expression known to man."[3]

By contrast, the tradition in the civil law countries of continental Europe has been to express rules in more general terms, leaving to the courts the detailed application of the rules in individual cases. The tradition of highly specific and complex legislation is not as strong in Australia as it once was. Increasingly, governments are realising the virtues of plain legal language, and there is a movement to make statutes more general, and easy to understand, than they have been hitherto.

9.1.3 *Types of ambiguity*

In the interpretation of statutes, courts must deal with a number of kinds of ambiguity. The first is semantic ambiguity. This arises where there is doubt as to the meaning of a particular word. There are a number of reasons why such doubts may arise in the course of interpreting legislation. Often this form of ambiguity occurs because general words are used. Legislation, being general in nature and intended to be applied to the public at large or a segment of it, necessarily contains generic words, which define a category or class. These words are capable of varying levels of interpretation from the narrow to the broad. Every generic word can be seen as consisting of concentric circles of meaning. One can identify certain objects which must be within the class, others which are probably within the class, and others still which may or may not be within the class. The task of the interpreter is to decide how broad an interpretation the word should be given, and at the outer limits of the meaning of the word, there is a penumbra of uncertainty. Semantic ambiguity may also arise because many words have more than one meaning. The word "light" for example, may be used as a noun, adjective or verb, and has a large variety of different meanings. Usually the sense in which such words are used is apparent from the context, but this is not always so.[4] Semantic ambiguity may further arise because words may be used in an ordinary or a technical sense. A word may be used in a technical sense in that it has a legal meaning which differs from that in ordinary usage, or the technical meaning may result from a particular trade or industry which is the subject matter of the legislation.

A second form of ambiguity is syntactical ambiguity which arises where the meaning of the individual words is clear but the difficulty in interpretation arises from the conjunction of one word, phrase or clause with another. Particular problems can arise from what grammarians call a hendiadys. A hendiadys exists where one idea is expressed by means of two words connected by "and". It is not uncommon for legislation to use two verbs in imposing an obligation upon a person. These may comprise two separate obligations (in which case each one is an independent obligation, and failure to comply with each will comprise a breach of duty) or there may only be one obligation expressed variously by the two verbs.

A third form of ambiguity is contextual ambiguity. Here, the cause of difficulty in interpreting a particular clause arises from the context in which that clause is found. A section may be ambiguous because of its position under a particular heading or within a particular group of sections, or because two sections within an Act conflict.

In order to reduce the degree of ambiguity in statutes, Parliamentary counsel, who are responsible for drafting, make use of a number of specific principles of interpretation which are understood by judges and other lawyers involved in statutory interpretation. For example, a statutory provision may identify the class not by use of a generic word but by using three or more specific words which all form a class, followed by a general phrase to include others of similar type. The rule of interpretation on which this drafting convention is based is the eiusdem generis rule[7] which requires the court to interpret the general phrase in the light of the class established by the three or more specific words. Another, similar rule is the noscitur a sociis rule.[8] This is a canon of interpretation which indicates that words take their meaning from their context. In resolving other forms of ambiguity, courts may have resort to general principles of interpretation. Traditionally, it has been said that the overriding goal is to interpret the statute in accordance with the intentions of Parliament, and there are general rules of interpretation which have been developed to assist the courts in reaching this goal.

9.2   The Intention of the Legislature

As a matter of constitutional theory, the notion that the court's task is to discover the intention of Parliament is a matter of fundamental importance for it emphasises the sovereignty of Parliament, and follows from the doctrine of the separation of powers. Basic to this doctrine is that Parliament makes the laws, while the role of the judiciary is to interpret and apply them.[9]

To a certain extent, the notion that the legislature has an intention is a fiction. It indicates, misleadingly, not only that a group of people may have a common intention—this is not such a strange concept—but that on the matter which is the subject of inquiry, the Parliament *must have had* an intention. This assumes that those who voted in favour of the Bill had a level of unanimity and of collective omniprescience which customarily is only ascribed to the Holy Trinity. Parliaments rarely demonstrate such divine qualities. Among those who voted for a Bill there may be as many intentions as to the meaning of a provision as there are political viewpoints represented in the assembly. Sometimes the form of wording is a compromise between those who would rather have a narrow provision and those who would like the provision to be drafted in much broader terms. It is not uncommon for the wording settled upon to involve a deliberate ambiguity in order for the compromise to be reached. The notion of parliamentary intention, understood in a subjective sense, also seems to

assume a considerable degree of foreknowledge of the circumstances which
may arise in the future and which may lead to consideration of the meaning
of a clause in the statute. Legislation must be applied in circumstances
which in all probability were not in the contemplation of the law makers
when the law was made, since it is not possible for law makers to foresee
all the circumstances in which a particular provision may need to be
interpreted and applied. The American jurist J C Gray has written: [8]

> "The fact is that the difficulties of so called interpretation arise when
> the legislature had no meaning at all; when the question which was
> raised on the statute never occurred to it; when what the judges have
> to do is, not to determine what the legislature did mean on a point
> which was not present in its mind, but to *guess* what it would have
> intended on a point not present in its mind, if the point had been
> present."

Put differently, the question which judges must often answer is whether,
given the circumstances which were clearly within the contemplation of the
legislature, the provision should be applied to the present circumstances
even if they are such that it is most unlikely that they were foreseen or
foreseeable when the statute was passed. It is by asking the question in this
manner that the court can deal with technological innovations. For
example, in *Lake Macquarie Shire Council v Aberdare County Council*
(1970)[9] the question arose whether a section in an Act which empowered
the local council to supply gas could be interpreted to include liquefied gas.
It was apparent that gas in this form could not have been within the
contemplation of the legislature at the time the Act was passed since coal
gas was the only form of gas then available. Nonetheless, it was held by the
High Court that liquefied gas was encompassed in the legislation. The law
established a class and the new invention fell within that class.

It is not possible, therefore, to speak of the intention of Parliament as
if one is thereby referring to the subjective intentions of those who voted
in favour of the Bill. The intention of the legislature is interpreted in an
objective sense to refer to the meaning of the words which Parliament has
used to express its intention. This does not necessarily mean that the ritual
invocation of the "intention of Parliament" is meaningless. It is possible
to give some content to the notion. First, one can speak readily of a *motive*
for legislation. New laws are introduced into Parliament for a reason.
Sometimes that reason is expressed in a preamble to the legislation. At other
times, it is apparent from the parliamentary debates or from an awareness
of the defects in the law which the Act was designed to correct. The motive,
or *purpose* of the legislation may provide some guidance as to how a
particular clause should be interpreted. Secondly, Acts of Parliament have
origins in the work of government, or committees and agencies appointed
by the government. That is, the detail of the Bill has emerged from the
considerations of public servants, of committees and of those drafting the
Bill. Sometimes these "travaux preparatoires" as they are known, are

available as a matter of public record. The legislation may have arisen out of an international convention, or the report of a law reform commission, or a public inquiry. Not uncommonly, law reform commissions append a draft bill to the final report. One cannot equate the intentions of those who wrote the reports with the intention of Parliament, but it may at least be inferred from the way in which the report's recommendations have been implemented that Parliament has adopted and endorsed the reasoning of the report.

Referring to the goal of statutory interpretation as being to discern the intention of Parliament acts as a reminder that the words of the statute should not be read in isolation. The words have a history, were enacted in pursuance of a motive, and have a context which assists in giving meaning to the words, or in choosing between two alternative explanations of the written text. In this sense, judges endeavour to determine the intention of Parliament through the words to which it has given its approval. The intention of Parliament is, however, only one of the factors at work in statutory interpretation. Judges must bridge the gap between that which Parliament evidently contemplated and that which falls for consideration at the given time. In this sense, judges must play a creative role, if not in deciding policy, then in discerning from the general policy in the given Act or in other enactments, a solution to the case before the court.

As the movement towards less detailed and complex statutes gathers pace, it is likely that the creative role which judges play in interpretation will increase. Reflecting on the movement towards more general language in statutes, Sir Anthony Mason has written: [10]

"The judge is also likely to become more of a constructive interpreter of legislation. That will happen as the so-called 'plain English' reforms in legislative drafting find their way into the statute book. The movement away from detailed regulation will leave the courts with more to do. The judges will be called upon to spell out the interstices of the legislative provisions. In doing so, they must resolve questions of interpretation by reference to the policies and purposes which are reflected in the legislation.

What I have just said may not be welcome news to those who believe that the courts do no more than apply precedents and look up dictionaries to ascertain what the words used in a statute mean. No doubt to those who believe in fairy tales that is a comforting belief. But it is a belief that is contradicted by the long history of the common law. That history is one of judicial law making which shows no signs of unaccountably coming to an end."

9.3   The Tradition of Statutory Interpretation

Sir Anthony Mason's approach to statutory interpretation is not new. In the period before the supremacy of Parliament was established through the political and military conflicts of the 17th century, the courts frequently resorted to creative interpretations of statutory language. In *Stradling v Morgan* (1560),[11] it is reported that various authorities were cited:

> "from which cases it appears that the sages of the law heretofore have construed statutes quite contrary to the letter in some appearance, and those statutes which comprehend all things in the letter they have expounded to extend but to some things, and those which generally prohibit all people from doing such an act they have interpreted to permit some people to do it, and those which include every person in the letter they have adjudged to reach some persons only, which expositions have always been founded on the intent of the legislature".

Even after the supremacy of Parliament was established, the primacy of the common law was such in the eyes of the judges that they tended to construe statutes restrictively where the legislation effected a change in the common law. They also adopted a strict construction to the criminal law where this would favour the defendant. Similarly, they showed a strong reluctance to fill in gaps in the statute even where this was necessary to make sense of the enactment. It was this restrictive approach to statutes which encouraged those who drafted them to specify the law's requirements with such particularity.[12]

Traditionally, the courts have applied numerous "rules" for the interpretation of statutes. They are not rules in any proper sense of that word. The word "rule" implies something which is fixed and must be applied in an all or nothing fashion. If followed, a rule is determinative of the outcome of a case, and the corollary of this is that if there are two or more "rules" which are equally applicable to the given facts, and which would produce contradictory outcomes, then one must conclude that there is no rule applicable to the case in hand unless and until the court has declared which of the conflicting rules should prevail. Understood in this sense, there are no rules for statutory interpretation. There are, however, principles and guidelines which influence the decisions of judges without in any sense compelling them to particular conclusions.

The three basic "rules" for the interpretation of statutes are known as the literal rule, the golden rule and the mischief rule. The "literal rule" provides that the courts must take the ordinary and plain meaning of the words as understood in their context. The assumption is that if the meaning is "clear" then the court is bound to apply the words in that literal sense. In very limited circumstances, the court may interpret the section in a way that requires a modification of the text. Words may be read in to make sense of a section which would not make sense otherwise. This is known generally as the golden rule and the classic statement is drawn from the speech of Lord Wensleydale in *Grey v Pearson* (1857)[13] in which he said that where the grammatical and ordinary sense of the words would lead to "some absurdity, or some repugnance or inconsistency with the rest of the instrument" then the ordinary sense of the words may be modified, so as to avoid that absurdity and inconsistency, but no further. Since this involves a modification of the ordinary meaning, not because there is an obvious semantic or syntactic ambiguity in the words used, but because the result is "absurd" or inconsistent with the statute read as a whole, the power to invoke the golden rule has traditionally been used sparingly. The use of the golden rule is dependent on whether the judge sees it as her or his role to correct obvious errors in the drafting of legislation or whether it should be left to Parliament to amend the statute.

These rules are applicable where the meaning of the words is unambiguous. Where there is an ambiguity, then the courts have traditionally used the "mischief rule" of interpretation. This rule is commonly dated to *Heydon's Case*, decided in the late 16th century. [14] In *Heydon's Case* the judges resolved that in construing statutes the court should look at the "mischief and defect" for which the common law did not provide and the cure which Parliament had laid down for that defect, with the result that the law should be so interpreted as to "suppress the mischief, and advance the remedy".

These traditional rules of interpretation have often been applied in Australia. In particular, it has been accepted as a central principle of interpretation that the courts must give effect to the ordinary and plain meaning of a statute where the words used are capable of only one construction. This is illustrated by the Western Australian case of *Higgon v O'Dea* (1962). [15] In this case the defendant was charged under s 84 of the *Police Act* 1892 (WA), which made it an offence for anyone who keeps "a house, shop or room, or any place of public resort" to "knowingly permit or suffer persons apparently under 16 years to remain therein". There was no qualification to this that the place should be one which would cause a young person some sort of moral harm or which was carrying on activities only suitable for adults. The defendant ran an amusement arcade, and the Full Court of the Supreme Court of Western Australia upheld his conviction because it was unable to construe the section in any alternative way, even though the provision was in the context of offences related to drunkenness, gaming and prostitution. Hale J commented:

"Under this section every shop-keeper, hotel-keeper and theatre proprietor who permits a child to enter his premises commits an offence, as does every local authority which permits a child to enter its parks or reserves. Such a result is clearly absurd but, to my mind, it is equally clear that this is what the section enacts. If an enactment is susceptible of two meanings, one rational and one absurd, it is not merely permissible but it is proper for the court to adopt the rational meaning: but where the language is clear and susceptible of only one meaning it is not permissible for the court in effect to legislate by refusing to accept the plain meaning of the words used." [16]

In this case, the golden rule could not be applied since there was no slight modification of the text which would have cured the defect. The section would have had to have been rewritten. Subsequently, it was amended by Parliament.

In other cases, Australian courts have been willing to read words into a statute in order to make sense of it. In *Re O'Reilly; Ex parte Australena Investments Pty Ltd* (1984)[17] Murphy J, deciding a case in which an order was being sought in the High Court against the Commissioner of Taxation, considered the words "within a reasonable time" should be read into a provision of the *Income Tax Assessment Act* 1936 with the effect that the Commissioner must give a ruling on an objection without undue delay. Similarly in *Cooper Brookes (Wollongong) Pty Ltd v FCT* (1981)[18] words were read in to overcome a clear drafting error. Aickin J dissented on the ground that it was not the role of the courts to fill gaps in the legislation. To do so, he argued, would be to usurp the legislative function.

9.4   The Modern Approach to Statutory Interpretation

While the literal rule, the golden rule and the mischief rule may still be referred to and invoked in particular cases, these rules are no longer regarded as being explanatory of the courts' approach to interpretation. Traditional expositions of statutory interpretation implied that courts may only look to the "mischief" to be remedied by the statute, or more generally, the purpose of the statute, where the wording of a particular section is ambiguous. However, it is apparent that in interpreting any written text, attention must be paid to the context in which the words are being used, and thus in the case of statutes, individual sections must be interpreted within the context of the entire statute and in the light of its purpose. Furthermore, the "mischief rule" is no longer an adequate approach to the identification of a statute's purpose. The assumption which underlay this rule is that the purpose of legislation is only to cure defects in the common law. This was substantially true at the time of *Heydon's Case*, but now only a small fraction of the legislation in Australia in any given year is enacted for the purpose of amending the common law. The common law is largely concerned with private rights, yet the significance of law in modern society is far more than in conferring such private rights and imposing duties between individuals. Most modern legislation is concerned with public life. It regulates and authorises the conduct of government, and provides the framework for the bureaucratic control of society in all its aspects whether social, economic or political.

9.4.1   Re-interpreting the traditional rules

Consequently, the traditional rules of interpretation have undergone some modification and restatement in recent years. The most important such restatement was made by judges of the High Court in *Cooper Brookes (Wollongong) Pty Ltd v FCT* (1981).[19] In this case, Mason and Wilson JJ were critical of a classical formulation of the literal rule given by Higgins J in *Amalgamated Society of Engineers v Adelaide Steamship Co Ltd* (1920).[20] Higgins J said in that case:

> "The fundamental rule of interpretation, to which all others are subordinate, is that a statute is to be expounded according to the intent of the Parliament which made it: and that intention has to be found by an examination of the language used in the statute as a whole. The question is, what does the language mean; and when we find what the language means, in its ordinary and natural sense, it is our duty to obey that meaning, even if we think the result to be inconvenient, impolitic or improbable."

In *Cooper Brookes*, Mason and Wilson JJ commented that the last clause of this statement would have been better omitted. They said:

> "Generally speaking, mere inconvenience of result in itself is not a ground for departing from the natural and ordinary sense of the language read in its context. But there are cases in which inconvenience of result or improbability of result assists the court in concluding that an alternative construction which is reasonably open is to be preferred to the literal meaning because the alternative interpretation more closely conforms to the legislative intent discernible from other provisions in the statute."[21]

For the same reasons, they also criticised the golden rule inasmuch as it appears to indicate that courts are entitled to depart from the plain meaning of an enactment only as far as is necessary to avoid an absurd result or some inconsistency with the rest of the statute.[22] They concluded that the rules of statutory interpretation are merely rules of common sense, and are aids to the interpretation of the intention of the legislature which need not be applied rigidly. It is legitimate for the court to depart from the literal meaning of the provision wherever "a literal reading does not conform to the legislative intent as ascertained from the provisions of the statute, including the policy which may be discerned from those provisions."[23]

The modern approach to statutory interpretation, in the light of *Cooper Brookes* and other cases, was expressed by McHugh JA in *Kingston v Keprose Pty Ltd* (1987)[24] in words which were subsequently cited by the High Court in *Bropho v Western Australia* (1990):[25]

> "Where the text of the legislative provision which embodies the proposition is grammatically capable of only one meaning and neither the context, the purpose of the provision nor the general purpose of the Act throws any real doubt on that meaning, the grammatical meaning must be taken as representing Parliament's intention as to the meaning of the law. A court cannot depart from the grammatical meaning of a provision because that meaning produces anomalies or injustices where no real doubt as to the intention of Parliament arises . . . If the grammatical meaning does give rise to an injustice or anomaly, however, a real doubt will usually arise as to whether Parliament

intended the grammatical meaning to prevail . . . if the grammatical meaning of a provision does not give effect to the purpose of the legislation, the grammatical meaning cannot prevail. It must give way to the construction which will promote the purpose or object of the Act."[26]

9.4.2   The ascendancy of the purposive approach

The "purposive approach", expressed by Mason and Wilson JJ in *Cooper Brookes*, represents the dominant approach to statutory construction. In most Australian States and Territories this approach has been reinforced by statute. For example, s 15AA of the *Acts Interpretation Act* 1901 (Cth) which was introduced by the *Statute Law Revision Act* 1981 (Cth), provides:

"In the interpretation of a provision of an Act a construction which would promote the purpose or object underlying the Act (whether that purpose or object is expressly stated in the Act or not) shall be preferred to a construction that would not promote that purpose or object."

Similar provisions are to be found in the laws of the Australian Capital Territory (passed in 1982), Victoria (1984) Western Australia (1984), New South Wales (1987) and Queensland (1991).[27] South Australia passed a similar provision in 1986 but qualified it by the preface that "where a provision is reasonably open to more than one construction" a purposive construction should be adopted.[28]

The immediate cause of the legislative change by the federal Parliament was the public controversy surrounding the literal interpretation of taxation legislation by the High Court in the 1970s, led by Barwick CJ. In particular, the court had taken a highly restrictive view of s 260 of the *Income Tax Assessment Act* 1936 (Cth) which was aimed at preventing tax avoidance. In a series of decisions,[29] the court adopted excessively literal interpretations which allowed artificial tax avoidance schemes to succeed.[30] During the course of the 1980s some of the taxation cases which had caused controversy were overruled and Parliament introduced a new Pt IVA into the *Income Tax Assessment Act* aimed at preventing artificial schemes to minimise taxation.

The ascendancy of the purposive approach is a comparatively recent development in Australian law, but it should not be seen as a radical development. At different stages in the history of statutory interpretation, the purposive approach has dominated, while a literal approach has prevailed often when the court has been most concerned to affirm that the law-making role rests only with Parliament and should not be seen as a function of the courts. The effect of this new ascendancy has been described by Justice Kirby, the President of the New South Wales Court of Appeal:[31]

"In a sense, the approach involves changing the focus of the camera through which a court views the words of the enactment. From the narrow field of the words in isolation or in their immediate surrounds, the centre of attention has shifted slightly to the ascertainment of the meaning of those words in the wider context of the legislation as a whole, other relevant laws, and the policy of Parliament as best it can be ascertained."

9.5   The Use of Extrinsic Materials

One of the major debates concerning statutory interpretation has been about the admissibility of extrinsic materials as aids to interpretation. These extrinsic materials include parliamentary debates, law reform commission or other committee reports, earlier versions of the bill, and explanatory memoranda.

9.5.1   The traditional approach

The traditional view at common law has been that such extrinsic materials are not admissible, except to determine the "mischief" which led to the passing of the legislation. [32] Many reasons have been given to justify this approach. In relation to parliamentary debates the argument is that the statements of individual members of Parliament cannot be taken to represent the views of the majority voting for the Bill. This argument is less cogent in relation to the second reading speech, since this is the occasion on which the minister responsible for introducing the Bill explains it to the House. To the extent that the Bill is passed by virtue of the government's majority in the House one may reasonably equate the views expressed in that speech with the intention of Parliament. Nonetheless, this argument did not hold sway with traditional judges who maintained the common law exclusionary rule.

Another reason often given is that to include the extrinsic materials would be to increase the cost of litigation since, in interpreting the Act, counsel would have to study a much greater range of material, and the reward of so doing might not justify the time. Furthermore, as Lord Wilberforce explained in a special Australian symposium on statutory interpretation:

"When one is considering extraneous aids, one has to bear in mind the difference of nature of the potential recipients. The magistrate or first instance judge has not the resources and he probably does not have counsel who can efficiently sort this material through . . . Higher courts, particularly the highest, have time to look at whatever may assist . . . If there is to be the same rule for all courts, it will have to compromise between the need for enlightenment and the need to simplify and shorten proceedings. We must avoid becoming too 'High Court oriented'." [33]

Considerations of the availability of extrinsic materials are especially significant in country areas where there may be no access to Hansard and other such documents. Even in cities, where such information might be more readily accessed, there is a risk that the right of recourse to such material will increase the costs of litigation, since the thorough preparation of a case requiring statutory interpretation would involve research into the background to the legislation, the preparatory materials, and the passage of the Bill through Parliament.

The traditional rule was reiterated by the High Court in *South Australian Commissioner for Prices and Consumer Affairs v Charles Moore (Aust) Ltd* (1977)[34] in which by a majority of 4-1, the court ruled inadmissible the original draft of the Bill and the relevant parliamentary debates. It had been argued that the history of the passage of the Bill through the South Australian Parliament would indicate that the relevant consumer credit statute was not intended to apply to department stores. This evidence was excluded on principle and the court interpreted the legislation as intended to include the stores.

9.5.2   Statutory reform

Significant changes to the common law position have been made by statute in a number of Australian jurisdictions. Section 15AB of the *Acts Interpretation Act* 1901 (Cth), introduced in 1984, now provides that extrinsic materials may be used either to confirm the ordinary meaning of a legislative provision or to determine the meaning where the provision is ambiguous or obscure, or the ordinary meaning would lead to a result which is manifestly absurd or unreasonable. The limitation in this section is significant. The High Court affirmed in a unanimous judgment in *Re Australian Federation of Construction Contractors; Ex parte Billing* (1986)[35] that it is a precondition of the use of extrinsic materials to challenge an ordinary meaning that the provision is, on its face, ambiguous or obscure or leads to a result which is manifestly absurd or unreasonable. If this precondition is not satisfied then no recourse may be had to the extrinsic materials.

Furthermore, unambiguous evidence of parliamentary intent which is evident from extrinsic materials may not prevail if the court determines that the intention has not been converted effectively into legislation. This was held to be the position in *R v Bolton; Ex parte Beane* (1987)[36] in which an American serviceman who, according to the American authorities, deserted the Marine Corps while serving in Vietnam, challenged the validity of a warrant issued for his arrest in Australia. Beane's argument was that the relevant legislation, under which the warrant was issued, only applied to deserters from foreign forces which were visiting Australia. Since the relevant events had occurred in Vietnam, the warrant was not lawful. This argument was accepted even though the Minister's second reading speech stated quite explicitly that the relevant section applied to deserters whether or not they were from a visiting force. The rest of the Act belied this express statement of intent. Mason CJ, Wilson and Dawson JJ, commented:

> "The words of a Minister must not be substituted for the text of the law. Particularly is this so when the intention stated by the Minister but unexpressed in the law is restrictive of the liberty of the individual. It is always possible that through oversight or inadvertence the clear intention of Parliament fails to be translated into the text of the law. However unfortunate it may be when that happens, the task of the court remains clear. The function of the court is to give effect to the will of Parliament as expressed in the law." [37]

Legislation in a number of States and Territories also allows recourse to extrinsic materials. The Australian Capital Territory, New South Wales, Queensland, Victoria, and Western Australia have all enacted legislation which allows such recourse, although, the terms of that legislation vary from jurisdiction to jurisdiction. [38] The availability of extrinsic materials does not mean, however, that there will be any major departure from the rule that words should be given their ordinary grammatical meaning. In *Mills v Meeking* (1990) [39] a case involving the interpretation of a Victorian statute, a majority of the High Court indicated a preference to be guided by the wording of the statute itself, which was unambiguous. Dawson J (in dissent) expressed considerable doubts about the usefulness of extrinsic materials: [40]

> "Whilst s 35(b)(ii) of the *Interpretation of Legislation Act* allows consideration to be given to any matter or document that is relevant, including reports of proceedings in any House of Parliament, the relevance of those proceedings must more often than not be questionable. The report of a speech of a member of Parliament other than that of the Minister moving the second reading of a Bill may often be unhelpful and even a second reading speech may be of little relevance. If greater significance is to be attributed to a second reading speech it seems that it must be based upon the assumption that it is less likely to express a mere individual view. Be that as it may, the words of a Minister cannot be substituted for the text of the law."

Similar views were expressed in the past by those opposed to the use of any extrinsic materials, and have been echoed by other judges since parliamentary reforms in the relevant jurisdictions allowed extrinsic materials to be used. [41] It is likely that the debate which preceded the introduction of the statutory reforms will continue as judges consider what weight to give to the extrinsic materials. No doubt, whatever the legislative formula, there will be some judges who will be swayed by extrinsic materials only when they point to a clear conclusion as to the meaning of a text which is ambiguous on its face. Other judges are likely to refer to the extrinsic materials and draw guidance from them more readily.

NOTES

1. For a full treatment of statutory interpretation, see Pearce, D and Geddes, R, *Statutory Interpretation in Australia* (3rd ed, Butterworths, Sydney, 1988); McAdam, A and Smith, T, *Statutes* (3rd ed, Butterworths, Sydney, 1993); Gifford, D, *Statutory Interpretation* (Law Book Co, Sydney, 1990).
2. Pearce and Geddes, op cit, pp 2-3. The court is not bound to select one of the interpretations offered by the parties. "Judges are more than mere selectors between rival views—they are entitled to and do think for themselves": Lord Wilberforce in *Saif Ali v Sydney Mitchell & Co* [1980] AC 198 at 212.
3. Allen, C K, *Aspects of Justice* (Stevens, London, 1958), p 284.
4. See, eg, *Murphy v Farmer* (1988) 79 ALR 1, in which the court had to determine whether the word "false" was being used in the sense of something being "wrong", or whether its other meaning, "deliberately untrue", was intended. On ambiguity generally see Evans, J, *Statutory Interpretation* (OUP, Auckland, 1988), ch 4.
5. Latin for "of the same kind".
6. For a detailed treatment, see the works cited in n 1, above.
7. *Duport Steels Ltd v Sirs* [1980] 1 All ER 529 at 541, per Lord Diplock.
8. Gray, J C, *The Nature and Sources of Law* (2nd ed, 1921), p 173, cited in Cross, R, *Statutory Interpretation* (Butterworths, London, 1976), p 25.
9. (1970) 123 CLR 327.
10. Mason, A, "The Australian Judiciary in the 1990s" (1994) 6 *Sydney Papers* 111 at 113-114.
11. (1560) 1 Plowd 199 at 205.
12. Cross, R, op cit, pp 8-12.
13. (1857) 6 HLC 61 at 106.
14. (1584) 3 Co Rep 7a at 7b; 76 ER 637 at 638.
15. [1962] WAR 140.
16. Ibid at 146.
17. (1984) 58 ALJR 36.
18. (1981) 147 CLR 297.
19. Ibid.
20. (1920) 28 CLR 129 at 161-162.
21. *Cooper Brookes (Wollongong) Pty Ltd v FCT* (1981) 147 CLR 297 at 320.
22. Ibid.
23. Ibid at 321.
24. (1987) 11 NSWLR 404.
25. (1990) 171 CLR 1 at 20.
26. *Kingston v Keprose Pty Ltd* (1987) 11 NSWLR 404 at 421-423.
27. *Interpretation Ordinance* 1967 (ACT), s 11A; *Interpretation Act* 1987 (NSW), s 33; *Acts Interpretation Act* 1954 (Qld), s 14A; *Interpretation of Legislation Act* 1984 (Vic), s 35(a); *Interpretation Act* 1984 (WA), s 18.
28. *Acts Interpretation Act* 1915 (SA), s 22.
29. For example, *Curran v Commissioner of Taxation* (1974) 131 CLR 409.
30. Commenting on this line of decisions in a dissenting judgment in 1980, Murphy J said: "In tax cases, the prevailing trend in Australia is now so absolutely literalistic that it has become a disquieting phenomenon. Because of it, scorn for tax decisions is being expressed constantly, not only by legislators who consider that their Acts are being mocked, but even by those who benefit. In my opinion, strictly literal interpretation of a tax Act is an open invitation to artificial and contrived tax avoidance. Progress towards a free society will not be advanced by attributing to Parliament meanings which no one believes it intended so that income tax becomes optional for the rich while remaining compulsory for most income earners." *FCT v Westraders Pty Ltd* (1980) 30 ALR 353 at 371.
31. *Bate v Priestly* (1990) FLC 92-102 at 77,663.
32. *Assam Railways and Trading Co Ltd v IR Commrs* [1935] AC 445; *Bitumen and Oil Refineries (Aust) Ltd v Commr for Government Transport* (1955) 92 CLR 200; *Wacando v Commonwealth* (1981) 148 CLR 1 at 25-26, per Mason J; *FCT v Whitfords Beach Pty Ltd* (1982) 150 CLR 355 at 373-375, per Mason J; *Hoare v R* (1989) 167 CLR 348 at 360.

33. Lord Wilberforce, "A Judicial Viewpoint" in *Symposium on Statutory Interpretation* (Attorney-General's Department, Canberra, 1983), p 5, at pp 7-8.
34. (1977) 139 CLR 449.
35. (1986) 68 ALR 416.
36. (1987) 162 CLR 514.
37. Ibid at 518.
38. *Interpretation Ordinance* 1967 (ACT), s 11B; *Interpretation Act* 1987 (NSW), s 34; *Acts Interpretation Act* 1954 (Qld), s 14B; *Interpretation of Legislation Act* (Vic), s 35; *Interpretation Act* 1984 (WA), s 19.
39. (1990) 169 CLR 214.
40. Ibid at 236-237.
41. *Commissioner of Police v Curran* (1984) 55 ALR 697 at 706-707, per Wilcox J; *Flaherty v Girgis* (1985) 4 NSWLR 248 at 259, per Kirby P.

Part Five

The Future of Australian Law

Chapter 10

THE CHALLENGE OF INCLUSION

The last quarter of the 20th century has proved to be a period of considerable change in Australian law. It has seen Australia achieve formal autonomy and legal independence as a result of the Australia Acts. This has coincided with the High Court's active reshaping of Australian common law in a manner which has led to an increasing gulf between the common law of Australia and that of other Commonwealth jurisdictions, including England. As the century, and indeed the millenium draws to a close, the severance of links with the British monarchy is being given serious consideration, and if Australia adopts the Republican path, this will necessitate substantial revisions to the federal Constitution. All these changes are deeply significant for the future of Australian law. A tradition received from Britain, and modified for Australian conditions from the earliest days of white settlement, has now evolved in such a way that it is possible to speak of a tradition of law in Australia which is distinct from the legal traditions of other common law countries.

Yet how "Australian" is the tradition? It is not Australian merely by virtue of the fact that the law has been shaped in a distinctive manner by Australian judges and the legislation of Australian Parliaments, both State and federal. Nor is it Australian merely because it differs from English law, New Zealand law, or the laws of other common law jurisdictions. Distinctiveness may be important to the formation of national identity, but distinctiveness from other legal systems is not sufficient to ensure that a country's legal system is "owned" by its people. For the tradition of law in Australia to be Australian, it needs to be a tradition which people accept as a valuable aspect of Australian life, and which reflects the composition, character and aspirations of the population. Furthermore, lawyers and the court system must be relevant to the general population as a last resort in the resolution of disputes, and not merely to corporations and organs of government. Despite all the changes in Australian law over the last quarter of a century, Australian law remains largely monocultural, and although women have been able to practice law for most of the century, the public face of the legal system—its judiciary and senior advocates—is predominantly a male face.

The challenge of inclusion is a challenge for the legal system to be more accommodating of the needs of the Australian population, and, in its public face, to be more representative of the diversity of that population. Perhaps the greatest challenge of all is that the legal system should be more accessible to private individuals, for the costs of justice are so high that they represent a major barrier to the legal system for a large proportion of the population. Increasing access to the court system is important, not merely so that all disputes which require a third party adjudicator can be resolved in accordance with the law, but so that the principle of the rule of law can be sustained.

10.1   Accommodating Diversity—A Legal System for All

For the tradition of law in Australia to reflect the composition and character of its population, its laws need to be drafted in a way which takes account of the diversity of that population, and the legal system needs to provide adequate protection for the rights of all. Many of these rights are the subject of international conventions to which Australia is a signatory such as the *International Covenant on Civil and Political Rights*, the *Convention on the Elimination of All Forms of Racial Discrimination*, the *Convention on the Elimination of All Forms of Discrimination Against Women*, and the *Convention on the Rights of the Child*. Treaties do not become part of Australian law merely because Australia is a signatory to them. In any event, many treaties and conventions are drafted with such a degree of generality and deliberate ambiguity that they could not usefully be adopted into Australian law as a source of specific rights and obligations. Furthermore, many specific provisions of conventions are not intended to be the source of individual rights but rather impose obligations upon governments to improve the welfare of the population through executive action and administrative measures. Nonetheless, numerous laws, both State and federal, prohibit discrimination, and provide remedies where discrimination is demonstrated, as well as conferring other legal rights which are consistent with the rights conferred under international law.

To a great extent, these international conventions on human rights reflect the values of the western legal tradition. The very language of human rights owes its origins to the western legal tradition, and in particular, the enlightenment precepts of the French and American Revolutions. The notion that the legal system should be the means by which social change is effected is also a peculiarly western idea, tracing its origins historically to the central role which law has had in all social ordering.[1] International law, with its use of moral and political pressure as a means of enforcing otherwise unenforceable obligations, is also dependent upon the notion of respect for law which is part of the western legal inheritance.[2] Thus, although international conventions on human rights are of quite recent origin, and laws prohibiting discrimination have only been enacted in the last few years, these developments find their origin and impetus within the western legal tradition, rather than by departure from it.

Nonetheless, the tradition of law in Australia, as in other western countries, has needed, and still needs, to undergo a transformation and renewal in order to become more relevant to the diverse population which the legal system serves and the range of demands upon that system. It should not be surprising that a legal tradition which developed in a time when the population was relatively homogenous, both ethnically and culturally, and in which men of Anglo-Celtic descent dominated and controlled public life, should, at times unwittingly, be insensitive to the needs of Aboriginal peoples, children, the disabled, ethnic minorities and women. The challenge of inclusion is a challenge to make the legal system more accessible, and the laws fairer to, a number of groups in society, so that it meets the needs of the diverse range of people who come into contact with the system.

10.1.1   Reconciliation with Aboriginal and Torres Strait Islander peoples

A particular need is for reconciliation between Aboriginal and Torres Strait Islander peoples and the white majority, and to reduce the justified suspicion of the legal system among Aboriginal people. The treatment of Aboriginal people within the legal system and by its laws has left a legacy of bitterness and suspicion among the Aboriginal community which it may take many generations to diminish. Elliott Johnston QC commented in the *National Report of the Royal Commission into Aboriginal Deaths in Custody* (1991) that "Aboriginal people have a unique history of being ordered, controlled and monitored by the State."[3] The process of dispossession from their traditional lands destroyed the Aboriginal economy which was based upon hunting and foraging, and led to an economic dependency upon white people. The subsequent history of race relations was one of control of every aspect of the lives of Aboriginal people, sometimes for the best of motives, but in the worst of ways. Aboriginal people were the victims not only of a racism which assumed the superiority of white ways and values, but also of a despotic benevolence which was equally destructive to their culture.[4]

The legal system provided the framework within which all this occurred, and the police were frequently the enforcers of government policies directed towards Aborigines, with the result that the tension between police and Aboriginal people has a long history. Still, the legal system is culturally alien to most Aboriginal people, and the suspicion of police and courts is deeply ingrained.

The *Mabo* decision[5] was an important step in the process of reconciliation, as was the *Native Title Act* 1993 (Cth).[6] The Australian Law Reform Commission in its report on the recognition of Aboriginal customary laws in 1986 made numerous recommendations for ways in which Aboriginal customary law could be integrated into the system of laws applicable to Aboriginal people.[7] An aspect of respect for Aboriginal people is respect for their traditions, however alien they may be to white Australian culture. These traditions need further recognition by the legal system.

10.1.2   Women and the law

Historically, the laws have also provided a framework for the exclusion of women from public life. Laws reserved the vote to adult males (and until the mid-19th century, only to those males with a particular level of wealth). Laws excluded women from the professions and from other forms of employment. The social structure, reinforced by law, placed women's role in the home, and subordinated their position to that of fathers and husbands.[8] Women did not have an autonomous legal status, rather their position was subsumed within the family unit and their interests identified with the interests of the family. Through the course of this century, this legal position has gradually changed. Women have been disaggregated from the family unit and allowed autonomy as individuals. The legal barriers to employment have been removed, and laws have been put in place to try to reinforce the principle of equal opportunity.

Coinciding with these changes, enormous changes have occurred in social structures in this century; the majority of women with dependent children now participate in the workforce,[9] although often this work is part time. Whereas once, women were subsumed within the family unit, there has been a loosening of the ties which bind people together in marriage simultaneously with a marked increase in the legal regulation of the employment relationship.[10] The changes in social structures have in turn produced new dilemmas for the law makers in determining the extent to which employers should be required to accommodate family commitments as a cost of employing staff, the way in which property should be allocated on marriage breakdown, and many other social issues associated with the changed social structures.

At a time when society is in such a stage of transition, and when so many aspects of male-female relationships are being renegotiated, an important aspect of the challenge of inclusion is the need to engage in a continual examination of our laws and policies to ensure that a fair balance is being struck between the rights of men and women in different areas of social life. Another aspect of the challenge is to ensure that laws which are apparently neutral on their face do not have a discriminatory impact in practice, and do not contain implicitly masculine assumptions.[11]

Changing laws is, however, only one dimension of the challenge. More difficult is changing attitudes. The structures of business and the professions do not readily accommodate the needs of women as the primary caretakers of children and other family members.[12] Consequently, women continue to pay a disproportionate share of the costs of caring.[13] Attitudes also need to be changed among lawyers and judges in order to eradicate examples of discrimination and gender insensitivity in the practice of the law. [14] The process of cross-examination in relation to complaints of domestic violence or sexual assault can be particularly alienating, as some defence lawyers seek to discredit the testimony of women by any means possible. They are aided and abetted in this by the adversarial system, which is predicated on the basis that each side should be able to present its case in whatever way it sees fit without much interference or control from the Bench. While judges have the power to disallow unfair questioning and to prohibit the harassment of witnesses, they are often reluctant to interfere with the manner in which the defence presents its case. This latitude given to defence lawyers in criminal trials is not infrequently at the expense of female witnesses.

10.1.3   Children and the courts

The legal system has also had to adapt to the needs of children to a much greater extent than hitherto. The awareness in recent years of the extent of child sexual assault, [15] and the public concern about the issue, has led to a considerable increase in the numbers of prosecutions for sexual offences against children, and also a reduction in the age at which children might be called to give evidence. In turn, this has led to greater attention being paid to the needs of children as witnesses. The laws of evidence have been amended in most States and Territories to reduce the number of situations when children are deemed incompetent to give evidence, and to remove provisions which required that their evidence be corroborated in order to be accepted. [16]

Court is nonetheless a frightening experience for many children. It is an environment which is quite alien from the world of home and school which children are used to, and they often have misconceptions about the process, for example, that the judge will punish them if they lie in court. [17] Many child witnesses are particularly afraid of seeing the perpetrator in the courtroom, [18] and for this, and other reasons, steps have been taken in most Australian jurisdictions to make the process of giving evidence an easier one for children. Most States and Territories now have the option of using closed circuit television for child witnesses. [19] Children give evidence from another room, which is connected to the courtroom by closed circuit television. [20] The child can see and hear the lawyers who conduct examination and cross-examination, while the lawyers, judge and jury are able to observe and listen to the child on the television monitor. Some jurisdictions also allow the child's evidence-in-chief to be given by means of a pre-recorded videotape. However, the child must normally be available for live cross-examination. [21]

The use of technnology is only one aspect of the challenge of including children in the court process. It is not only the courtroom which is strange for children, but also the language used by the lawyers. Prosecutors and judges who are not used to dealing with children, and defence lawyers endeavouring to cast a reasonable doubt upon the accuracy of the child's testimony, may confuse a child witness by using language which is inappropriate to the child's age and linguistic capabilities.

The use of abstract rather than concrete language, sentences with multiple clauses, multifaceted questions, and questions with double-negatives can all serve to confuse children,[22] while a focus upon peripheral rather than central details of their story may give a false impression of unreliability.[23] Judges and magistrates who have an understanding of child development and the needs of child witnesses can intervene to ensure that children are able to understand the questions asked and to prevent them from being subjected to unfair cross-examination. However, a lack of awareness of the problems children have in giving evidence, together with an unwillingness to interfere significantly in the presentation of the defence case, combine to make the experience of giving evidence unnecessarily upsetting and difficult for many children.

Different issues arise in relation to children who are defendants in criminal trials. Almost all children accused of breaking the law are dealt with in special Children's Courts or Juvenile Courts. These are generally much more informal than adult courts and sentencing practices have an explicit orientation towards rehabilitation, with custodial sentences being a last resort only used for repeat offenders convicted of serious crimes. Diversion schemes, including the use of police cautioning, are also an integral part of the response to juvenile crime.[24]

In the past, the welfare orientation of juvenile courts has been a source of injustice for some children. The use of vague "status offences" such as being in moral danger or being beyond the control of parents has been a means whereby adolescents have been placed in state care "for their own good", but against their will, as a means of controlling their behaviour.[25] Furthermore, the informal nature of court proceedings has justified failures to observe due process.[26] Under modern juvenile court principles, due process is meant to be observed, while courts are required in sentencing to show a proportionality between the offence and the sentence. Nonetheless, many problems remain. Because juvenile offenders are often represented in court by publicly funded duty solicitors, there can be a tendency for representation to be based upon brief consultations with the defendant, and for a discontinuity in representation to occur where there is more than one hearing. Juvenile defendants are amongst the many groups in society who suffer from the pressure to reduce the public costs of justice.

10.1.4   Multiculturalism and the legal tradition

The challenge of inclusion is also the challenge of adapting the legal system to the demands of a multicultural society.[27] The Australian government's official policy on multiculturalism, the *National Agenda for a Multicultural Australia* (1989)[28] stated that one of the government's objectives for its multicultural policy was "to promote equality before the law by systematically examining the implicit cultural assumptions of the law and the legal system to identify the manner in which they may unintentionally act to disadvantage certain groups of Australians".[29]

Multiculturalism means different things to different people.[30] In terms of the legal system, the claim to respect for the rights of minorities may take five different forms. First, an acceptance of cultural diversity means that the freedom of particular groups to enjoy their culture or religion should not be restricted unless this is necessary to protect the human rights of others. The rights of minorities to be able to practise their religion and maintain their culture are protected by various conventions in international law. For example, Art 27 of the *International Covenant on Civil and Political Rights* provides that in States which have ethnic, religious or linguistic minorities, persons belonging to such minorities shall not be denied the right, in community with other members of their group, to enjoy their own culture, to profess and practise their own religion, and to use their own language.[31] This is subject to the qualification, contained in Art 18(3), that States are entitled to impose such limitations on the exercise of people's freedom to manifest their religion or beliefs as are necessary in the interests of public safety, order, health or morals, or for the protection of the fundamental rights and freedoms of others. In the western legal and political tradition, the rights of minorities are primarily protected by the principles of freedom of speech, religion and assembly. Laws which single out particular ethnic minorities or religious groups by prohibiting cultural or religious practices which are particular to them violate the principle of equality before the law.[32] Nonetheless, laws which are neutral on their face and apparently of universal application may in practice have a discriminatory impact upon particular groups by inhibiting the enjoyment of their culture or exercise of their religion.

The second dimension of multiculturalism which is expressed in international conventions and covenants is that governments should act to prevent discrimination based upon religion or ethnicity. Article 26 of the *International Covenant on Civil and Political Rights* prohibits discrimination on the grounds of race and national origin, as does the *Convention on the Elimination of All Forms of Racial Discrimination*. These international obligations are given effect in domestic law by legislation such as the *Racial Discrimination Act* 1975 (Cth). State anti-discrimination laws are also consistent with the aims of the international conventions.

The third dimension is that the legal system should be accessible to people irrespective of their cultural background and first language. If people from a non-English speaking background are to be able to understand court cases in which they are involved, this means that they will need interpreter services both in court and in the earlier stages of the legal process, such as interviews with police and legal representatives.[33] The Australian Law Reform Commission, reporting on multiculturalism and the law in 1992,[34] recommended that the right to give evidence through an interpreter should be enshrined in the law of the Commonwealth, and that professional interpreters should be used at public expense. Defendants who do not understand what is being said in the trial should also be provided with an interpreter. The Commission also recommended the expansion of interpreter services in other branches of the legal system.[35]

A fourth possible dimension of multiculturalism in relation to the law is that government officials and courts should take account of particular cultural factors in the application of the general laws of the land to individuals. Thus, in child custody and access cases involving children of mixed race, account might be taken of such factors as the importance for the child's cultural development and sense of identity of maintaining links with her or his extended family. The willingness or unwillingness of one parent seeking custody to allow contact with the family of the other parent might be an important factor in the ultimate decision.[36] In criminal cases, officials or courts might take account of the cultural context in which the offence occurred in deciding whether to prosecute, whether to convict, or how to sentence.[37] Specific exemptions, whether de facto or de jure, might be given to particular ethnic groups where the interference with their religious freedom outweighs any public benefit of the application of the law to them. For example, in a multicultural society, it would be consistent with good policy both to require the wearing of safety helmets by motor cyclists generally, and to take account of the objections of the Sikh community, who wear turbans for religious reasons, either by exempting them from the helmet requirement or by exercising a discretion not to prosecute them.[38]

A fifth potential dimension for multiculturalism is that the law should be sufficiently pluralistic to allow different communities to be governed by their own laws on matters where cultural values differ significantly between different groups. This fifth claim for multiculturalism is controversial. Sensitivity to cultural practices conflicts with the principle, which is a fundamental premise of western legal systems, that all members of society should be governed by the same laws. Apart from adherence to the fundamental precepts of the western legal tradition, there are other reasons for not allowing different communities to be governed by different legal norms. The recognition and enforcement of certain cultural norms and rules by the law of the country could, in certain instances, violate the principle that the government should protect the rights of vulnerable members of minority groups from practices which are regarded by the dominant culture as oppressive. The Australian Law Reform Commission gave as its reasons for rejecting the possibility of separate laws that:

> "Imposing special laws on people because they belong to a particular ethnic group could introduce unjustified discriminations into the law, lead to unnecessary and divisive labelling of people, and possibly be oppressive of individual members of that group."[39]

The first four dimensions of multiculturalism have gained support from federal government policy. The extent and limits of the government's commitment to multiculturalism is expressed in the *National Agenda for a Multicultural Australia*.[40] There, multiculturalism is defined as having three aspects, cultural identity, social justice and economic efficiency. The right to cultural identity means that all Australians have the right to express and share their individual cultural heritage, including their language and religion. This right is subject to carefully defined limits. Australians are required to accept the basic structure and principles of Australian society, defined as comprising the Constitution and the rule of law, tolerance and equality, Parliamentary democracy, freedom of speech and religion, English as the national language and equality of the sexes. Social justice, in the context of a multicultural policy means the right of all Australians to equality of treatment and opportunity, and the removal of barriers of race, ethnicity, culture, religion, language, gender or place of birth. The third aspect, economic efficiency, means the need to maintain, develop and utilise effectively the skills and talents of all Australians, regardless of background.

Australia's multicultural policy thus seeks to allow linguistic and cultural diversity within a framework of commitment to values which are seen to be fundamental to Australian society. The notion of the rule of law is a protected principle, but individual rules are not. Nonetheless, the goal of having a multiculturally sensitive legal system is harder to realise in practice than it may sound in theory. The right to cultural expression may conflict with other rights in international conventions to which Australia is a signatory, such as the Convention on the Elimination of All Forms of Discrimination Against Women and the Convention on the Rights of the Child. The protection of the rights of women and children may at times conflict with particular cultural practices which would otherwise have a claim to recognition.[41] The competing rights contained within these various international covenants and conventions create a difficult balancing operation for governments in a multicultural society. On the one hand, they must respect the cultural practices of minority groups within the society. On the other hand, they must protect "minorities within minorities", that is, the vulnerable members of ethnic minorities, from cultural practices which are oppressive.[42]

In resolving these conflicts, governments and courts have to steer between the twin dangers of cultural insensitivity and cultural relativism. There is scope for individual laws to be much more sensitive culturally than they are at present,[43] but at the same time, there is a danger that culture will be used as an excuse for practices which should not be tolerated and which violate human rights.[44]

10.2   Access to Justice: Making Legal Rights Effective

The challenge of inclusion is the challenge of making the law more representative of the character and composition of the population. But beyond the need for diversity is a need to lower the barriers to justice which inhibit a large proportion of the population from exercising their legal rights. Without access to justice, there is a gulf between the law on the books and the law in action.

In many legal systems, this gulf can be vast. Many totalitarian regimes, both past and present, offer examples of legal systems in which fundamental human rights are guaranteed on paper, but are violated in practice. Yet even in countries with traditions of democratic government, a similar discrepancy between theory and practice can occur. Laws can be passed which are presented as the solution to social problems, but which only provide rights on paper without changing institutions and practices in a way which will make those rights effective. Legislation is cheap. Governments can point to the legislation when claiming compliance with international conventions or when responding to criticism. Yet sometimes the rhetoric of the law is not supported by the resources necessary to give effect to the stated intentions of the legislators. The law on the books justifies inaction, precisely because it gives the appearance of action.

A failure to provide proper access to justice is a major cause of the dichotomy between the law on the books and the law in action. Access to justice is a fundamental right which makes other rights effective.[45] The formal conferral of a right is of no value unless adequate means exist to protect that right and to enforce corollary obligations. It is also an important aspect of the rule of law. As King CJ of the South Australian Supreme Court has said:[46]

> "We cannot be said to live under the rule of law, in the full meaning of that expression, unless all citizens are able to assert and defend their legal rights effectively and have access to the courts for that purpose. Under our legal system, and indeed under the legal systems obtaining in all complex modern societies, that requires professional assistance. If that professional assistance is denied to any citizen who reasonably needs it to assert or defend his legal rights, the rule of law in the society is to that extent deficient."

Many people do not so much need the means to go to court, as they need the capacity to make litigation a realistic threat if the other party continues to deny their legal rights. The vast majority of disputes are settled informally between the parties or by negotiations which are conducted through lawyers. The threat of litigation is itself an important element in negotiations, for it gives an incentive for settlement.

For many people, the costs of access to justice, and the risks associated with litigation, are often too great for them to use the legal system to protect their legal rights. Perhaps it is an ideal that all citizens should be able to defend their legal rights effectively. It is tempting to contrast the existing situation with a historic golden age in which justice was available to all at moderate expense, and was meted out without fear or favour. It is doubtful that such a legal "garden of Eden" has ever existed in a developed western society. Yet it is vital if the law is to be effective at all, that a sufficient number of citizens are able to get access to justice to enforce their rights.

10.2.1 Bargaining in the shadow of the law

The significance of the courts does not lie only in their role as the final adjudicators of individual disputes when all other means of dispute resolution have failed. More than this, the decisions of the courts send messages to the community at large. Marc Galanter has written that:

> "The principal contribution of courts to dispute resolution is providing a background of norms and procedures against which negotiations and regulation in both private and governmental settings take place. This contribution includes, but is not exhausted by, communication to prospective litigants of what might transpire if one of them sought a judicial resolution. Courts communicate not only the rules that would govern adjudication of the dispute, but possible remedies, and estimates of the difficulty, certainty and costs of securing particular outcomes." [47]

Thus, courts send messages which allow people to bargain in the law's shadow. [48] At a fundamental level, the message which the courts send to the community is that the law will be enforced, and that a person who resists compliance with the law and who violates the rights of others will be required not only to comply with the orders of the court, but also to pay the costs of the litigation. Furthermore, the cases which are litigated help to provide the legal norms against the background of which the negotiations take place. These norms confer "bargaining chips" [49] on those engaged in negotiation, and affect the outcomes of those negotiations.

The role of the courts in sending messages is thus important to the resolution of disputes without the need for an adjudication. If only a few cases reach the courts, or only certain kinds of cases are adjudicated, involving plaintiffs who have the knowledge, means and will to litigate, then the law will be ineffective in providing the background of norms against which the rights of individuals can be protected through negotiation.

10.2.2 Pathways to justice

There is considerable evidence that the legal system does not adequately provide means of giving redress for at least some of the legal wrongs suffered by citizens. In one Australian study, reported by Jeffrey Fitzgerald, a telephone survey was conducted in which members of households were asked to report on problems entailing injury, harm or loss within a three year period. [50] The aim was to discover "middle-range" grievances of a variety of types, rather than to obtain an exhaustive litany of problems. These respondents were asked about personal injuries and other tortious damage where $1000 or more was at stake, consumer complaints over $1000, claims of discrimination, property disputes, grievances concerning landlords, claims against the government and post-divorce disputes, amongst others. The numbers of grievances reported varied from category to category—24 per cent of households reported grievances involving road accidents, accidents at work and other damage caused by someone else; 16 per cent reported landlord and tenant problems; 77 per cent led to claims against the alleged wrongdoer; 56 per cent of claims were disputed in whole or in part.

Fitzgerald's study indicates that the chances of success in making a claim depends substantially on the type of injury or loss suffered. Ninety four per cent of tort claimants got all or part of what they claimed. By contrast, only 65 per cent of consumers received total or partial satisfaction, compared with only 55 per cent of those in property disputes and only 38 per cent of those complaining of discrimination. The high rate of recovery in tort cases is not surprising. There are well understood procedures for making claims against insurers in the case of road traffic accidents, and lawyers do not often need to be involved even if there is for a time some dispute about the amount the insurer will pay. Motorists often belong to associations which can assist them in such claims. Those who suffer injuries at work similarly have established procedures for claiming against employers under workers' compensation schemes and frequently have access to union assistance if need be. It may well be that these advisory organisations also play a role in screening out cases which are unmeritorious so that the person does not reach the stage of making a claim.

In other sorts of grievance where the path to a successful resolution is not nearly so well marked, nor advice and assistance so readily available, the number of successful claims is likely to be much lower. Although there are established procedures for making claims against the government, and the Administrative Appeals Tribunal has been established at federal level to hear appeals from administrative decisions, a social security claimant does not necessarily have the same assistance from advisory organisations as is readily available to an employee who is injured in an industrial accident. This sort of claim against the government requires greater personal commitment and access to information for it to succeed. This is even more true of claims of discrimination.

10.3   Obstacles to the Enforcement of Rights

10.3.1   Access to information

There are a number of obstacles inhibiting access to justice. A fundamental one is the lack of information about the possibility of a legal claim. Before there can be a claim, the aggrieved person must be aware that a legal remedy is available and confident that it is worthwhile for a claim to be made, using lawyers if need be. Access to information about the law thus plays an important part in providing access to justice.

People with grievances need encouragement to pursue a claim from informed non-legal professionals before they take what is for them the major step of seeking legal advice. In one English study, only 26 per cent of those victims of accidents who were incapacitated for two weeks or longer considered claiming damages.[51] Most who did claim did so because someone else first suggested it to them. In general these were people with some knowledge and understanding of the legal system—police, trade union officials, doctors and hospital personnel. Victims of accidents in the home were less likely to come into contact with knowledgeable professionals even if blame could be attributed in law to a third party, and less likely to realise that the accident concerned might be grounds for a legal claim.

The major source of information about the law ought to be the large number of solicitors in private practice who are available for consultation by members of the general public. Yet numerous studies in Australia and in other English—speaking countries show that when lawyers are consulted, it is largely in regard to certain types of problem which are perceived as matters on which lawyers can give assistance.[52] Conveyancing and other matters concerning property, the making of a will and the legal consequences of marriage breakdown are all matters on which lawyers are readily consulted. Landlord and tenant disputes, consumer problems and discrimination matters are less likely to result in visits to lawyers.[53] This is indicated by Cass and Sackville's study of recourse to lawyers in three relatively disadvantaged areas of Sydney.[54] They asked 548 respondents whether they had experienced problem situations in the last five years where they might have needed legal assistance. Twenty four such situations were presented to them broadly classified into problems concerning accommodation, accidents, consumer matters, money, marriage and family matters and problems with the police. Sixty nine per cent of the sample claimed to have experienced at least one problem situation.[55] Forty four per cent had consulted a lawyer, although if conveyancing is excluded, the proportion fell to 25.4 per cent. Possibly, some people who consulted a lawyer about a conveyance also had a consultation on a non-conveyancing matter.[56] However, consultation with a solicitor was much more common in regard to certain injuries than others. Cass and Sackville commented:

> "The sample of 548 respondents reported a significant number of matters in respect of which, in our opinion, legal advice should have been sought but was not. Some respondents had failed to pursue claims that might have been of considerable material value to them, such as those for damages for personal injuries arising out of work-related accidents. Others had failed to seek advice when charged with criminal offences and found themselves convicted without having had the benefit of legal advice. In many cases the respondents who did not seek legal assistance had experienced accommodation, consumer and money

problems which, although not involving large sums, were of some importance to the respondents themselves and were not resolved satisfactorily."[57]

This tendency to see lawyers as relevant only to certain sorts of legal problems is not confined to disadvantaged social groups. The findings that people tend only to consult lawyers about certain kinds of legal problems are consistent with overseas studies drawn from surveys of the general population.[58] While it is true that use of lawyers is more likely for those of higher socio-economic status and educational level, those with higher incomes are more likely to be involved in buying or selling property or in making a will.[59]

10.3.2   Cost

A second obstacle to using the legal system is the cost. Indeed for individuals in need of legal advice and representation, this is likely to be the greatest obstacle to seeking legal services. A person's fear that the costs of taking legal action will be far beyond her or his reach is a strong disincentive even to take the first step of seeking legal advice. Often, such fears are likely to be misplaced. Where the person has a clear legal entitlement, as will often be the case, the cost of legal advice, and whatever action is necessary to pursue the claim further, may be only a small fraction of the amount recovered. Nonetheless, a person will only realise this once that advice has been obtained.

Another source of anxiety about legal costs is the fear that the matter will have to go to court. Not only will the litigant be liable for the court fees and the costs of legal representation, but he or she might be liable for some or all of the costs of the other party. In Australia, the normal rule is that the loser will bear the reasonable costs of the winning party.[60] These costs are usually assessed by reference to a scale of fees set by the courts. The costs which are allowed to a successful litigant are known as party and party costs. Where the successful litigant has not been charged the scale fees by her or his lawyer, but has been charged higher fees, then the difference between the scale amount and the actual fees charged must be met by that litigant. These actual fees are known as the solicitor-client costs. While the normal approach in most jurisdictions and courts is to award party-party costs only, in some circumstances, and in some courts, a successful litigant may be awarded costs on a solicitor-client basis as long as those costs were reasonably incurred.[61]

The cost of legal services delivered by the private profession varies considerably from practitioner to practitioner, firm to firm and State to State. It also varies according to the nature of the legal work being done. Typically, in most law firms, some areas of practice are more lucrative than others, and those areas where higher charges can be sustained—in particular, in commercial work—subsidise other aspects of the practice.

Charges are levied on a variety of bases. Frequently, solicitors charge in accordance with the number of hours spent in relation to that matter, and detailed time sheets are kept in relation to each client. Another common way of charging is by reference to the court scales.[62]

Where litigation is necessary in order to protect a person's legal rights, the costs of taking the matter to court may run into many thousands of dollars. While much of this may be recovered from the other party in the event of success, the recovery of costs depends on the extent to which one's own solicitor-client costs are allowed, and the extent of the defendant's capacity to meet an order for costs. The costs of litigation may be such as to require the sacrifice of many years of savings or to necessitate extensive borrowing. It is thus not surprising that people only litigate when they have no choice in the matter (for example, when they are defending against an unjustified claim), where they are seeking compensation and realise that they have a strong chance of success, or where they place a value on what is thereby protected or preserved which is greater than the costs of litigation. For many others, even those with watertight legal claims, a common response when the claim is resisted is to find other ways of dealing with the problem—changing jobs, moving house or finding other means of exit and avoidance as the case may be.

10.4   Improving Access to Justice

10.4.1   Providing information and advice

A starting point in improving access to justice and in making the legal system more relevant to people's lives is to increase the levels of community education about law generally, so that people realise when legal advice may be necessary. The growth in popularity of legal studies courses in secondary schools is a positive development in this respect, but such courses have only become part of the school curriculum comparatively recently, and then only as an optional subject.

There is a need for general community education with respect to legal rights. For a large percentage of the population, the reticence about taking legal action is so strong that people need considerable encouragement through education campaigns and by other means, to take the first steps necessary to enforce their rights. When governments bring in reforming legislation which gives extensive rights on paper, people need to be told in plain English not only what those legal rights are, but also the avenues through which they can make their complaints, enforce their rights and pursue their claims.

Education about the law is especially necessary for migrants. Migrants may need explanation of basic aspects of the legal process with which the majority of the population could expect to be familiar, for example, the role of juries. Education about the law is also an aspect of overcoming the cultural gulf which inhibits members of ethnic minorities from having greater access to the legal system. Education is necessary not only to convey basic information to people about their rights and obligations under Australian law, but also to overcome misconceptions people may have about the requirements of Australian law, based upon their experiences in their countries of origin.[63] The Australian Law Reform Commission report on multiculturalism recommended that a number of steps be taken to improve community awareness of legal rights.[64]

In addition to the private profession there are numerous other sources of legal advice. Legal aid solicitors and community legal centres (see below) provide legal advice, and advice on legal rights given by informed non-lawyers may also be provided by government departments, Law Society advisory services and advice bureaux. For many years, New South Wales has had a successful scheme of Chamber Magistrates in Local Courts. These are court officials with legal training who provide legal advice.[65] A similar service is provided by the clerks of court.

10.4.2   Reducing legal costs

A number of inquiries have been set up into the costs of justice, and various proposals have been made to reduce the high cost of legal advice and representation.[66] Many steps have already been taken at both State and federal levels to reform the legal profession and to remove restrictive practices which have a tendency to increase costs. Many of these practices were the product of traditions which had survived long after the reasons for them had disappeared. The pattern of reform in recent years has been either to ensure a fused profession, or to eliminate most of the practical divisions between solicitors and barristers which had ceased to be justifiable.[67]

Some of the reforms which have been made, and others which have been proposed, relate to the levels of consumer information about legal services which are designed to allow them to make more informed choices in deciding who should represent them. Legal practitioners are now permitted to advertise in all States and Territories, but the various jurisdictions differ considerably in the extent to which restrictions upon advertising are imposed. The Trade Practices Commission, in its report on the legal profession in 1994, recommended that all restrictions on advertising should be lifted except to the extent that they prohibit false, misleading or deceptive conduct.[68]

Another means of promoting consumer choice, as well as giving clients a greater degree of control over the costs of legal services, is to require that an estimate of costs be given or that there should be an explanation of the basis upon which costs will be charged. For example, in family law matters, the Family Court requires that solicitors provide clients with written information on the approximate costs to the client up to and including the conciliation conference (the Order 24 conference), the estimated future costs of the preparation for trial, and the estimated costs of the first day of trial.[69] Similar disclosure rules have been introduced by some State law societies,[70] or by State legislation.[71]

Providing information on costs is important to help clients evaluate all the options available to them in pursuing a claim, and in deciding on legal representation. However, providing such information can only be a small part of providing access to justice. Consumers of legal services are not used to shopping around to obtain the most reasonably priced advice, and the nature of legal advice is that often only after a quite extensive interview can the legal problems be identified, and a preliminary assessment of the options available be made.

It has also been recommended that surveys be conducted of the fees lawyers charge for different kinds of services, with appropriate adjustments being made for the different levels of seniority of the lawyer and the size of the firm, so that consumers are able to make a more informed assessment of the estimated charges in their own cases.[72]

Where lawyers preparing matters for litigation charge according to court scales, the costs may be assumed to be competitive with other practitioners. However, this can depend upon the way in which the scale is constructed. If the scale allows many of the costs to be calculated by reference to the time spent on a matter, then the actual cost of the legal representation will depend to some extent upon the efficiency of the practitioner. In relation to family law, the *Joint Select Committee on Certain Aspects of the Operation and Interpretation of the Family Law Act* 1975, reporting in 1992, recommended that costs agreements, by which the client agrees that charges should be levied on some basis other than the scale rates, should only be enforceable if an independent solicitor certifies that the client entered into the agreement freely and voluntarily.[73]

10.4.3   Contingency Fees

A further reform which has been implemented in South Australia and New South Wales and which is under consideration elsewhere, is the use of contingency fees. Contingency fees are widely used in North America. Typically, the arrangement is used when the claim is for a monetary sum such as damages. The lawyer agrees not to charge if the client loses, (other than court fees in some cases) but is allowed to charge more than her or his normal rate if the client is successful. In North America, it is common for the contingency fee to be calculated as a percentage of the sum recovered. However, this is not the only form of contingency fee arrangement. For example, the *Legal Profession Reform Act* 1993 (NSW) allows "conditional costs agreements" by which lawyers may charge a premium on their normal fees of up to 25 per cent, if the litigation succeeds.[74] In South Australia, contingency fees are permitted, subject to certain requirements, and the practitioner is allowed to charge up to double the scale rates if the client succeeds.[75]

Contingency fee agreements, while superficially attractive, have their disadvantages. First, as long as the cost-indemnity rule continues, by which the loser pays some or all of the winner's legal costs, contingency fee agreements only protect the litigant from having to bear her or his own costs. Failure in the litigation may still leave the client with the responsibility of paying a very large legal bill incurred by the defendant. Secondly, contingency fees usually only benefit plaintiffs, since they are premised on the basis that the legal fees will be paid out of the compensation recovered in the litigation. Therefore, they do nothing to reduce the problem of costs for the defendant. Thirdly, their success is dependent either on practitioners having high ethical standards, or on strict independent scrutiny, or both. Contingency fees ought only to be used when the client has a significant risk of failure in the litigation as well as of success. There is an obvious danger that clients with clear entitlements to receive damages will be persuaded to accept a contingency fee arrangement even though the risks of losing the case are negligible.

The Access to Justice Advisory Committee, set up by the federal Attorney-General, recommended in a report in 1994 that contingency fees be allowed of up to 100 per cent above the practitioner's normal charges, so that if the chances of success are only 50 per cent, the practitioner ought to be able to charge double her or his ordinary fees, while the percentage increase would be lower if the chances of success in the litigation were higher. It is recommended that such contingency fees should be permitted in all cases other than criminal law cases and family law cases, and that the reasons for offering a contingency fee, and for the percentage increase involved, should be recorded in writing. Such agreements could be set aside if the client complained subsequently. Furthermore, the client should be given the opportunity to seek independent legal advice.[76]

While this may increase access to justice, it is questionable whether it provides sufficient safeguards against abuse. Obtaining independent legal advice will incur additional expense for the client, and for a client already worried about legal costs, this may be a deterrent. Furthermore, once an agreement is entered into, the safeguard against abuse lies in the client's ability and willingness to complain. This presupposes that he or she will have access to the information that the chances of success in the litigation were much higher than the lawyer had represented. A better approach would be to combine the recommendations of the Access to Justice Advisory Committee with random scrutinising of contingency fee agreements by an ethics committee of the relevant law society, together with scrutiny by the trial judge in those cases which go to trial.

10.4.4   Legal Aid

Legal aid schemes exist in all the States and Territories to provide access to the legal system for many people who are unable to afford a lawyer, and to provide legal advice. Statutory legal assistance schemes have existed in Australia since the 1930s. The first was established in South Australia by the *Poor Persons' Legal Assistance Act* 1936 (SA).[77] Similar statutory schemes were established in other States between 1954 and 1971.[78] These schemes operated through State Law Societies and involved the employment of private solicitors at public expense. Some States, such as New South Wales, provided salaried Public Solicitors and Public Defenders as a primary means of meeting the legal needs of the poor.

The federal government entered the arena in 1973 with the establishment of the Australian Legal Aid Office (ALAO). In conception, this was an ambitious scheme to achieve a significant increase in the access of poorer people to legal services. The aim was for a network of shopfront law centres which would not only act in individual cases but play a role in public interest advocacy. This scheme for improving access to justice was an integral part of the Whitlam government's vision for a more equitable social order. However, the vision was never realised. From its inception, the ALAO was heavily reliant on solicitors in private practice and thus the idea of salaried lawyers on a "shopfront" basis was not fulfilled. Constitutional problems limited the scope of matters which the ALAO could handle, and the salaried lawyers who were employed by the ALAO met with resistance from the private profession.[79]

With the change of government in 1975, the policy towards legal aid changed. The Fraser government's policy of a "new federalism" led to a shift in responsibility for legal aid from the Commonwealth to the States, although the Commonwealth continued to participate in the funding of State schemes. State Legal Aid Commissions were established, and now exist in all States and Territories. The ALAO merged with the State Commissions. Thus, the initiative to establish a major legal aid service at federal level gave way to an integrated service on a State by State basis in which people could seek assistance in matters both of Commonwealth and State law at the same office. Since the founding of the ALAO there has been a significant increase in the public funding of legal aid. State and Commonwealth funding is not the only source of finance. The income from solicitors' trust accounts, contributions from assisted persons and costs received by the Commission have all been additional sources of revenue. In all States and Territories, the majority of governmental legal aid funding still comes from the Commonwealth.[80]

Various models for legal aid schemes have been tried around the world. In some jurisdictions, the legal aid scheme operates through the private profession. In others, there has been an emphasis on salaried full time legal aid lawyers.[81] Australia combines the two approaches. In 1992-1993, the Legal Aid Commissions paid 57.2 per cent of their budgets to private practitioners, although the percentages varied from State to State.[82] There are advantages in having salaried lawyers as the basis for a legal aid scheme. It provides an opportunity for lawyers to develop expertise in areas of law most likely to be of concern to indigent people (although private practitioners may choose to specialise in this way as well). Against this must be offset the problem of retention of marketable legal aid lawyers in the face of higher salaries in the private sector.

Legal aid schemes have two major functions, that of providing advice, and assistance. Legal representation is subject to means tests and merit tests. It may be available only for certain categories of legal problems. Legally aided persons may be asked to make a contribution, and costs may be recovered out of the proceeds of a successful legal claim. The merit test is a requirement that the applicant has a reasonable prospect of success in the case. Legal assistance and representation may also be available through duty solicitor schemes in various courts. These services, provided either by salaried legal aid lawyers or by rostered private practitioners, provide assistance to people who appear in court without legal representation.

The priority in the granting of legal aid has traditionally been for defendants in criminal trials, in particular, in cases where a prison sentence may be imposed. This prioritisation of criminal matters was reinforced by the decision of the High Court in *Dietrich v R* (1992). [83] The court held that if an indigent person who is facing trial on a serious criminal charge is unable to obtain legal representation through no fault of her or his own, then the trial should be adjourned or stayed until such representation is available. Mason CJ and McHugh J acknowledged that this decision would probably require a re-ordering of the priorities for legal aid unless further government funds were made available to the legal aid commissions.

A decision of the Full Court of the Family Court is also likely to have an impact on the way in which legal aid funds are allocated. In *Re K* (1994), [84] the court listed 13 different circumstances in which the Family Court should order separate representation for the child or children in custody and access cases. The effect of this decision is that separate representatives will be appointed in a much larger number of cases than previously. Since separate representation for children is provided from legal aid funds, the decision in *Re K*, like the decision in *Dietrich*, is likely to affect the way in which legal aid is allocated between deserving claimants.

The Australian Law Reform Commission has pointed out that the priority given to defendants in criminal trials, which was reinforced by *Dietrich*, has a discriminatory impact. [85] Since most criminal defendants are men, and most applicants for legal aid in criminal trials are men, the majority of recipients of legal aid are men. In 1992-1993, men received 63 per cent of legal aid funding and women received 37 per cent. [86] Apart from criminal law, the other area of law which accounts for a significant proportion of legal aid expenditure is family law, [87] and in 1992-1993, almost 70 per cent of applicants were women. [88] While the right to legal representation in criminal trials ought to be regarded as of very great importance, it has been argued that the loss of custody of one's children may be as significant a loss for many women as is the loss of liberty. [89]

Indeed, the Family Court has strongly criticised the movement away from legal aid provision in family law matters in favour of criminal law cases in recent years, and urged that legal aid funding should be increased in custody and access cases. [90]

Another area in which the allocation of legal aid funds may be discriminatory is in the restrictions imposed upon the grant of legal aid for women who seek protection orders as a result of domestic violence. In States and Territories where the police do not often seek protection orders on behalf of victims, and the onus is upon the complainant to bring her own application, the effect of legal aid allocations may be that the government does much more to provide legal assistance to the perpetrators of domestic violence than it does to assist the victims. [91]

The problems which Legal Aid Commissions have in prioritising very scarce resources amongst different categories of needy claimants are immense. Ultimately, the decisions which must be made are political decisions, concerning the respective priorities of criminal law, family law and other categories of case, and the extent to which the society will tolerate the denial of justice to claimants who cannot afford to litigate, or to defend themselves in litigation, without legal representation.

The existing problems in providing adequate means of access to the legal system through legal aid suggest that questions need to be asked about the multiplication of laws, legal rights and new tribunals as a means of dealing with social problems. Every new set of legal rights is likely to give rise to greater demands on legal services for the enforcement of those rights and therefore, more claims for legal aid, unless the possibility of obtaining legal aid is arbitrarily excluded. Another by-product of creating new rights is that pressure upon the court system is also increased, exacerbating the problems of delays in obtaining a court hearing and escalating the costs of providing courts and judges.

There is a tendency for some governments to multiply laws, rights and tribunals without adequately considering the additional strains this might place upon the legal system, and the extent to which the existence of the new category of rights will mean that less public resources are devoted to the protection of existing rights. [92] A question which needs to be asked is how much justice the society can afford to have, and how many rights it can afford to protect at a reasonable level of effectiveness. Legal rights and remedies are only one means of dealing with social problems, and as legal aid commissions have to make hard decisions about priorities, so perhaps, do Parliaments.

10.5   Legal Services for the Disadvantaged

In response to the need for access to justice for those who cannot afford legal representation or who are otherwise disadvantaged, a number of organisations and community legal centres have been established to provide legal advice and assistance.

10.5.1   The Aboriginal Legal Service

A number of Aboriginal Legal Services operate in different parts of Australia providing legal advice and assistance to people of Aboriginal and Torres Strait Islander descent (and their spouses).[93] These are funded by the federal government. The genesis of the Service was in Redfern, Sydney in 1970; Redfern is an inner city area with a sizeable urban Aboriginal community and it was seen that they had particular needs in coping with policing in that area. The claims of police harassment made by Aboriginal activists were made known to academics and practitioners and as a result of these discussions, the Aboriginal Legal Service was established.

The Aboriginal Legal Services have played an important role in bridging the gap between white legal culture and Aboriginal society and have found considerable acceptance in Aboriginal communities. They are controlled by Aboriginals even though often the lawyers are white. In the main, Aboriginal Legal Service work is confined to criminal defence work, but the Services have increased their involvement in civil matters and endeavour to make Aboriginals aware of the use which can be made of the legal system to achieve particular goals.

The Australian Law Reform Commission has recommended that a separate legal service should be established for Aboriginal women.[94] Aboriginal women have a particular need for representation from other women which is separate from the representation of men. One reason for this is that in traditional Aboriginal culture, there are some things which are "women's business" and may only be revealed to other women. Furthermore, there are some matters in which women's needs are not met by Aboriginal Legal Services. It is the policy of most services not to act for one indigenous client against another. This means that Aboriginal women often do not have the legal representation from a culturally sensitive service which they need in cases of physical or sexual violence at the hands of an Aboriginal perpetrator.[95] Furthermore, the priorities of Aboriginal Legal Services are to represent defendants in criminal cases. Aboriginal women's needs for protection from family violence and for representation in family law matters are thus less likely to be met.[96]

10.5.2   Community Legal Centres

An important aspect of the movement to give disadvantaged people access to justice has been the development of Community Legal Centres. These are publicly funded, "shopfront" centres for legal advice and assistance which either operate in disadvantaged localities or as specialist agencies dealing with particular problems such as tenancy advice. Inasmuch as they are publicly funded and generally employ salaried lawyers providing free legal advice, they have some features in common with the Legal Aid Commission offices. However, in origin, philosophy, and modus operandi they are quite different and operate alongside the formal legal aid structures rather than being subsumed under the organisational system of State Legal Aid Commissions. Indeed, they endeavour to remain strictly independent of such institutional control.

The first non-Aboriginal community legal centre to be founded in Australia was the Fitzroy Legal Service in Melbourne which was opened in December 1972.[97] Other legal centres were opened in Melbourne in the course of 1973. In 1977, the Redfern Legal Centre was opened in Sydney. Subsequently, legal centres were opened in other States, some rooted in local communities, others with links, formal or informal, to university law schools, and others providing specialist legal services to the poor and disadvantaged.

There are variations between different legal centres in regard to their precise functions and means of working. Case work is of course a central aspect of the work of most legal centres. Full time lawyers and volunteer lawyers combine to provide legal services to clients. Often the centres operate evening sessions staffed by volunteers. Qualified lawyers are frequently assisted by law students and non-lawyers. The first full time worker to be employed at Redfern Legal Centre was not a lawyer but a social worker, and this is symptomatic of an important emphasis in the legal centres movement on a multi-disciplinary approach to people's problems. The legal aspect of a person's housing problems may be an eviction notice, but her or his needs go beyond assistance with resisting an eviction order. Thus, many legal centres endeavour to function in local communities alongside other welfare services and agencies, to provide a co-ordinated and multi-disciplinary response to the problems which clients face.

Legal centres vary in the extent to which lawyers are willing to undertake legal representation in court. Some prefer to leave court work to the legal aid system because of its time-consuming nature, and to confine their work primarily to giving advice, writing letters, assisting with legal aid applications, and other such non-court work. Others take "referrals back" from Legal Aid Commissions more readily. Clients thereby apply for legal aid but are represented in the matter by the solicitor from the community legal centre.

Case work is not the only function of many legal centres. They are also active in publishing and community education. Handbooks, published by legal centres, exist in a number of States and provide a readable guide to the law for those who are not legally trained. Legal centres are also active in law reform and in campaigning for change on various issues of importance to the disadvantaged. As one writer has said:

"The element which most clearly distinguishes legal centres from other legal agencies in the public and private sector is their commitment to effecting structural change on behalf of the poor through the legal system. This contrasts with traditional rhetoric about legal service delivery which focuses on the provision of legal services to specific individuals on a case by case basis. . . . Essentially it is a political objective, aimed at re-ordering power relations between 'the haves' and the 'have-nots', which has formed the cornerstone in the ideology of the legal centres movement."[98]

Reality has not always matched rhetoric. Early visions that the centres would be managed and controlled by "the community" through open and public management meetings have failed to reach fruition. The idea that hierarchies would be avoided, and that pay differentials between lawyers and non-lawyers would be minimised have had to compete with other constraints imposed by government award wages and the need to retain experienced staff. Nonetheless, an egalitarian spirit remains. A movement which was intended as a critique of the establishment has had to cope with its acceptance by that establishment. Legal Centres have representatives on some Legal Aid Commissions, and have played a significant role in the development of policy in the delivery of legal services to the disadvantaged. [99]

An important development in the legal centres movement has been the emergence of specialised legal centres, notably in New South Wales. [100] As the legal centres movement developed, it was realised that there were advantages in specialised services meeting the needs of those with a community of interests. Specialised services, dealing with consumer credit, immigration, intellectual disability and welfare rights are examples of such specialised centres.

In its 1994 report, *Equality Before the Law: Justice for Women*, the Australian Law Reform Commission pointed to the effectiveness of the few women's legal centres, and those which specialise in assisting women who have been victims of domestic violence, as an indication of the value of such services as a means of providing greater access to justice for women. The Commission recommended that the government should fund one extra women's legal service in each State and Territory. [101] Such legal centres can fulfil a valuable role in offering legal advice, referral and representation in areas of the law which are most likely to concern women. The identification of such centres as women's legal services can also help to overcome some of the estrangement which some women feel within a male-dominated legal system.

10.6   Alternative Dispute Resolution

Another response to the problems of access to justice has been the vast increase in services offering alternative dispute resolution (ADR) and, in particular, mediation. The common feature of all ADR mechanisms is that they involve the use of a neutral third party who endeavours to facilitate a settlement of a dispute without having the power to adjudicate on the matter. Mediation, conciliation, negotiation, facilitation and independent expert appraisal are all forms of such dispute resolution.[102] Arbitration is sometimes listed as a form of alternative dispute resolution, but it differs from the others—and resembles court-based adjudication—in that a neutral third party decides the case for the parties.

The form of alternative dispute resolution process which has attracted most attention in recent years is mediation. This is a form of structured negotiation in which the mediator (or mediators) controls the process while the parties control the outcome. Folberg and Taylor's widely used definition is that mediation "can be defined as the process by which the participants together with the assistance of a neutral person or persons, systematically isolate disputed issues in order to develop options, consider alternatives, and reach a consensual settlement that will accommodate their needs."[103] There are a number of different models of mediation. In family disputes, it is common for there to be two mediators, one male and one female.[104] Where co-mediators are used, the mediators may also bring different professional backgrounds to the process of mediation. Mediation sessions are highly structured. Typically, the parties are each given the opportunity to present their story and to state what they are seeking in the mediation. The mediator identifies points of agreement and disagreement and encourages the generation of possible solutions to the matters in dispute. The possible solutions are then evaluated, and the parties are encouraged to attempt to reach an agreement on a solution which would be mutually acceptable. The final stage is to endeavour to formulate an agreement which is realistic for the parties to carry out.

Mediation is encouraged by the court system in a number of ways. The Family Court began a pilot mediation programme in 1992, using a co-mediation model.[105] Mediation is voluntary. It has been extended to a number of registries of the court, and it is planned that the provision of mediation be expanded further.[106] This is in addition to the counselling facilities and other ADR processes which have been an aspect of the court's work since its inception.[107] There are also a number of other family mediation services, which receive government funding.

The Federal Court has also introduced a programme of "assisted dispute resolution" and has the power to refer proceedings to a mediator with the consent of the parties.[108] Over 90 per cent of cases referred to mediation are consumer protection cases under the *Trade Practices Act* 1974 (Cth). Some intellectual property cases are also referred to mediation.[109] Mediation conferences are usually conducted by the registrars of the court, but some have been conducted by judges.[110] A mediation programme has also been introduced into the Administrative Appeals Tribunal.[111]

Mediation is also used as a process of dispute resolution in a number of State courts. "Settlement weeks" have been used in a number of States as a means of reducing court waiting lists in civil matters. Parties are encouraged to settle their cases in the course of that week with the assistance of the officers of the court. The resulting agreements are embodied in consent orders.

While many courts have thus introduced mediation programmes, ADR is not primarily an adjunct to court processes. Independently of the courts, ADR has flourished in a variety of different contexts. The Australian Commercial Disputes Centre in Sydney was established to provide a forum for the resolution of commercial disputes, and mediation is increasingly used by government and business. In certain States, the governments fund dispute resolution centres[112] which were established to mediate disputes between neighbours, family members and other such private disputes.

Alternative dispute resolution mechanisms have many advantages. They are generally cheaper and more speedy than court processes. For these reasons they are popular with governments which want to reduce legal aid bills, court costs and court waiting lists. They allow the parties the opportunity to tell their stories in their own way: parties are not confined by rules of evidence nor are they limited to presenting those facts which are relevant to prove a particular cause of action. They are not confined either by the range of remedies available to courts. They may devise remedies and solutions which are most appropriate to them.

Despite these many advantages of alternative dispute resolution, there are many dangers in this shift towards ADR. One is that ADR, together with tribunals, will become the justice system for the majority of private citizens, while government and commerce monopolise the civil courts. There are some indications that this is happening in the range of matters which are currently sent to ADR—family matters, consumer complaints, social security claims, disputes between neighbours. Mediation and conciliation may offer useful means of resolving many such disputes, but it should not be assumed that dispute resolution equates with justice.

The limitations of ADR are first, that alternative dispute resolution mechanisms presuppose that the claim can and should be compromised. In some disputes, compromise is quite appropriate, especially where the parties are likely to continue in a relationship with one another, as parents must do even after divorce, and neighbours must do for as long as they remain neighbours. But if people need to compromise on their rights in order to get any justice at all, then mediation offers, not justice in the shadow of the law, but dispute resolution outside of the law.

Secondly, mediation and other forms of facilitated dispute resolution presuppose that the parties are both articulate and able to defend their own interests. In many cases, this is simply not so. Linguistic and cultural barriers to assertiveness are likely to diminish the capacity of the person to participate effectively in mediation, and this is likely to be a problem especially for women of non-English speaking backgrounds. A history of domestic violence also has a serious detrimental effect on the capacity of the victims of violence to stand up to perpetrators,[113] as well as allowing for the possibility of further violence occurring before or after the mediation session. For these reasons, some mediation services do not mediate between couples where there is a history of domestic violence, and endeavour to screen for indications of such violence when assessing the suitability of the couple for mediation.[114]

Thirdly, the effectiveness of mediation as a means by which parties may protect and assert their legal rights depends on the extent to which they are aware of those rights. Frequently, the advantages of mediation are contrasted with the disadvantages of litigation. However, since the great majority of all disputes are settled without an adjudication by a judge, the proper comparison to be made is between mediation and negotiation between solicitors. Negotiations take place against the background of solicitors' awareness of the parties' legal rights and their assessment of the chances of success in litigation. Negotiations between solicitors, properly conducted, have many of the same advantages of cheapness and flexibility which are attributed to mediation, with the added advantage that the client is represented by a knowledgeable and articulate representative who will endeavour to gain the best possible settlement for the client. Negotiation is a form of alternative dispute resolution which has been at the heart of legal practice for generations.

There must be concerns therefore about whether governments' enthusiasm for ADR is motivated by the best interests of vulnerable citizens or by an overriding concern to process as many disputes as cheaply as possible. Those who are in a position of bargaining strength in a dispute are much more likely to favour mediation than negotiation between solicitors or litigation in the courts. The more vulnerable party in the mediation will not have the advantage of a representative, and if he or she has not received—and understood—proper legal advice, will not have the bargaining chips derived from knowledge of her or his legal entitlements.

Mediation, supported by legal advice and with agreements scrutinised for their fairness by legal representatives after the mediation, has a valuable role to play in the legal system for some people and in some kinds of disputes. However, where the primary motivation for its introduction or encouragement by governments is to cut costs, there is the danger that it will be used inappropriately, and that people will be forced to attend mediation as a precondition to receiving what they really want—an adjudication by the court in accordance with the law.[115]

10.7   Access to Justice and the Problem of Centripetal Law

While governments are increasingly encouraging people to settle their own disputes by alternative dispute resolution, and withdrawing legal aid for civil litigation, they have so far failed to recognise the problem of centripetal laws which have the effect of drawing parties inexorably towards a judicial resolution, rather than conferring upon them the clear bargaining endowments which would facilitate settlements.

Many Australian laws are written on the premise that they will be used by courts in deciding cases, rather than by parties in settling disputes in the shadow of the law. Numerous laws confer broad discretions on judges, for example, to set aside unfair contracts or to compensate for deceptive and misleading practices in trade and commerce.[116] Discretion is a particular feature of family law. Judges have a broad discretion in dividing the property of a husband and wife following marriage breakdown, and in resolving conflicts concerning with whom the children will live and how often the other parent will have contact with them. The legislation does not offer rules or fixed entitlements, but rather it lists the factors which judges should consider.[117] In New South Wales, Victoria and the Northern Territory, the courts also have a discretion to divide the property of couples who have been in a de facto relationship.[118]

The argument in favour of conferring broad discretions upon judges is that it gives them the necessary flexibility to tailor the relief awarded to the particular circumstances of each case rather than being fettered by fixed rules. However, this presupposes that a large number of cases will be the subject of judicial decision, and that governments are willing to bear the costs of providing access to the courts so that judges are able to achieve fair outcomes in each case. The greater the degree of discretion, the more difficult it is to bargain in the shadow of the law, for where there is a broad discretion, the law casts only an uncertain shadow. Judges may reasonably disagree on the appropriate outcomes of individual cases, and although experienced practitioners learn to predict outcomes with a certain degree of reliability, the complex messages concerning people's "entitlements" conveyed by the courts through the process of adjudication become simplified into some basic categories of case in order to make negotiations easier.[119]

Centripetal laws assume that courts will make the decisions, and regulate the conduct and adjudication of cases within the court setting. Centrifugal laws send clear messages to people about their rights, obligations and entitlements, so that judicial resolution of disputes is made necessary only where the facts of the case or the scope of the rule are in dispute.[120] For example, centripetal laws concerning family property guide judges on how to exercise their discretion when a dispute comes before the courts concerning the allocation of that property on marriage breakdown. Centrifugal laws would give the parties fixed entitlements, such as equal shares in all the property acquired after the marriage other than by gift to one party, by inheritance or as an award of damages for personal injury, subject to a power to vary those equal shares on application by one of the parties.[121] Centripetal laws give judges a discretion to vary the terms of a person's will after death where a dependant has not been adequately provided for.[122] Centrifugal laws would provide that the surviving spouse and dependent children should receive fixed proportions of the estate. Centripetal laws empower judges to set aside or vary standard form contracts which contain unfair terms. Centrifugal laws would provide model standard form contracts, and place the onus upon the business which is relying on the standard form contract to justify variations from the legislative model.

Centrifugal laws may sometimes be arbitrary, but they simplify the messages the law gives, thereby reducing the numbers of disputes and assisting in the resolution of disputes by conferring bargaining chips. They provide a framework within which alternative dispute resolution may operate successfully. An emphasis upon private ordering combined with the conferral of broad discretions on judges in the few cases which come to courts, is the worst of all worlds; but it is the direction in which the Australian legal system is heading rapidly.

10.8   Conclusion: The Future of Tradition

At the end of the 20th century, Australians find themselves at a time when they are reflecting, and must reflect on their future. Questions are being asked not only about whether it is time for Australia to become a republic, but also about what it means for Australia to be a truly multicultural society, about the suitability of the federal constitution for a nation soon to enter the 21st century, and about basic aspects of the legal system. How relevant are traditional modes of dispute resolution through adversarial litigation for the needs of modern society? Does Australia have a "Rolls-Royce" system of justice, when it can only afford a Holden? To what extent are traditional means of legal reasoning based upon premises which are unsustainable? How does the legal system incorporate the needs, aspirations and particular insights of groups which have not hitherto been part of the mainstream of public life?

To these questions about the future, the past may seem only faintly relevant. In one sense, Australia's future cannot rest in recollecting its past, for the ties with Britain are no longer as significant as they once were, either economically, politically or culturally. It is a declining proportion of the population who trace their ancestry to Britain or even to Europe. Far fewer still, hark back to their origins with the longing of the displaced and uprooted. To face the future, Australians must be secure in their identity, and embrace the unknown, or at least the little known.

Yet there is another sense in which Australians must recollect their past—the historical and ideological origins of their ideas and institutions—in order to chart successfully a new course for the future. It is only in understanding the origins of those aspects of law and society which constitute foundational ideas and assumptions, that we can assess them properly. With a profound understanding of the past, traditions which seem to be superfluous in the modern era may be seen to have a basis in the hard-fought struggles of another age, with implications for the present.

Above all, traditions have an intrinsic value merely for being traditions. The legitimacy of institutions is conferred as much by emotion as by reason, and as much by memory as by present consent. Sometimes, great trees must be felled in order to make way for new growth; but new saplings do not have the roots of the great trees. They are less able to withstand storms, and are more vulnerable to the winds of change. Vibrant new growth may sometimes be purchased only at the price of instability. Traditions can insulate societies from what Alvin Toffler described as "future shock".[123]

The strongest traditions have grown from shared values which have energised a society towards the development of new structures and institutions. The energy which created the French and American revolutions and other revolutions before and since, was born not only from dissatisfaction with the existing situation, but from an ideological commitment, at least among some of the leaders, to a new order. None of the great revolutions in western society, whether social, political, or intellectual, were won without cost. It is in times when shared values are weak, and individual preoccupation displaces a commitment to the common good, that those traditions born in very different times have their greatest value, as representing a shared heritage.

Above all, it is the strength of traditions that, once established, they can outlast the disappearance of those conditions which were essential to their formation and early development. Many of the most significant ideas of the western legal tradition, respect for law, its prominence as a means of social ordering, the importance of law's moral quality, the virtue of the rule of law, have all survived for a long time after the reasons which made them important values have disappeared from public consciousness. Similarly, the idea of natural human rights continues in our political discourse long after any consensus has gone about the basis for the existence or identification of these rights. Traditions have the virtue that at times, they can take on a life of their own.

Western societies are at a stage of history when they are living off their reserves. The intellectual conditions which gave birth to the traditions and values of legal and political life in western societies are no longer with us in the same way that they once were. The ideas of natural law, which, at their best, gave to positive law a standard of accountability, and called it onward to greater integrity, have been displaced from their prominence in jurisprudential thought. The Judaeo-Christian worldview, which gave to people a respect for law as intrinsically valuable, and called people to obey that law not only out of fear but out of civic duty, is not internalised in the values of the populace to the extent that it once was. Locke's theory of natural rights, and Rosseau's social contract are but a dim memory. Yet through all these changes in the beliefs and value systems of the population, the legal and political traditions of western societies continue on.

The western legal tradition has changed much over the centuries of its life. No one century has left it unaltered. It is an evolving tradition, not a static one. The future, in Australia, as elsewhere, depends upon recollecting this past, valuing it, and allowing it to be the basis for further change.

Nonetheless, the tradition of law in Australia is in urgent need of renewal. The challenge of inclusion is a challenge to make the legal system relevant and accessible to all Australians, irrespective of age, disability, ethnicity, gender or wealth. As the century comes to an end, the challenge of inclusion is the most urgent challenge of all.

NOTES

1. See above, 2.1.2.
2. See above, 2.1.3.
3. Johnston, E, *National Report of the Royal Commission into Aboriginal Deaths in Custody* (AGPS, Canberra, 1991), Vol 1, p 4.
4. For histories, see Johnston, E, *National Report of the Royal Commission into Aboriginal Deaths in Custody* (AGPS, Canberra, 1991), Vol 2, Ch 10; Reynolds, H, *Dispossession* (Allen and Unwin, Sydney, 1989).
5. *Mabo v Queensland (No 2)* (1992) 175 CLR 1.
6. See above, 5.1.3.
7. Australian Law Reform Commission, *Recognition of Aboriginal Customary Law*, Report No 31 (Sydney, 1986).
8. Graycar, R and Morgan, J, *The Hidden Gender of Law* (Federation Press, Sydney, 1990); Scutt, J, *Women and the Law* (Law Book Co, Sydney, 1990).
9. Where the youngest child is under five, 47 per cent of women are in the workforce. Where the youngest child is of school age, the proportion rises to 66 per cent. Australian Bureau of Statistics, *Labour Force Status and Other Characteristics of Families* (Canberra, 1993).
10. Glendon, M, *The New Family and the New Property* (Butterworths, Toronto, 1981).
11. Australian Law Reform Commission, *Equality Before the Law*, Report No 31 (Sydney, 1986); Naffine, N, *Law and the Sexes* (Allen and Unwin, Sydney, 1990), Ch 5; Graycar, R (ed), *Dissenting Opinions* (Allen and Unwin, Sydney, 1990).
12. Women are not only the primary caretakers of children. They also constitute 72.6 per cent of those caring for the elderly, 75.9 per cent of those caring for adults with a mental illness and over 60 per cent of those caring for disabled adults: Australian Law Reform Commission, *Equality Before the Law: Justice for Women*, Report No 69 (Sydney, 1994), Vol 1, p 12.
13. Joshi, H, "The Cost of Caring" in Glendinning, C and Millar, J (eds) *Women and Poverty in Britain* (Wheatsheaf, Brighton, 1987), p 112.
14. See, eg, Australian Law Reform Commission, *Equality Before the Law: Interim Report*, Report No 67 (Sydney, 1994).
15. Goldman, R and Goldman, J, "The Prevalence and Nature of Child Sexual Abuse in Australia" (1988) 9 *Australian Journal of Sex, Marriage and the Family* 94; Finkelhor, D, *Sexually Victimised Children* (Free Press, New York, 1979); Finkelhor, D, *Child Sexual Abuse: New Theory and Research* (Free Press, New York, 1984).
16. See generally, Parkinson, P, "The Future of Competency Testing for Child Witnesses" (1991) 15 Crim LJ 186; Warner, K, "Child Witnesses in Sexual Assault Cases" (1988) 12 Crim LJ 286.
17. Cashmore, J and Parkinson, P, "The Competency of Children to Give Evidence" (1991) 3(1) *Judicial Officers Bulletin* (Judicial Commission of NSW) 1.
18. Flin, R, Stevenson, Y and Davies, G, "Children's Knowledge of Court Proceedings" (1989) 80 *British Journal of Psychology* 285.
19. Cashmore, J, "The Use of Video Technology for Child Witnesses" (1990) 16 Monash Univ LR 228; on the position in the Australian Capital Territory, see Australian Law Reform Commission, *Children's Evidence: Closed Circuit TV*, Report No 63 (Sydney, 1992).
20. In Western Australia, a variation on this has also been used: the defendant is in another room, watching proceedings through closed circuit television, and is able to communicate with defence lawyers.

21. Of all States and Territories, Western Australia has the greatest variety of means by which children can give evidence: *Acts Amendment (Evidence of Children and Others) Act* 1992 (WA).

22. Brennan, M and Brennan, R, *Strange Language: Child Victims Under Cross Examination* (2nd ed, Riverina-Murray Institute, Wagga Wagga, 1988); Cashmore, J, "Problems and Solutions in Lawyer-Child Communication" (1991) 15 Crim LJ 193.

23. Parkinson, P, "Child Sexual Abuse Allegations in the Family Court" (1990) 4 *Australian Journal of Family Law* 60 at 66-72; Oates, K, "Children as Witnesses" (1990) 64 *Australian Law Journal* 129; Bussey, K, "The Competence of Child Witnesses" in Calvert, G, Ford, A and Parkinson, P (eds), *The Practice of Child Protection: Australian Approaches* (Hale and Iremonger, Sydney, 1992), p 69.

24. See generally, Seymour, J, *Dealing With Young Offenders* (Law Book Co, Sydney, 1988); Borowski, A and Murray, T (eds), *Juvenile Delinquency in Australia* (Methuen Australia, Sydney, 1985).

25. Andrews, R and Cohn, A, "Ungovernability: The Unjustifiable Jurisdiction" (1974) 83 Yale LJ 1383; Teitelbaum, L and Gough, A (eds), *Beyond Control: Status Offenders in the Juvenile Court* (Ballinger, Cambridge, Mass, 1977); Garlock, P, " 'Wayward' Children and the Law, 1820-1900: The Genesis of the Status Offense Jurisdiction of the Juvenile Court" (1979) 13 Georgia LR 341.

26. Morris, A, Giller, H, Szwed, E and Geach, H, *Justice for Children* (Macmillan, London, 1980).

27. See Bird, G (ed), *Law in a Multicultural Australia* (National Centre for Crosscultural Studies in Law, Melbourne, 1991); Bird, G, *The Process of Law in Australia: Intercultural Perspectives* (2nd ed, Butterworths, Sydney, 1993).

28. *National Agenda for a Multicultural Australia* (Office of Multicultural Affairs, Canberra, 1989).

29. Ibid, p 17.

30. See, eg, Bullivant, B, "Australia's Pluralist Dilemma: An Age-old Problem in a New Guise" (1983) 55 *Australian Quarterly* 136; Jupp, J, "Multiculturalism: Friends and Enemies, Patrons and Clients" (1983) 55 *Australian Quarterly* 149; Jayasuriya, L, "Rethinking Australian Multiculturalism: Towards a New Paradigm" (1990) 62 *Australian Quarterly* 50.

31. See also Art 30 of the *Convention on the Rights of the Child*.

32. In the constitutional law of the United States, this fundamental principle was expressed by Stone J in his famous footnote 4 in *United States v Carolene Products Co* (1938) 304 US 144 at 152. He stated that one of the grounds on which legislation could be subjected to "more exacting judicial scrutiny" was if it was directed at particular religious, national or racial minorities, or expressed prejudice against "discrete and insular minorities".

33. D'Argaville, M, "Serving a Multicultural Clientele: Communication Between Lawyers and Non-English-speaking Background Clients" in Bird, G (ed), op cit, p 83.

34. Australian Law Reform Commission, *Multiculturalism and the Law*, Report No 57 (Sydney, 1992).

35. Ibid, Ch 3.

36. Australian Law Reform Commission, *Multiculturalism and the Law*, Report No 57, op cit, Ch 6. See also *Goudge and Goudge* (1984) FLC 91-534 (Evatt CJ dissenting); *DKI and OBI* [1979] FLC 90-661; *In the Marriage of McL; Minister for Health and Community Services (NT) (Intervener)* [1991] FLC 92-238.

37. For example, in *R v Isobel Phillips* (Northern Territory Court of Summary Jurisdiction, 19 September 1983, unreported) the defence of duress was allowed to an Aboriginal woman from the Warumungu tribe because the evidence demonstrated that she was required by tribal law to fight in public with any woman involved with her husband, and was under a threat of death or serious injury if she did not respond. Australian Law Reform Commission, *Recognition of Aboriginal Customary Law*, Report No 31, op cit, para 430, fn 82. See also the recommendations of the Australian Law Reform Commission on the need to take account of cultural factors in the application of the criminal law. Australian Law Reform Commission, *Multiculturalism and the Law*, Report No 57, op cit, Ch 8.

38. There is a specific legislative exemption for Sikhs in England: *Motor Cycle Crash Helmets (Religious Exemption) Act* 1976. For the position in Australia, see Australian Law Reform Commission, *Multiculturalism and the Law*, Report No 57, op cit, pp 175-176.

39. Australian Law Reform Commission, *Multiculturalism and the Law*, Report No 57, op cit, pp 11-12. Legal pluralism, in relation to tribal Aboriginal communities, was also rejected by the Australian Law Reform Commission in its report on Aboriginal customary law, in favour of the limited recognition of customary laws for specific purposes: Australian Law Reform Commission, *Recognition of Aboriginal Customary Law*, Report No 31, op cit. For comment, see Poulter, S, "Cultural Pluralism in Australia" (1988) 2 Int J of Law and the Family 127.

40. *National Agenda for a Multicultural Australia*, op cit, vii.

41. For example, in relation to arranged marriages where pressure is exerted by parents to enter the marriage despite the reluctance of the young woman to do so. On arranged marriages and the law of nullity in Australia, see *In the Marriage of S* (1980) FLC 90-820.

42. Sadurski, W, "Last Among Equals: Minorities and Australian Judge-Made Law" (1989) 63 ALJ 474 at 481.

43. See, eg, Parkinson, P, "Taking Multiculturalism Seriously: Marriage Law and the Rights of Minorities" (1994) 16 Syd LR (forthcoming).

44. On the issue of child abuse, see New South Wales Child Protection Council, *Culture—No Excuse* (Sydney, 1994); Korbin, J, "Child Sexual Abuse: A Cross-Cultural View" in Oates, K (ed), *Understanding and Managing Child Sexual Abuse* (Harcourt Brace Jovanovich, Sydney, 1990), p 42.

45. Cappelletti, M and Garth, B, "Access to Justice: The Newest Wave in the Worldwide Movement to Make Rights Effective" (1978) 27 Buffalo LR 181.

46. Opening address, Commonwealth Legal Aid Council Conference (1984) quoted in Disney, J, Redmond, P, Basten J and Ross, S, *Lawyers* (2nd ed, Law Book Co, Sydney, 1986), p 461.

47. Galanter, M, "Justice in Many Rooms: Courts, Private Ordering and Indigenous Law" (1981) 19 *Journal of Legal Pluralism & Unofficial Law* 1 at 6.

48. Mnookin, R and Kornhauser, L, "Bargaining in the Shadow of the Law: The Case of Divorce" (1979) Yale LJ 950.

49. Ibid at 968.

50. Fitzgerald, J, "Grievances Disputes and Outcomes: A Comparison of Australia and the United States" (1983) 1 *Law in Context* 15. See also Galanter, M, "Reading the Landscape of Disputes: What We Know and Don't Know (and Think We Know) About Our Allegedly Contentious and Litigious Society" (1983) 31 UCLALR 4.

51. Harris D et al, *Compensation and Support for Illness and Injury* (Clarendon, Oxford, 1984).

52. For a review of American, British and Australian data see Cass, M and Western, J, *Legal Aid and Legal Need* (Commonwealth Legal Aid Commission, Canberra, 1980), Chs 3 and 4.

53. In Fitzgerald's study, (above), most claims were made without recourse to lawyers. In all those cases where the claim was disputed, only 21 per cent of people consulted lawyers. Lawyers were not consulted at all in regard to landlord and tenant disputes, and were consulted in only 3.4 per cent of discrimination claims. Even in consumer and tort problems where the amount involved was over $1000, lawyers were consulted in only 47 per cent of tort disputes and 12 per cent of consumer disputes. Lawyers were involved additionally, however, in some cases where the claim was not contested. About 19 per cent of instances in which lawyers were involved could be so categorised.

54. Cass, M and Sackville, R, *Legal Needs of the Poor* (Commission of Inquiry into Poverty, AGPS, 1975).

55. Ibid, p 8.

56. Ibid, pp 75-76.

57. Ibid, p 89.

58. Cass, M and Western, J, op cit, Ch 3.

59. Significantly, Cass and Sackville found that there was no difference between the income level of those who consulted a lawyer and the whole sample (Cass, M and Sackville, R, op cit, p 77).

60. In some courts and tribunals, the cost-indemnity rule does not apply, or is only applied in certain situations (where, eg, a reasonable offer of settlement has been refused). See, eg, *Family Law Act* 1975 (Cth), s 117; Access to Justice Advisory Committee, *Access to Justice: An Action Plan* (Canberra, 1994), pp 167-168.

61. In New South Wales, a completely different approach to the calculation of costs has been introduced. The *Legal Profession Reform Act* 1993 (NSW), amending the *Legal Profession Act* 1987, abolished scales and provides that costs should be assessed by a cost assessor who is a practising lawyer. The assessor should consider whether it was reasonable to carry out the work done, and also the reasonableness of the amounts charged. See *Legal Profession Act* 1987, ss 208F-208s.
62. Researchers, examining the basis for charging in personal injury litigation in Victoria and New South Wales found that in New South Wales, 83 per cent charged wholly or mainly by reference to time. In Victoria, 68.8 per cent used court scales. Worthington, D and Baker, J, *The Costs of Civil Litigation: Current Charging Practices, New South Wales and Victoria* (Civil Justice Research Centre, Sydney, 1993).
63. See, eg, Australian Legal Reform Commission, *Multiculturalism and the Law, Research Paper No 1, Family Law: Issues in the Vietnamese Community* (ALRC, Sydney, 1991), pp 24-30.
64. ALRC, *Multiculturalism and the Law*, Report No 57, op cit, Ch 2.
65. Studies in the 1970s indicated that Chamber Magistrates were the most well known source of legal advice in the community in New South Wales. See Cass, M and Sackville, R, op cit, and Tomasic, R, *Law, Lawyers and the Community* (Law Foundation of New South Wales, Sydney, 1976).
66. See, eg, Law Reform Commission of Victoria, *Access to the Law: Restrictions on Legal Practice*, Report No 47 (Melbourne, 1992); Senate Standing Committee on Legal and Constitutional Affairs, *The Cost of Justice, Foundations for Reform* (Commonwealth of Australia, Canberra, 1993) and *The Cost of Justice, Second Report, Checks and Imbalances* (Commonwealth of Australia, Canberra, 1993); Access to Justice Advisory Committee Report, op cit.
67. See Weisbrot, D, *Australian Lawyers* (Longman Cheshire, Melbourne, 1990).
68. Trade Practices Commission, *Study of the Professions—Legal, Final Report* (Canberra, 1994), p 178.
69. Family Court of Australia, Practice Direction 2/91.
70. For example, Queensland and South Australia: see Access to Justice Advisory Committee Report, op cit, pp 133-134.
71. *Legal Profession Reform Act* 1993 (NSW), amending the *Legal Profession Act* 1987 (NSW), s 175.
72. Trade Practices Commission Final Report, op cit, pp 158-160; Access to Justice Advisory Committee Report, op cit, pp 145-147.
73. Joint Select Committee on Certain Aspects of the Operation and Interpretation of the Family Law Act 1975, *The Family Law Act 1975: Aspects of its Operation and Interpretation* (AGPS, Canberra, 1992), pp 343-345.
74. *Legal Profession Act* 1987 (NSW), ss 186-188 (as amended).
75. *Legal Practitioners Act* 1981 (SA), ss 41-42.
76. Access to Justice Advisory Committee, op cit, Ch 6, action 6.2.
77. Basten, J, Graycar, R and Neal, D, "Legal Centres in Australia" (1983) 6 UNSWLJ 163 at 164.
78. Ibid at n 13.
79. Armstrong, S, "Labor's Legal Aid Scheme: the Light that Failed" in Scotton, R B and Ferber, H (eds), *Public Expenditures and Social Policy: Vol 1, The Whitlam Years 1972-1975* (Longman Cheshire, Melbourne, 1980), p 220.
80. Access to Justice Advisory Committee Report, op cit, pp 231-236.
81. See Cappelletti, M and Garth, B, op cit, Pt III.
82. Commonwealth Attorney-General's Department, *Annual Report 1992-1993*, Vol 2, p 177.
83. (1992) 177 CLR 292.
84. (1994) FLC 92-461.
85. Australian Law Reform Commission, *Equality Before the Law*, Report No 31, op cit, pp 95-98.
86. Ibid, p 95.
87. In 1992-1993, 72 per cent of approvals were for criminal law matters, compared with 21 per cent for family law and 7 per cent for other civil law claims. Legal Aid and Family Services, *Gender Bias in Litigation. Legal Aid: An Issues Paper* (Attorney-General's Department, Canberra, 1994), p 24.
88. Australian Law Reform Commission, *Equality Before the Law*, Report No 31, op cit, p 96.

89. Mossman, M J, "Gender Equality and Legal Aid Services: A Research Agenda for Institutional Change" (1993) 15 Syd LR 30 at 48.
90. *Sajdak and Sajdak* (1993) FLC 92-348; *McOwan and McOwan* (1994) FLC 92-451 at 80,691.
91. Australian Law Reform Commission, *Equality Before the Law*, Report No 31, op cit, pp 100-101.
92. The Access to Justice Advisory Committee noted that the Commonwealth, and some States such as New South Wales, require legal services impact statements when considering new legislation, and this may involve consultation with Legal Aid Commissions. While this may lead to an increase of funding for legal aid to cope with the increased demand, it is by no means certain that legislation which is likely to result in a significant increase in demand for legal services will be accompanied by an appropriate increase in legal aid provision. Access to Justice Advisory Committee Report, op cit, p 247.
93. For a full account and evaluation, see Lyons, G, "Aboriginal Legal Services" in Hanks, P and Keon-Cohen, B (eds), *Aborigines and the Law* (Allen and Unwin, Sydney, 1984), p 137.
94. Australian Law Reform Commission, *Equality Before the Law*, Report No 31, op cit, pp 117-128.
95. For discussion of physical and sexual violence against women in Aboriginal communities see Greer, P with Breckenridge, J, " 'They Throw the Rule Book Away': Sexual Assault in Aboriginal Communities" in Breckenridge, J and Carmody, M (eds), *Crimes of Violence* (Allen and Unwin, Sydney, 1992), p 189.
96. Australian Law Reform Commission, *Equality Before the Law*, Report No 31, op cit, pp 123-124.
97. For a history and critique of the legal centres movement see Basten, J, Graycar, R and Neal, D, op cit.
98. Neal, D (ed), *On Tap, Not on Top, Legal Centres in Australia 1972-1982* (Legal Services Bulletin, Melbourne, 1984), Introduction, p 3.
99. See Basten, J, Graycar, R and Neal, D, op cit, pp 178-187.
100. See Petre, C, "Specialisation: The Sydney Push" in *On Tap, Not on Top*, op cit, p 12.
101. Australian Law Reform Commission, *Equality Before the Law*, Report No 31, op cit, pp 111-117.
102. Astor, H and Chinkin, C, *Dispute Resolution in Australia* (Butterworths, Sydney, 1992), Ch 3.
103. Folberg, J and Taylor, A, *Mediation: A Comprehensive Guide to Resolving Conflict Without Litigation* (Jossey-Bass, San Francisco, 1984), p 7.
104. Gribben, S, "Mediation of Family Disputes" (1994) 6 *Australian Journal of Family Law* 126 at 129.
105. Bordow, S and Gibson, J, *Evaluation of the Family Court Mediation Service* (Family Court of Australia, Sydney, 1994), p 33. For the legislative framework, see *Family Law Act* 1975 (Cth), ss 19A-19C.
106. Office of the Attorney-General, *Family Law Act 1975, Directions for Amendment* (Canberra, 1993), pp 4-5, 48.
107. See above, 7.5.
108. *Federal Court of Australia Act* 1976 (Cth), ss 53A-53C.
109. Access to Justice Advisory Committee Report, op cit, p 281.
110. Ibid.
111. *Administrative Appeals Tribunal Act* 1975 (Cth), s 34A. Mediation was introduced on a trial basis in 1991: O'Connor, D, "Future Directions in Australian Administrative Law: The Administrative Appeals Tribunal" in McMillan, J (ed), *Administrative Law: Does the Public Benefit?* (Australian Institute of Administrative Law, Canberra, 1992), pp 194, 200. For criticism, see De Maria, W, "The Administrative Appeals Tribunal in Review: On Remaining Seated During the Standing Ovation" in McMillan, J (ed), op cit, pp 96, 108-114.
112. In New South Wales, these are known as Community Justice Centres.
113. Astor, H, "Violence and Family Mediation: Policy" (1994) 8 *Australian Journal of Family Law* 3.
114. Gribben, S, "Violence and Family Mediation: Practice" (1994) 8 *Australian Journal of Family Law* 22; Family Law Rules, O 25A, r 5.
115. For other criticisms, see Astor, H and Chinkin, C, op cit, Ch 2.

116. See, eg, *Trade Practices Act* 1974 (Cth) and the *Fair Trading Acts* in the States and Territories; see also *Contracts Review Act* 1980 (NSW). See generally, Clarke, P and Parkinson, P (eds), *Unfair Dealing, Laws of Australia* (Law Book Co, Melbourne, 1993), Vol 35.

117. *Family Law Act* 1975 (Cth). It is planned to amend the *Family Law Act* 1975 in the light of recommendations made by the *Joint Select Committee on Certain Aspects of the Operation and Interpretation of the Family Law Act 1975*, op cit, and the Family Law Council. See Attorney-General, *Directions for Amendment*, op cit. The proposed amendments will enact a presumption of equality in the division of the property between husband and wife, subject to variation on a number of different grounds. These reforms may narrow the discretion of judges to some extent. Changes are also planned in relation to the law concerning children, in particular by replacing custody and access orders with residence and contact orders.

118. *De Facto Relationships Act* 1984 (NSW); *Real Property Act* 1958 (Vic), Pt IX; *De Facto Relationships Act* 1991 (NT).

119. Parker, S, Parkinson, P and Behrens, J, *Australian Family Law in Context* (Law Book Co, Sydney, 1994), pp 430-432.

120. The terminology of centripetal and centrifugal law is derived from Galanter, M, op cit.

121. This is the position under community property regimes. For a survey, see Parkinson, P, "Who Needs the Uniform Marital Property Act?" (1987) 55 *University of Cincinnati Law Review* 677.

122. Dickey, A, *Family Provision After Death* (Law Book Co, Sydney, 1992).

123. Toffler, A, *Future Shock* (Random House, New York, 1970).

INDEX

significance, 255
terra nullius, doctrine of, 7, 21, 126-127
abolition of, 129-131

Magistrates
Chamber, in Local Courts, 268, 286
courts of summary jurisdiction
equitable rights and remedies, powers
in respect of, 185
jurisdiction of, 184-185
stipendiary, use of in Australia, 181-182

Magna Carta of 1215
due process, establishment by, 117
monarchical power, limitations laid down
by, 97
versions of, 92

Maoris
white settlers in New Zealand, treaty
with, 7

Marriage
ecclesiastical courts, jurisdiction in
respect of law of, 89

Mediation—*see* **Alternative dispute
resolution**

Monarchy
abolition of, after reign of Charles I,
105-106
Australian legislative process, role of
Queen in, 155
conflicts, constitutional, of 17th century,
100-110
common law courts and Crown,
relationship between, 101-102
Crown and Parliament, relationship
between, 102-104
constitutional, after Restoration, 107-109
divine right of kings, 103, 107
establishment of, in England, 69
federal and state legislation, power to
withhold Royal Assent, 164
feudal era, royal authority in, 95-98
Head of State of Australia, English
monarch as, 171-172
limited, as principle of constitutionality,
114
ministry, extinguishment of power of
monarch to choose, 113
prerogative courts, 89-90
abolition of, 105
Restoration, constitutional monarchy
after, 107-109

Montesquieu
empirical attack on natural law by, 52
separation of powers, expression of
constitutional principle by, 117

Moral authority
law, of, as characteristic of western legal
tradition, 28-29, 60

Morality
law and, conceptual distinction, 24

Multiculturalism
cultural identity, right to, 261
definition, 261
development of multicultural society, 8
different communities, government by
different legal norms, 260
economic efficiency, as aspect of
government policy on, 261
education about law, need for, 267-268
inclusion, challenge of, 258
legal tradition, and, 258-261
particular cultural factors, relevance to
application of general laws, 260
social justice, in context of multicultural
policy, 261

Nation state
laws higher than, and independent of, 58

Native title
land, to, recognition of, 129-131

Native Title Act 1993 (Cth)
effect, 131

Natural law, 38-46
Aquinas
civil disobedience, view of, 43-44
eternal law, and, 41-43
natural law after, 45-46
Aristotle, writings concerning, 39-40
Bentham, criticism for subjectivism by,
53-54
Cicero, writings concerning, 40-41
civil law and, discordance between, 41
defence of, by Finnis, 53
definition of, by Ulpian, 39
empirical attack on, 52
Greek ideas of, 38-41
Hobbes' theory of, 47
legal positivism and—*see* **Legal
positivism**
Locke's idea of fundamental human
rights, 48-50
method of legal reasoning associated
with, 207
philosophical attack on, 52
positivist critique of—*see* **Legal
positivism**
Roman ideas of, 38-41
Rousseau's view of, 50-52
secularisation of, 45-46
ultimate authority ascribed to, 15

Natural rights—*see* **Rights**

New South Wales Act 1823
inferior courts, establishment of
hierarchy by, 180-181
Supreme Court, establishment by, 180